THE UN CONVENTION ON THE RIGHTS OF THE CHILD AND DOMESTIC COURTS

This important contribution to children's rights scholarship brings fresh perspectives to the complicated relationship between domestic law and international law in the practice of domestic courts. Through a critical assessment of the judicial application of the Convention on the Rights of the Child in four jurisdictions (Australia, France, South Africa, and the United Kingdom), the book demonstrates that the traditional rules of reception remain an essential starting point in understanding how national courts apply the Convention but are unable to explain all forms of judicial engagement therewith. The book shows that regardless of the legal system (monist, dualist, hybrid), courts can apply the Convention meaningfully, especially when the domestic structure of reception converges with it. The comparative international law perspective used in the book and the heterogenous sample of jurisdictions analysed enable the author to distil insights valid for other jurisdictions.

MEDA COUZENS is a children's rights scholar currently based in the School of Law, Western Sydney University, Australia, and a Research Fellow with the School of Law, University of KwaZulu-Natal, Durban, South Africa. Meda holds a doctorate from the University of Leiden and master's degrees from the Universities of Bucharest, London, and KwaZulu-Natal. She has researched children's rights in Australia, France, Myanmar, Romania, South Africa, Tanzania, and the United Kingdom.

THE UN CONVENTION ON THE RIGHTS OF THE CHILD AND DOMESTIC COURTS

A Comparative International Law Perspective

MEDA COUZENS

Western Sydney University

&

University of KwaZulu-Natal

CAMBRIDGE
UNIVERSITY PRESS

CAMBRIDGE
UNIVERSITY PRESS

Shaftesbury Road, Cambridge CB2 8EA, United Kingdom

One Liberty Plaza, 20th Floor, New York, NY 10006, USA

477 Williamstown Road, Port Melbourne, VIC 3207, Australia

314–321, 3rd Floor, Plot 3, Splendor Forum, Jasola District Centre, New Delhi – 110025, India

103 Penang Road, #05-06/07, Visioncrest Commercial, Singapore 238467

Cambridge University Press is part of Cambridge University Press & Assessment, a department of the University of Cambridge.

We share the University's mission to contribute to society through the pursuit of education, learning and research at the highest international levels of excellence.

www.cambridge.org
Information on this title: www.cambridge.org/9781108833714

DOI: 10.1017/9781108981163

When citing this work, please include a reference to the DOI 10.1017/9781108981163

First published 2025

A catalogue record for this publication is available from the British Library

Library of Congress Cataloging-in-Publication Data

Names: Couzens, Meda, author.
Title: The UN Convention on the Rights of the Child and domestic courts / Meda Couzens, Western Sydney University.
Description: Cambridge, United Kingdom ; New York, NY : Cambridge University Press, 2024. | Includes bibliographical references and index.
Identifiers: LCCN 2024029261 (print) | LCCN 2024029262 (ebook) | ISBN 9781108833714 (hardback) | ISBN 9781108986663 (paperback) | ISBN 9781108981163 (epub)
Subjects: LCSH: International and municipal law. | Convention on the Rights of the Child (1989 November 20) | Municipal courts.
Classification: LCC KZ1263 .C68 2024 (print) | LCC KZ1263 (ebook) | DDC 341.4/8572–dc23/eng/20240627
LC record available at https://lccn.loc.gov/2024029261
LC ebook record available at https://lccn.loc.gov/2024029262

ISBN 978-1-108-83371-4 Hardback

To my family and the readers.

CONTENTS

ACKNOWLEDGEMENTS

This book originates in the PhD thesis I completed with the Leiden Law School, The Netherlands, in 2019, under the supervision of Professors Ton Liefaard and Julia Sloth-Nielsen, for whose guidance and support I remain grateful. Since then, the project has changed shape and evolved into the current book.

I am grateful for the support I received along the way while completing this book, ranging from guidance to reassurance to critical reading and editing. I thank Dr Alison Pert, Dr Rayner Thwaites, Professor Claire Fenton-Glynn, Professor Azadeh Dastyari, Professor Catherine Renshaw, and my other colleagues at the School of Law, Western Sydney University, for engaging constructively with my work. I thank Ms Michelle Nichols for editing this book.

I thank my family, especially my husband Ed and our son Kay, and my friends for putting up with me during this long journey.

TABLE OF CASES

International Courts

African Court on Human and Peoples' Rights

Tanganyika Law Society v. United Republic of Tanzania (Application Nos. 009/2011 and 011/2011, 14 June 2013) 2.2.1

European Court of Human Rights

A.B. v. France (Application No. 11593/12, 12 July 2016) 3.5.1.1

Advisory Opinion concerning the recognition in domestic law of a legal parent–child relationship between a child born through a gestational surrogacy arrangement abroad and the intended mother (Request No. P16–2018-001, 10 April 2019) 3.6.2.2

Costello-Roberts v. United Kingdom (Application No. 13134/87, 25 March 1993) 6.7.2.1

Labassée v. France (Application No. 65941/11, 26 June 2014) 3.6.2.2

Mennesson v. France (Application No. 65192/11, 26 June 2014) 3.6.2.2

Odièvre v. France (Application No. 42326/98, 13 February 2003) 3.3, 3.5.2, 3.6.2.2

Osungu and Lokongo v. France (Applications Nos. 76860/11 and 51354/1) 3.3, 3.6.2.2

Popescu v. Romania (No. 2) (Application No. 71525/01, 26 April 2007) 2.3.1.2

Popov v. France (Application Nos. 39472/07 and 39474/07, 19 January 2012) 3.5.1.1, 3.6.2.1

Swedish Engine Drivers' Union v. Sweden (Application No. 5614/72, 6 February 1976) 2.3.1.2

European Court of Justice

NV Algemene Transport- en Expeditie Onderneming van Gend and Loos v. Netherlands Inland Revenue Administration – Reference for a preliminary ruling: Tariefcommissie – Pays-Bas, Case 26–62 of 1963 2.3.1.2

Permanent Court of International Justice

Jurisdiction of the Courts of Danzig, Advisory Opinion [1928] PCIJ (ser B) No. 15 (3 March) 2.3.1.2

Domestic Courts

Australia

Minister for Immigration and Multicultural and Indigenous Affairs, Re; Ex parte Lam [2003] HCA 6 4.4.1, 4.4.4, 4.6.1, 4.6.2, 7.4.1
Momcilovic v. The Queen [2011] HCA 34 4.6.1
Murray v. Director, Family Services, ACT [1993] FamCA 103 4.4.1, 4.4.2
Northern Territory of Australia v. GPAO [1999] HCA 8 4.4.2, 4.6.1, 4.6.2, 7.2, 7.3.2, 7.3.2.1
Oram & Lambert [2019] FamCAFC 4 4.4.1
Purvis v. New South Wales (Department of Education and Training) [2003] HCA 62 4.4.1
R v. A2 [2019] HCA 35 4.4.2, 4.6.1
Ralton & Ralton [2017] FamCAFC 182 4.4.1
Rilak & Tsokas [2017] FamCAFC 26 4.4.1
Sharma v. Minister for the Environment [2021] FCA 560 4.6.1
TLB, In re [2007] VSC 439 4.4.5, 4.6.2, 7.4
Tomasevic v. Travaglini [2007] VSC 337 4.5.2, 4.6.1, 4.6.2
Victoria v. Commonwealth [1996] HCA 56 4.4.1
VYZ v. Chief Executive Officer of the Department of Justice [2022] WASC 274 4.6.1
Western Australia v. Ward [2002] HCA 28 4.2
Woolley, Re; Ex parte M276/2003 [2004] HCA 49 4.4.2, 4.6.1, 4.6.2, 7.3.2, 7.3.2.3, 7.4
XYZ v. Commonwealth [2006] HCA 25 4.4.1
Z, Re [1996] FamCA 89 4.4.1, 4.4.2, 4.6.1, 4.6.2, 7.3.2, 7.4, 7.4.1
ZD v. Secretary to the Department of Health and Human Services [2017] VSC 806 4.5.1
Zlotnik & Gerasimov [2015] FamCAFC 174 4.4.1
ZZ v. Secretary, Department of Justice [2013] VSC 267 4.5.2, 4.6.2, 7.4.1

Bangladesh

Bangladesh Legal Aid and Service Trust (BLAST) v. Secretary, Ministry of Education, Writ Petition No. 5684 of 2010 (13 January 2011) 2.3.2.2

Belgium

Council of State, Decision No. 69715 of 21 November 1997 2.3.1.2
Court of Cassation, Case No. P.99.0276.F (Justel No. F-19990331-5) of 31 March 1999 2.3.1.2

Canada

Baker v. Canada (Minister of Citizenship and Immigration) [1999] 2 SCR 817 2.3.2.1, 2.3.2.2
Canadian Foundation for Children, Youth and the Law v. Canada (Attorney General) [2004] 1 SCR 76 2.3.2.2
Suresh v. Canada [2002] 1 SCR 3 2.3.2.1

Fiji

France

Court of Cassation

Civil Section

Criminal Section

Crim, No. 98-84538, 1999 Non publié au bulletin 3.3
Crim, No. 00-84429, 2001 Non publié au bulletin 3.3
Crim, No. 05-86947, 2006 Non publié au bulletin 3.6.1
Crim, No. 09-81239, 2009 Non publié au bulletin 3.5.2.1
Crim, No. 09-81710, 2009 Non publié au bulletin 3.5.2.1
Crim, No. 09-83032, 2010 Non publié au bulletin 3.5.2.1
Crim, No. 09-83351, 2009 Non publié au bulletin 3.5.2.1
Crim, No. 10-86237, 2010 Non publié au bulletin 3.5.2.1
Crim, No. 10-87811, 2011 Non publié au bulletin 3.5.2.1

Social Section

Soc, No. 11-40090, 2012 Bulletin 2012, V, No. 28 3.6.2.2

Assembly

Ass, No. 09-69052, 2011 Bulletin 2011, No. 6 3.3, 3.5.1.1, 3.5.1.2, 3.6.2.2
Ass, No. 09-71352, 2011 Bulletin 2011, No. 5 3.3, 3.5.1.1
Ass, No. 10-17049, 2011 Bulletin criminel 2011, No. 1 3.6.2.2
Ass, No. 11-17520, 2013 Bulletin 2013, No. 2 3.3, 3.5.1.1
Ass, No. 13-28369, Bulletin 2014, No. 1 3.6.1
Ass, No. 14-21323, 3 July 2015 3.6.2.2
Ass, No. 10-19053, 2018 Publié au bulletin (ECLI:FR:CCASS:2018:AP00638) 3.6.2.2
Ass, No. 15-50002, 2015 Publié au bulletin (ECLI:FR:CCASS:2015:AP00620) 3.6.2.2

Council of State

CE, No. 136601, 1993 Mentionné dans les tables du recueil Lebon 3.4
CE, No. 141083, 10 March 1995 (*Demirpence*) Mentionné dans les tables du recueil Lebon 3.4
CE, No. 155096, 1998 Mentionné dans les tables du recueil Lebon 3.4
CE, No. 161364, 22 September 1997 Publié au recueil Lebon (*Cinar)* 3.4, 3.5.1.2, 3.5.2, 3.5.2.1, 7.3.1, 7.4, 7.4.1
CE, No. 163043, 23 April 1997 Publié au recueil Lebon (*GISTI)* 3.2
CE, No. 191232, 1999 Publié au recueil Lebon 3.4
CE, No. 214664, 2002 Inédit au recueil Lebon 3.4
CE, No. 216521, 2001 Publié au recueil Lebon 3.4
CE, No. 220271, 2001 Publié au recueil Lebon (*Nezdulkins*) 3.5.1.1
CE, No. 220434, 2004 Inédit au recueil Lebon 3.5.1.2, 3.5.2, 3.5.2.1, 3.6.2.2
CE, No. 238724, 2003 Inédit au recueil Lebon 3.4
CE, No. 247587, 2004 Inédit au recueil Lebon 3.4
CE, No. 249369, 2004 Publié au recueil Lebon (ECLI:FR:CESSR:2004:249369.20040324) 3.5.1.2, 3.5.2, 3.5.2.1, 3.6.2.2

Constitutional Council

Other Courts

New Zealand

Norway

South Africa

Coetzee v. Government of the Republic of South Africa v. Commanding Officer Port Elizabeth Prison 1995 (10) BCLR 1382 5.2.2, 5.5.1
De Gree v. Webb 2007 (5) SA 184 (SCA) 5.4.2.1, 5.5.2
De Reuck v. Director of Public Prosecutions (Witwatersrand Local Division) 2003 (12) BCLR 1333 (CC) 7.4.1
Director of Public Prosecutions, KZN v. P [2006] 1 All SA 446 (SCA) 5.4.4
Director of Public Prosecutions, Transvaal v. Minister for Justice and Constitutional Development 2009 (7) BCLR 637 (CC) 5.4.2.1, 5.4.3, 5.5.2, 7.3.1, 7.4.1
Director of Public Prosecutions, YG v. S [2017] ZAGPJHC 290 5.5.1
Du Toit v. Ntshinghila [2016] 2 All SA 328 (SCA) 5.4.2.3, 7.2
F v. F [2006] 1 All SA 571 (SCA) 5.4.1, 5.5.1
Freedom of Religion South Africa v. Minister of Justice and Constitutional Development [2019] ZACC 34 5.5.1
Geldenhuys v. The State 2009 (1) SACR 1 (SCA) 5.4.4, 5.5.1, 5.5.2, 7.2
Glenister v. President of the Republic of South Africa 2011 (7) BCLR 651 (CC) 1.3.2, 5.2, 5.2.2, 5.5.1
Governing Body of the Juma Musjid Primary School v. Essay NO 2011 (8) BCLR 761 (CC) 5.3, 5.5.1
Government of the Republic of South Africa v. Grootboom 2001 (1) SA 46 (CC) 5.2.2, 5.5.1
J v. National Director of Public Prosecutions 2014 (7) BCLR 764 (CC) 5.4.2.1, 7.3.2.3
Khosa v. Minister of Social Development 2004 (6) SA 505 (CC) 5.5.2
Le Roux v. Dey 2011 (6) BCLR 577 (CC) 5.4.2.1, 5.5.1, 5.5.2, 7.4
M v. S (Centre for Child Law Amicus Curiae) 2007 (12) BCLR 1312 (CC) 5.3, 5.4.2.1, 5.5.1, 5.5.2, 7.2, 7.3.1, 7.4, 7.4.1
MEC for Education: Kwazulu-Natal v. Pillay 2008 (1) SA 474 (CC) 5.5.2
Minister for Welfare and Population Development v. Fitzpatrick 2000 (7) BCLR 713 (CC)
Minister of Health v. Treatment Action Campaign 2002 (10) BCLR 1033 (CC) 5.4.1, 7.2.1
Raduvha v. Minister of Safety and Security 2016 (10) BCLR 1326 (CC) 5.3, 5.5.1, 5.5.2
R v. H 2005 (6) SA 535 (C) 5.4.1
S v. Makwanyane 1995 (3) SA 391 (CC) 5.2, 5.2.2, 5.5.1
S v. P 2000 (2) SA 656 (SCA) 5.4.4, 5.5.1
S v. Williams 1995 (3) SA 632 (CC) 5.2, 5.2.2
Teddy Bear Clinic for Abused Children v. Minister of Justice and Constitutional Development 2014 (2) SA 168 (CC) 5.5.2

Switzerland

D v. Family Allowance Fund of Zug Canton, Swiss Federal Tribunal Arrêts du Tribunal fédéral 136 I 297, 2010 2.3.1.2

United Kingdom

AL (Serbia) v. Secretary of State for the Home Department [2008] UKHL 42 6.6
Ali (Iraq) v. Secretary of State for the Home Department [2016] UKSC 60 6.5.2.1, 6.5.2.2, 6.7.2
ANS v. ML [2012] UKSC 30 6.4
Christian Institute v. Lord Advocate (Scotland) [2016] UKSC 51 6.3, 6.5.1, 6.7.2
D (a child), In re [2006] UKHL 51 6.4, 6.7.1, 6.7.2.1, 7.4
D (a child), In the matter of [2019] UKSC 42 6.6
E (a child) (Northern Ireland), In re [2008] UKHL 66 (*E (a child)* 6.5.1, 6.5.2.1, 6.5.2.2, 7.4
Ghaidan v. Godin-Mendoza [2004] UKHL 30 6.5
HH v. Deputy Prosecutor of the Italian Republic, Genoa [2012] UKSC 25 6.5.1, 6.5.2.1, 6.5.2.2, 6.7.1, 6.7.2, 6.7.2.1, 7.4.1
Hunter v. Canary Wharf Ltd [1997] UKHL 14 6.4, 6.7.1, 6.7.2
J v. C (an infant) [1970] AC 668 6.7.2
JR38 for Judicial Review (Northern Ireland), In the matter of an application by [2015] UKSC 42 6.3, 6.5.1, 6.5.2.2, 6.7.1, 6.7.2, 6.7.2.1, 7.3.2.3, 7.4
Makhlouf v. Secretary of State for the Home Department (Northern Ireland) [2016] UKSC 59 6.5.1, 6.5.2.1, 6.5.2.2, 6.7.2
Mathieson, a deceased child v. Secretary of State for Work and Pensions [2015] UKSC 47 6.3, 6.5.1, 6.5.2.1, 6.5.2.2, 6.6, 6.7.1, 6.7.2
McLaughlin for Judicial Review (Northern Ireland), In the matter of an application by [2018] UKSC 48 6.5.1, 6.5.2.1, 6.6, 6.7.1
Nzolameso v. City of Westminster [2015] UKSC 22 6.4, 6.5.1, 6.5.2.1, 6.7.1, 6.7.2
PJS v. News Group Newspapers Ltd [2016] UKSC 26 6.5.2.2, 6.7.2
Public Law Project v. Lord Chancellor [2015] EWCA Civ 1193 6.3, 7.5
R v. Durham Constabulary [2005] UKHL 21 6.3, 6.4, 6.5.1, 6.5.2.1, 6.7.1, 6.7.2, 7.2
R v. G [2003] UKHL 50 6.4, 6.7.2, 7.3.2.3, 7.4
R v. London Borough of Barnet ex parte G [2003] UKHL 57 6.7.2
R v. Secretary of State for Education and Employment ex parte Williamson [2005] UKHL 15 6.6, 6.7.2, 7.2
R v. Secretary of State for the Home Department ex parte Venables and Thompson [1997] UKHL 25 6.4, 6.5.2.1, 6.6, 6.7.1, 6.7.2, 6.8
R (on the application of AA) v. Secretary of State for the Home Department [2013] UKSC 49 6.7.2
R (on the application of DA) v. Secretary of State for Work and Pensions [2019] UKSC 21 6.3, 7.2, 7.4.1
R (on the application of MM (Lebanon)) v. Secretary of State for the Home Department [2017] UKSC 10 6.5.1, 6.5.2.1, 6.7.2
R (on the application of SG (previously JS)) v. Secretary of State for Work and Pensions [2015] UKSC 16 6.3, 6.5.1, 6.5.2.1, 6.5.2.2, 6.7.1, 6.7.2, 6.7.2.1, 7.2

R (on the application of T) v. Secretary of State for the Home Department [2014] UKSC 35 6.5.1, 6.6, 6.7.1, 6.7.2, 6.7.2.1, 7.2

Reference by the Attorney General and the Advocate General for Scotland – United Nations Convention on the Rights of the Child (Incorporation) (Scotland) Bill [2021] UKSC 42 6.3

S (a child), In re [2004] UKHL 47 6.5.1, 6.7.2

Sanderson v. McManus [1997] UKHL 1 6.4, 6.7.1

Smith v. Secretary of State for Work and Pensions [2006] UKHL 35 6.4, 6.5.1, 6.7.1, 6.7.2.1

TN and MA (Afghanistan) v. Secretary of State for the Home Department [2015] UKSC 40 6.7.2

ZH (Tanzania) v. Secretary of State for the Home Department [2011] UKSC 4 6.5.1, 6.5.2.1, 6.5.2.2, 6.6, 6.7.1, 6.7.2, 6.7.2.1, 7.2, 7.3.1, 7.4, 7.4.1

Zoumbas v. Secretary of State for the Home Department [2013] UKSC 74 6.5.1, 6.5.2.1, 6.5.2.2, 6.7.2

United States

Foster v. Nielson 27 US (2 Pet) 253 (1829) 2.3.1, 2.3.1.1

Medellin v. Texas, 552 US 491 (2008) 2.3.1.2

TABLE OF STATUTES

Australia

France

South Africa

United Kingdom

TABLE OF TREATIES

ABBREVIATIONS

A1P1	Protocol No. 1 to the Convention for the Protection of Human Rights and Fundamental Freedoms
ACRWC	African Charter on the Rights and Welfare of the Child, 1990
AHRCA	Australian Human Rights Commission Act 1986 (Cth)
CC	Court of Cassation (France)
CE	Conseil d'État (Council of State, France)
CEDAW	Convention on the Elimination of All Forms of Discrimination against Women
CERD	International Convention on the Elimination of All Forms of Racial Discrimination
CRC	United Nations Convention on the Rights of the Child, 1989
CYFA	Children, Youth and Families Act 2005 (Vic)
ECHR	European Convention on Human Rights and Fundamental Freedoms (Convention for the Protection of Human Rights and Fundamental Freedoms), 1950
ECJ	European Court of Justice
ECtHR	European Court of Human Rights
EU	European Union
FLA	Family Law Act 1975 (Cth Australia)
HRA	Human Rights Act 1998 (UK)
ICCPR	International Covenant on Civil and Political Rights, 1966
QPC	*question prioritaire de constitutionalité*
SCA	Supreme Court of Appeal (South Africa)
UNHCHR	United Nations High Commissioner for Human Rights
VSC	Supreme Court of Victoria (Australia)

1

Introduction

1.1 Why the Courts Matter

Following its adoption and wide ratification, the 1989 United Nations Convention on the Rights of the Child[1] (CRC or Convention) became an important rallying tool for improving the lives of children around the world. Progress has been made in giving effect to the CRC, with many domestic and international actors – including domestic courts – contributing to its implementation. The focus of this book is on domestic courts, whose engagement with the CRC has, until recently, been under-analysed.[2] This shift in attention reflects the evolution of the CRC from a standard-setting instrument with influence on domestic laws and policies[3] to one that is expected to be effectively implemented.

The focus on the courts is not meant to suggest that they are the apex implementation mechanism for the CRC. The Convention is complex

[1] Convention on the Rights of the Child, 20 November 1989, in force 2 September 1990, 1577 UNTS 3.

[2] Recent publications include Ton Liefaard and Jaap E. Doek (eds.), *Litigating the Rights of the Child: The UN Convention on the Rights of the Child in Domestic and International Jurisprudence* (Dordrecht: Springer, 2015); John Tobin, 'Judging the Judges: Are They Adopting the Rights Approach in Matters Involving Children?' (2009) 33(2) *Melbourne University Law Review* 579; Kirsten Sandberg, 'The Role of National Courts in Promoting Children's Rights: The Case of Norway' (2014) 22(1) *International Journal of Children's Rights* 1; Meda Couzens, 'Romanian Courts and the UN Convention on the Rights of the Child: A Case Study' (2016) 24(4) *International Journal of Children's Rights* 851.

[3] John Tobin, 'Increasingly Seen and Heard: The Constitutional Recognition of Children's Rights' (2005) 21(1) *South African Journal on Human Rights* 86; Venice Commission, *Report on the Protection of Children's Rights: International Standards and Domestic Constitutions* (CDL-AD(2014)005, 2014); Beatrice Duncan, *Global Perspectives on Consolidated Children's Rights Statutes* (UNICEF, Legislative Reform Initiative, 2008) 35–36; Laura Lundy, Ursula Kilkelly, and Bronagh Byrne, 'Incorporation of the United Nations Convention on the Rights of the Child in Law: A Comparative Review' (2013) 21 (3) *International Journal of Children's Rights* 442.

and speaks to all echelons of power and all levels of society. Courts have limitations as an implementation mechanism. Their institutional position channels them towards a 'compliance model of human rights'.[4] Courts do not capitalise on the multidimensionality of the CRC, including its political, advocacy, policy, planning, and programming dimensions.[5] They perform best in times of peace and respect for the rule of law, and they must be 'willing and capable'[6] of sanctioning rights violations. None of these aspects can be taken for granted. Also, courts seldom address systemic children's rights issues (except, perhaps, in constitutional litigation) and, as Tobin points out, children's rights remain disputed concepts and are hampered by difficulties in access to courts and by procedural impediments.[7]

Although the courts are not a panacea for the successful implementation of the CRC, the judicial application of the Convention is sought and valued. The Committee on the Rights of the Child (Committee or CRC Committee), which monitors the implementation of the CRC, has made an intrinsic link between the realisation of the rights of children and their protection by national courts.[8] Many courts engage with the CRC and, while the quality of such engagement varies, this has often led to positive legal developments, with courts sometimes acting as a safety net when children's rights fall victim to political oversight.[9]

[4] John Tobin, 'Understanding a Human Rights Based Approach to Matters Involving Children: Conceptual Foundations and Strategic Considerations' in Antonella Invernizzi and Jane Williams (eds.), *The Human Rights of Children: From Vision to Implementation* (Burlington: Ashgate, 2011) 61, 66.

[5] James Himes, 'Monitoring Children's Rights: Cutting through the Confusion and Planning for the Effective Action' in Eugeen Verhellen (ed.), *Monitoring Children's Rights* (The Hague: Martinus Nijhoff, 1996) 113, 119; Tobin, 'Understanding a Human Rights Based Approach', 66.

[6] Emilia Justyna Powell and Jeffrey K. Staton, 'Domestic Judicial Institutions and Human Rights Treaty Violation' (2009) 53(1) *International Studies Quarterly* 149, 154.

[7] Tobin, 'Judging the Judges', 581; John Tobin, 'Article 4: A State's General Obligation of Implementation' in John Tobin (ed.), *The UN Convention on the Rights of the Child: A Commentary* (Oxford: Oxford University Press, 2019) 108, 117.

[8] CRC Committee, *General Comment No. 5 (2003): General Measures of Implementation of the Convention on the Rights of the Child (arts. 4, 42 and 44, para. 6)*, 27 November 2003, CRC/GC/2003/5, para. 21.

[9] See Aoife Nolan, *Children's Socio-Economic Rights, Democracy and the Courts* (Oxford: Hart 2011).

1.2 The CRC: A Special Treaty?

Consistent attention to the domestic implementation of the CRC has created an expectation that the courts, as part of the state structure, apply the Convention. However, judicial application of the CRC has escaped close attention, the focus often being on the Convention as a guide for legal and policy reform.[10] Recent studies have analysed the role of the courts in giving effect to international treaties,[11] but the peculiarities of the CRC warn against simply importing such analyses. This is not to say that *only* factors inherent to the CRC impact on its judicial application,[12] or to advocate for a CRC-specific theory of judicial application.[13] Nonetheless, it is relevant to acknowledge that some special features of the CRC may influence its judicial application. The discussion below selects the features that, in the author's view, are most relevant to the judicial application of the CRC and are best able to provide a context for the rest of the book.[14]

1.2.1 The CRC as an Enforceable Legal Instrument

More than that of other human rights treaties, the legal nature of the CRC has been criticised. The criticism concerns two issues: the very *legal* nature of the Convention and its justiciability. These issues are distinct, albeit intersecting, but seldom differentiated.

[10] Himes, 'Monitoring Children's Rights', 119–120; Jonathan Todres, 'Emerging Limitations on the Rights of the Child: The U.N. Convention on the Rights of the Child and Its Early Case Law' (1998) 30(1) *Columbia Human Rights Law Review* 159, 193.

[11] Magnus Killander (ed.), *International Law and Domestic Human Rights Litigation in Africa* (Pretoria: Pretoria University Law Press, 2010); David Sloss (ed.), *The Role of Domestic Courts in Treaty Enforcement: A Comparative Study* (New York: Cambridge University Press, 2009); Dinah Shelton (ed.), *International Law and Domestic Legal Systems: Incorporation, Transformation, and Persuasion* (Oxford: Oxford University Press, 2011); André Nollkaemper, *National Courts and the International Rule of Law* (Oxford: Oxford University Press, 2011).

[12] In fact, this book later shows that factors beyond the Convention affect its application.

[13] Cf. Daniel Hill, 'Estimating the Effects of Human Rights Treaties on State Behavior' (2010) 72(4) *Journal of Politics* 1161, 1172. Hill supports a treaty-specific approach to assessing the impact of human rights treaties.

[14] For a more comprehensive discussion of the Convention's special features, see Wouter Vandenhole, 'Distinctive Characteristics of Children's Human Rights Law' in Eva Brems, Ellen Desmet, and Wouter Vandenhole (eds.), *Children's Rights Law in the Global Human Rights Landscape: Isolation, Inspiration, Integration?* (Oxon: Taylor & Francis Group, 2017) 21.

Courts apply *law*; therefore, the judicial application of the CRC depends on it being cognisable as law (i.e., being *legal* or juridical). Some authors have questioned the Convention's legal pedigree, indirectly suggesting that courts have a limited role in giving it effect.[15] Thus, it has been argued that the Convention is a 'bewildering hotchpotch of provisions',[16] 'rather a political instrument than an ensemble of judicially enforceable elements',[17] and yet to 'mature into a solid legal instrument'.[18] The Convention, it is argued, lacks some markers of legal-ness: a general limitations provision[19] and a rigorous interpretation that avoids rights inflationism.[20] The absence of an enforcement mechanism has also been seen as a sign of legal vulnerability.[21] Indeed, the absence until 2014 of an individual communications procedure[22] has limited the opportunities for the CRC to be applied in court-like processes that validate its juridical nature. Differences between article 4 of the CRC and general implementation provisions of other treaties, explored in Chapter 2, have left the CRC vulnerable to claims that it was not intended to be applied by the courts. Further, there may be a perception of a 'softer' legal nature reinforced by the prominence in the CRC discourse

[15] Paradoxically, the CRC has also been criticised for being too legal because it reduces the rights of children to the 'law's binary code of lawful/unlawful' (Michael King, 'Children's Rights as Communication: Reflections on Autopoietic Theory and the United Nations Convention' (1994) 57(3) *Modern Law Review* 385, 390) and conceals the complexities of child-related issues (John I'Anson, Ann Quennerstedt, and Carol Robinson, 'The International Economy of Children's Rights: Issues in Translation' (2017) 25(1) *International Journal of Children's Rights* 50).

[16] Jane Fortin, *Children's Rights and the Developing Law*, 3rd ed. (Cambridge: Cambridge University Press, 2009) 40–41.

[17] Johan Vande Lanotte and Geert Goedertier, 'Monitoring Human Rights: Formal and Procedural Aspects' in Eugeen Verhellen (ed.), *Monitoring Children's Rights* (The Hague: Martinus Nijhoff, 1996) 73, 109–110.

[18] Wouter Vandenhole, Gamze Erdem Türkelli, and Sara Lembrechts, *Children's Rights: A Commentary on the Convention on the Rights of the Child and Its Protocols* (Cheltenham: Edward Elgar Publishing, 2019) 28.

[19] Vandenhole, Erdem Türkelli and Lembrechts, *Children's Rights*, 30.

[20] Nigel Cantwell, 'Are Children's Rights Still Human?' in Antonella Invernizzi and Jane Williams (eds.), *The Human Rights of Children: From Visions to Implementation* (Burlington, VT: Ashgate, 2011) 37, 53.

[21] Jane Fortin, 'Children's Rights: Flattering to Deceive?' (2014) 26(1) *Child and Family Law Quarterly* 51–52.

[22] This was rectified in 2014 with the coming into force of the Optional Protocol to the Convention on the Rights of the Child on a Communications Procedure, New York, 19 December 2011, in force 14 April 2014 (adopted by United Nations General Assembly resolution A/RES/66/138 of 19 December 2011).

of the best interests of the child – a concept traditionally associated with decisions informed primarily by empirical information rather than hard legal principles.[23]

The misgivings about the CRC's juridical nature have been expressed at times as criticism of its vagueness or aspirational nature.[24] Clarity is an important element of the rule of law and distinguishes legal norms from other official instruments, such as policies, strategies, and the like. This criticism is relevant to the courts' ability to apply the Convention, touching on both its legal nature and its justiciability. Many authors disagree that the CRC is beyond the reach of *legal* interpretation. Also, the Committee interprets the CRC and contributes to clarifying its meaning. The very application by the courts illustrates that they consider the CRC not as being inherently vague but rather as being capable of legal interpretation through repeated application. De Búrca captures well this gradual clarification of the Convention when she approaches it as an experimental instrument.[25] Accordingly, its vagueness is not a concern because the content of rights is built through the reiteration of interpretations among the users of the Convention, both domestic and international. This clarification by reiteration reminds us that law is not static and that what is vague today is no longer so tomorrow. This is plentifully demonstrated by, inter alia, the increasing acceptance of the justiciability of socio-economic rights and the evolution of the general principles of the CRC from half-baked concepts to its flag bearers, as discussed in Section 1.2.2.

The multidimensional nature of the CRC may have created angst about its *legal* nature. The CRC is a complex socio-political *and* legal instrument.[26] A theory of how its various dimensions articulate is

[23] I borrow from Roux, who makes this point about family law and child protection: Theunis Roux, 'Judging the Quality of Legal Research: A Qualified Response to the Demand for Greater Methodological Rigour' (2014) 24(1) *Legal Education Review* 178, 181.

[24] Fortin, *Children's Rights and the Developing Law*, 40–41. Other authors, however, use an affirming language, referring to the 'broad formulation' and the 'high level of abstraction' of the CRC: John Tobin, 'Introduction: The Foundation for Children's Rights' in John Tobin (ed.), *The UN Convention on the Rights of the Child: A Commentary* (Oxford: Oxford University Press, 2019) 1, 3, 13.

[25] Gráinne de Búrca, 'Human Rights Experimentalism' (2017) 111(2) *American Journal of International Law* 277.

[26] Himes, 'Monitoring Children's Rights', 119; Ann Quennerstedt, 'Transforming Children's Human Rights: From Universal Claims to National Particularity' in Michael Freeman (ed.), *Law and Childhood Studies: Current Legal Issues Volume 14* (Oxford:

lacking, but, to use Michael King's terminology,[27] the Convention has more than a 'legal message' and it transcends what is 'amenable to legal understanding'.[28] The multidimensionality of the CRC reflects the coexistence therein of equally valid and autonomous codes for children's issues. Accordingly, *legal* imperfections in the CRC are not destructive of its *legal*-ness. Instead, they may signal that some of its aspects cannot (yet) be decoded by the law and they may speak to the Convention's non-legal audiences.

The above discussion calls for reflection on how *being legal/juridical* (or 'of the law') is understood in a CRC context. An oversimplified approach that equates being legal with justiciability (i.e., enforceability resulting in individual remedy) may have projected the CRC as having a weak legal nature. However, what is legal or non-legal is nuanced and often depends on the context. For example, failure to pass legislation to give effect to the CRC is a legal matter for the CRC Committee that may find the state in violation of the CRC. For a domestic ordinary court, however, this may be a political rather than legal matter. Different types of judicial use may place different demands on an international norm and thus colour the perception of its legal nature. Thus, as discussed in the Chapter 2, for direct application, a CRC norm must be complete because it becomes the rule of decision. For indirect application, completeness is less important if the court can extract *some* aspects relevant to the legal interpretation process. The jurisdiction of the courts that engage with the CRC is also relevant. There are, for example, constitutional and ordinary courts, administrative and judicial courts, federal and state courts, and ordinary and specialist courts. The varied jurisdiction of these courts may have consequences for the CRC where not *all* domestic courts have the power to respond to *all* the domestic violations of international treaties.

In brief, certain features of the CRC may have created the perception of a legally weak instrument, with the courts having only a limited role in its implementation. However, as Scheinin argues, judicial rulings have persuaded national audiences that 'human rights law is really law, by all

Oxford University Press, 2012) 104–105; Tara M. Collins, 'The General Measures of Implementation: Opportunities for Progress with Children's Rights' (2019) 23(3) *International Journal of Human Rights* 338, 349; Tobin, 'Introduction', 3.

[27] I am adapting slightly Michael King's approach. He considers the CRC to be the *legal* coding of child-related issues, while I use his ideas to argue that the Convention itself contains both legal and non-legal codes.

[28] Michael King, 'Against Children's Rights' (1996) 50 *Acta Juridica* 28, 30, 34.

international and domestic standards'.[29] While the Convention may not be flawless, this book is replete with examples of judicial application that validate its legal-ness. Nonetheless, the discussion above remains relevant for a better understanding of the context in which the CRC is judicially applied and as a call for a better understanding of its legal nuances.

1.2.2 The Novelty of the CRC

Some of the strengths in the CRC lie in its diversity of rights – which transcend the dichotomy between civil and political rights and socio-economic rights – and its general principles in articles 2, 3, 6, and 12. These features are not neutral when it comes to judicial application.

The CRC has created new rights (see articles 6, 7, 8, 12, 18, and 31), including rights whose nature is difficult to ascertain (see articles 3, 5, and 31). While alternative categorisations of rights are sometimes used in relation to the CRC rights – provision, protection, and participation rights[30] – these categories are not analytically developed,[31] leaving the distinctiveness of the CRC rights insufficiently clarified. Courts may be cautious about rights that are difficult to unpack in a traditional paradigm or they may fail to capitalise fully on the diversity of rights created by the Convention.

The four general principles of the CRC identified by the Committee[32] are a distinctive feature of the Convention but are 'thinly

[29] Martin Scheinin, 'General Introduction' in Martin Scheinin (ed.), *International Human Rights Norms in the Nordic and Baltic Countries* (The Hague: Martinus Nijhoff, 1996) 11, 17.

[30] For critical views, see Ann Quennerstedt, 'Children, But Not Really Humans? Critical Reflections on the Hampering Effect of the "3 P's"' (2010) 18(4) *International Journal of Children's Rights* 619; Didier Reynaert et al., 'Introduction: A Critical Approach to Children's Rights' in Wouter Vandenhole et al. (eds.), *Routledge International Handbook of Children's Rights Studies* (London: Routledge, 2015) 1.

[31] They are said to be of 'pedagogical' value only: Quennerstedt, 'Children, But Not Really Humans?', 621.

[32] These were identified by the Committee as articles 2 (non-discrimination), 3 (best interests of the child), 6 (survival and development), and 12 (right to be heard): CRC Committee, *General guidelines regarding the form and content of initial reports to be submitted by States parties under article 44, paragraph 1 (a), of the Convention*, 30 October 1991, CRC/C/5, para. 13. See generally Karl Hanson and Laura Lundy, 'Does Exactly What It Says on the Tin? A Critical Analysis and Alternative Conceptualisation of the So-called "General Principles" of the Convention on the Rights of the Child' (2017) 25(2) *International Journal of Children's Rights* 285; Laura Lundy and Bronagh Byrne, 'The Four General Principles of the United Nations

conceptualised'[33] and have an uneven profile. The most popular are articles 3(1) and 12, while article 6 is in its infancy[34] and article 2 remains underutilised. Although theoretically vulnerable, as Hanson and Lundy argue, the general principles are 'an accessible shorthand for the child's rights project as a whole'.[35] They capture the essence of the CRC in provisions that have a high degree of generality, enabling their judicial application in a wide range of contexts and the identification of convergence with the domestic law, thereby increasing the opportunities for the Convention to be applied by the courts. This is demonstrated by the case law on article 3 in the jurisdictions analysed in this book.

To conclude, some of the features of the CRC add a distinctive note to its judicial application. They create opportunities and tensions that are absent in other human rights instruments, and they influence whether and how the courts apply the CRC. The judicial application of the CRC is, however, influenced by more than its features, as shown in the case studies in this book. As Tobin suggests, there is a 'a strong onus on proponents of a more active judicial approach in this area' to articulate a more coherent approach to the judicial application of the CRC.[36] This book seeks to make a modest contribution in that regard.

1.3 What Does This Book Do?

This book addresses the impact of domestic rules concerning the relationship between international treaties and domestic law on the ability of domestic courts to engage effectively with the Convention. It considers the implications of the findings of this study with regard to the role of domestic courts in giving effect to the CRC. The book explores issues such as how the courts apply the CRC, to what effect, and the factors that influence that engagement.

Convention on the Rights of the Child: The Potential Value of the Approach in Other Areas of Human Rights Law' in Eva Brems, Ellen Desmet, and Wouter Vandenhole (eds.), *Children's Rights Law in the Global Human Rights Landscape: Isolation, Inspiration, Integration?* (Oxon: Taylor & Francis Group, 2017) 52.

33 Hanson and Lundy, 'Does Exactly What It Says', 292.

34 Noam Peleg, 'Developing the Right to Development' (2017) 25(2) *International Journal of Children's Rights* 380.

35 Hanson and Lundy, 'Does Exactly What It Says', 298.

36 Tobin, 'Judging the Judges', 581.

1.3.1 Focus on Reception or Engagement Rules and Legal Status

This research considers the judicial application from the perspective of the basic rules that govern the domestic status of the Convention (the reception or engagement rules) in four selected legal systems – Australia (dualist), France (monist), South Africa (hybrid), and the United Kingdom (dualist)[37] – with civil and common law traditions.

Dividing legal systems into monist, dualist, and hybrid systems,[38] with the consequent distinction between the direct and indirect application of international treaties, may seem too basic and outdated as an analytical tool in the context of significant theoretical developments concerning the relationship between international treaties and domestic law. Although formal rules regarding the interaction between the CRC and domestic legal systems cannot fully explain the dynamic of judicial engagement with the CRC, they remain important analytical tools for several reasons.

First, the formal reception scaffold allows the courts to 'find ways to treat international law as law',[39] as opposed to approaching the CRC as simply being relevant to the development of legislation, policies, and practice. As the courts continue to engage with the formal aspects of reception as 'an unavoidable first step'[40] in the application of international norms, it remains distinctly relevant to give such rules

[37] For the distinction between monism and dualism, and between monist and dualist *legal systems*, see David Sloss, 'Non-Self-Executing Treaties: Exposing a Constitutional Fallacy' (2002) 36(1) *University of California Davis Law Review* 1, 9. Sloss points out that the adjectives 'monist' and 'dualist' are used 'to describe different types of domestic legal systems' and not just 'two different theoretical perspectives on the relationship between domestic and international law': David Sloss, 'Treaty Enforcement in Domestic Courts: A Comparative Analysis' in David Sloss (ed.), *The Role of Domestic Courts in Treaty Enforcement: A Comparative Study* (New York: Cambridge University Press, 2009) 1, 5. It is in the former sense that the terms are used in this work.

[38] Hybrid systems are those in which at least some international norms can be applied directly by the courts. Hybrid monist states are said to include Germany, the Netherlands, Poland, Russia, South Africa, and the United States: Sloss, 'Treaty Enforcement in Domestic Courts', 1, 7. Sloss credits Van Alstine with the creation of the term. See Michael P. Van Alstine, 'The Role of Domestic Courts in Treaty Enforcement: Summary and Conclusions' in David Sloss (ed.), *The Role of Domestic Courts in Treaty Enforcement: A Comparative Study* (New York: Cambridge University Press, 2009) 555.

[39] Benedetto Conforti, *International Law and the Role of Domestic Legal Systems* (Dordrecht: Springer, 1993) 13.

[40] René Provost, 'Judging in Splendid Isolation' (2008) 56(1) *American Journal of Comparative Law* 125, 135. See similarly Helen Keller and Alec Stone Sweet, 'Assessing the Impact of the ECHR on National Legal Systems' in Helen Keller and Alec Stone Sweet (eds.), *A Europe of Rights: The Impact of the ECHR on National Legal Systems* (New York: Oxford University Press, 2008) 678, 682.

heightened attention. The initial interest in the domestic legal status of the CRC[41] has faded in favour of a preoccupation with its substance, but occasionally the interest in legal status[42] resurfaces, showing that the issue remains unsettled.[43] The CRC Committee itself remains preoccupied by it and has urged for clarification in this regard.[44]

Second, the formal rules governing the interaction between the CRC and domestic law reflect a domestic agreement regarding the means that the courts can use to give effect to the CRC in a consistent and meaningful way. Within the limits of this agreement, the courts have uncontested powers to engage with the Convention and can be held accountable for their deployment or otherwise. Third, by being public and accessible both domestically and internationally, these norms shape expectations in relation to how the courts should engage with the CRC.

Fourth, a focus on formal rules of reception has the potential to show whether the courts engage with the CRC in ways not captured by these rules. Knop is critical of engaging with the courts' application of international law as 'dependent on the conviction of bindingness'[45] and of the 'traditional "bindingness" model of international law'.[46] In her view,

[41] André Alen and Wouter Pas, 'The UN Convention on the Rights of the Child's Self-Executing Character' in Eugeen Verhellen (ed.), *Monitoring Children's Rights* (The Hague: Martinus Nijhoff, 1996) 165; Eugeen Verhellen, *Convention on the Rights of the Child: Background, Motivation, Strategies, Main Themes* (Leuven: Garant, 1994).

[42] 'Legal status' is understood here to refer not only to whether a treaty is incorporated, but also to other methods of using the CRC that are authorised by the domestic law (i.e., as an interpretation aid).

[43] CRC Committee, *List of issues to be taken up in connection with the consideration of the third periodic report of the Netherlands*, 22 October 2008, CRC/C/NLD/Q/3; CRC Committee, *List of issues to be taken up in connection with the consideration of the third and fourth periodic reports of Romania*, 9 March 2009, CRC/C/ROM/Q/4.

[44] CRC Committee, *General Comment No. 5*, para. 19. See generally Meda Couzens, 'CRC Dialogues: Does the Committee on the Rights of the Child "Speak" to the National Courts?' in Ton Liefaard and Julia Sloth-Nielsen (eds.), *The United Nations Convention on the Rights of the Child: Taking Stock After 25 Years and Looking Ahead* (Leiden: Brill/Nijhoff, 2016) 103.

[45] Karen Knop, 'Here and There: International Law in Domestic Courts' (2000) 32(2) *New York University Journal of International Law and Politics* 501, 503. The term 'bindingness' may mislead and requires some qualification. Even when the consideration of international law is mandated (see the South African case study in Chapter 5), international law does not become binding. Further, in some dualist states (see the Australian case study in Chapter 4), the consideration of international law is, without more, not mandated. Knop associates 'bindingness' with a status or use of international law that derives its authority and legitimacy from its formal authorisation by the domestic law. This is the meaning given to 'bindingness' when the term is used in this work.

[46] Knop, 'Here and There', 504.

trying to understand how the courts engage with international law by considering exclusively the legally endorsed methods of engagement prevents a full understanding of the judicial application of international law.[47] That observation is ultimately supported by this book, which identifies *sui generis* methods of judicial engagement with the Convention. Nonetheless, it is by using these formal rules as a demarcation tool that such alternative methods can be identified and the complexity of judicial engagement with the CRC illustrated.

To move away from the traditional focus on bindingness, Knop has suggested relating to international treaties as comparative law (persuasive rather than authoritative). This author sits uneasily with that suggestion.[48] Even if the CRC is not domestically incorporated, it cannot be reduced to the same legal position as laws of foreign jurisdictions. The CRC has been ratified by the state, while the same state is a complete outsider in relation to the laws of any other state. The CRC has a history of its juridical nature being contested, and this approach may encourage an unwarranted revisionism. A comparative law approach could perhaps circumvent some of the counterproductive debates that take place when discussing the legal status of the CRC,[49] offering an outlet for its values and principles while its status continues to be debated. However, similar outcomes can be obtained without eroding the legal strength of the CRC. This can be achieved by acknowledging the diversity of what it means to be 'legal' or 'binding' and by recognising the evolving nature of the CRC's normativity, which is gradually discovered through the interaction of the Convention with the domestic courts that use a variety of domestic tools to decipher it.

Lastly, the variances between how the courts engage with human rights treaties across the divide between monist and dualist legal systems may be shrinking,[50] but some distinctions remain. Monist and dualist systems

[47] Knop, 'Here and There', 503.

[48] Admittedly, this approach could be used as an analytical tool to unpack the judicial reasoning in some cases and in some legal systems. It remains, however, uncertain whether the approach is intended to displace traditional approaches or work alongside them, and whether it is intended to be universally valid or selectively applied. If Knop's approach has universal aspirations, then it is likely to encounter major resistance from some legal systems, in which the constitutional provisions proclaim that international law is part of the domestic law (e.g., see the French case study in Chapter 3).

[49] See especially the French and Australian case studies in Chapters 3 and 4, respectively.

[50] See generally Dinah Shelton, 'Introduction' in Dinah Shelton (ed.), *International Law and Domestic Legal Systems: Incorporation, Transformation, and Persuasion* (Oxford: Oxford University Press, 2011) 1, 3; Melissa A. Waters, 'Creeping Monism: The Judicial Trend

legitimise prima facie different legal enquiries and methods of engagement – that is, respectively, application versus no application in the absence of legislative effect, and direct versus indirect application.[51] Direct application may lead to outcomes that are not available in dualist systems: immediate legal effect, regardless of legislative inaction; potential access to remedies in cases of violation; and, in certain legal systems, the possibility of setting aside domestic norms that conflict with the Convention. Indirect application, however, permits a more flexible and diverse engagement with the Convention by allowing the courts to select only those aspects of a provision that are relevant to the case at hand.

This book returns therefore to the basic tools of the rules of reception, which can still yield useful insights for a better conceptualisation of the role of the courts in applying the CRC. The perspective of the book is enhanced by a closer attention to the structure of reception than has previously been afforded. The systematic attention to reception rules as a domestic entry point for treaties highlights the importance of the structure of reception ('*structure d'accueil du droit interne*'[52]) to the judicial operation of the Convention, meaning the legal context in which it applies – which may include the legislative context, judicial powers, existing case law, the structure of the government, membership of regional organisations, and so on. By highlighting the interconnectedness between the formal rules of engagement and the structure of reception, this book introduces much-needed nuance to the analysis of the judicial application of human rights treaties. It draws attention to the multiple sources of, inter alia, children's rights, which occupy the same legal space as the Convention, and to the importance of *local* legal knowledge for a full understanding of the dynamic between the courts and the CRC.

toward Interpretive Incorporation of Human Rights Treaties' (2007) 107(3) *Columbia Law Review* 628; Scheinin, 'General Introduction', 13; André Nollkaemper, 'The Duality of Direct Effect of International Law' (2014) 25(1) *European Journal of International Law* 105; David Sloss, 'Domestic Application of Treaties' (Santa Clara Law Digital Commons, 2011) 3, https://digitalcommons.law.scu.edu/facpubs/635.

51 Van Alstine, 'The Role of Domestic Courts', 566.

52 Claudia Sciotti-Lam, *L'applicabilité des traités internationaux relatifs aux droits de l'homme en droit interne* (Brussels: Bruylant, 2004) 441. The term is borrowed from Verhoeven (Joe Verhoeven, 'La notion d'"applicabilité directe" du droit international' (1980) 15(2) *Revue belge de droit international* 243, 260), who cites P. Comte.

1.3.2 Meaningful or Effective Engagement

This book looks beyond establishing whether reception rules simply enable courts to apply the CRC: it considers whether the courts have been able to do so meaningfully within those rules. Only meaningful engagement can be effective and thus an appropriate measure to give effect to the CRC, as required by article 4. Meaningful engagement looks different in each jurisdiction because it is informed by the constitutional limitations on court powers. For example, courts in dualist systems cannot be expected to apply the CRC directly. Similarly, courts cannot be expected to assert the domestic priority or supremacy of the Convention if this is not open to them under the domestic law.

In this book, meaningful engagement is understood as engagement with an ascertainable purpose, which is justified by the relevance and usefulness of the CRC. Meaningful engagement can be procedural and substantive. Procedural meaningful engagement exists when CRC norms and their domestic implications are analysed and a reasoned decision is made as to why the Convention is followed or rejected.[53] Substantive meaningful engagement exists when the engagement is effective in that a court extracts something relevant from the CRC that contributes to the reasoning by adding *something unique* (i.e., an 'added value'[54]) that cannot be sourced to other instruments. A favourable outcome is not essential for meaningful engagement because the law can develop even in the absence of positive outcomes in concrete cases. A contribution to the child-friendly development of domestic law can take place in many ways, including by clarifying the domestic law, enabling and encouraging child-friendly reasoning, providing a framework for analysing and understanding the domestic law, and highlighting issues that are otherwise overlooked.

Value-added, which implies complementarity with other legal sources, is more realistic than dominant influence or sole application as a marker

[53] I draw here from Juha Tuovinen, 'The Role of International Law in Constitutional Adjudication: *Glenister v President of the Republic of South Africa*' (2013) 130(4) *South African Law Journal* 661.

[54] The term 'added value of the Convention' is used in a similar way by de Graaf: Coby de Graaf, 'The Application of the United Nations Convention on the Rights of the Child in Dutch Legal Practice' in Alison Diduck, Noam Peleg, and Helen Reece (eds.), *Law in Society: Reflections on Children, Family, Culture and Philosophy* (Leiden: Brill Nijhoff, 2015) 589, 591. The term 'value-added' has a different meaning for Waters, who uses it to refer to cases in which courts rely on international treaties simply to provide support for reasoning that is well anchored in the domestic law: Waters, 'Creeping Monism', 654.

of substantive meaningful engagement because domestic legal reasoning is seldom dominated by international law or informed by it alone. Further, value-added helps distinguish the CRC from convergent or overlapping legal instruments and constitutes an incentive for its sustainable application. In most cases, the procedural dimension is a stepping stone to substantive engagement and thus to uncovering the added value of the CRC.

1.3.3 The Selection of Jurisdictions

The four jurisdictions analysed here would probably be strange bedfellows in a classic comparative study. France is a monist legal system in which the CRC is part of the domestic legal order, and thus directly applicable. Australia is a dualist system in which the CRC is not fully incorporated but courts can give it effect in statutory interpretation and the development of the common law. South Africa is a hybrid system that permits the direct application of the CRC, but this has been shied away from in favour of constitutional interpretation. The United Kingdom is a dualist system in which the unincorporated CRC can be used to develop the common law or to interpret statutes, but its application is almost always mediated by the European Convention on Human Rights and Fundamental Freedoms (ECHR).[55]

The diversity of the sample nonetheless reflects the reality of the cosmopolitan context in which the CRC operates and aligns with the comparative international law perspective used in this research and discussed in Section 1.4 below. The findings do not purport to be universally applicable, but they do provide some insights of general value that can contribute to conceptualising the role of the courts in giving effect to the CRC and that can invite further exploration of the field. The four jurisdictions are used to illustrate rather than represent various approaches to the judicial application of the Convention, and thus, their diversity is a suitable tool for learning about the CRC. In keeping with the comparative international law perspective of this study, the primary focus is on learning about the CRC through the experience of the domestic courts, rather than learning about the domestic jurisdictions

[55] Convention for the Protection of Human Rights and Fundamental Freedoms, as amended by Protocol Nos. 11 and 14, 4 November 1950, ETS 5.

that are compared.[56] The more diverse the jurisdictions we observe, the more we learn about the Convention. Further, this 'bricolage'[57] elicits insights that are not available when analysing a more homogenous sample. It demonstrates in a CRC context that no reception rules are inherently more enabling of judicial engagement than others. In addition, it allows for different dimensions of the CRC to be revealed and explored. Thus, courts look closely at the legal features of the CRC (i.e., clarity and completeness or norms) to decide whether it can be applied directly or not, but they are content with considering its 'softer' aspects – such as its values and objectives – for the purposes of indirect application. Lastly, the bricolage brings to the fore the significance of the structure of reception for the judicial application of the CRC by showing that jurisdictions with common features can vary widely in terms of their judicial application of the Convention.[58]

The judgments analysed in this book come from the highest courts with jurisdiction to engage with the CRC – except in the case of Australia, where three courts are considered: the High Court, the Full Court of the Family Court, and the Supreme Court of Victoria. Initially, only the High Court was selected, but, for the reasons explained in Chapter 4, such a limited focus would have provided an incomplete image of how the Australian judiciary engages with the Convention.

Only cases in which the CRC was explicitly mentioned have been considered, but there remains much to be learned from cases in which the Convention was not mentioned but was relevant. The sampling and the analysis follow slightly different patterns due to the particularities of the legal systems involved. In the Australian, South African, and UK case studies, all cases in which the CRC was mentioned by the relevant courts were considered. That approach was not possible in France because of the much higher number of cases that have reached the highest courts. For that jurisdiction, the cases were primarily selected purposefully, using relevant French literature as a guide to their significance. Further, the different styles of judgment writing in civil and common law

[56] If this approach prompts self-reflection and stimulates cross-learning between the analysed jurisdictions, those are welcome by-products.

[57] Mark Tushnet, 'The Possibilities of Comparative Constitutional Law' (1999) 108(6) *Yale Law Journal* 1225. Tushnet uses the term to refer to comparative research conducted in relation to jurisdictions at hand or available to a researcher.

[58] For example, while the Australian and UK systems have similar reception rules and share a legal tradition, the human rights scaffolding present in the United Kingdom (but absent in Australia) has clearly facilitated the application of the CRC.

jurisdictions account for the closer attention given to specific judgments in the case studies on Australia, South Africa, and the United Kingdom.

1.4 The Theoretical Perspective of This Work

This research is doctrinal and fits within the emerging field of comparative international law. The field entails 'identifying, analyzing, and explaining similarities and differences in how actors in different legal systems understand, interpret, apply, and approach international law'.[59] Roberts et al. argue that the field sits at the intersection between international law and comparative law. It borrows insights and methods from comparative law to understand more fully how international law is approached by diverse domestic and international actors.[60] Roberts et al. point out that this field is 'primarily descriptive and explanatory'.[61] The descriptive bend of comparative international law is fitting for this study, which investigates an issue that has been insufficiently explored on a systematic basis and seeks to illustrate the importance of the domestic reception frameworks for the application of the CRC. The descriptive nature of this perspective does not prevent it from raising normative and theoretical questions, including in relation to the implications of the identified differences and similarities for how international law is conceptualised.[62] This theoretical question is indeed addressed in Chapters 7 and 8, where attention is given to the implications of the findings for understanding the role of domestic courts.

There is a potential overlap between comparative international law and comparative constitutional law,[63] but Roberts et al. argue that they are distinct – ostensibly because the former's focus is on 'cross-national understandings, interpretations, applications, and approaches to international law rather than constitutional law'.[64] That distinction is relevant for this work, wherein the focus is on the operation of domestic rules that often have a constitutional nature – that is, the reception rules. As the purpose of this study is to learn about the *international* (i.e., the CRC)

[59] Anthea Roberts et al., 'Conceptualizing Comparative International Law' in Anthea Roberts et al. (eds.), *Comparative International Law* (New York: Oxford University Press, 2018) 3, 6 (footnote omitted).

[60] Roberts et al., 'Conceptualizing', 4.

[61] Roberts et al., 'Conceptualizing', 6; see also at 28.

[62] Roberts et al., 'Conceptualizing', 6; see also at 28.

[63] Roberts et al., 'Conceptualizing', 9.

[64] Roberts et al., 'Conceptualizing', 9.

while comparing the domestic, the better framework is that of comparative international law, with due acknowledgement for its intersection with, in this case, comparative constitutional law.

Comparative international law is said to lack 'an implicit normative agenda'.[65] This makes it a suitable perspective from which to study the vast, free-flowing cosmopolitan space in which different domestic and international approaches to giving judicial effect to the CRC unapologetically coexist in a horizontal relationship void of formal hierarchy.[66] This perspective captures the reality of the autonomous engagement with the CRC by domestic courts and international bodies, such as the Committee, all of which make available to all others their take on the CRC.

The theoretical framing of this work would not be complete without acknowledging the influence of some selected cosmopolitan insights. The comparative international law perspective and the form of cosmopolitanism used here align in various ways, which make them good enquiry partners. They enable observation and description without judgement and hierarchy, and the rich description celebrated by both approaches domestic law as more than a passive recipient of the CRC. Further, they both allow the portrayal of domestic law not as a threat to the universalist promises of international law but as central to its raison d'être and operation.

A 'cosmopolitan context'[67] for understanding the operation of the CRC is perhaps inevitable for a treaty whose wide ratification creates an espace juridique with enormous diversity. This diversity will continue for the foreseeable future, and cosmopolitanism is a good tool to normalise, accept, and respect this diversity in a space that is resistant to hierarchical ordering. Cosmopolitanism is an amorphous concept, broadly associated with, inter alia, individualism and universalism.[68]

[65] Roberts et al., 'Conceptualizing', 28.

[66] The relationship between the CRC Committee and the courts could be seen as vertical but only in a descriptive rather than normative sense, because the Committee's output is not technically binding on domestic courts.

[67] Concept used by Zlatko Skrbiš and Ian Woodward, 'Cosmopolitan Openness' in Maria Rovisco and Magdalena Nowicka (eds.), *The Ashgate Research Companion to Cosmopolitanism* (Farnham: Ashgate, 2011) 53, 55.

[68] Robert Cryer et al., *Research Methodologies in EU and International Law* (Oxford: Hart Publishing, 2011) 46. See also Roland Pierik and Wouter Werner, 'Cosmopolitanism in Context: An Introduction' in Roland Pierik and Wouter Werner (eds.), *Cosmopolitanism in Context: Perspectives from International Law and Political Theory* (Cambridge: Cambridge University Press, 2010) 1, 3.

Its boundaries are ill-defined,[69] cosmopolitan views permeating areas as diverse as legal, cultural, political, civic, and global justice studies.[70] The cosmopolitanism that has influenced this work is not the 'avowedly normative, idealistic'[71] *legal* cosmopolitanism, which aspires to institutionalisation and uniformity. It is instead what Porras calls the 'thin cosmopolitanism'[72] that 'expresses an attitude, an approach, a sensibility, or a way of being in the world',[73] which is specific to cultural cosmopolitanism. This form of cosmopolitanism enables observation and communication of what one sees, without expecting hierarchies and value judgements. Like comparative international law, placing the enquiry in a cosmopolitan context validates the centrality of the domestic legal experience for understanding the Convention, which is 'discovered' primarily through its interaction with the diverse domestic realities on which it is dependent.

There is another aspect of the cosmopolitanism literature to which I am indebted: the concept of the 'cosmopolitan stranger',[74] with which I associate as far as this work is concerned. This figure is a person with the 'cosmopolitan way of seeing'[75] of an observer who has a 'greater allegiance'[76] to the international than to the national. A cosmopolitan stranger sees the local as a tool for understanding the international, in much the same way as does an international comparatist. The stranger, however, acknowledges limitations that an international comparatist may not – namely, uncertainty about the accuracy of their understanding of

[69] Samuel Scheffler, 'Conceptions of Cosmopolitanism' (1999) 11(3) *Utilitas* 255; Vince P. Marotta, 'The Cosmopolitan Stranger' in Stan van Hooft and Wim Vandekerckhove (eds.), *Questioning Cosmopolitanism, Studies in Global Justice 6* (Dordrecht: Springer, 2010) 105, 110; Garrett Wallace Brown and David Held, 'Editor's Introduction' in Garrett Wallace Brown and David Held (eds.), *The Cosmopolitan Reader* (Cambridge: Polity Press, 2010) 1, 9.

[70] Wallace Brown and Held, 'Editor's Introduction', 9.

[71] Cryer et al., *Research Methodologies*, 47.

[72] Ileana M. Porras, 'Liberal Cosmopolitanism or Cosmopolitan Liberalism?' in M. N. S. Sellers (ed.), *Parochialism, Cosmopolitanism, and the Foundations of International Law* (Cambridge: Cambridge University Press, 2011) 118, 136.

[73] Porras, 'Liberal Cosmopolitanism', 121. Others refer to it as 'an intellectual disposition': Marotta, 'The Cosmopolitan Stranger', 110.

[74] Marotta, 'The Cosmopolitan Stranger', 105. Nussbaum talks about cosmopolitanism as a 'lonely business', an exile 'from the comfort of local truths': Martha C. Nussbaum, 'Patriotism and Cosmopolitanism' in Garrett Wallace Brown and David Held (eds.), *The Cosmopolitan Reader* (Cambridge: Polity Press, 2010) 155, 161.

[75] Skrbiš and Woodward, 'Cosmopolitan Openness', 55.

[76] Marotta, 'The Cosmopolitan Stranger', 113.

the realities of the host place. There is, nonetheless, a silver lining to this limitation. Because 'estrangement is pedagogy'[77] and the stranger questions 'nearly everything that is taken for granted by the host',[78] the cosmopolitan stranger brings a perspective that transcends domestic and international essentialism.[79] Thus, I am a cosmopolitan stranger in relation to the four jurisdictions studied here, with the proviso that I am a more informed stranger in relation to Australia and South Africa.[80] My learning curve has been steep and perhaps I have missed some (or many) of the autochthonous legal subtleties, or I might not have fully understood the local potential for CRC advancement. Intellectual caution and integrity have, however, guided this work so as to avoid legal error. I hope that by holding multiple mirrors to these diverse legal spaces, this book raises meaningful questions that are waiting to be explored.

1.5 The Structure of the Book

Following this introductory Chapter 1, Chapter 2 paints the context in which judicial application is considered in this book. It shows that internationalist expectations on the judicial application of the CRC, such as those voiced by the Committee, do not fully articulate what the courts are able to do under the domestic rules that govern the direct and indirect application of treaties. Chapters 3, 4, 5, and 6 contain the case studies, which present the case law followed by an analysis of judicial application as enabled by the reception rules. Chapters 7 and 8 consider the implications of the findings of this book for understanding the role of the courts in applying the Convention.

[77] Expression used by Sneja Gunew, 'Estrangement as Pedagogy: The Cosmopolitan Vernacular' in Rosi Braidotti Patrick Hanafin and Bolette Blaagaard (eds.), *After Cosmopolitanism* (London: Routledge, 2012) 132, 136, building on the work of Paul Gilroy. Mark Tushnet, however, argues that learning from the experience of foreign cultures can only be meaningful if excessive local detail is avoided: Tushnet, 'The Possibilities', 1308.

[78] Marotta, 'The Cosmopolitan Stranger', 108.

[79] Marotta, 'The Cosmopolitan Stranger', 118.

[80] Although I received my legal training and practised law in Romania, I subsequently lived and taught law in both South Africa and Australia.

2

The CRC and the Courts

International and Domestic Perspectives

2.1 Introduction

The CRC is concomitantly an international instrument *and* an instrument with municipal legal relevance.[1] When applying the Convention, courts operate at the intersection of domestic and international legal orders.[2] This dual operation of both the CRC and the courts has generated inconsistent perspectives on the judicial application of the Convention. The international perspective is maximalist: the courts ought to apply the CRC domestically;[3] while the domestic perspective is more reserved: courts bear primary allegiance to domestic law and their role in applying the Convention is limited by constitutional considerations, including its domestic legal status.

It is not the aim of this work to reconcile those perspectives, which, as argued in Chapter 8, are better left discrete, but their canvassing is useful as a context for the four case studies that follow and for a more nuanced understanding of the judicial application of the CRC. The international perspective on judicial application is presented in Section 2.2 with reference to article 4 of the CRC and the views of the CRC Committee, while the domestic perspective is presented in Section 2.3 with reference to the direct and indirect application of the CRC – the two paradigm engagement methods in monist, dualist, and hybrid states. The chapter shows that while the international perspective strongly favours judicial

[1] Writing generally about treaties, Curtis A. Bradley, 'Self-Execution and Treaty Duality' (2008) 1 *Supreme Court Review* 131, 133.

[2] André Nollkaemper, 'The Duality of Direct Effect of International Law' (2014) 25(1) *European Journal of International Law* 105, 108–109.

[3] For discussion, see Karen Knop, 'Here and There: International Law in Domestic Courts' (2000) 32(2) *New York University Journal of International Law and Politics* 501, 516; René Provost, 'Judging in Splendid Isolation' (2008) 56(1) *American Journal of Comparative Law* 125, 168.

application, the Convention itself does not, in general, demand this, unless it is the appropriate implementation measure for specific provisions. This leaves the judicial application of the CRC largely dependent on domestic laws and dynamics, which calls for close attention to be paid to domestic realities. That is the approach taken in the case studies.

2.2 The International Perspective on the Judicial Application of the CRC

2.2.1 Article 4 of the CRC and the Courts

Article 4 of the CRC, the general implementation provision, reads:

> States Parties shall undertake all appropriate legislative, administrative, and other measures for the implementation of the rights recognized in the present Convention. With regard to economic, social and cultural rights, States Parties shall undertake such measures to the maximum extent of their available resources and, where needed, within the framework of international co-operation.

Courts and remedies for violations are not mentioned in article 4, although corresponding provisions in other human rights treaties contain such references.[4] Some treaties even require that treaty bodies be provided with information about their judicial application.[5] A question arises, therefore, as to the significance of those omissions from article 4. John Tobin argues that the drafting history of article 4 indicates an attempt to 'adapt and fuse'[6] the general implementation provisions in

4 Article 2(3) of the International Covenant on Civil and Political Rights, 16 December 1966, in force 23 March 1976, 999 UNTS 171 (ICCPR); articles 1 and 13 of the Convention for the Protection of Human Rights and Fundamental Freedoms, 4 November 1950, in force 3 September 1953, 213 UNTS 221 (ECHR); article 6 of the International Convention on the Elimination of All Forms of Racial Discrimination, 21 December 1965, in force 4 January 1969, 660 UNTS 195 (CERD); article 2(1) of the Convention against Torture and Other Cruel, Inhuman or Degrading Treatment or Punishment, 10 December 1984, in force 26 June 1987, 1465 UNTS 85; article 2(c) of the Convention on the Elimination of All Forms of Discrimination against Women, 18 December 1979, in force 3 September 1981, 1249 UNTS 13 (CEDAW); and article 13 (1) of the Convention on the Rights of Persons with Disabilities, 13 December 2006, in force 3 May 2008, 2515 UNTS 3.

5 Article 9 of CERD, article 18 of CEDAW, and article 73 of the International Convention on the Protection of the Rights of All Migrant Workers and Members of Their Families, 18 December 1990, in force 1 July 2003, 2220 UNTS 3.

6 John Tobin, 'Article 4: A State's General Obligation of Implementation' in John Tobin (ed.), *The UN Convention on the Rights of the Child: A Commentary* (Oxford: Oxford University Press, 2019) 108.

the International Covenant on Civil and Political Rights (ICCPR)[7] and the International Covenant on Economic, Social and Cultural Rights.[8] Thus, the different wording of article 4 has no important consequences for the obligations incurred by states.[9] For other authors, however, the absence of reference to courts in article 4 remains a 'significant oversight',[10] especially if one searches for an *international* obligation for states to ensure the judicial application of a treaty.[11]

Generally, international law does not prescribe the means of its domestic implementation[12] because its focus is on compliance, rather than on the means to achieve it.[13] Furthermore, there is no *general* international obligation to provide access to courts to address violations of treaty rights.[14] Specific treaties may explicitly create such obligation by referring to courts or tribunals or to remedies in their general implementation provisions;[15] or they may imply it in their language, their object and purpose, the subsequent practice of states, and, possibly, the negotiation history.[16] An international obligation to provide access to courts cannot be implied when treaties similar in nature and scope provide victims with access to courts, while the treaty in discussion does not.[17]

[7] ICCPR, 16 December 1966, in force 23 March 1976, 999 UNTS 171.

[8] International Covenant on Economic, Social and Cultural Rights, 16 December 1966, in force 3 January 1976, 993 UNTS 3.

[9] Tobin, 'Article 4', 108.

[10] Jonathan Todres, 'Emerging Limitations on the Rights of the Child: The U.N. Convention on the Rights of the Child and Its Early Case Law' (1998) 30(1) *Columbia Human Rights Law Review* 159, 178. Todres contrasts this with the mentioning of the courts in article 3(1).

[11] Sean D. Murphy, 'Does International Law Obligate States to Open Their National Courts to Persons for the Invocation of Treaty Norms That Protect or Benefit Persons?' in David Sloss (ed.), *The Role of Domestic Courts in Treaty Enforcement: A Comparative Study* (New York: Cambridge University Press, 2009) 61.

[12] Thomas Buergenthal, 'Modern Constitutions and Human Rights Treaties' (1998) 36 *Columbia Journal of Transnational Law* 211. Occasionally, international law may require a specific form of implementation, such as legislative measures e.g., article 2(1) of the Convention against Torture).

[13] Murphy, 'Does International Law Obligate States', 70; Marc Bossuyt, 'The Direct Applicability of International Instruments on Human Rights' (1980) 15(2) *Revue belge de droit international* 317, 318, 321–322.

[14] Murphy, 'Does International Law Obligate States', 63.

[15] A right to a remedy supports a right of access to courts, although a right to remedy can be satisfied by access to non-judicial remedies. However, because the effective remedies are most often judicial remedies, it is likely that where a treaty mentions access to remedies, it refers to judicial remedies.

[16] Murphy, 'Does International Law Obligate States', 96–105.

[17] Murphy, 'Does International Law Obligate States', 105–108.

That is because the treaty has designed its implementation mechanisms to include means other than access to the courts. In relation to the CRC, Murphy argued that

> [u]nlike other UN human rights treaties, however, such as the treaties on civil and political rights, racial discrimination, and torture, the Convention on the Rights of the Child contains no express, general provisions calling for access to national organs, including national courts, for vindication of personal rights. The absence of such a provision, when it was included in earlier human rights treaties, weighs against implying such access to national courts on the basis of that convention.[18]

Some courts have come close to that reasoning. A majority of the Norwegian Supreme Court held that the absence of a reference in the CRC (incorporated verbatim by legislation) to an obligation for the state to secure access to effective national remedies meant that the Court could not make a finding of violation.[19] The Court contrasted the CRC with other treaties, pointing out that orders declaring violations of the ECHR and the ICCPR were justified by their recognition of the right to an effective remedy.[20]

However, the history of the drafting of the CRC and a consideration of other provisions of the Convention suggest that the omission of a reference to courts and/or remedies in article 4 does not substantially weaken the role of the courts in giving effect to the CRC. Although no prominent role was anticipated for the courts when article 4 was drafted,[21] a restrictive formulation that referred only to administrative and legislative implementation measures was rejected in favour of a formulation that also refers to 'other measures'[22] – including, therefore,

[18] Murphy, 'Does International Law Obligate States', 106 (footnotes omitted). He nonetheless mentions specific provisions referring to courts: articles 9(2), 12, 37(d), 40(2)(b)(iii): 106 n 152.

[19] *A, B, C and the Norwegian Association for Asylum Seekers (NOAS) (third party intervener) v. The State, represented by the Immigration Appeals Board*, Supreme Court of Norway (HR-2012-02399-P) at paras. 96, 101. For a compelling dissent, see Justice Bårdsen.

[20] *A, B, C* at para. 99. See also at paras. 94–95.

[21] Todres, 'Emerging Limitations', 178.

[22] Paragraphs 57–61 of the 1981 report of the Working Group to the Commission on Human Rights (E/CN.4/L.1542), which is quoted in paragraph 289 of the 1981 report of the Commission on Human Rights (E/CN.4/1475), reprinted in Office of the United Nations High Commissioner for Human Rights (UNHCHR), *Legislative History of the Convention on the Rights of the Child: Volume I* (New York: United Nations, 2007) 351. See also E/CN.4/1989/WG.1/CRP.1, pages 17–20, quoted in UNHCHR, *Legislative History*, 353.

the courts. This inclusion suggests that access to courts can be *the* effective and appropriate implementation measure under article 4.[23] This is especially so for those provisions closely aligned with the judicial function for which judicial application meets the requirements of effectiveness (i.e., enabling state compliance with a treaty) and appropriateness (i.e., advancing the rights protected by the treaty).[24]

The references to courts during the drafting process are not numerous, but some state representatives did anticipate a remedial process through the courts.[25] It emerges that, although regrettable, the absence of a reference to the courts in article 4 does not undermine the judicial application of the Convention. The states parties did not *exclude* the involvement of the courts in giving effect to the CRC; instead, they favoured a wording of article 4 that maximises, rather than restricts, opportunities for judicial application. The rule on the exhaustion of domestic remedies in the 2011 Optional Protocol to the Convention on the Rights of the Child on a Communications Procedure is a clear statement of principle that remedies must be domestically available.[26] This does not create an international obligation for states to ensure that the CRC is applied by the courts, but considering that effective remedies are often judicial remedies,[27] the Protocol supports the role of the courts in giving effect to the Convention.

The role of the courts in giving effect to the CRC cannot be understood through a literal reading of article 4. While discussion often gravitates around the remedial or reactive role of the courts in cases of alleged violations of CRC rights, the courts also play an implementing role for

[23] Todres, 'Emerging Limitations', 178.

[24] Venice Commission, *Report on the Implementation of International Human Rights Treaties in Domestic Law and the Role of the Courts* (CDL-AD(2014)005, 2014) 14, para. 40; Tobin, 'Article 4', 112–113.

[25] Statements by the Ugandan and US representatives respectively: A/C.3/44/SR.41 (20 November 1989), para. 27, quoted in UNHCHR, *Legislative History*, 258; E/CN.4/1988/WG.1/WP.17 (29 January 1988), quoted in UNHCHR, *Legislative History*, 351.

[26] Optional Protocol to the Convention on the Rights of the Child on a Communications Procedure, New York, 19 December 2011, in force 14 April 2014 (adopted by United Nations General Assembly resolution A/RES/66/138 of 19 December 2011).

[27] It has even been stated that the remedies envisaged by human rights treaties are primarily of a judicial nature because they meet the criteria of availability, effectiveness, and sufficiency. See the African Court on Human and Peoples' Rights in *Tanganyika Law Society v. United Republic of Tanzania* (Application Nos. 009/2011 and 011/2011, 14 June 2013) at paras. 82.1, 82.3.

provisions that are closely related to the judicial function.[28] For example, some articles refer explicitly to the courts, signalling that they are the effective and appropriate mechanism for implementation according to article 4. Provisions in relation to the best interests of the child, the removal of a child from the family environment, participation in relevant proceedings, protection proceedings, and juvenile justice, for example, fall into this category.[29] There are also provisions that imply judicial involvement without necessarily mentioning the courts.[30]

The distinction between the enforcement and implementation roles of the courts, respectively, is relevant to how courts give effect to the CRC and the factors that may affect it. When courts act as an *enforcement* mechanism, much depends on the powers bestowed upon them vis-à-vis other state organs. However, when they act as an *implementation* mechanism, there is often scope to apply the CRC in the day-to-day administration of justice, over which courts themselves have much control. Ultimately, whatever role the courts assume, whether enforcement or implementation, the absence of judicial application of the CRC may lead to international responsibility. This does not, by itself, create a *de jure* obligation to ensure domestic judicial application, although it may give rise to a *de facto* obligation in this regard.

2.2.2 The CRC Committee's View on the Judicial Application of the CRC

The position of the CRC Committee has evolved from sidelining the courts as general implementation measures[31] to requiring states to accompany their reports with, inter alia, copies of 'principal ... judicial decisions' relevant to the CRC,[32] to provide information on the judicial

[28] For example, it is a primary judicial function to use detention as a last resort under article 37(b), but it is not the primary duty of courts to register the child immediately after birth under article 7(1).

[29] See, for example, articles 3(1), 9(1), 12(2), 18(2), 37(d), 40(2)(b)(iii), 40(2)(b)(v).

[30] For example, articles 21, 37(a), 37(b), 40(2)(b)(i), 40(2)(b)(iv).

[31] CRC Committee, *General guidelines regarding the form and content of initial reports to be submitted by States parties under article 44, paragraph 1 (a), of the Convention*, 30 October 1991, CRC/C/5, para. 9.

[32] CRC Committee, *General guidelines regarding the form and content of periodic reports to be submitted by States parties under article 44, paragraph 1 (b), of the Convention*, 29 November 2005, CRC/C/58/Rev.1, para. 7 (*General guidelines* 2005). See also CRC Committee, *Treaty-specific guidelines regarding the form and content of periodic reports to be submitted by States parties under article 44, paragraph 1 (b), of the Convention on the*

application of some CRC provisions[33] and on remedies available and their accessibility to children,[34] and to inform the Committee about the impact of jurisprudence on children.[35] It has even taken to criticising or praising courts for how they engage with the Convention.[36]

In General Comment No. 5,[37] the Committee discusses the courts among the general implementation mechanisms.[38] Accordingly, the ability of children's rights to be invoked before the courts is the ultimate test of an effective implementation: '[t]he test must be whether the applicable rights are truly realized for children and can be directly invoked before the courts'.[39] Furthermore, a children's rights perspective needs to be applied, inter alia, throughout the judiciary[40] because '[f]or rights to have meaning, effective remedies must be available to redress violations'.[41] The Committee acknowledges that the access to effective remedies is 'implicit', rather than explicit in the CRC, but it supports this with reference to other human rights treaties.[42] It stresses that all rights in the CRC (economic, social, cultural, civil, and political) 'must be

Rights of the Child, 25 November 2010, CRC/C/58/Rev.2, para. 15 (*Treaty-specific guidelines* 2010).

33 CRC Committee, *General guidelines* 2005, paras. 13, 15–16, 19, 21–23, 25, 31.

34 CRC Committee, *General guidelines* 2005, para. 16; CRC Committee, *Treaty-specific guidelines* 2010, para. 7.

35 CRC Committee, *Treaty-specific guidelines* 2010, para. 13.

36 CRC Committee, *Concluding observations of the Committee on the Rights of the Child: France*, 22 June 2009, CRC/C/FRA/CO/4, para. 10; CRC Committee, *Concluding observations on the second periodic report of South Africa*, 27 October 2016, CRC/C/ZAF/CO/2, para. 5; CRC Committee, *General Comment No. 8 (2006): The right of the child to protection from corporal punishment and other cruel or degrading forms of punishment (arts. 19; 28, para. 2; and 37, inter alia)*, 2 March 2007, CRC/C/GC/8, para. 25.

37 CRC Committee, *General Comment No. 5 (2003): General measures of implementation of the Convention on the Rights of the Child (arts. 4, 42 and 44, para. 6)*, 27 November 2003, CRC/GC/2003/5.

38 In *General Comment No. 16*, the Committee is even more specific and includes judicial measures as implementation measures under article 4: CRC Committee, *General Comment No. 16 (2013) on State obligations regarding the impact of the business sector on children's rights*, 17 April 2013, CRC/C/GC/16, part IV.B.3.

39 CRC Committee, *General Comment No. 5*, para. 21.

40 CRC Committee, *General Comment No. 5*, para. 12.

41 CRC Committee, *General Comment No. 5*, para. 24. The Committee gives the term 'justiciability' a wide meaning, which includes access to other 'independent complaint procedures': at para. 24. Generally, however, a matter is considered justiciable if it is amenable to *judicial* determination.

42 CRC Committee, *General Comment No. 5*, para. 24. Tobin adds that providing effective remedies is a necessary and appropriate measure under article 4: Tobin, 'Article 4', 115.

regarded as justiciable'[43] and that states should ensure access to remedies, including the courts. Lastly, the Committee highlights the need to clarify 'the extent of applicability of the Convention in States where the principle of "self-execution" applies and others where it is claimed that the Convention ... has been incorporated into domestic law'.[44] The Committee does not acknowledge the courts as the custodians of this process, but it implies as much when referring to incorporation[45] and self-execution, as discussed in Section 2.3.

The Committee envisages both implementation and remedial roles for the courts. It sees the courts playing a primarily implementation role for provisions connected to the judicial function. This is reflected in the general comments, which contain numerous statements in relation to how children ought to be treated by the courts.[46] The Committee mentions the remedial role in relation to breaches of CRC rights or as a corrective to inadequate implementation by the political branches of the

[43] CRC Committee, *General Comment No. 5*, para. 25.

[44] CRC Committee, *General Comment No. 5*, para. 19.

[45] That is, '[i]ncorporation should mean that the provisions of the Convention can be directly invoked before the courts and applied by national authorities and that the Convention will prevail where there is a conflict with domestic legislation or common practice': CRC Committee, *General Comment No. 5*, para. 20.

[46] Some general comments – such as CRC Committee, *General Comment No. 10 (2007): Children's rights in Juvenile Justice*, 9 February 2007, CRC/C/GC/10; CRC Committee, *General Comment No. 12 (2009): The right of the child to be heard*, 20 July 2009, CRC/C/GC/12; and CRC Committee, *General Comment No. 14 (2013) on the right of the child to have his or her best interests taken as a primary consideration (art. 3, para. 1)*, 29 May 2013, CRC/C/GC/14 – deal extensively with what the Committee sees as requirements arising from the CRC in relation to the courts' treatment of children. Others include CRC Committee, *General Comment No. 11 (2009): Indigenous children and their rights under the Convention*, 12 February 2009, CRC/C/GC/11, para. 33; Committee on the Protection of the Rights of All Migrant Workers and Members of Their Families and CRC Committee, *Joint General Comment No. 3 (2017) of the Committee on the Protection of the Rights of All Migrant Workers and Members of Their Families and No. 22 (2017) of the Committee on the Rights of the Child on the general principles regarding the human rights of children in the context of international migration*, 16 November 2017, CMW/C/GC/3-CRC/C/GC/22, para. 30; CRC Committee, *General Comment No. 13 (2011): The right of the child to freedom from all forms of violence*, 18 April 2011, CRC/C/GC/13, para. 54; Committee on the Elimination of Discrimination against Women and CRC Committee, *Joint General Recommendation No. 31 of the Committee on the Elimination of Discrimination against Women/General Comment No. 18 of the Committee on the Rights of the Child on harmful practices*, 14 November 2014, CEDAW/C/GC/31-CRC/C/CG/18, para. 87(d); CRC Committee, *General Comment No. 9 (2006): The rights of children with disabilities*, 27 February 2007, CRC/C/GC/9, paras. 73–74.

state.[47] It often associates access to courts (rather than other bodies) with effective individual remedies and enjoins states to provide access to judicial redress in a wide variety of contexts.[48] To support the courts' role as a corrective to inadequate implementation, the Committee supports direct application and giving priority to the CRC over domestic law or practice:

> Incorporation should mean that the provisions of the Convention can be directly invoked before the courts and applied by national authorities and that the Convention will prevail where there is a conflict with domestic legislation or common practice. In case of any conflict in legislation, predominance should always be given to the Convention, in the light of article 27 of the Vienna Convention on the Law of Treaties.[49]

In sum, the Committee contemplates an extensive role for the courts, with maximum implementation benefits for the CRC. Its vision is pervaded by features such as the justiciability of all CRC rights, no differentiation between types of legal systems in terms of the role of the courts, a role for the courts in ensuring the prevalence of the CRC over conflicting domestic law, and the direct application of the CRC in relevant legal systems. Articulated by an international monitoring body, the Committee's vision overlooks the position of the courts as domestic institutions and has at times resulted in questionable legal views. For example, the Committee relies on article 27 of the Vienna Convention on the Law of Treaties[50] to argue that courts should give priority to the CRC

[47] Recently, the Committee created a special part on remedies in some general comments: CRC Committee, *General Comment No. 12 (2009)*, CRC/C/GC/12, paras. 46–47; CRC Committee, *General Comment No. 15 (2013) on the right of the child to the enjoyment of the highest attainable standard of health (art. 24)*, 17 April 2013, CRC/C/GC/15, part VI.F; CRC Committee, *General Comment No. 16*, part VI.B; CRC Committee, *General Comment No. 21 (2017) on children in street situations*, 21 June 2017, CRC/C/GC/21, para. 22.

[48] CRC Committee, *General Comment No. 4 (2003): Adolescent health and development in the context of the Convention on the Rights of the Child*, 1 July 2003, CRC/GC/2003/4, para. 9; CRC Committee, *General Comment No. 13*, para. 55(e); CRC Committee, *General Comment No. 15*, part VI.F; Committee on the Elimination of Discrimination against Women and CRC Committee, *Joint General Recommendation No. 31/General Comment No. 18*, para. 55(o), (q); CRC Committee, *General Comment No. 21*, para. 22.

[49] CRC Committee, *General Comment No. 5*, para. 20. See also CRC Committee, *General Comment No. 6 (2005): Treatment of unaccompanied and separated children outside their country of origin*, 1 September 2005, CRC/GC/2005/6, para. 14.

[50] Vienna Convention on the Law of Treaties, 23 May 1969, in force 27 January 1980, 1155 UNTS 331.

when in conflict with the domestic law,[51] but this is an *international* obligation incumbent on states, rather than a *domestic duty* with which the courts must, without more, comply.[52] Also, the Committee has been inconsistent on the thorny issue of direct application.[53] While it supports the direct application of the CRC, the Committee has questioned only some relevant states in relation to it.[54] Further, although it expects the entire Convention to be directly applied,[55] the Committee singled out article 3(1) to declare it as directly applicable,[56] possibly undermining its earlier statement about the direct application of the entire CRC.

Thus, the Committee's maximalist vision and its scant consideration of the domestic anchoring of the courts illustrate the rift between international expectations of judicial application of the CRC and domestic reality. This is reflected in the coexistence of two judicial application narratives – one international and one domestic – that may sometimes overlap and at other times diverge, as illustrated here.

2.3 The Domestic Perspective on the Judicial Application of the CRC

Unlike the Committee, the courts are institutions that are deeply embedded in their domestic legal systems. It is within their purview to decide the domestic legal status of the Convention when it is invoked before them. This is an important task, as acknowledged by the Committee

[51] CRC Committee, *General Comment No. 5*, para. 20; CRC Committee, *General Comment No. 6*, para. 14. This view is also reflected in some concluding observations. For example, in relation to Australia, the Committee expressed concern that the CRC 'cannot be used by the judiciary to override inconsistent provisions of domestic law': CRC Committee, *Concluding observations: Australia*, 20 October 2005, CRC/C/15/Add.268, para. 9. This is not constitutionally tenable in Australia. See Chapter 4.

[52] André Nollkaemper, 'The Netherlands' in David Sloss (ed.), *The Role of Domestic Courts in Treaty Enforcement: A Comparative Study* (New York: Cambridge University Press, 2009) 326, 333.

[53] Meda Couzens, 'CRC Dialogues: Does the Committee on the Rights of the Child "Speak" to the National Courts?' in Ton Liefaard and Julia Sloth-Nielsen (eds.), *The United Nations Convention on the Rights of the Child: Taking Stock after 25 Years and Looking Ahead* (Leiden: Brill/Nijhoff, 2016) 103, 111–112.

[54] France has been questioned often by the Committee in relation to the direct application of the CRC, but states such as Belgium, the Netherlands and Romania have seldom or only recently been so questioned: see Couzens, 'CRC Dialogues'.

[55] CRC Committee, *Concluding observations: France*, 22 June 2009, CRC/C/FRA/CO/4, para. 11.

[56] CRC Committee, *General Comment No. 14*.

itself,[57] and, in Provost's words, '[w]hile the issue of the binding nature of domestic norms rarely arises, it will often constitute an unavoidable first step in the application of international norms'.[58] The courts decide on the domestic legal status of the CRC according to the domestic legal rules that govern its interaction with the domestic law (i.e., the rules of reception or engagement). These formal rules differ between states. A distinction is commonly made between dualist and monist systems,[59] with an accompanying distinction between direct and indirect applications of the CRC. Direct and indirect applications of international treaties, which are widely accepted as descriptions of the interaction between the courts and international law, are used in this work as a point of departure for analysing the judicial application of the CRC.

2.3.1 *The Direct Application or Self-Execution of the CRC*

2.3.1.1 An Introduction to Direct Application/Self-Execution

Some legal systems, monist or hybrid, operate with the linguistically simple but conceptually complex principle that ratified treaties are automatically part of the domestic legal order, without legislative transposition, and may be applied directly by courts. Direct application, or self-execution,[60] is a powerful tool: it equates treaties (generally) with domestic statutes, makes them direct sources of domestic rights, and allows them to fill gaps in domestic law.[61] When direct application is complemented by domestic treaty supremacy, the effects are enhanced in that domestic norms that conflict with a treaty can be set aside (i.e., not

[57] It called for a clarification of self-execution, constitutional status, and domestic incorporation of the CRC: CRC Committee, *General Comment No. 5*, para. 19.

[58] Provost, 'Judging in Splendid Isolation', 135.

[59] See Section 1.3.1. Hybrid systems are not discussed separately in this chapter because they combine the essential features of monist and dualist systems.

[60] The term 'self-execution' is preferred in the United States and Japan, while 'direct application' is favoured in Europe: Dinah Shelton, 'Introduction' in Dinah Shelton (ed.), *International Law and Domestic Legal Systems: Incorporation, Transformation, and Persuasion* (Oxford: Oxford University Press, 2011) 1, 11. Because self-execution is the 'defining feature of direct effect' (André Nollkaemper, *National Courts and the International Rule of Law* (Oxford: Oxford University Press, 2011) 118), the terms 'direct application' and 'self-execution' are used interchangeably in this work.

[61] Arne Vandaele and Wouter Pas, 'International Human Rights Treaties and Their Relation with National Law: Monism, Dualism and the Self-Executing Character of Human Rights' in Arabella Weyts (ed.), *Understanding Children's Rights: Collected Papers Presented at the Seventh International Interdisciplinary Course on Children's Rights* (Ghent: Children's Rights Centre, University of Ghent, 2004) 269, 271.

applied in a specific case) and, when relevant, substituted with the international norm. The direct application of international treaties is, however, complex. In relation to the CRC, views have ranged between enthusiastic support[62] and complete rejection.[63] Courts have been similarly inconsistent.[64]

A full analysis of the intricacies of direct application cannot be undertaken here,[65] but some context is relevant with regard to the CRC. The complexity of direct application arises from a confluence of factors, including fundamental domestic principles such as the separation of powers, legality, and democracy;[66] having both international and domestic legal dimensions;[67] the terminological complexities inherent in a

[62] CRC Committee, *Concluding observations: France*, 2009, para. 11.

[63] See generally David Smolin, 'Overcoming Religious Objections to the Convention on the Rights of the Child' (2006) 20(1) *Emory International Law Review* 81; Eric Engle, 'The Convention on the Rights of the Child' (2011) 29 *Quinnipiac Law Review* 793.

[64] Jean-Pierre Rosenczveig, 'The Self-Executing Character of the Children's Rights Convention in France' in Eugeen Verhellen (ed.), *Monitoring Children's Rights* (The Hague: Martinus Nijhoff, 1996) 187; Manuela Limbeek and Marielle Bruning, 'The Netherlands: Two Decades of the CRC in Dutch Case Law' in Ton Liefaard and Jaap E. Doek (eds.), *Litigating the Rights of the Child: The UN Convention on the Rights of the Child in Domestic and International Jurisprudence* (Dordrecht: Springer, 2015) 89; Wouter Vandenhole, 'The Convention of the Rights of the Child in Belgian Case Law' in Ton Liefaard and Jaap E. Doek (eds.), *Litigating the Rights of the Child: The UN Convention on the Rights of the Child in Domestic and International Jurisprudence* (Dordrecht: Springer, 2015) 105; Meda Couzens, 'Romanian Courts and the UN Convention on the Rights of the Child: A Case Study' (2016) 24(4) *International Journal of Children's Rights* 851.

[65] See generally Antonio Cassese, *International Law*, 2nd ed. (New York: Oxford University Press, 2005), 227; Eric Claes and Arne Vandaele, 'L'effet direct des traités internationaux: Une analyse en droit positif et en théorie du droit axée sur les droits de l'homme' (2001) 34(2) *Revue belge de droit international* 411, 423; Tim Wu, 'Treaties' Domain' (2007) 93 (3) *Virginia Law Review* 571, 579; Nollkaemper, 'The Duality of Direct Effect', 106.

[66] Carlos Manuel Vázquez, 'Treaties as Law of the Land: The Supremacy Clause and the Judicial Enforcement of Treaties' (1995) 122 *Harvard Law Review* 599; Venice Commission, *Report on the Implementation*, para. 30.

[67] For the controversies raised by the dual nature of direct application or self-execution, see generally Jacques Velu, 'Les effets directs des instruments internationaux en matière de droits de l'homme' (1980) 15(2) *Revue belge de droit international* 293–294; Joe Verhoeven, 'La notion d'"applicabilité directe" du droit international' (1980) 15(2) *Revue belge de droit international* 243; Bradley, 'Self-Execution', 151; David Sloss, 'Executing *Foster v. Neilson*: The Two-Step Approach to Analyzing Self-Executing Treaties' (2012) 53(1) *Harvard International Law Journal* 301, 303; David Sloss, 'Non-Self-Executing Treaties: Exposing a Constitutional Fallacy' (2002) 36(1) *University of California Davis Law Review* 1; Didier Chauvaux and Thierry-Xavier Girardot, 'Les clauses d'un traité international dépourvues d'effet direct ne peuvent être invoquées à

globalised concept that is explicated through domestic tools; the conflation of direct application with justiciability, the supremacy of international law, and other related legal concepts; and the opacity of the criteria for direct application. Some of these issues are discussed in the following paragraphs, alongside the functional definition of direct application relied on in this work.

Conceptual Distinctions and the Definition of Direct Application Terms such as 'direct effect', 'direct application', 'direct applicability', 'self-executing', 'justiciability', 'invocation', and 'being automatically a part of the domestic law' are used in the context of direct application.[68] These terms are often left undefined or with divergent definitions.[69] Justiciability and direct application are court-centred doctrines that may intersect but remain conceptually distinct and are triggered by different criteria. Conflating them has sometimes led to the denial of direct application because a treaty provision did not meet *justiciability* criteria, rather than the criteria for direct application.[70] Further, 'being automatically a part of the domestic law' is not equivalent

l'encontre d'un acte réglementaire' (1997) *L'Actualité juridique: Droit administratif* 435; Wu, 'Treaties' Domain', 573.

68 See Jean-François Akandji-Kombé, 'De l'invocabilité des sources européennes et internationales du droit social devant le juge interne' (2012) 11 *Droit social* 1014; Claudia Sciotti-Lam, *L'applicabilité des traités internationaux relatifs aux droits de l'homme en droit interne* (Brussels: Bruylant, 2004) 335; Michael P. Van Alstine, 'The Role of Domestic Courts in Treaty Enforcement: Summary and Conclusions' in David Sloss (ed.), *The Role of Domestic Courts in Treaty Enforcement: A Comparative Study* (New York: Cambridge University Press, 2009) 555.

69 Akandji-Kombé, 'De l'invocabilité', part I.a. For example, some authors distinguish between self-execution and direct application (Thomas Buergenthal, 'Self-Executing and Non-Self-Executing Treaties in National and International Law' in The Hague Academy of International Law, *Collected Courses of the Hague Academy of International Law/Recueil des cours*, vol. 235 (Leiden: Brill, 1992) 303, 321), while others argue that self-execution is the 'defining feature of direct effect' (Nollkaemper, *National Courts*, 118), or direct effect is but one of the elements of direct applicability, thus making a distinction between direct application and direct effect (Akandji-Kombé, 'De l'invocabilité', part I.b).

70 On the availability of judicial remedies and self-execution, see Anne Woolhandler, 'Judicial Enforcement of Treaties: Self-Execution and Related Doctrines: Remarks' (2006) 100 *Proceedings of the American Society of International Law* 439, 448; David Sloss, 'Self-Executing Treaties and Domestic Judicial Remedies' (2004) 98 *Proceedings of the American Society of International Law* 346; David Sloss, 'When Do Treaties Create Individually Enforceable Rights?: The Supreme Court Ducks the Issue in *Hamdan* and *Sanchez-Llamas*' (2006) 45(1) *Columbia Journal of Transnational Law* 20.

to direct application. It simply indicates that the treaty has been domestically 'received'[71] or has entered the domestic order *as is*[72] (i.e., with its own wording) and thus has *some* legal force therein. However, that legal force is not always given effect by courts.[73]

Another important relevant distinction is between the domestic supremacy of international treaties and their direct effect. The *domestic* supremacy (or prevalence or priority) of ratified international treaties operates only if it is recognised in the domestic law.[74] Its judicial effect can be to invalidate or prevent reliance on the domestic norm that conflicts with an international treaty, depending on the legal system. Domestic supremacy and direct application are distinct concepts. For example, when a treaty provision is used to fill a gap in the domestic law, that provision is applied directly but does not assert its supremacy.[75] Domestic supremacy and direct effect have different legal sources,[76] but they are closely associated[77] and some courts approach them as being interdependent.[78] The conflation of these two distinct concepts prevents treaty supremacy from operating effectively in jurisdictions with a restrictive approach to direct application, as seen in the French case study in Chapter 3.

The definition of direct application is, predictably, marred by complexities. In *Foster v. Nielson*,[79] the US Supreme Court stated,

[71] Van Alstine, 'The Role of Domestic Courts', 597–598; Verhoeven, 'La notion', 251.

[72] Nollkaemper, *National Courts*, 118.

[73] Buergenthal, 'Self-Executing and Non-Self-Executing Treaties', 318, 369; Nollkaemper 'The Netherlands', 339.

[74] Treaty supremacy cannot be *domestically* 'forced' by article 27 of the VCLT: Nollkaemper 'The Netherlands', 333.

[75] Verhoeven, 'La notion', 247. Also, direct effect may be immaterial to supremacy. The EU directives, for example, have no direct effect but 'can preclude reliance on a provision of national law' inconsistent therein: Paul Craig and Gráinne de Búrca, *EU Law: Texts, Cases and Materials*, 4th ed. (Oxford: Oxford University Press, 2008) 271.

[76] For example, articles 93 and 94 of the Dutch Constitution deal respectively with direct effect and supremacy (Nollkaemper 'The Netherlands', 331–333), paragraph 14 of the Preamble to the 1946 French Constitution deals with automatic incorporation, and article 55 of the 1958 French Constitution deals with supremacy. See Alain Pellet, *Quelle place la Constitution de 1958 fait-elle au droit international?* (2008), www.conseil-constitutionnel.fr/la-constitution.

[77] Verhoeven, 'La notion', 247.

[78] For example, France (see Chapter 3) and the Netherlands: Nollkaemper, 'The Netherlands', 351.

[79] 27 US (2 Pet) 253 (1829) (*Foster*).

> Our constitution declares a treaty to be the law of the land. It is, consequently, to be regarded in courts of justice as equivalent to an act of the legislature, whenever it operates of itself without the aid of any legislative provision.[80]

Academic definitions of direct application or self-execution refer to a treaty that is 'capable of judicial application without additional implementing legislation',[81] or that applies 'as is, and not as potentially transformed by national legislation'.[82] While some authors argue that self-execution has multiple dimensions that require distinct definitions,[83] others maintain that there are degrees of direct application or legal effect.[84] Some definitions of direct application include references to individual rights. According to Buergenthal, a self-executing treaty gives rise to legal rights or obligations that are enforceable in the domestic courts.[85] Similar views have been expressed in Europe, where direct application is closely associated with the protection of individual rights.[86] This association restricts the direct application of international treaties[87] and has prompted authors to distinguish between wide and narrow meanings of direct application.[88]

In this confusing space, there are two certainties: first, courts make 'a basic distinction'[89] between directly applicable treaties and other treaties,

80 *Foster* at 314.

81 Buergenthal, 'Modern Constitutions', 213. See similarly Neville Botha, 'Rewriting the Constitution: The "Strange Alchemy" of Justice Sachs, Indeed!' (2009) 34(1) *South African Yearbook of International Law* 253, 266; Shelton, 'Introduction', 11.

82 Nollkaemper, *National Courts*, 118.

83 See generally Vázquez, 'Treaties as Law of the Land', 1995.

84 André Alen and Wouter Pas, 'The UN Convention on the Rights of the Child's Self-Executing Character' in Eugeen Verhellen (ed.), *Monitoring Children's Rights* (The Hague: Martinus Nijhoff, 1996) 165; Gaëlle Dumortier, 'L'effet direct des conventions internationales' (2012) 3 *Revue française de droit administratif* 547; Sciotti-Lam, *L'applicabilité*, 340–341.

85 Buergenthal, 'Self-Executing and Non-Self-Executing Treaties', 317.

86 Akandji-Kombé, 'De l'invocabilité', part I.c. See also Ronny Abraham, 'Les effets juridiques, en droit interne, de la Convention de New York relative aux droits de l'enfant' (1997) 3 *Revue française de droit administratif* 585, part III.B.

87 Sciotti-Lam, *L'applicabilité*, 336; Van Alstine, 'The Role of Domestic Courts'.

88 A *sensu lato* direct application can be limited to creating obligations for states parties, filling gaps in national law, setting aside inconsistent domestic norms, or substituting itself to the domestic law: Sciotti-Lam, *L'applicabilité*, 439–440. A *sensu stricto* directly applicable norm must create individual rights: Sciotti-Lam, *L'applicabilité*, 337. This distinction mirrors the relationship between objective and subjective direct effect under European Union law: see generally Craig and Gráinne de Búrca, *EU Law*.

89 Van Alstine, 'The Role of Domestic Courts', 600–601.

and second, a norm is directly applicable if it is capable of being applied in the absence of legislative measures that complete or clarify it.[90] For the purposes of this work, direct application is approached pragmatically to mean the use by courts of an international norm as a self-standing source of domestic law '*as is*',[91] without legislative transposition, to produce a legal effect that could not be obtained through the application of domestic law alone.[92]

2.3.1.2 Direct Application, Its Criteria, and the CRC

Direct application depends on certain criteria that, although objective in appearance, are 'fundamentally open to multiple interpretations'.[93] Even if courts do not always give them explicit attention or apply them consistently, these criteria continue to be used. Generally, the courts look at the intent of the states, the creation of individual rights, and the aptitude of a norm to be applied directly.[94] Each of these criteria is contested in terms of its relevance or meaning, or both.

The Intent of the Parties Treaties do not refer explicitly to direct application, and thus, courts sometimes resort to ascertaining the intent of states to determine their direct applicability. The intent criterion has been contested on different grounds, including that self-execution is generally a domestic matter, rather than one of international obligation,[95]

90 Sciotti-Lam, *L'applicabilité*, 336.

91 Nollkaemper, *National Courts*, 118. Sloss refers to a directly applied norm as the 'rule of decision': David Sloss, 'Treaty Enforcement in Domestic Courts: A Comparative Analysis' in David Sloss (ed.), *The Role of Domestic Courts in Treaty Enforcement: A Comparative Study* (New York: Cambridge University Press, 2009) 1, 11.

92 This is a composite definition that builds on the general structure of the definition advocated by Sciotti-Lam (*L'applicabilité*, 349), to which it adds the outcome of direct application (a solution for 'the inertia of the state', according to Verhoeven, 'La notion', 245, or a remedy 'where national law fails', according to André Nollkaemper, 'The Duality of Direct Effect', 105, 112).

93 Nollkaemper, 'The Duality of Direct Effect', 124.

94 For different formulations, see Shelton, 'Introduction', 11; Buergenthal, 'Self-Executing and Non-Self-Executing Treaties', 328; Arne Vandaele and Eric Claes, 'L'effet direct des traités internationaux. Une analyse en droit positif et en théorie du droit axée sur les droits de l'homme' (Institut de droit international, Working Paper No. 15, 2001) 12; Carine Laurent-Boutot, 'La Cour de cassation face aux traités internationaux protecteurs des droits de l'homme' (unpublished PhD thesis, University of Limoges, 2006); Sciotti-Lam, *L'applicabilité*, 357.

95 European community law is a rare example where states took an international obligation to make a treaty directly applicable. See Chauvaux and Girardot, 'Les clauses'.

and thus cannot be decided by referring to the intent of the treaty drafters.[96]

In a CRC context, its wording as a carrier of state intent has been used in various ways to deny its direct application. Indeed, the wording of the CRC (especially article 4) and its *travaux préparatoires* do not suggest an intention to make the CRC directly applicable.[97] However, during negotiations, the parties did not raise or oppose its direct application,[98] suggesting that this was a matter left to each individual state. The absence of references to effective remedies[99] and the reference to implementation measures in article 4[100] have been taken as reflecting an intent not to create a self-executing treaty. These views are rejected by international bodies. For the European Court of Human Rights (ECtHR), the reference to remedies in article 13 of the ECHR does not create obligations in relation to the *type* of measures (judicial or others) that states ought to take to ensure rights effectiveness.[101] The mention of implementation measures in the CRC does not create a presumption of non-self-execution. International bodies have rejected such a presumption,[102] which would undermine the long-accepted direct effect of equivalent provisions

[96] Sloss, 'Self-Executing Treaties'; Sloss, 'Executing *Foster v. Neilson*'.

[97] Sciotti-Lam, *L'applicabilité*, 381.

[98] Sciotti-Lam, *L'applicabilité*, 380. Only Germany raised direct application-related issues by making a declaration that the CRC was not directly applicable by its courts. It withdrew the declaration in 2010: 'Status of Treaties: Convention on the Rights of the Child', *United Nations Treaty Collection*, https://treaties.un.org/Pages/ViewDetails.aspx?src=IND&mtdsg_no=IV-11&chapter=4#10.

[99] By contrast, some courts have inferred self-execution from the formulation of article 1 of the ECHR, which provides that states 'shall secure' the rights in the Convention: Julien Pieret, 'L'influence du juge belge sur l'effectivité de la Convention: retour doctrinal et jurisprudentiel sur le concept d'effet direct' in Vincent Chapaux, Julien Pieret, and Annemie Schaus (eds.), *Entre ombres et lumières: cinquante ans d'application de la Convention européenne des droits de l'homme en Belgique* (Brussels: Bruylant, 2008) 83.

[100] Courts in France, Belgium, and Luxembourg have done so: see Sciotti-Lam, *L'applicabilité*, 387; for France, see Chapter 3. For a Belgian example, see Belgian Court of Cassation, Case No. P.99.0276.F (Justel No. F-19990331-5) of 31 March 1999.

[101] See Anja Seibert-Fohr, 'Domestic Implementation of the International Covenant on Civil and Political Rights Pursuant to Its Article 2 Para. 2' (2001) 5 *Max Planck Yearbook of United Nations Law* 399, 422. See also *Swedish Engine Drivers' Union v. Sweden* (Application No. 5614/72, 6 February 1976) at para. 50; *Popescu v. Romania No. 2* (Application No. 71 525/01, 26 April 2007) at para. 104.

[102] Committee on Economic, Social and Cultural Rights, *General Comment No. 9: The domestic application of the Covenant*, 3 December 1998, E/C.12/1998/24, para. 11.

in other human rights treaties.[103] As correctly stated, implementation measures are important for the non-self-executing norms in a treaty, but they do not erase the self-executing nature of those that are directly applicable.[104]

It has also been argued that the intent of states is not a useful criterion,[105] as it is surrounded by much uncertainty. Thus, it is not clear whose intent matters (i.e., individual states, states collectively, or the executive or other branches of states).[106] This has been notoriously controversial in a CRC context, with the literature pointing to situations where the views of the parliament have differed from those of the executive that ratified the CRC,[107] or where the views of courts on direct application have differed from those of parliament.[108] Further uncertainty exists in relation to what the intent is about (i.e., substantive rights or self-execution)[109] and how to determine that intent.[110]

Individual Rights The creation of individual rights is also a contested criterion. It has been argued that treaty provisions can be applied directly,[111] as a legitimate constraint on the power of the

[103] The direct application of ICCPR rights is accepted despite references to legislative measures in article 2(2): Christopher Harland, 'The Status of the International Covenant on Civil and Political Rights (ICCPR) in the Domestic Law of State Parties: An Initial Global Survey through UN Human Rights Committee Documents' (2000) 22 (1) *Human Rights Quarterly* 187, 195–196.

[104] Abraham, 'Les effets juridiques', part III.B; Benedetto Conforti, *International Law and the Role of Domestic Legal Systems* (Dordrecht: Springer, 1993) 32.

[105] Nollkaemper, *National Courts*, 135; Pieret, 'L'influence', 83, 86.

[106] For details, see Bradley, 'Self-Execution'; Sciotti-Lam, *L'applicabilité*, 357, 418; Pieret, 'L'influence', 107.

[107] Sonja Neudorfer and Claudia Wernig, 'Implementation of International Treaties into National Legal Orders: The Protection of the Rights of the Child within the Austrian Legal System' (2010) 14 *Max Planck Yearbook of United Nations Law* 409, 417.

[108] See the discussion in Coby de Graaf, 'The Application of the United Nations Convention on the Rights of the Child in Dutch Legal Practice' in Alison Diduck, Noam Peleg, and Helen Reece (eds.), *Law in Society: Reflections on Children, Family, Culture and Philosophy* (Leiden: Brill Nijhoff, 2015) 589–590; Limbeek and Bruning, 'The Netherlands', 98.

[109] See the discussion by Jean-Pierre Ancel, 'La Cour de cassation et la Convention internationale relative aux droits de l'enfant' (2001) 5(205) *Journal du droit des jeunes* 20–21; Nollkaemper, 'The Netherlands', 341.

[110] Vázquez, 'Treaties as Law of the Land', 705; Buergenthal, 'Self-Executing and Non-Self-Executing Treaties', 380.

[111] See generally Van Alstine, 'The Role of Domestic Courts'; Verhoeven, 'La notion', 264; Sciotti-Lam, *L'applicabilité*, 336, 343; Vandaele and Claes, 'L'effet direct', 15.

state[112] that can operate without creating individual rights.[113] The emergence of the individual rights criterion is linked to, for example, procedural requirements[114] and historical developments,[115] and has been reinforced by the jurisprudence of some supranational courts.[116] To ascertain if a treaty creates rights, courts have considered the general implementation provisions,[117] the wording of the treaty (i.e., whether it refers to obligations for states or rights for individuals),[118] and treaty context.[119] Nonetheless, a lack of clarity remains, making the criterion difficult to apply.[120]

For example, courts such as the Belgian Council of State,[121] the French Court of Cassation and Council of State,[122] and the Swiss Federal Tribunal[123] have denied direct effect to CRC norms on the ground that they refer to state obligations and not individual rights. Endorsement of such a literal reading would lead to absurd conclusions. There would be, for example, a 'right of the child to be protected from economic exploitation' (article 32 of the CRC), but not a right to be protected against drugs, sexual exploitation, or trafficking, because articles 33–36 do not use the term 'right'. This literal approach has been duly criticised. Authors have argued that the 'content and nature of the obligation are decisive'.[124] Also, the CRC Committee has identified individual rights in

112 Nollkaemper, 'The Netherlands', 351. See also Alen and Pas, 'The UN Convention'; Claes and Vandaele, 'L'effet direct'; Van Alstine, 'The Role of Domestic Courts'.

113 Alen and Pas, 'The UN Convention', 173–174.

114 Sciotti-Lam, *L'applicabilité*, 354.

115 Sciotti-Lam (*L'applicabilité*, 346) links this requirement with *Jurisdiction of the Courts of Danzig, Advisory Opinion* [1928] PCIJ (ser B) No. 15 (3 March) at 17–18.

116 Verhoeven, 'La notion', 245, with reference to the ECHR and ECJ jurisprudence. See the ECJ decision in *NV Algemene Transport- en Expeditie Onderneming van Gend and Loos v. Netherlands Inland Revenue Administration – Reference for a preliminary ruling: Tariefcommissie – Pays-Bas*, Case 26–62 of 1963 (*Van Gend and Loos*) at 12.

117 Sciotti-Lam, *L'applicabilité*, 398–400.

118 Murphy, 'Does International Law Obligate States', 101.

119 *Van Gend and Loos* at 11–13.

120 See generally Sloss, 'When Do Treaties Create'; Sital Kalantry, 'The Intent-to-Benefit: Individually Enforceable Rights under International Treaties' (2008) 44 *Stanford Journal of International Law* 63.

121 Belgian Council of State, Decision No. 69715 of 21 November 1997 (in relation to article 20).

122 See the discussion in Chapter 3.

123 The Tribunal considered articles 3(1) and 26 to be declaratory provisions that do not create rights: *D v. Family Allowance Fund of Zug Canton*, Swiss Federal Tribunal Arrêts du Tribunal fédéral 136 I 297, 2010.

124 Alen and Pas, 'The UN Convention', 171 (footnote omitted).

CRC provisions that are not drafted in a rights language.[125] This aligns with *Van Gend and Loos*, where the European Court of Justice (ECJ) deduced the existence of an individual right from the context of the relevant treaty – although the term 'right' was not used in that case.[126]

Clarity and Completeness The aptitude of a provision to be directly applied – variously expressed as a requirement for clarity, completeness, precision, or sufficiency – has been the most influential in deciding direct application.[127] This criterion requires that international norms be 'clear enough to serve as objective law'.[128]

The CRC may be vulnerable in relation to this criterion, as some of its provisions are, arguably, vague.[129] However, open-ended provisions are not unusual in human rights treaties, and this characteristic should not be an insurmountable challenge to direct application. Legal principles, for example, have an open-ended wording, but courts do not refuse their application.[130] The alleged indeterminacy of CRC provisions can be addressed through contextual interpretation.[131] Further, what courts

[125] For example, *General Comment No. 14* declared that article 3(1) of the CRC contains a right of the child to have his or her interests taken as a primary consideration. In *General Comment No. 13*, the CRC Committee declared that article 5 contains a right for the child to be directed and guided in the exercise of rights by caregivers (para. 59) and that article 19 contains 'a right to protection from all forms of violence' (para. 65).

[126] *NV Algemene Transport- en Expeditie Onderneming van Gend and Loos v. Netherlands Inland Revenue Administration – Reference for a preliminary ruling: Tariefcommissie – Pays-Bas*, Case 26–62 of 1963. The court relied on, for example, the 'spirit, the general scheme and the wording of those provisions' (at 11) and the clear obligations they created for other individuals, the states, or international institutions (at 12).

[127] Buergenthal, 'Self-Executing and Non-Self-Executing Treaties', 343; Shelton, 'Introduction', 12.

[128] Nollkaemper, 'The Netherlands', 342. Or 'self-sufficient' (Bossuyt, 'The Direct Applicability', 318), or 'sufficiently precise and complete' (Sciotti-Lam, *L'applicabilité*, 439).

[129] Ursula Kilkelly, 'The Convention on the Rights of the Child after Twenty-five Years: Challenges of Content and Implementation' in Martin D. Ruck, Michele Peterson-Badali, and Michael Freeman (eds.), *Handbook of Children's Rights: Global and Multidisciplinary Perspectives* (New York: Routledge, 2016) 80, 85; John Tobin, 'Judging the Judges: Are They Adopting the Rights Approach in Matters Involving Children?' (2009) 33(2) *Melbourne University Law Review* 579, 581; Michael King, 'Children's Rights as Communication: Reflections on Autopoietic Theory and the United Nations Convention' (1994) 57(3) *Modern Law Review* 385, 395; Vande Lanotte and Goedertier, 'Monitoring Human Rights', 109–110.

[130] Conforti, *International Law*, 28–29.

[131] Ursula Kilkelly and Laura Lundy, 'Children's Rights in Action: Using the Convention on the Rights of the Child as an Auditing Tool' in André Alen et al. (eds.), *The UN*

perceive as vague changes with the times, as the courts are increasingly exposed to international law and open-ended legal texts.[132] Also, the wider availability of treaty case law influences the assessment of clarity arguably more than the intrinsic features of the concerned provisions. Clarity is often obtained through repeated judicial application,[133] which makes the interpreted provisions appear clearer because it enhances their ability to be absorbed in judicial reasoning. This perception bias is reflected in the practice of some European courts that favour the application of the ECHR in cases concerning children, despite the CRC being equally relevant and of equivalent domestic legal status.[134]

Importantly, assessments of completeness do not depend exclusively on the wording of international provisions.[135] They may, for example, be informed by 'the vagueness of the normative implications of the various rights'.[136] Thus, if certain rights are not justiciable domestically, a court may decide that they are not clear or precise enough despite their intrinsic clarity. Further, courts or bodies with competence to apply open-ended norms, such as constitutions, assess completeness differently from courts that habitually apply more specific norms.[137] Finally, a domestic structure of reception (or '*structure d'accueil du droit interne*'[138]) that converges with a treaty facilitates a finding of completeness. Procedural requirements such as standing and justiciability, the

Children's Rights Convention: Theory Meets Practice, 2nd ed. (Antwerp: Intersentia, 2007) 57, 66.

132 Viorel Ciobanu, 'Independenţa judecătorului şi principiul legalităţii în procesul civil' (2010) 2 *Revista Română de Drept Privat* 43, 47, 49; Lech Garlicki, 'Constitutional Courts versus Supreme Courts' (2007) 5(1) *International Journal of Constitutional Law* 44, 49; Claes and Vandaele, 'L'effet direct', 430.

133 Craig Scott and Patrick Macklem, 'Constitutional Ropes of Sand or Justiciable Guarantees? Social Rights in a New South African Constitution' (1992) 141 *University of Pennsylvania Law Review* 1, 84.

134 Vandenhole, 'The Convention of the Rights of the Child in Belgian Case Law', 121; Limbeek and Bruning, 'The Netherlands', 101; Couzens, 'Romanian Courts'.

135 Buergenthal, 'Self-Executing and Non-Self-Executing Treaties', 395; Sciotti-Lam, *L'applicabilité*, 443; Velu, 'Les effets directs', 314; Pieret, 'L'influence', 6.

136 Philip Alston, 'Out of the Abyss: The Challenges Confronting the New U.N. Committee on Economic, Social and Cultural Rights' (1987) 9(3) *Human Rights Quarterly* 332, 351.

137 Buergenthal, 'Self-Executing and Non-Self-Executing Treaties', 395; Carole Nivard, 'Précision et organes institués par des conventions internationales et européennes' (2015) 7 *Revue des droits de l'homme* paras. 5, 20.

138 Sciotti-Lam, *L'applicabilité*, 441 (see Section 1.3.1). Dugard also links self-execution with the ability of the domestic system to accommodate the application of the international norm: John Dugard, *International Law: A South African Perspective* (Lansdowne: Juta, 2005) 62.

likelihood of 'constitutional controversy'[139] following direct application, and judicial attitudes towards international law[140] also influence direct application, as does the strength of a treaty enforcement mechanism. European courts have carefully considered ECtHR judgments following findings of violations against their states, which over time has influenced the recognition of direct effect to many ECHR provisions.[141] As Buergenthal argues, courts tend to approach treaties differently 'when they know that they do not have the last word when it comes to determining the meaning or relevance of an international agreement'.[142]

Thus, the absence of clarity and precision is a complex criterion that does not depend exclusively on the wording of the CRC. It should, therefore, not be an autonomous criterion to refuse its direct application;[143] at a minimum, there must be caution in its application.

To conclude, the direct application of international treaties is a troubled institution, with complexities that erode its potential as an implementation mechanism for the CRC. The CRC is vulnerable in relation to the criteria for direct application, although those vulnerabilities are disputed. How the pitfalls and successes of direct application operate in practice is explored in the French and South African case studies in Chapters 3 and 5.

2.3.2 *The Indirect Application of the CRC*

2.3.2.1 An Introduction to Indirect Application

The indirect application of international treaties is premised on the idea that although such treaties are not domestic law if they are not incorporated, they can be given some legal effect by courts. In other words, unincorporated treaties have 'a variable and mitigated [domestic] normativity'.[144] Indirect application appears less conceptually difficult than direct application, but, in reality, its complexities are of a different kind. Thus, the intrinsic legal qualities of treaty provisions do not appear

139 *Medellin v. Texas*, 552 US 491 at 550 (2008) (Breyer J dissenting).
140 Buergenthal, 'Self-Executing and Non-Self-Executing Treaties', 383; Sciotti-Lam, *L'applicabilité*, 331.
141 Buergenthal, 'Self-Executing and Non-Self-Executing Treaties', 384.
142 Buergenthal, 'Self-Executing and Non-Self-Executing Treaties', 394.
143 Claes and Vandaele, 'L'effet direct', 431.
144 Provost, 'Judging in Splendid Isolation', 153.

central to indirect application. Instead, the main concern, at least in dualist states, seems to be with the legitimacy of relying on such provisions and deriving certain outcomes. This means that indirect application may raise separation of powers concerns. Further, indirect application encompasses a far greater variety of application techniques than direct application. Such judicial techniques differ between legal systems and include, for example, constitutional[145] and statutory interpretation with consideration of international law; the use of international law to control administrative discretion or inform judicial discretion; declarations of incompatibility of national law with international law; and reliance on international treaties to develop the common law. As demonstrated later in this book,[146] there are complexities in the recognition of some of these techniques and their boundaries.

Courts in both monist and dualist systems apply treaties indirectly,[147] but indirect application is critical for courts in dualist systems because it is the only way to give judicial effect to unincorporated treaties such as the CRC. In light of the selected jurisdictions in this book,[148] indirect application is discussed here in relation to dualist systems and those hybrid systems in which the approach to treaties bears primary allegiance to dualism (such as South Africa).

There are two important features of a dualist approach to treaties with relevance for this study. First, unlike in monist systems, treaties are not automatically incorporated domestically upon ratification. It is accepted that treaties bind a state *internationally* upon ratification/accession but become *domestically* binding only if given the force of law through an act of the legislature.[149] This arises from the doctrine of separation of powers: the executive enters international agreements, which are binding internationally, but it is not entitled to make domestic laws, which can

[145] This may be contentious, depending on the jurisdiction. Compare, for example, Australia (Chapter 4) and South Africa (Chapter 5).

[146] See especially the case studies on Australia (Chapter 4), South Africa (Chapter 5), and the United Kingdom (Chapter 6).

[147] The Netherlands and Romania, for example, are two monist systems in which the CRC is applied indirectly by courts. See Limbeek and Bruning, 'The Netherlands'; Couzens, 'Romanian Courts'.

[148] It may be interesting to compare the indirect application of the CRC in dualist and monist systems, but this is a matter for another day.

[149] On legislative mechanisms, see Malcolm N. Shaw, *International Law*, 8th ed. (Cambridge: Cambridge University Press, 2017) 115.

only be made by legislatures.[150] Second, in dualist states that embrace the doctrine of parliamentary supremacy (such as Australia and the United Kingdom discussed in this book), parliaments can make laws contrary to the state's international obligations.[151] The consequence is that international treaties cannot prevail over domestic statutes, unlike in monist systems that embrace treaty supremacy.

Behind its generic description as 'indirect', this form of application is fairly heterogeneous. Thus, there are variations in terms of a duty to consider international law and/or comply with it. For example, consideration of international law is mandatory for courts in some states but discretionary in others.[152] This can be altered by legislation[153] and selected treaties can be assigned an elevated interpretive role that distinguishes them from other treaties within the same jurisdiction.[154] Expectations of legal interpretations consistent with a treaty also vary. Such consistency is variably required,[155] encouraged,[156] favoured,[157] or simply left to the courts.[158] The impact of the interpretive techniques may vary in intensity,[159] ranging from simply 'gilding the domestic lily',[160] or confirming the reasoning already developed based on domestic rules, to developing the

150 Christof Heyns and Frans Viljoen, *The Impact of the United Nations Human Rights Treaties on the Domestic Level* (The Hague: Kluwer Law International, 2002) 8; Shaw, *International Law.*

151 See Chapters 4 and 6 discussing Australia and the United Kingdom, respectively. For Canada, see Provost, 'Judging in Splendid Isolation', 132–133.

152 Compare, for example, South Africa (Chapter 5) and Australia (Chapter 4).

153 Legislation can make unincorporated treaties mandatory considerations in administrative decision-making: see Andrew Edgar and Rayner Thwaites, 'Implementing Treaties in Domestic Law: Translation, Enforcement and Administrative Law' (2018) 19(1) *Melbourne Journal of International Law* 24.

154 In the United Kingdom, the Human Rights Act 1998 mandates the consideration of the ECHR but not of other human rights treaties: see primarily sections 2 and 3.

155 *Tavita v. Minister of Immigration* [1994] 2 NZLR 257 at 266.

156 For Australia, see, for example, Anne Devereux and Sarah McCosker, 'International Law and Australian Law' in Donald Rothwell and Emily Crawford (eds.), *International Law in Australia* (Sydney: Thomson Reuters, 2017) 23, 36, 39. For Canada, see, for example, Melissa A. Waters, 'Creeping Monism: The Judicial Trend toward Interpretive Incorporation of Human Rights Treaties' (2007) 107(3) *Columbia Law Review* 628, 695. See also *Baker v. Canada* [1999] 2 SCR 817 at para. 70; *Suresh v. Canada* [2002] 1 SCR 3 at para. 59.

157 See the position in the United Kingdom in relation to the ECHR under the Human Rights Act 1998.

158 See the South African case study in Chapter 5.

159 Waters, 'Creeping Monism', 687.

160 Waters, 'Creeping Monism', 654.

common law and interpreting constitutional provisions. In some cases, the effect has been so intense that terms such as 'interpretive incorporation'[161] or 'creeping monism'[162] have been coined.

There are also variations in the prerequisites for the indirect application of international treaties. In some states, reliance on international treaties is conditional on an ambiguity in the domestic law, while in others it is not. For example, ambiguity in statutes is required in Australia, the United Kingdom, and New Zealand,[163] but not in Canada or South Africa.[164] The meaning of 'ambiguity' can also vary from narrow to wide definitions, with the latter being more accommodating of international law.

Therefore, although surrounded by less controversy than direct application, indirect application is characterised by a wide variety of application techniques, some of which are jurisdiction specific.

2.3.2.2 The Indirect Application of the CRC

The implications of the above are that if the CRC is not legislatively incorporated in dualist states, it is in a fairly vulnerable position because it does not have the legal status of domestic law. Thus, reliance on the CRC may be discretionary, with domestic law prevailing in cases where inconsistency is irreconcilable through interpretation. This presumed vulnerability is not always borne out by reality, as illustrated in the Australian, South African, and UK case studies in Chapters 4, 5, and 6. India, another dualist jurisdiction, has a vibrant judicial application of the CRC, with notable practical and policy impacts in fields such as labour law, care and protection, juvenile justice, and maintenance, to name but a few.[165] These jurisdictions are not isolated examples. The selected immigration and corporal punishment cases briefly mentioned

[161] 'Interpretive incorporation' is a term coined by Justice Michael Kirby of the High Court of Australia: Waters, 'Creeping Monism', 652 n 92).

[162] Waters, 'Creeping Monism', 654.

[163] For Australia and the United Kingdom, see Chapters 4 and 6, respectively. For New Zealand, see Melissa Poole, 'International Instruments in Administrative Decisions: Mainstreaming International Law' (1999) 30(1) *Victoria University of Wellington Law Review* 91.

[164] Gib van Ert, 'Canada' in David Sloss (ed.), *The Role of Domestic Courts in Treaty Enforcement: A Comparative Study* (New York: Cambridge University Press, 2009) 166, 173; sections 39(1)(b) and 233 of the Constitution of the Republic of South Africa, 1996.

[165] See the discussion in Enakshi Ganguly Thukral and Anant Kumar Asthana, 'Children's Rights in Litigation: Use of the CRC in Indian Courts' in Ton Liefaard and Jaap E. Doek

in the following chapters further warn against underestimating indirect application as a means of giving effect to the CRC.

The CRC was indirectly applied in three iconic immigration cases from New Zealand, Australia, and Canada, in which the courts reshaped the law in their respective countries and recognised some legal effect to unincorporated treaties – an effect that had previously been denied. In *Tavita v. Minister of Immigration*,[166] the New Zealand Court of Appeal decided that immigration authorities ought to consider article 9 of the CRC when deciding the removal from New Zealand of the foreign father of a New Zealand child.[167] In *Minister for Immigration and Ethnic Affairs v. Teoh*,[168] discussed extensively in Chapter 4, the Australian High Court decided that an unincorporated treaty such as the CRC gave rise to a legitimate expectation that administrative authorities would act accordingly. *Baker v. Canada (Minister of Citizenship and Immigration)*,[169] like *Tavita* and *Teoh*, concerned the role of unincorporated treaties in informing administrative discretion in decisions to remove from the jurisdiction the foreign parents of domestically born children.[170] The majority decided that although the CRC was not domestically incorporated, it could inform statutory interpretation and the assessment of the reasonableness of the decision.[171] These three judgments converge in rejecting the traditional view that unincorporated treaties have no domestic effect, although they do not go so far as requiring administrative compliance with the CRC.[172]

The CRC was relied on with mixed results in cases concerning corporal punishment. In *Ali v. The State*,[173] the High Court of Fiji interpreted constitutional provisions with reference to the CRC and decided

(eds.), *Litigating the Rights of the Child: The UN Convention on the Rights of the Child in Domestic and International Jurisprudence* (Dordrecht: Springer, 2015) 31.

166 [1994] 2 NZLR 257 (*Tavita*). For comment, see Poole, 'International Instruments'.

167 *Tavita* at 266.

168 [1995] HCA 20 (*Teoh*).

169 [1999] 2 SCR 817 (*Baker*).

170 For the innovative aspects of the judgment, see Knop, 'Here and There', 510; Provost, 'Judging in Splendid Isolation', 198; van Ert, 'Canada', 196.

171 *Baker* at paras. 69–71 (L'Heureux-Dubé J). Judges Iacobucci and Cory dissented.

172 Michel Bastarache, 'La révision judiciaire des décisions ministérielles à la lumière de l'arrêt *Baker c. Canada*' (2004) 5(2) *Revue de la common law en français* 399, 415; Margaret Allars, 'One Small Step for Legal Doctrine, One Giant Leap towards Integrity in Government: *Teoh's* Case and the Internationalisation of Administrative Law' (1995) 17(2) *Sydney Law Review* 204, 231–232.

173 [2001] FJHC 123 (relied on articles 19 and 28).

that the use of corporal punishment in schools was unconstitutional. In *BLAST v. Secretary, Ministry of Education*,[174] the Supreme Court of Bangladesh relied on the CRC to conclude that corporal punishment in schools and other settings is inconsistent with the country's constitution. However, in the case of *Canadian Foundation for Children, Youth and the Law v. Canada (Attorney General)*,[175] a majority of the Supreme Court of Canada upheld the constitutional validity of reasonable corporal punishment applied by parents and teachers.[176] Both the majority and the minority judges endorsed the relevance of the CRC and relied on it, albeit with different results.[177]

To conclude, while the CRC is more vulnerable from a legal status point of view in dualist systems, there are substantial opportunities for courts to meaningfully engage with it through indirect application.

2.4 Conclusion

This chapter canvassed the multi-polar framework of the judicial application of the CRC. The Convention itself is overall neutral in terms of the role of the courts – although, in the context of certain provisions, courts may be the appropriate mechanism of implementation under its article 4. The omission of the courts from its general mechanisms of implementation means that the CRC has largely left it to the states, and thus implicitly to the courts, to decide on its judicial application based on the reception rules specific to each system. As discussed above, these reception rules can be complex and vary greatly between jurisdictions, and they constrain the courts in terms of how and to what effect they can rely on the Convention. As this brief account of direct and indirect applications shows, there are opportunities and challenges to the judicial application of the CRC regardless of whether the state is monist or

[174] *Bangladesh Legal Aid and Service Trust (BLAST) v. Secretary, Ministry of Education*, Writ Petition No. 5684 of 2010 (13 January 2011) (relied on articles 19, 28, and 37).

[175] [2004] 1 SCR 76. See Gib van Ert, 'Canadian Cases in Public International Law in 2003–4' (2004) 42 *Canadian Yearbook of International Law* 583, 601.

[176] See *Canadian Foundation* at para. 1 (McLachlin CJ).

[177] The majority held, for example, that the CRC did not explicitly require the banning of all forms of corporal punishment and that some of its articles could be used to give a constitutionally compatible interpretation to the impugned law: *Canadian Foundation* at paras. 31–33 (McLachlin CJ). Arbour J, in minority, relied on the views of the CRC Committee to hold that the law that excused corporal punishment was unconstitutional: *Canadian Foundation* at paras. 186–188 (Arbour J).

dualist. It may be, however, that the opportunities and challenges differ, as illustrated in the case studies that follow. The constraints that hinder the courts in their engagement with the CRC do not apply to the CRC Committee, which has put forward a maximalist view on the role of the judiciary in this regard. Its vision encompasses, for example, the direct application of the entire Convention, remedies for its violation, and ensuring its supremacy over conflicting domestic law.

A divergence is obvious between the courts and the Committee's views on their role. This is an observation with no normative undertones, as the intrinsic validity of these diverse views is largely accepted by this author as a product of their distinct institutional positions – that is, domestic organs and an international monitoring body, respectively. This divergence is not, however, immaterial for this work. It is an adequate analytical tool to interrogate both the international and the domestic perspectives on judicial application and to identify their strengths, weaknesses, and potential synergies. It provides the context for a better understanding of the role of the courts as 'border' institutions for the implementation of the CRC, with the courts acutely aware of both the expectations that they will give effect to the Convention and the domestic rules that legitimise but also constrain that effect. The four case studies that follow illustrate how the courts have managed that task.

3

France

3.1 Introduction

The French case law illustrates the intricacies of direct application as the primary means of giving judicial effect to the CRC.[1] In the absence of a consolidated children's rights statute and explicit constitutional protection, the CRC is the main domestic source of children's rights in France. Its effectiveness depends on its direct application, which is the almost exclusive method of judicial engagement with the CRC in a context where interpretation consistent with *general* (rather than European Union) international law, habitual in the other jurisdictions discussed in this book, is 'ambiguous, even underground'.[2]

The direct application in France has been afflicted by the 'textbook' problems discussed in Chapter 2 and, historically, it has been domestically contentious. Even the CRC Committee criticised the French courts for their reluctance to apply the CRC directly.[3] Gradually, this reluctance

[1] France ratified the CRC on 7 August 1990: 'Status of Treaties: Convention on the Rights of the Child', *United Nations Treaty Collection*, https://treaties.un.org/Pages/ViewDetails.aspx?src=IND&mtdsg_no=IV-11&chapter=4. The Convention came into force for France on 8 October 1990, with its publication in the official gazette.

[2] Jean-François Akandji-Kombé, 'De l'invocabilité des sources européennes et internationales du droit social devant le juge interne' (2012) 11 *Droit social* 1014. The reasons for this reluctance include the fact that general international law does not explicitly require its use in the interpretation of national law and the Constitution does not explicitly endorse such use: Akandji-Kombé, 'De l'invocabilité'. See also Elisabeth Lambert Abdelgawad and Anne Weber, 'The Reception Process in France and Germany' in Helen Keller and Alec Stone Sweet (eds.), *A Europe of Rights: The Impact of the ECHR on National Legal Systems* (New York: Oxford University Press, 2008) 108, 117. However, the courts seem to be slowly developing this possibility: Carine Laurent-Boutot, 'La Cour de cassation face aux traités internationaux protecteurs des droits de l'homme' (unpublished PhD thesis, University of Limoges, 2006) 42, 44; Franck Latty, 'Observations, *GISTI et FAPIL*' in Alain Pellet and Alina Miron (eds.), *Les grandes décisions de la jurisprudence française de droit international public* (Paris: Dalloz, 2015) 674.

[3] The Committee has consistently criticised France for its record of direct application: CRC Committee, *Concluding observations: France*, 25 April 1994, CRC/C/15/Add.20, para. 12;

was overcome through a consistent, multi-jurisdictional engagement with the Convention and robust academic commentary. The trend has generally been favourable to direct application, but a gap remains between the expectations created by the constitutional principle that the CRC is part of the domestic law and has supra-legislative status, and the reality of its somewhat cautious direct application. The winding road towards direct application shows that the factors that determine it go beyond its intrinsic features to include policy reasons and the plural legal and jurisdictional space in which the Convention applies (i.e., the structure of reception, as suggested in Chapter 1).

The case law on which this chapter is based emanates from the Court of Cassation or *Cour de cassation* (the Court), the highest judicial court, and the Council of State or *Conseil d'État* (CE or the Council), the highest administrative court.[4] These apex courts do not issue binding precedents, but they are extremely influential. They unify judicial practice and are the last domestic defenders of human rights,[5] including the rights of children.

This chapter proceeds with an introduction to the direct application of international treaties in France. It then presents and critically analyses the jurisprudence of the Court and the Council and the impact of the direct application of the CRC in France.

3.2 The Direct Application of International Human Rights Treaties in France

According to its Constitution, France is a monist state in which ratified treaties are automatically incorporated into the domestic legal order[6] and

CRC Committee, *Concluding observations: France*, 22 June 2009, CRC/C/FRA/CO/4, paras. 10–11; CRC Committee, *Concluding observations on the fifth periodic report of France*, 23 February 2016, CRC/C/FRA/CO/5, para. 7.

4 Conseil d'État, https://conseil-etat.fr/; Cour de cassation, https://www.courdecassation.fr/. The cases were accessed on Legifrance (www.legifrance.gouv.fr/), an official database of French law, and will therefore be cited in accordance with the identifications provided there (the court, appeal number, and year). All translations from French into English are by this author, unless otherwise indicated.

5 Laurent-Boutot, 'La Cour de cassation', 34. On the French legal system, see John Bell, Sophie Boyron, and Simon Whittaker, *Principles of French Law*, 2nd ed. (Oxford: Oxford University Press, 2008).

6 Paragraph 14 of the Preamble to the 1946 French Constitution. The Constitution is a composite text, consisting of the Constitution of 1958 (of the Fifth Republic) and the texts to which it refers, such as the Declaration of the Rights of Man and the Citizen of 1789, the

thus become binding sources of law for domestic judges.[7] This automatic incorporation creates a vocation for direct application by courts in relation to those treaty provisions (rather than the treaties as a whole) that satisfy the criteria discussed below. Ratified treaties enjoy supremacy or primacy over statutes but not over the Constitution.[8] Direct application and treaty supremacy are distinct principles, but French courts approach them as being intrinsically linked and recognise the supremacy of only those treaty provisions that are of direct application.[9]

The assertion of treaty supremacy needs to be distinguished from constitutional review. The courts rule on direct application and treaty primacy in concrete disputes, while the Constitutional Council decides the validity of statutes[10] upon their assessment against a 'constitutional bloc' (*bloc de constitutionnalité*[11]), which contains domestic norms with constitutional value. International treaties are not part of the

Preamble of the 1946 Constitution, and the 2004 Charter for the Environment: Bertrand Mathieu, 'Qu'est-ce que la Constitution?', *Conseil constitutionnel* (2008), www.conseil-constitutionnel.fr/. For commentary on French monism, see Alain Pellet, 'Quelle place la Constitution de 1958 fait-elle au droit international?', *Conseil constitutionnel* (2008), www.conseil-constitutionnel.fr/la-constitution; Emmanuel Decaux, 'Le régime du droit international en droit interne' (2010) 62(2) *Revue internationale de droit comparé* 467, 469; Didier Chauvaux and Thierry-Xavier Girardot, 'Les clauses d'un traité international dépourvues d'effet direct ne peuvent être invoquées à l'encontre d'un acte réglementaire' (1997) *L'Actualité juridique: Droit administratif* 435.

[7] Bell, Boyron, and Whittaker, *Principles of French Law*, 14.

[8] Article 55 of the 1958 Constitution. See generally Jean Rivero and Jean Waline, *Droit administrative* (Paris: Dalloz, 2002) 68–69; Jean-François Lachaume, 'Droit international et juridiction judiciaire', *Répertoire de droit international Dalloz*, October 2009, paras. 107, 126; Louis Dubouis, 'Droit international et juridiction administrative', *Répertoire de droit international Dalloz*, January 2006, para. 3; Latty, 'Observations', 679.

[9] Jean-François Lachaume, 'Jurisprudence française relative au droit international (année 1997)' (1998) 44 *Annuaire français de droit international* 663 paras. 17, 95, 127; Pierre Lagarde, 'La convention de New York du 26 janvier 1990 sur les droits de l'enfant n'est pas directement applicable en droit interne' (1993) 3 *Revue critique de droit international privé* 449, para. 1. Nonetheless, treaties not applied by courts enjoy domestic primacy and bind the Parliament: Jean-Pierre Ancel, 'La Cour de cassation et la Convention internationale relative aux droits de l'enfant' (2001) 5(205) *Journal du droit des jeunes* 20–21.

[10] *A priori* (under article 61 of the 1958 Constitution) or *a posteriori* (*question prioritaire de constitutionalité* (QPC) at the request of individuals in disputes before courts: article 61-1 of the 1958 Constitution, introduced on 23 July 2008 and effective March 2010. See Vlad Constantinesco and Stéphane Pierré-Caps, *Droit constitutionnel Français* (Paris: Presses Universitaires de France, 2010) 221–222.

[11] These are 'norms of constitutional nature' with different sources: Decaux, 'Le régime', 478. In addition to the norms in note 6, these include fundamental principles of French law as recognised from time to time by the Constitutional Council. See Constantinesco and Pierré-Caps, *Droit constitutionnel Français*, 224.

constitutional bloc. French statutes are, therefore, subject to a dual control: by the Constitutional Council against constitutional norms, and by courts against international treaties (*contrôle de conventionnalité*). Constitutional control decides the validity of the statutory norm, while the *contrôle de conventionnalité* informs the application of the norm in concrete disputes. Thus, a statutory norm that is inconsistent with an international treaty can be ignored (although not declared invalid) by a court in a *specific dispute* and, sometimes, the international norm can be applied instead.

Direct application has far-reaching consequences, as discussed in Chapter 2. Therefore, in specific disputes, the international provision may cover a gap in the domestic law, create rights not explicitly recognised by the domestic law, or set aside and/or substitute domestic norms that are inconsistent with the provision. A directly applicable provision also informs the lawfulness of administrative acts or delegated legislation (decrees).[12]

As explained in Chapter 2, the terms 'direct effect' and 'direct application' are used interchangeably in this work, but a distinction is sometimes made between them in France. Thus, direct effect is seen as a high-order form of direct application that is triggered when a norm creates individual rights that are enforceable by courts.[13] The distinction between direct effect and direct application, inspired by the European Union law, is controversial when applied to general international law,[14] but it has been used to signal to the courts that incorporated treaty norms have a nuanced domestic normativity. The concept of 'invocability' emerged as an umbrella term to capture the diverse normative capacity of incorporated international norms,[15] which ranges from the 'maximum normativity'[16] of norms with direct effect to the more limited

[12] Rivero and Waline, *Droit administrative*, 67. See CE, No. 163043, 23 April 1997 (known as *Groupe d'information et de soutien des travailleurs immigré*, or *GISTI*); comment by Chauvaux and Girardot, 'Les clauses'.

[13] Akandji-Kombé, 'De l'invocabilité', part I.c.

[14] Akandji-Kombé, 'De l'invocabilité', part I.c.

[15] For more on the concept, see Ronny Abraham, 'Les effets juridiques, en droit interne, de la Convention de New York relative aux droits de l'enfant' (1997) 3 *Revue française de droit administratif* 585; Gaëlle Dumortier, 'L'effet direct des conventions internationales' (2012) 3 *Revue française de droit administratif* 547; Serge Slama, 'Adoption de nouveaux critères de détermination de l'effet direct des normes internationales sans consacrer leur invocabilité systématique' (CREDOF, 2012) para. 4; Saida El Boudouhi, 'The National Judge as an Ordinary Judge of International Law: Invocability of Treaty Law in National Courts' (2015) 28(2) *Leiden Journal of International Law* 283, 285.

[16] Dumortier, 'L'effet direct'.

normativity of other norms. This limited normativity may include primacy over inconsistent national norms, the substitution of domestic norms, or the use of international law to interpret domestic laws.[17]

These arguments have not persuaded the courts. In 1997, in *GISTI*[18] (discussed in Section 3.4), the *commissaire du gouvernement*, Rony Abraham (later a President of the International Court of Justice), unsuccessfully attempted to persuade the Council that an international provision need not have direct effect *sensu stricto* in order to control the lawfulness of government decrees.[19] Fifteen years later, in *GISTI and FAPIL*,[20] the *commissaire du gouvernement* Gaëlle Dumortier also argued that to serve as a 'reference norm', it was enough for an international norm to have a sufficient degree of normativity that allows it to perform that function.[21] These arguments were rejected by the Council, which appears determined to exclude from its adjudicatory function any norms not recognised as having direct effect.[22]

The courts have largely lacked a systematic approach to direct application,[23] but some central features emerge. They assess direct applicability on an article-by-article basis and, beyond the formal ratification and publication requirements, two criteria must be satisfied. The *subjective criterion* requires the norm to create individual rights and thus not only concern the relationships between states. The *objective criterion* refers to the degree of normativity of the provision,[24] or the 'quality of the norm'.[25] It requires that a norm be sufficiently clear and precise or complete to assist in resolving a concrete dispute, without the need to take any further domestic measures.[26]

As discussed in Sections 3.3 and 3.4, the CRC has been particularly affected by the courts' narrow application of the subjective criterion.

[17] Akandji-Kombé, 'De l'invocabilité', part I.c.
[18] CE, No. 163043, 23 April 1997 (*GISTI*) (see note 12).
[19] Abraham, 'Les effets juridiques', part III.B.2. This view is endorsed by, among others, Chauvaux and Girardot, 'Les clauses'; Dumortier, 'L'effet direct'.
[20] CE, No. 322326, 11 April 2012 (*GISTI and FAPIL*).
[21] Dumortier, 'L'effet direct'.
[22] Latty, 'Observations', 681.
[23] Latty, 'Observations', 676; Cour de cassation, *Rapport annuel 2013* (2014) 111.
[24] Bérangère Taxil, 'Les critères de l'applicabilité directe des traités internationaux aux États-Unis et en France' (2007) 59(1) *Revue internationale de droit comparé* 157, 159.
[25] Laurent-Boutot, 'La Cour de cassation', 40.
[26] Dumortier, 'L'effet direct'. See also Abraham, 'Les effets juridiques', part III.A.2-3; Taxil, 'Les critères', 166–167.

To assess compliance therewith, courts consider the state's intention, scrutinising the wording of the relevant provisions[27] and the object of the treaty.[28] Formulations requiring states to take implementation measures led to a denial of direct application by the Court.[29] For some time, the Council rejected the application of provisions *addressed to states* (*critère rédactionnel*[30]) that included formulations such as 'states undertake to guarantee' or 'undertake to recognise',[31] which were considered to create obligations between states and not individual rights capable of direct domestic application. The Council abandoned this approach with *GISTI and FAPIL* in 2012, when it decided that a norm addressed to states does not inherently lack direct applicability. Instead, its normative value must be established by analysing its wording and the possibility of its immediate application.

The courts are not always clear on their engagement with the two criteria and the reasons for rejecting direct application.[32] The analysis of direct application in judgments is limited and the reasoning is stereotypical.[33] These deficiencies are compounded by the notorious brevity of the judgments[34] and the unpredictability of direct application generated by the article-by-article approach.[35]

In brief, direct application can deliver significant legal dividends in France, but it takes place in a context where the Convention may struggle

[27] Cour de cassation, 'L'application direct de la Convention de New York relative aux droits de l'enfant' in Cour de cassation, *Rapport annuel 2009* (2010) 81, 83.

[28] Lachaume, 'Droit international', para. 94; Cour de cassation, *Rapport annuel 2009*, 84.

[29] Lachaume, 'Droit international', para. 93.

[30] Claudia Sciotti-Lam, *L'applicabilité des traités internationaux relatifs aux droits de l'homme en droit interne* (Brussels: Bruylant, 2004) 383.

[31] Abraham ('Les effets juridiques', part III.A.2.c), who also notes that formulations such as 'states recognise' or 'states guarantee' have led to the recognition of direct effect. See also Lagarde, 'La convention', para. 3.

[32] Dubouis, 'Droit international', para. 40; Chauvaux and Girardot, 'Les clauses'.

[33] Latty, 'Observations', 684.

[34] On the historical, political, and legal reasons for this approach to judgment writing, see Michel de S.-O.-l'E. Lasser, 'Judicial (Self-)Portraits: Judicial Discourse in the French Legal System' (1995) 104(6) *Yale Law Journal* 1325; Bertrand Louvel, 'Discours prononcé en ouverture des travaux de la commission de réflexion dédiés à la motivation' (14 September 2015) 1; Conseil d'État, *Groupe de travail sur la rédaction des décisions de la juridiction administrative: rapport final* (May 2012) 10. The brevity of judgments should not be mistaken for a lack of sophistication. The comprehensive arguments of the *commissaire du gouvernement/commissaire public* or *conseilleurs*, who are members of the Council and the Court, respectively, reveal rich deliberations with references to a multitude of sources, including international law.

[35] Latty, 'Observations', 684.

to meet the direct application criteria as interpreted by the courts. The next two sections illustrate how the Court and the Council have navigated the volatile institution of direct application when engaging with the CRC. The two courts are discussed separately because of their distinct jurisdictions and, importantly, because in the first fifteen years of CRC application they have taken different approaches to its direct application. As discussed later, the practice of the two courts is now better aligned, albeit not uniform. Nonetheless, a presentation of their historical differences illustrates the domestic complexity of direct application (unacknowledged internationally by the CRC Committee, as discussed in Chapter 2) and highlights the many factors that influence it – some going well beyond the rules of reception and the formulation of CRC provisions.

3.3 The Direct Application of the CRC by the Court of Cassation

The Court moved from an initial quiet acceptance of the direct application of the CRC to its firm rejection and then in 2005 to the current cautious approach. Contrary to prevailing practice, in the 1993 case of *Lejeune*,[36] the Court decided that the *entire* CRC lacked direct applicability. In a custody matter, the appellant argued that a lower court had breached articles 1, 3, 9, and 12 of the CRC because it had decided what was in the best interests of the child by relying on the views conveyed by the child to a psychologist rather than the court, and ignored concerns that the child's views had been influenced by the mother.[37] The First Civil Division decided that the CRC was not directly applicable because it created obligations only for states and could not be invoked directly by individuals. In subsequent judgments, the Court supplemented its reasoning by pointing out that article 4 indicates that the CRC creates obligations 'only for the states, so that it cannot be invoked before the courts'.[38] By 1997, all other divisions of the Court adopted this reasoning, which was welcomed by some as the display of a 'beautiful unanimity'.[39]

[36] Civ 1, No. 91-11310, 10 March 1993 (*Lejeune*).

[37] The same reasoning was used in Civ 1, No. 91-17487, 2 June 1993 and Civ 1, No. 91-18735, 15 July 1993.

[38] Civ 1, No. 91-18735, 15 July 1993. See also Civ 1, No. 94-05075, 24 October 1995.

[39] Jean Massip, 'La cour de cassation et le caractère directement exécutoire en France de la Convention sur les droits de l'enfant' (1998) 39 *Les petites affiches* 25.

However, this position was not universally supported. Some lower courts continued to apply the CRC, facing Court admonishment,[40] and the Court itself did not consistently pursue an article 4-based reasoning.[41] Some judges, writing extrajudicially, argued that article 4 requires domestic implementation measures only when 'necessary' and not when CRC provisions can be given effect immediately.[42] Because the Court has no practice of writing dissenting judgments,[43] these views had no authoritative platform from which to speak.

Academics criticised the Court for its departure from the habitual article-by-article approach to direct application,[44] and for ousting the direct application of the CRC for reasons not used in relation to other human rights conventions.[45] Others, however, defended the position of

40 Jean Massip, 'La Convention relative aux droits de l'enfant, qui ne crée des obligations qu'à la charge des États parties, n'est pas directement applicable en droit interne' (1993) *Recueil Dalloz* 361n2; Jean Hauser, 'Droits de l'enfant: il y a CIDE et CIDE!' (1994) *Revue trimestrielle de droit civil* 581; Jean-Luc Rongé, 'La Convention internationale relative aux droits de l'enfant: on avance ou on recule?' (2004) 10(240) *Journal du droit des jeunes* 9, 15n60; Jean-Pierre Rosenczveig, 'The Self-Executing Character of the Children's Rights Convention in France' in Eugeen Verhellen (ed.), *Monitoring Children's Rights* (The Hague: Martinus Nijhoff, 1996) 187; Lagarde, 'La convention', para. 7.

41 Jean-Pierre Marguénaud, 'De l'indifférence des juridictions judiciaires à l'égard de la Convention internationale relative aux droits de l'enfant' (1999) *Revue trimestrielle de droit civil* 509; Claire Neirinck, 'L'application de la Convention internationale de l'enfant à la découpe: à propos d'un revirement de jurisprudence' (2005) 5 *Revue de droit sanitaire et social* 814. See also Crim, No. 98-84538, 16 June 1999; Crim, No. 00-84429, 5 September 2001.

42 Ancel, 'La Cour de cassation', 21; Jean-Pierre Ancel, 'La protection des droits de la personne dans la jurisprudence récente de la Cour de cassation' in Cour de cassation, *Rapport de la Cour de cassation 2000* (2001), www.conseil-constitutionnel.fr/conseil-constitutionnel/francais/la-constitution/la-constitution-de-1958-en-20-questions/quelle-place-la-constitution-de-1958-fait-elle-au-droit-international.17499.html.

43 They are a 'quasi-taboo' and a 'profoundly foreign' tool for the French judiciary: Jean-Pierre Ancel, 'Les opinions dissidents' (5ème conférence du Cycle de conférences annuelles sur les méthodes de jugement, 18 October 2005).

44 Baptiste Bonnet, 'Le Conseil d'État et la Convention internationale des droits de l'enfant à l'heure du bilan: de l'art du pragmatisme' (2010) 17 *Recueil Dalloz* 1031; Dominique Bureau, 'De l'application directe en France de la Convention de New York du 26 janvier 1990 sur les droits de l'enfant' (2005) 4 *Revue critique de droit international privé* 679; Françoise Monéger, 'Enfant (droits de l')', *Répertoire de droit international Dalloz*, January 2006, 1. See, more generally, Françoise Dekeuwer-Défossez, 'La convention relative aux droits de l'enfant, qui ne crée des obligations qu'à la charge des États parties, n'est pas directement applicable en droit interne' (1994) *Recueil Dalloz* 34; Rosenczveig, 'The Self-Executing Character', 190; Marguénaud, 'De l'indifférence'; Lagarde, 'La convention'.

45 Lagarde, 'La convention', paras. 6–7; Rongé, 'La Convention', 15.

the Court as straightforward[46] or of little consequence, either because the French law largely complied with the CRC or because the latter could be given effect through alternative legal means, including through the application of the ECHR and legal reform.[47] The Court itself rejected the criticism that its en bloc rejection of direct application deprived the CRC of domestic effect, arguing that the Council had jurisdiction to ensure that state organs comply with the CRC.[48]

Legal and policy reasons informed the position of the Court.[49] Article 4 constituted the main *legal* reason, with its reference to implementation measures taken as reflecting the parties' intention to create obligations for states rather than individual rights that are enforceable domestically.[50] That many specific provisions are addressed to states was taken to reflect state undertakings rather than individual rights.[51] As the right to approach an international body to obtain a remedy was considered a marker of direct applicability,[52] the absence of an individual communication mechanism implied that the CRC was not intended to have direct effect.[53] It was thus argued that 'it would be a paradox'[54] to apply the Convention directly in France if the Committee itself was not able to do something similar.

From a *policy* perspective, the Court was concerned that a too eager application of the CRC instead of domestic law would destabilise the domestic legal order.[55] The Court was keen to avoid 'artificial litigation

[46] Benhamou, cited by Françoise Monéger, 'La Convention des droits de l'enfant devant les juridictions administratives' (1996) *Revue de droit sanitaire et social* 137.

[47] Dekeuwer-Défossez, 'La convention relative aux droits de l'enfant'.

[48] Cour de cassation, *Rapport annuel 2009*, 84; Jean-Pierre Ancel, 'La Convention de New York relative aux droits de l'enfant devant la Cour de cassation' (2011) *Justice & Cassation* 13, 15.

[49] Rongé uses the term *politique judiciaire:* Rongé, 'La Convention', 15.

[50] Massip, 'La Convention'; Jean Massip, 'L'application par la Cour de cassation de conventions internationales récentes relatives à l'enfance' (1995) 53 *Les petites affiches* 41.

[51] Bénédicte Vassallo, 'La Convention des droits de l'enfant à la cour de cassation' (2010) 296 *Journal du droit des jeunes* 25. See also Dekeuwer-Défossez, 'La convention relative aux droits de l'enfant'; Ancel, 'La Convention', 14; Cour de cassation, *Rapport annuel 2009*, 84; Massip, 'L'application', part I.B.

[52] Ancel, 'La Cour de cassation', 20; Cour de cassation, *Rapport annuel 2009*, 84.

[53] Dekeuwer-Défossez, 'La convention relative aux droits de l'enfant'; Massip, 'La Convention'; Massip, 'L'application', part I.B.

[54] Dekeuwer-Défossez, 'La convention relative aux droits de l'enfant'. Certainly, the absence of an individual communication mechanism deprived the CRC of an important pressure tool to support its direct application: Sciotti-Lam, *L'applicabilité*, 411.

[55] The manipulation of the CRC by adults and the multiplication of appeals were further concerns: Sciotti-Lam, *L'applicabilité*, 411–412.

encouraged by the terms often vague and less precise of the Convention'[56] and the legal uncertainty resulting from a case-by-case approach to direct application.[57] Also of concern were the potential manipulation of the CRC by adults;[58] the tensions between the rights of the child, the public order and the rights of parents;[59] and the prospect of engaging with socio-economic rights.[60] Faced with these difficulties, the Court resolved to issue a 'decision of principle'[61] in *Lejeune*, although one was not required by the facts of the case.[62] Subsequently, article 4 was relied on as a convenient *legal* cover by a court that made 'a deliberate strategic choice',[63] indicating that it was for the legislature to bring the law into line with the Convention.[64]

In May 2005, the Court changed its approach. In two decisions rendered on the same day, the Court de facto applied articles 3 and 12, the 'two stars'[65] of the CRC. In one case, the Court decided that by not considering the request of a child to be heard in an appeal against a custody decision, the court breached articles 3(1) and 12(2) of the CRC.[66] A second case concerned a child born to a lesbian couple through artificial insemination. After separation, one of the partners changed her sex and recognised the *paternity* of the child. The biological mother challenged the recognition for being contrary to the biological reality. The court of appeal agreed, but recognised visitation rights for the transsexual parent. The Court endorsed the visitation rights and accepted

56 Massip, 'L'application', part I.B.

57 Massip, 'L'application', part I.B.

58 Sciotti-Lam, *L'applicabilité*, 411–412.

59 Hauser, 'Droits de l'enfant'; Laurent-Boutot, 'La Cour de cassation', 58. Some courts, for example, allowed children to intervene in their parents' divorce proceedings, and judges endorsed applications by children who refused to join their parents at religious shrines: Rosenczveig, 'The Self-Executing Character', 194.

60 Laurent-Boutot, 'La Cour de cassation', 59–60.

61 Massip, 'L'application', part I.A; Dekeuwer-Défossez, 'La convention relative aux droits de l'enfant'.

62 The child had been listened to by the relevant professionals in compliance with article 12: Massip, 'La Convention'; Massip, 'L'application', part I.A.

63 Eric Claes and Arne Vandaele, 'L'effet direct des traités internationaux: Une analyse en droit positif et en théorie du droit axée sur les droits de l'homme' (2001) 34(2) *Revue belge de droit international* 411, 449. See similarly Sciotti-Lam, *L'applicabilité*, 411.

64 Bonnet, 'Le Conseil d'État'. Some judges explicitly endorsed this view: Massip, 'La Convention'.

65 Adeline Gouttenoire, 'L'application de la Convention internationale des droits de l'enfant' (2012) 50 *Les petites affiches* 17.

66 Civ 1, No. 02-20613, 18 May 2005.

that the legal justification for the decision was article 3(1).[67] In June 2005, the Court was more explicit and declared that article 3(1) had direct effect. The appellant mother challenged the order for the immediate return of an abducted child to the country of habitual residence, arguing that it violated, inter alia, article 3(1). Uprooting the child from France, where she was already integrated, risked severely affecting her. This was relevant to the exception to immediate return in article 13(b) of the 1980 Hague Convention on the Civil Aspects of International Child Abduction (Hague Convention).[68] The Court decided that article 3(1) was of direct application and required that the best interests of the child be given primary importance in assessing the risk of danger posed by the immediate return.[69]

In its May and June 2005 judgments, the Court abandoned its en bloc rejection of the direct application of the CRC and reverted to the habitual article-by-article approach. Having invoked the CRC ex officio, the Court was clearly determined to change its approach. It later referred to these decisions as 'decisions of principle'.[70] The judgments inspired mixed reactions. There were reservations about article 3(1) becoming a norm of control for domestic statutes,[71] in parallel with views that the direct application was largely symbolic[72] or a 'sacrifice to the fashion of international norm'.[73]

Regrettably, the Court did not justify the change, but commentators argued that it was influenced by legal and extra-legal factors.[74] Thus, the Court accepted that the reference to implementation measures in article 4

[67] Civ 1, No. 02-16336, 18 May 2005.

[68] Hague Convention on the Civil Aspects of International Child Abduction, 25 October 1980, in force 1 December 1983, Hague XXVIII.

[69] Civ 1, No. 04-16942, 14 June 2005.

[70] Cour de cassation, *Rapport annuel 2009*, 86. For further discussion, see Ancel, 'La Convention', 19; Bureau, 'De l'application directe'; Vassallo, 'La Convention'.

[71] Bureau, 'De l'application directe', III.A.20; Philippe Bonfils and Adeline Gouttenoire, *Droit des mineurs* (Paris: Dalloz, 2008).

[72] Because article 12(2) had already been given effect in a statute applied alongside this article: Françoise Dekeuwer-Défossez, 'La Convention internationale des droits de l'enfant: quelles répercussions en droit français?' (2006) 5 *Cahiers de la recherche sur les droits fondamentaux* 39, 42.

[73] Jean Hauser, 'La référence à la Convention internationale des droits de l'enfant (CIDE) fait recette à la Cour de cassation mais est-elle nécessaire?' (2006) *La revue trimestrielle de droit civil* 101.

[74] Patrick Courbé, 'L'application directe de la Convention des Nations unies sur les droits de l'enfants' (2006) *Recueil Dalloz* 1487.

did not characterise the legal nature of *all* CRC provisions,[75] as some provisions are not dependent on legislative intervention.[76] The long-held views of the judges opposing the *Lejeune* reasoning eventually prevailed, once the presidency of the First Civil Division had changed.[77] The absence of a communications mechanism ceased to be considered an obstacle to direct application, demonstrating the *ab initio* vulnerability of the argument.[78] The cautious direct application of the CRC by the Council allayed the Court's fear about the destabilising effect of the CRC[79] and encouraged it to harmonise the approaches of the two institutions.[80] The evolution of human rights jurisprudence favoured the recognition of direct effect: the Court applied other treaties directly;[81] the best interests of the child had penetrated the ECtHR jurisprudence,[82] with that court issuing judgments against France in which it referred to the CRC;[83] and lower courts had started to rebel,[84] signalling that it was time for change.

After the 2005 decisions, the Court engaged more freely with the CRC – although much of its jurisprudence concerns article 3(1)[85] and only rarely other provisions. For example, article 8 was implicitly applied when the Court decided that statutory provisions that allowed children born out of wedlock to take the surname of one of the parents, but not

[75] Bureau, 'De l'application directe', III.B.15–16.

[76] Bureau, 'De l'application directe', III.B.15-16; Ancel, 'La Cour de cassation'; Ancel, 'La protection'.

[77] Laurent-Boutot, 'La Cour de cassation', 68–69. See especially the extrajudicial writings of Jean-Pierre Ancel, the presiding judge of the First Civil Division at the time of 2005 decisions.

[78] The argument is now further weakened by the 2011 addition of a communications procedure to the CRC, which was ratified by France in 2016: Optional Protocol to the Convention on the Rights of the Child on a Communications Procedure, New York, 19 December 2011, in force 14 April 2014 (adopted by United Nations General Assembly resolution A/RES/66/138 of 19 December 2011).

[79] Courbé, 'L'application'.

[80] Bureau, 'De l'application directe'; Cour de cassation, *Rapport annuel 2005* (2006) 416.

[81] Courbé, 'L'application'; Lachaume, 'Droit international', para. 96, referring to the ECHR and the ICCPR.

[82] François Boulanger, 'Applicabilité directe de la Convention de New York et intérêt supérieur de l'enfant' (2006) *Recueil Dalloz* 554; Dekeuwer-Défossez, 'La Convention internationale', 40. The advocate general, for example, supported the direct application of article 3(1), relying on its use by the ECtHR: Laurent-Boutot, 'La Cour de cassation', 71–72.

[83] Rongé, 'La Convention', 15.

[84] Ancel, 'La Cour de cassation', 21; Rongé, 'La Convention', 15.

[85] Vassallo, 'La Convention', 27; Cour de cassation, *Rapport annuel 2009*, 85.

their united surnames, were consistent with it.[86] The Court relied on article 9(3) to justify the refusal to order the return of a child unlawfully removed from Morocco, because the interests of the child were better served by keeping her in France.[87] In the *Benjamin* case,[88] the father of a child born *sous X*[89] had recognised the child prior to his birth. The Court raised article 7(1) ex officio[90] and recognised the child's right to know and be raised by his parent. Notably, that right was not provided under French law.

Socio-economic rights have generally been avoided by the Court, which has preferred to base its decision on article 3(1). In several cases, it was argued that it was contrary to, inter alia, articles 3(1), 24(1), and 26 for child grants to be denied to legal migrants whose children joined them in France without following the required family reunification procedures.[91] The Assembly of the Court decided that making the grant conditional upon following a procedure that proved the legality of the children's entry into France had an

> objective character justified by the necessity within a democratic state to control the influx of children, [and] did not constitute a disproportionate interference with the right to family life guaranteed by articles 8 and 14 of the ECHR, and did not disregard the dispositions of article 3-1 of the Convention on the Rights of the Child.[92]

[86] Civ 1, No. 08-18871, 6 January 2010.

[87] Civ 1, No. 06-12687, 22 May 2007.

[88] Civ 1, No. 05-11285, 7 April 2006 (*Benjamin*).

[89] A practice by which the mother can require that the birth and her identity be kept secret and that her child be made available for adoption. The mother has two possibilities: to not disclose her name (anonymous birth); or to disclose her name to the relevant institution, requesting that it be kept secret and disclosed only to the child upon reaching the age of 18 (secret birth). See Fanny Vasseur-Lambry, 'Les message troublants du juge de la filiation: l'accouchement sous X en question' (2012) 137 *Les petites affiches* 13; *Odièvre v. France* (Application No. 42326/98, 13 February 2003) at paras. 15–18.

[90] Vassallo, 'La Convention', 33. For another case concerning article 7(1), see Civ 1, No. 10-19028, 1 June 2011 (no breach).

[91] See Claire Coutou and Bénédicte Vassallo, 'Rapport de Mmes Coutou et Vassallo, Conseillers référendaires' (2008) 674 *Bulletin d'information* 12; Françoise Monéger, 'Rapport de Mme Monéger, Conseiller rapporteur (Pourvoi no 09-69.052' (2011) 747 *Bulletin d'information* 20.

[92] Ass, No. 09-69052, 3 June 2011; Ass, No. 09-71352, 3 June 2011. See also Ass, No. 11-17520, 5 April 2013. The position of the Court was later endorsed by the ECtHR in *Osungu and Lokongo v. France* (Application Nos. 76860/11 and 51354/1), 1 October 2015.

In brief, after a decade of rejecting the direct application of the CRC, the Court is now cautiously applying it. The demise of the subjective criterion in 2005 should have generated more engagement with the objective criterion, and thus more upfront engagement with issues such as the completeness and clarity of CRC provisions. The domination of article 3(1) might have made that less urgent. However, some judges have argued that many CRC provisions fall short of the objective criterion because they are 'so general or even so vague that it cannot be seen how their violation can be invoked by individuals',[93] since a court 'cannot . . . make a decision referring exclusively to the New York Convention as its justification'.[94] Although compliance with the objective criterion lurks in the background, the Court has avoided explicitly engaging with it and has allowed direct application to develop organically, as the cases have required it.

3.4 The Direct Application of the CRC by the Council of State

The Council applied the CRC directly on an article-by-article basis from the outset. Its case law is dominated by article 3(1), which was recognised as having direct effect in 1997 in *Cinar*.[95] That case concerned a Turkish mother who resided lawfully in France but had brought her four-year-old son to the country illegally. The mother applied for a residence permit for the child, but the application was rejected because it was made from France rather than overseas, as required by the law. The mother appealed, arguing that the ECHR and the CRC had been breached. The *commissaire du gouvernement*, Rony Abraham, supported the direct application of article 3(1), which he considered the only well-founded reason for the appeal. Abraham argued that the article was of direct application because no additional measure was needed for its application. Its general nature and propensity to multiple interpretations did not prevent its application because administrative judges were accustomed to the application of general norms, such as general legal principles. Thus, despite the illegal entry of the child into France, a separation from the mother in the circumstances (i.e., an unknown father and no family members able to care for the child in Turkey) was contrary to

93 Massip, 'La Convention'. See similarly Ancel, 'La Cour de cassation', 20; Ancel, 'La Convention', 14.

94 Massip, 'La Convention'. See similarly Dekeuwer-Défossez, 'La convention relative aux droits de l'enfant'; Neirinck, 'L'application'; Boulanger, 'Applicabilité directe'.

95 CE, No. 161364, 22 September 1997 (known as *Cinar*).

article 3(1).[96] The administrative decision was invalidated and article 3 (1) was applied instead to permit the child to stay in France.

In relation to other articles, the Council has been inconsistent, 'even incoherent'.[97] Most articles were declared without direct effect,[98] although at times the Council tacitly applied them – especially when it concluded that no breach had occurred.[99] Some articles moved between direct application and denial thereof, without explanation by the Council. Articles 7, 9, 10, 12, and 16 were initially denied direct application but were eventually applied directly. Thus, a decision to deport a foreign national, who was married to a French resident and the father of four children, did not violate article 7(1) because the family could move overseas, where the children could be raised by both parents.[100] Article 9, together with article 3(1), the Preamble of the 1946 Constitution, and article 8 of the ECHR, justified granting permission to reside in France to the parents of girls granted refugee status because of their risk of female genital mutilation in their country of origin.[101] Article 10 was rejected as irrelevant, rather than without direct effect, when raised by a child living in France who sought reunification with her siblings who lived abroad.[102] Article 12(2) was explicitly declared of direct application in an immigration appeal where administrative authorities were criticised for not having listened to the child concerned. The Council rejected the appeal because the view of the child was conveyed to the authorities by the child's grandmother.[103] In 2004, the Council decided that the

[96] See the discussion of the case in Michel Reydellet, 'La convention des droits de l'enfant n'est pas un traité "hors-jeu"' (1998) 11 *Les petites affiches* 17.

[97] Roger Errera, 'L'application de la Convention Internationale relative aux droits de l'enfant et l'incidence de la Convention européenne des droits de l'homme sur les droits de l'enfant' (Comité franco–britannique de coopération judiciaire, Colloque de Rennes sur l'enfant en justice, 19–21 May 2005) 7.

[98] Articles explicitly denied direct effect included articles 2, 3(2), 3(3), 4, 5, 6, 7, 8, 9, 10, 11, 12, 14, 16, 18, 19, 20, 24(1), 26(1), 27(1), 28, and 29.

[99] Reliance on articles 9 and 19 was rejected as 'unfounded', rather than with the usual formula of 'creating obligations between states', in CE, No. 136601, 28 July 1993. The Council implicitly applied article 16 (CE, No. 141083, 10 March 1995 (known as *Demirpence*)) and even assessed certain provisions of the Civil Code against articles 3 (1) and 16 (CE, No. 191232, 30 June 1999), but in 2002 it decided that article 16, together with articles 7 and 9, creates obligations only between states and cannot be applied directly (CE, No. 214664, 18 January 2002).

[100] CE, No. 247587, 27 February 2004.

[101] CE, No. 368676, 20 November 2013.

[102] CE, No. 155096, 1 April 1998. See similarly CE, No. 238724, 10 March 2003.

[103] CE, No. 291561, 27 June 2008.

deportation of an undocumented migrant, who was thereby separated from his children who resided lawfully in France, did not constitute a violation of article 16 because it was not an *arbitrary* interference with the children's private life and family life.[104]

In many decisions in which it denied direct effect, the Council relied on what became the hallmark of its engagement with the CRC: that some of its provisions create obligations between states (rather than individual rights that can be applied directly by courts) because they are addressed to the states. The Council has used this reasoning overwhelmingly in relation to the CRC,[105] and often in relation to article 9 when applied in immigration cases.[106] The reasoning was stretched beyond those articles that are addressed primarily to states to articles such as 7, 14, and 16.

This literal approach, which enabled a simplistic disregard for some CRC provisions, has been displaced by *GISTI and FAPIL.*[107] Consequently, the Council can no longer dismiss the direct application of the CRC simply because some of its provisions are addressed to states. This shift is slowly influencing the case law. Although the literal approach has not been completely abandoned, the Council has used it in only one CRC-related decision concerning articles 7 and 8 combined.[108] Further, when the Council assessed the lawfulness of decrees against articles 20,[109] 21 and 22,[110] and 32,[111] it considered their substance rather than rejecting their application because they were addressed to states. Recently, the Council decided that 'because of its imprecision, [article 6] lacks direct effect'[112] and cannot be applied. Why article 6 was deemed imprecise is not explained, but it is encouraging that the Council did not avoid dealing with its direct application by hiding behind article 3(1),

[104] CE, No. 265003, 29 December 2004.

[105] Of the 112 cases that used the formula creating 'seulement des obligations entre États' ('exact phrase' search on Legifrance) between 8 October 1990 and 24 September 2022, only ten relate to other international treaties. Of those ten, only one refers to another human rights treaty (i.e., the Convention on the Elimination of All Forms of Discrimination against Women).

[106] It was also used in relation to articles 2, 4, 6, 7, 8, 10, 12, 14, 16, 18, 28, and 29.

[107] See Section 3.2.

[108] CE, No. 364895, 10 April 2013. The only other decision (as of 24 September 2022) in which the classic formula was used concerned an extradition treaty: CE, No. 439436, 30 July 2021.

[109] CE, No. 428478, 5 February 2020.

[110] CE, No. 370459, 18 December 2015 at para. 14.

[111] CE, No. 373968, 18 December 2015.

[112] CE, No. 440154, 1 February 2022.

which was also invoked. Unfortunately, the shift to the objective criterion did not advantage article 6, which in the past had been implicitly applied.[113] Thus, while the post-2012 approach taken by the Council is encouraging, it is unlikely to result in an unfiltered direct application of the entire CRC.

As discussed in Section 3.4, the Council can assess the lawfulness of secondary legislation (decrees) against international treaties. The Council defined its approach in this regard in *GISTI*, where the applicants requested the invalidation of a decree that made access to social security conditional on proof of legal residence in France, arguing that the decree was contrary to, inter alia, articles 24(1), 26(1), and 27(1) of the CRC. The Council took the narrow view that only international norms that have direct effect (i.e., create individual justiciable rights) can be used for this purpose and the invoked CRC provisions do not meet that requirement. This position was endorsed in *GISTI and FAPIL*. This restrictive approach significantly impacts the effectiveness of the CRC in administrative judicial review and is compounded by the limited number of provisions applied directly by the Council and the exceptional use of the CRC as an interpretation aid.[114]

To conclude, the direct application of the CRC challenged both the Court and the Council. The inconsistencies in the case law are difficult to reconcile because of the cryptic nature of the judgments and a lack of transparency in how the direct application criteria are used. Ironically, being considered part of the domestic law brought upon the CRC a literal approach to interpretation that courts use for domestic statutes – to its disadvantage. The demise of the subjective criterion should have led to a closer engagement with the objective criterion and matters such as the clarity and completeness of CRC provisions, over which concerns still linger.[115] This is yet to be achieved. However, despite these trials and tribulations, direct application has contributed to giving domestic effect

[113] In 2001, the Council found that a decision to authorise the commercialisation of an oral contraceptive was not contrary to article 6 (read with article 2 of the ECHR and article 6 of the ICCPR): CE, No. 216521, 25 April 2001.

[114] For such exceptional use, see CE, No. 253973, 30 July 2003; CE, No. 349624, 26 July 2011.

[115] See, for example, Abraham, 'Les effets juridiques', part III.A.3; Ancel, 'La Cour de cassation', 21; Massip, 'La Convention'; Vassallo, 'La Convention'. In its 2009 annual report, the Court of Cassation comments that many CRC provisions do not recognise 'precise and determined rights' because they are 'very general, even vague': Cour de cassation, *Rapport annuel 2009*, 84.

to the Convention and has generally enriched domestic law and improved the legal protection of children's rights. It has done so by operating as domestic law and by adding value to judicial reasoning, as discussed below.

3.5 The Impact of the Direct Application of the CRC in France

3.5.1 The CRC as Domestic Law: Scope and Legal Force

3.5.1.1 Scope of Application

Direct application equates the CRC with domestic law and opens numerous opportunities for application. Although few CRC provisions have been recognised as having direct effect, the Convention is applied across many legal matters. Protection-oriented provisions are most popular. Article 3(1) dominates, as discussed below, but juvenile justice-related provisions are also applied. For example, the Council decided that article 37(b) and (c) do not prohibit the extradition of a minor to a country that has special rules concerning child offenders.[116] A decree requiring detention centres for immigrant families awaiting deportation to provide child-specific materials was not contrary to articles 3(1) and 37 because it did not encourage the use of detention but was rather intended to set special detention standards for children.[117] Autonomy-oriented rights have begun to be applied. For example, the Council found that a media regulator did not breach article 13 when it prohibited the broadcasting of an interview with a child offender whose mother opposed the broadcasting.[118] Articles 16 and 3(1) were not breached by a decree that created a database that sought to prevent threats to public security by retaining the personal data of, inter alia, children below the age of 13.[119]

Many cases are immigration-related, but there is an increasing diversity of matters in which the CRC is invoked, including abduction,[120] taxation,[121] same-sex parenthood,[122] the use of performance-enhancing

[116] CE, No. 220271, 14 February 2001 (known as *Nezdulkins*).

[117] CE, No. 282275, 12 June 2006. The Council's position may be problematic under the ECHR. See *Popov v. France* (Application Nos. 39472/07 and 39474/07, 19 January 2012); *A.B. v. France* (Application No. 11593/12, 12 July 2016).

[118] CE, No. 334289, 16 March 2011. The Council also found that there was no disproportionate interference with article 10 of the ECHR.

[119] CE, No. 332886, 11 March 2013; CE, No. 389815, 21 September 2015.

[120] Civ 1, No. 16-20858, 7 December 2016.

[121] CE, No. 320321, 24 August 2011.

[122] CE, No. 370459, 18 December 2015.

drugs,[123] children joining the Islamic State,[124] legal aid,[125] the choice of a name,[126] the sale of female hygiene products,[127] and the extradition of child offenders[128] or primary caregivers.[129] Notably absent are socio-economic rights, which are shunned even when explicitly raised,[130] although, surprisingly, article 32(1) and (2)(b) of the CRC were used to assess the lawfulness of two decrees that authorised the involvement of children aged 15–18 in hazardous work involving asbestos-contaminated environments.[131]

Article 3(1) dominates the case law of both courts, having generated an application 'comfort zone'. The consequence is that courts prefer to apply article 3(1) and eschew articles with a direct effect that is less clear. In some cases, article 3(1) has absorbed the substance of norms denied direct effect,[132] including socio-economic rights. In *L'Association Aides*,[133] for example, the Council formally applied article 3(1) but gave effect to the substance of article 24, which it had previously declared as not having direct

[123] CE, No. 363376, 19 June 2013.

[124] CE, No. 386817, 9 December 2015 (article 3(1) did not create an obligation for the state to require that French minors have the written authorisation of their parents to leave France).

[125] CE, No. 370989, 17 February 2016.

[126] Civ 1, No. 10-27512 11-19963, 15 February 2012 (naming a child after a cartoon character – 'Titeuf', which sounds like *petit oeuf*, or little egg – was not in the child's interests).

[127] CE, No. 440154, 1 February 2022. It was argued with reference to articles 3 and 6 that an advertisement for hygiene products for girls was indecent and had a pornographic character. The Council decided that the metaphorically intimate images of young girls were in relation to hygiene and did not have an indecent or pornographic nature: at paras. 9, 11.

[128] *Nezdulkins* (see note 116 and the accompanying text).

[129] CE, No. 385927, 9 December 2015 at para. 6 (see the text accompanying note 171 and see also note 223).

[130] Ass, No. 09-69052, 3 June 2011; Ass, No. 09-71352, 3 June 2011. See also Ass, No. 11-17520, 5 April 2013.

[131] CE, No. 373968, 18 December 2015 at para. 13. The Council decided that the decrees were not contrary to these provisions because they did not prohibit exposure to asbestos below a dangerous or harmful level.

[132] The Council applied article 3(1) to protect the relationship between parents and children in immigration matters prior to accepting the direct application of articles 9 and 10: Françoise Monéger, 'Le Conseil d'État met en avant l'intérêt supérieur de l'enfant contenu dans la Convention des Nations Unies sur les droits de l'enfant' (1998) 3(1) *Revue de droit sanitaire et social* 174.

[133] CE, No. 285576, 7 June 2006 (known as *L'Association Aides*).

effect.[134] The Council also decided that the eviction of a family, which included children, that did not have title over their dwelling could not be prevented, but that the best interests of the child must be a primary consideration according to article 3(1).[135] The convergence of the reasoning with the substance of article 27 is clear. Recently, the Court assessed the conformity with article 3(1) of certain statutory provisions, although the values sought to be protected related to articles 24 and 26 of the CRC.[136] Further, some articles were denied direct effect when applied independently, but were thereafter applied in conjunction with article 3(1).[137] Thus, the dominance of article 3(1) may have removed the incentive for the courts to wrestle with the direct application of other articles – but, on the other hand, the article has lent its legal clout to other CRC provisions or served as a vehicle to protect their substance.

At first glance, the ascendancy of article 3(1) is surprising, considering that it is the 'most explosive'[138] CRC provision, it is not formulated as a typical directly applicable norm,[139] and it is not exemplary in its precision. Several factors may have facilitated the rise. For example, the norm is not addressed to the states but rather to their institutions,[140] resonating perhaps with the literal approach to interpretation taken by the courts. The provision is general and flexible,[141] it lacks a reference to implementation measures,[142] and the courts are familiar with the concept of the 'interests of the child',[143] which is also used by the

[134] Laurence Gay, 'L'affirmation d'un droit aux soins du mineur étranger ou l'inconventionnalité partielle d'une loi jugée conforme à la Constitution' (2006) 11 *Revue de droit sanitaire et social* 1047.

[135] CE, No. 395911, 28 July 2017.

[136] Ass, No. 09-69052, 3 June 2011; Ass, No. 09-71352, 3 June 2011. See also Ass, No. 11-17520, 5 April 2013 (see notes 92 and 130).

[137] For example, the Council applied article 7(1) directly together with article 3(1) (CE, No. 300721, 8 April 2009), but it denied its direct application together with article 8, reasoning that they created obligations exclusively between states (CE, No. 364895, 10 April 2013).

[138] Courbé, 'L'application'.

[139] Bureau, 'De l'application directe'.

[140] Rongé, 'La Convention', 14; Pierre Bordry, 'Le Conseil d'État français et la Convention internationale relative aux droits de l'enfant' (2001) 205 *Journal du droit des jeunes* 16, 19.

[141] Neirinck, 'L'application'; Rémy Schwartz, 'La jurisprudence du Conseil d'État et les droits de l'enfant' (2010) 296 *Journal du droit des jeunes* 37–38 (footnote omitted).

[142] Reydellet, 'La convention'.

[143] See Michelle Gobert, 'Le droit de la famille dans la jurisprudence de la Cour de cassation' (Neuvième conférence le droit de la famille dans la jurisprudence de la Cour de cassation, 11 December 2006); Gilles Lebreton, 'Le droit de l'enfant au respect de son

ECtHR.[144] Although controversy about article 3(1) remains,[145] a comprehensive and increasingly diverse best interests jurisprudence has developed, as discussed below.

3.5.1.2 Legal Force

When recognised as having direct effect, the CRC has considerable legal force, as discussed in Section 3.2. It operates as an autonomous source of law with supra-legislative status, incompatibility with which may result in disregarding domestic rules or invalidating administrative action or secondary legislation. The courts have a mixed, albeit not negligible, record in capitalising on this powerful legal status.

The CRC has been relied on as an autonomous source of law and occasionally this has led to the recognition of rights or benefits beyond those provided by the national law. In *Benjamin*, the Court recognised the right of a child to know his parents based on article 7(1), although the right was not explicitly provided for in French law. In *Cinar*, the Council mainstreamed the concept of the best interests of the child, which was not provided by the relevant statutes, into the administrative jurisprudence through the direct application of article 3(1).[146] Similarly, although a child's right to be heard is not recognised in administrative statutes, the Council applied article 12(2) directly to uphold the right of a *makfoul* (a child placed in *kafala*) to be heard in administrative and judicial

"intérêt supérieur". Critique républicaine de la dérive individualiste de droit civil français' (2003) 2 *Cahiers de la recherche sur les droits fondamentaux* 77; Hauser, 'La référence'. However, prior to the ratification of the CRC, the concept of the best interests of the child did not receive statutory recognition: Adeline Gouttenoire, 'Les droits de l'enfant en droit français' in Olga Cvejić Jančić (ed.), *The Rights of the Child in a Changing World* (Cham: Springer, 2016) 109.

144 Dekeuwer-Défossez, 'La Convention internationale', 40.

145 Françoise Dekeuwer-Défossez, 'L'effectivité de la CIDE: rapport de synthèse' (2010) 200 *Les petites affiches* 35; Pierre Verdier, 'Pour en finir avec l'intérêt de l'enfant' (2008) 280 *Journal du droit des jeunes* 34; Bonfils and Gouttenoire, *Droit des mineurs*; Gobert, 'Le droit de la famille'; Lebreton, 'Le droit de l'enfant'; Vassallo, 'La Convention'. The Court has questioned the reliance on article 3(1) when the interests of the child are mentioned in domestic law, but it concluded that its usage emphasises the importance of the concept: Cour de cassation, *Rapport annuel 2009*, 90.

146 A search of the Council's case law on Legifrance for the period from 1 January 1960 to 22 September 1997 (the date of the *Cinar* decision) using the exact phrase '*l'intérêt de l'enfant*' produced five results; no result was obtained for the phrase '*l'intérêt supérieur de l'enfant*'. For the period from 23 September 1997 to 1 September 2022, 722 results were obtained for '*l'intérêt supérieur de l'enfant*' and 151 for '*l'intérêt de l'enfant*'.

proceedings concerning the issuing of a visa to join the *kafil* (*kafala* carer) in France.[147]

An autonomous application of article 3(1) permitted the Council to justify individual exceptions from the application of laws that may otherwise disproportionately affect some children. For example, children born overseas through surrogacy to French commissioning parents could be issued with French travel documents because, although surrogacy was contrary to French public order and thus legally invalid, the administration had an obligation to give a primary consideration to the best interests of children.[148] *Makfouls* could benefit from the family reunification process, despite the relevant statute not explicitly providing for this, if the denial of reunification would constitute an excessive interference with the private life and family life of the *kafil* and a violation of article 3(1).[149] The *makfouls* living with their *kafils* in France could be issued with French travel documents, despite the law not explicitly providing for it, if it is established that denying such documents would breach article 3(1) by preventing the children maintaining ties with their biological family overseas.[150] In 2003, the French Section of the Observatoire International des Prisons argued that a decree providing disciplinary procedures for incarcerated children was contrary to article 3(1) because it was not adapted to the age of the children.[151] The Council upheld the validity of the decree, but determined that it was incumbent on prison authorities to inform the children's guardians of the disciplinary proceedings and allow them to make representations or arrange legal representation for the children. Another case concerned a decree that abrogated legal provisions requiring that the family and protection services be immediately informed of the detention of a child, and that the probation services pay a timely visit to the child. The Observatoire International des Prisons argued that the decree was contrary to articles 3(1) and 37(c).[152] The Council disagreed and further

[147] CE, No. 291561, 27 June 2008.

[148] CE, No. 348778, 4 May 2011; CE, No. 401924, 3 August 2016. The Council is mindful not to trespass into the jurisdiction of the Court and indicates that issues of nationality and filiation are decided by the judicial courts.

[149] CE, No. 249369, 24 March 2004; CE, No. 220434, 24 March 2004. See also Monéger, 'Enfant (droits de l')'; Isabelle Guyon-Renard, 'Rapport de Mme Guyon-Renard, Conseiller rapporteur' (2012) 777 *Bulletin d'information* 7.

[150] CE, No. 351906, 3 October 2012.

[151] CE, No. 253973, 30 July 2003.

[152] CE, No. 369766, 24 October 2014.

decided that those articles have direct effect and must be applied by prison authorities themselves.[153] In individual cases, this may lead in fact to an immediate notification of the family and a probation services visit. The Council's approach in these cases was to leave the regulatory framework undisturbed and use the CRC to justify child-focused exceptions from the application of the domestic law in individual cases.

The Court of Cassation is less inclined to carve out individual exceptions relying directly and exclusively on the CRC. The Court has explained its strict adherence to the letter of the law by pointing out that 'it respects the texts voted by the legislator'.[154] Thus, unlike the Council, it has not extended to the *makfoul*s benefits that are not explicitly bestowed upon them by statute. It set aside, for example, a lower court decision based on article 3(1) of the CRC and articles 8 and 14 of the ECHR, which ordered the state to pay a *kafil* the child benefit reserved by statute for adoptive or prospective parents.[155] There are, however, exceptions to this strict legalism. For example, in addition to *Benjamin*, the Court relied on articles 3(1) and 12(2) to justify the appointment of a legal representative for a child when the statutory conditions for the appointment had not been met.[156]

As mentioned above, the supra-legislative domestic status of the CRC enables the Council to use it as an autonomous standard against which to assess the lawfulness of secondary legislation (decrees). The Council has declared unlawful a small number of decrees for the reason of inconsistency with the CRC. In *L'Association Aides*, it invalidated decrees that prevented undocumented immigrant children who have not been in France for a certain amount of time from accessing healthcare services other than emergency care.[157] In *L'Observatoire International des Prisons*, the Council invalidated a ministerial decree that permitted the use of solitary confinement for children, relying on articles 3(1) and 37, which require that detention regimes take into account the age of the child.[158]

153 CE, No. 369766, 24 October 2014 at para. 10. For another decision in which the Council explicitly stated that the administration must apply article 3(1), see CE, No. 305031, 9 December 2009 (visa for *makfouls*).

154 Cour de cassation, *Rapport annuel 2009*, 93.

155 Civ 2, No. 08-15571, 11 June 2009. See also Vassallo, 'La Convention', 27.

156 Civ 1, No. 03-17912, 22 November 2005. See Boulanger, 'Applicabilité directe', 4.

157 CE, No. 285576, 7 June 2006.

158 CE, No. 293785, 31 October 2008 (known as *L'Observatoire International des Prisons*) (*L'Observatoire*).

In both cases, the Council invalidated the decrees only to the extent of their applicability to children, on the grounds that they did not offer sufficient guarantees for a special treatment of children. The accompanying claims in relation to adults were rejected.

Both the Court and the Council can use CRC provisions recognised as having direct application as 'norms of control' for statutes. In the event of inconsistency with the Convention, the relevant statutory provision is to be disregarded in the case at hand. Both courts have shown a willingness to evaluate statutes against the CRC, but they have rarely declared them to be inconsistent with the Convention. This reluctance is not specific to the CRC; more generally, the combination of direct effect and treaty supremacy have provoked a 'considerable upheaval'[159] among judges. The Court has never made a finding of inconsistency with the CRC,[160] although it has accepted in principle that the Convention can serve as a standard against which to evaluate domestic law. It assessed, for example, the Civil Code against article 20[161] and it affirmed that the primacy of article 3(1) can be asserted in contentious cases.[162]

All successful assertions of CRC precedence over statutes have so far taken place before the Council and have involved article 3(1).[163] Thus, in *Cinar*, discussed above, national law was set aside because of its inconsistency with article 3(1) and the latter was applied instead. In *L'Association Aides*,[164] the Council declared incompatible with the CRC a statute that limited access to healthcare for undocumented immigrant children. The Council decided that this limitation disregarded articles 1 and 3(1), which require the state not to limit children's access to medical services that are necessary to protect their health. More recently, the Council articulated its expectation that lower courts enquire, where relevant, into the compatibility of domestic statutes with article 3(1) before proceeding to their application. It decided that by 'not assessing if the *law*

[159] M. Guy Canivet, 'Vision prospective de la Cour de cassation' (l'Académie des sciences morales et politiques, 13 November 2006) 6. See also Decaux, 'Le régime', 468.

[160] Ancel, 'La Convention'; Gouttenoire, 'L'application', 18; Monéger, 'Rapport', 34–35; Vassallo, 'La Convention', 33.

[161] Civ 1, No. 09-10439, 15 December 2010; Civ 1, No. 08-11033, 25 February 2009; Guyon-Renard, 'Rapport'.

[162] Civ 1, No. 17-70039, 7 March 2018.

[163] The Council did, however, assess the lawfulness of decrees against other articles, but found no inconsistency. See Section 3.4.

[164] CE, No. 285576, 7 June 2006.

itself was compatible with these stipulations [article 3(1)], the court committed an error of law'.[165]

Recent developments have diversified the effect of the CRC's supremacy over the domestic law. In 2016, the Council decided that even if *in abstracto* a statute is consistent with an international treaty, judges must ensure that, in specific disputes, its application does not disproportionately interfere with the rights engaged.[166] The decision authorises administrative judges to carve out exceptions to the application of otherwise valid statutes that in specific individual cases may disproportionately interfere with human rights. Arguably, the Council used this approach in a CRC context before its formal recognition when it relied on article 3(1) to craft exceptions from the application of statutes that disproportionately affected certain children.[167] In a similar vein is a 2019 advisory opinion in which the Court advised that the supra-legal status of article 3(1) permitted a court exceptionally to refuse to terminate parental rights, even when all the statutory requirements are met, if the termination would be antithetical to giving a primary consideration to the best interests of the child concerned.[168] The supra-legislative status of article 3(1) was the justification for the Court recognising a judicial discretion to deviate from the letter of the law in order to respond to the needs of individual children. Although the Court's opinion does not appear to be a decision of principle that stretches beyond its narrow factual context, it is a leap for a court that has repeatedly declared its allegiance to the letter of the law.[169] It appears, therefore, that either boldly or more mutedly, both courts agree that CRC supremacy justifies the recognition of a decisional discretion necessary to apply the law so as to accommodate the special needs of children.

The above developments pose interesting questions about how the proportionality assessment suggested by the Council would be carried out in relation to article 3(1). No such assessment is explicitly conducted by the courts, and one may argue that it is being avoided. For example,

[165] CE, No. 375887, 10 July 2015 at para. 10 (emphasis added).

[166] CE, No. 396848, 31 May 2016, especially at paras. 2, 9. Although this decision concerned an alleged breach of article 8 of the ECHR, the wording used by the Council does not appear to be limited to that convention.

[167] See especially the cases concerning *kafala* (discussed above in Section 3.5.1.2) and surrogacy (discussed below in Section 3.5.2).

[168] Civ 1, No. 19-70007, 19 June 2019.

[169] Cour de cassation, *Rapport annuel 2009*, 93; Civ 1, No. 09-66486, 6 April 2011 (see the reference to *l'état du droit positif*).

when article 8 of the ECHR and article 3(1) of the CRC were invoked together, the courts' decisions in relation to the former were based on an assessment of the proportionality of interference therewith, while the reasoning in relation to the latter simply indicated that article 3(1) was breached or otherwise.[170] The Court has, however, obliquely made proportionality remarks. When upholding the deportation of a father convicted of criminal offences, it endorsed the balancing between the interests of the victim, society, and the child that was made by the lower court.[171] Proportionality assessments in a CRC context are thus looming over the French courts.

The limited number of incompatibility findings in relation to statutes may suggest that courts are too ready to assume that national law complies with the CRC and/or that they may engage in problematic interpretations of the CRC. For example, the Council decided that article 12(2) was not breached because a child conveyed her views through her grandmother, but it did not enquire into the effectiveness of listening to the child through a representative.[172] Further, when it applied article 13, the Council gave no attention to the tension between a teenager's consent to the broadcasting of his interview and his mother's opposition to it.[173]

The courts may also be anxious that article 3(1), the most widely applied article, is not a suitable standard for *in abstracto* evaluation of legal norms. Traditionally, the Constitution did not entrench the best interests of the child, leaving France with no domestic precedent for an abstract application of this concept. Concerns were raised, for example, about using the best interests test to assess legislation when it was designed to be applied in individual cases,[174] and about placing the interests of the child above the parliament-made law[175] and thus risking a lack of legal security.[176] Nonetheless, these difficulties do not alleviate

[170] Ass, No. 09-69052, 3 June 2011 (see the text accompanying note 92); CE, No. 249369, 24 March 2004; CE, No. 220434, 24 March 2004 (see Section 3.5.1.2).

[171] CE, No. 385927, 29 December 2015.

[172] CE, No. 291561, 27 June 2008.

[173] CE, No. 334289, 16 March 2011.

[174] Bonfils and Gouttenoire, *Droit des mineurs*; Lucette Khaïat, 'La défense des droits de l'enfant, un combat inachevé' (2010) 296 *Journal du droit des jeunes* 20, 23.

[175] Adeline Gouttenoire, 'Le domaine de l'article 3-1 de la CIDE: la mise en oeuvre du principe de primauté de l'intérêt supérieur de l'enfant' (2010) 200 *Les petites affiches* 24.

[176] Bonfils and Gouttenoire, *Droit des mineurs*. It is not clear, for example, when the application of article 3(1) could lead to a dislocation of statutory provisions that are clear and precise: Cour de cassation, *Rapport annuel 2009*, 92; Monéger, 'Rapport', 34–35.

the constitutional obligation of judges to assess domestic norms against article 3(1).[177] Moreover, the recent recognition by the Constitutional Council of the best interests of the child as a constitutional value[178] may ease concerns that article 3(1) is not fit for abstract application.

Lastly, political and legal complexities may sometimes deter findings of incompatibility with the CRC. For example, a CRC-based challenge to the regressive social assistance legislation of 2005–2006 would have required the Court to reverse the effects of legislation enacted by the parliament specifically to overturn the previous jurisprudence of the Court, which maximised access to family benefits for legal migrants.[179] Further, setting aside, for reason of inconsistency with the CRC, the norm that prevented the adoption of *makfouls* by *kafils* raised concerns about diplomatic relations with the children's country of origin.[180]

In brief, the Court and the Council have applied directly a modest number of CRC provisions and have given effect to the domestic supremacy of the Convention, albeit cautiously. The application of the CRC has had positive consequences for how courts engage with child-related matters, as expanded upon below.

3.5.2 The Added Value of the CRC

In France, as in other jurisdictions, the Convention applies alongside other legal instruments. The domestic contentiousness of the direct application of the CRC, combined with the existence of potentially overlapping legal instruments, has raised questions about the relevance of the direct application of the CRC.[181] A comparison between the case law of the Court and the Council and that of the Constitutional Council shows the continued relevance of the direct application of the CRC as a solid foundation for child-focused legal reasoning that is unavailable

177 Gouttenoire, 'Le domaine'.

178 See, for example, Decision No. 2018-768 QPC, 21 March 2019 (*Adama S*) (radiological bone scans to determine age).

179 See Coutou and Vassallo, 'Rapport', 23–24; Patrice Maynial, 'Observations de M. Maynial, Premier avocat général' (2008) 674 *Bulletin d'information* 33.

180 Jean-Paul Jean, 'Observations de M. Jean, Avocat général' (2013) 777 *Bulletin d'information* 31. Some *makfouls*, for example, still have biological families in the country of origin. Adoption might not be the best solution for them, as it leads to the severance of ties with the biological family.

181 Cour de cassation, *Rapport annuel 2009*, 92; Hauser, 'La référence'; Schwartz, 'La jurisprudence'; Vassallo, 'La Convention'.

under other instruments. The Constitutional Council does not apply the CRC, which is not a part of the 'constitutional bloc',[182] and – with a limited number of child-specific provisions in the Constitution,[183] none of them formulated as individual rights – its jurisprudence has been less child-focused than that of the courts. For example, in relation to births *sous X*, the Constitutional Council preserved the status quo, which negates the legal relationship between the birth mother and the child. It decided that by seeking to avoid births that endanger the mother and the child, and to prevent infanticide and child abandonment, the parliament struck a correct balance between the interests of the mother in remaining anonymous and those of the child.[184] In *Benjamin*, however, the Court of Cassation used article 7 of the CRC to address the relationship between *fathers* and children born *sous X*, recognising the right of those children to know the fathers who were willing to recognise them. Similarly, the Constitutional Council declared a budget-related statute to be consistent with the Constitution[185] but, in *L'Association Aides*, the Council of State decided that the same statute was inconsistent with article 3(1) and invalidated its implementing decrees. The difference in reasoning is stark. While article 3(1) was central to the Council of State's view that children as a vulnerable group needed special protection, the Constitutional Council gave no independent attention to children as a distinct group affected by the law.[186] In both cases, the direct application of the Convention enabled the courts to differentiate their position from that of the Constitutional Council and arrive at child-centred solutions.

In addition to enabling child-focused reasoning, direct application has led to the recognition and protection of rights not provided by national

[182] See Section 3.2. For examples of cases where the Constitutional Council affirmed that it does not apply the CRC, see Decision No. 2013-669, 17 May 2013 at para. 57; Decision No. 2016-739, 17 November 2016 at para. 53.

[183] These constitutional provisions are paragraphs 11 (health, security, rest, and leisure) and 13 (education) of the 1946 Preamble. The constitutional protection has been extended, however, by the Constitutional Council, which declared the special system of juvenile justice (Decision No. 2002-461 DC, 29 August 2002 at para. 26) and the best interests of the child (*Adama S*), respectively, as constitutional principles. See further Christine Lazerges, 'Les limites de la constitutionnalisation du droit pénal des mineurs' (2008) 1 *Archives de politique criminelle* 5; Hugues Fulchiron, 'La constitutionnalisation de l'intérêt supérieur de l'enfant' (2019) 13 *Recueil Dalloz* 709 para. 2.

[184] Decision No. 2012-248 QPC, 16 May 2012 at paras. 6, 8. Notably, the ECtHR sees this practice as falling within the state's margin of appreciation: *Odièvre* at para. 49.

[185] Decision No. 2003-488 DC, 29 December 2003 at paras. 14–20.

[186] Gay, 'L'affirmation'.

statutes.[187] Further, following the direct application of article 3(1) in *Cinar* in 1997, the best interests of the child were not simply introduced but also mainstreamed in the administrative jurisprudence. What this demonstrates is that direct application can contribute to mainstreaming children's rights in *all* decisions concerning them, even in the absence of domestic legislation.

One of the difficulties in discerning the value added by the CRC is the complex legal context in which it is applied. The joint invocation and the overlap of the CRC with other national and international legal sources have prompted views that the Convention plays a secondary or 'complementary role'.[188] It was argued, for example, that article 8(1) of the ECHR absorbs article 3(1) and that decisions are based on the latter when the parties 'forget' to invoke the former.[189] These concerns about the Convention's value must be interrogated. Whether the CRC is paired with other legal instruments depends on the legal context. In administrative case law, for example, article 12(2) is relied on independently, as there is no explicit legislative or ECHR support for it.[190] The CRC is used independently by the Council and the Court when they wish to distinguish the treatment of children from that of adults, in order to provide children with additional protection.[191] Article 3(1) is useful when there is tension with the rights of parents in matters such as abduction, the termination of parental rights,[192] and the recognition of filiation.[193] Features such as the need to take positive action or to enquire into the situation of individual children are associated with the application of this article.[194] These normative consequences are clearly derived by the courts from the CRC rather than other legal instruments.

While some normative overlap may exist between the CRC and other legal instruments, it should not be automatically assumed. For instance,

[187] The right to know one's parents (*Benjamin*) and the right to be heard in administrative litigation (CE, No. 291561, 27 June 2008; see the text accompanying notes 103, 147, and 172).

[188] Schwartz, in relation to articles 3(1) of the CRC and 8 of the ECHR: Schwartz, 'La jurisprudence', 39. Vassallo notes the pairing of article 3(1), 7(1), and 12(2) with statutes that refer to the interests of the child, filiation, and the child's right to be heard: Vassallo, 'La Convention'.

[189] Schwartz, 'La jurisprudence', 40.

[190] CE, No. 291561, 27 June 2008.

[191] For example, *L'Association Aides* and *L'Observatoire*.

[192] Civ 1, No. 19-70007, 19 June 2019.

[193] Civ 1, No. 18-50080, 19-11251, 16 September 2020 at para. 19.

[194] For an example, see CE, No. 392191, 11 May 2016 at para. 3.

in surrogacy cases where it upheld requests for travel documents for children to join their commissioning parents in France, the Council justified its decisions exclusively on the basis of article 3(1).[195] The Council used article 3 to distinguish between the legal treatment of children and that of adults. It did the same in some decisions concerning family reunification in a *kafala* context, which it justified based on article 8 of the ECHR in relation to the *kafils* and article 3(1) in relation to the *makfouls*.[196] In cases concerning socio-economic rights, where the link with article 8 of the ECHR is tenuous or even lacking, the courts have applied article 3(1).[197] Decisions compatible with the ECHR may not always be compatible with article 3(1). For example, a deportation order against a mother was compatible with the mother's rights under article 8 of the ECHR but its execution after the birth of the child would have been inconsistent with article 3(1).[198] Further, the deportation of a child was found not to contravene article 3 of the ECHR (protection against torture and ill-treatment) but to seriously breach article 3(1) of the CRC and could not be carried out.[199]

In some cases, the CRC is more useful than domestic law or the ECHR and this enhances its value. In abduction cases, for example, article 8 of the ECHR is not considered by the Court. Instead, the Court applies the Hague Convention and article 3(1) (or occasionally article 9(3) of the CRC[200]), which are useful in deciding the immediate return (or otherwise) of a child to the country of habitual residence when there is some risk to the child.[201] In decisions concerning the issuing of travel documents to *makfouls*, the Council relied only on article 3(1) because article 8 of the ECHR was not relevant.[202]

The critical reflections on the joint application of the CRC with other sources of law may suggest some apprehension about its value for

195 CE, No. 348778, 4 May 2011; CE, No. 401924, 3 August 2016 at para. 6.

196 CE, No. 220434, 24 March 2004; CE, No. 249369, 24 March 2004.

197 *L'Association Aides* (access to medical care); *L'Observatoire* (the treatment of children in detention). Delay in the payment of a social grant owed to a child in a precarious situation was found to be contrary to article 3(1) only, with article 8 of the ECHR not being invoked: CE, No. 406637, 19 May 2017 at para. 7.

198 CE, No. 274713, 7 April 2006.

199 CE, No. 386865, 9 January 2015.

200 Civ 1, No. 06-12687, 22 May 2007.

201 Civ 1, No. 19-14464, 27 June 2019 (ECHR not invoked); Civ 1, No. 04-16942, 14 June 2005 (ECHR invoked but not dealt with by the Court).

202 This is because the family life of the *makfoul* was with the *kafil* in France, rather than with the biological family abroad. See CE, No. 351906, 3 October 2012.

domestic judges. This apprehension is not justified. First, directly applicable norms rarely operate independently as they need some supporting national law to facilitate their application.[203] Second, a legal norm remains valuable even if it does not generate by itself the legal outcome of a case. In a legal context characterised by norm inflation, the contribution of the CRC to judgments may be subtle but not less important, as most clearly illustrated in decisions where child-focused reasoning is not overtly supported by other sources of law. Third, the joint application of the CRC with other relevant legal norms is not an existential crisis for the former. The principle of subsidiarity provides a legitimate justification for the priority application of the national law, and article 41 of the CRC itself requires that national or international standards offering superior protection be applied with priority. A positive working relationship with other legal sources, in which the CRC retains its autonomous value for the courts, is possible. It rests on the courts avoiding assumptions that the CRC has little to add to the reasoning and acknowledging that perceptions that it may have more limited value for courts are influenced by familiarity with more jurisprudentially developed legal instruments.[204]

3.5.2.1 The Value Added by Article 3(1)

As already observed, much of the value added by the CRC to the reasoning of the courts arises from article 3(1). Even the intransigent Court of Cassation succumbed to its appeal by using the internationalised phrase the 'best interests of the child' (rather than the domestic phrase the 'interest of the child') before recognising direct effect to article 3(1).[205] As for the Council, it has so accepted the 'best interests' standard that article 3(1) can inform its reasoning without even being acknowledged.[206]

Two features of the best interests jurisprudence illustrate the distinct contribution of this article to case law development: asserting children's

[203] André Nollkaemper, 'The Duality of Direct Effect of International Law' (2014) 25(1) *European Journal of International Law* 105.

[204] Schwartz mentions that, as an administrative judge, he finds the ECHR 'easier to use', with article 8 of the ECHR being applied more frequently and more comfortably than article 3(1) of the CRC: Schwartz, 'La jurisprudence', 39–40.

[205] Ancel, 'La protection'; Ancel, 'La Convention', 19; Cour de cassation, *Rapport annuel 2009*, 85–86: Lebreton, 'Le droit de l'enfant'.

[206] See CE, No. 400074, 13 July 2016, where, although article 3(1) is not mentioned, it permeates the reasoning, as reflected in the use of the 'best interests of the child' formula (absent from other legal texts relied on) and the general tenor of the judgment.

interests and their uniqueness, and giving these interests prominence in matters affecting children indirectly.

Children as Independent Holders of Unique Rights and Interests Article 3(1) has been used by the courts to assert the position of children as independent rights holders. This is reflected in the courts' attention to children's own interests, independently of the interconnected adult interests. Article 3(1) was used by the courts as a *legal* tool to give expression to the unique nature of children's interests and to disentangle them (at least for analytical purposes) from the collective family interests protected under article 8 of the ECHR. The courts made it clear that this uniqueness is not there for contemplation: it demands that decision-makers identify children's own interests and explain how they have been considered. Examples are numerous and a few will suffice. Thus, the choice of language for education cannot be informed by a father's interest to preserve his relationship with the children and without considering what is in their best interests.[207] A residence decision made without ascertaining the best interests of the child and on grounds extraneous to those interests is unlawful.[208] In parental abduction cases, the Court relies on article 3(1) to identify the interests of children, as distinct from those of their parents, and to give them priority.[209] Thus, a court cannot decide on a child's return by considering the difficulties faced by the abducting parent but not the situation of the child.[210]

The Council of State gives effect to this autonomy of interests in various ways. First, it demands that children's specific legal needs be considered in individual cases but also when drafting statutes or delegated legislation. For example, in the often-mentioned cases of *L'Association Aides* and *L'Observatoire*, the Council invalidated the challenged decrees *only* to the extent of their application to children because of the failure to take into consideration their specific needs. Conversely,

[207] Civ 1, No. 02-18360, 9 November 2005.

[208] Such as the late recognition of paternity, the permission for overseas travel given by the father, and the mother's amenability to the development of the father–child relationship: Civ 1, No. 06-17869, 13 March 2007. See also Cour de cassation, *Rapport annuel 2009*, 90.

[209] Civ 1, No. 16-20858, 7 December 2016; Civ 1, No. 17-11840, 12 July 2017. In Hague Convention cases, the Court relies on article 3(1) to decide if there is a severe risk or the possibility of an intolerable situation that would justify the Court applying an exception from the rule of immediate return.

[210] Civ 1, No. 11-28424, 13 February 2013; Civ 1, No. 17-11927, 13 July 2017.

decrees regarding the collection, processing, and retention of personal data that differentiated between children and adults did not breach articles 3(1) and 16.[211] Second, the Council sought to avoid visiting on children the negative consequences of their parents' illicit behaviour in cases concerning, for example, family reunification,[212] deportation,[213] and the issuing of travel documents to children born through surrogacy overseas.[214] Recently, the Council applied this approach to anti-terrorism measures. It declared unlawful an order that severely restricted the freedom of movement of a mother, the sole primary caregiver of three young children, who was suspected of having supported persons involved in terrorist activities. The Council found that the order violated, inter alia, article 3(1), as it was a serious interference with the children's best interests.[215] Third, article 3(1) allowed the Council to support flexible decision-making by justifying individual exceptions to the application of rules whose blanket application may severely affect some children.[216] For example, it decided that children who are accompanied by adult carers may be deported, but article 3(1) requires special guarantees for their protection, including information about the conditions the child will face in the country of reception and the relationship with the accompanying adult.[217] Further, although the state has no obligation to provide emergency accommodation for families with children awaiting deportation,[218] or to pay financial support for children who reunited with their French-residing parents without following the required procedure,[219] if the

[211] CE, No. 332886, 11 March 2013 at paras. 21, 26.
[212] *Cinar.*
[213] CE, No. 274713, 7 April 2006.
[214] CE, No. 348778, 4 May 2011.
[215] CE, No. 395622, 6 January 2016. Concomitantly, the Council found a violation of article 8 of the ECHR because of the excessive interference with family life. The order required the mother to report three times a day to a police station in a different town. She did not have a car and relied on public transport. The Council ordered the minister to amend the order.
[216] *Kafala* and family reunification (CE, No. 249369, 24 March 2004; CE, No. 220434, 24 March 2004) and the issuing of travel documents (CE, No. 351906, 3 October 2012); the issuing of travel documents to children born through surrogacy abroad (CE, No. 348778, 4 May 2011); and family and social services visits to arrested children (CE, No. 369766, 24 October 2014).
[217] CE, No. 386865, 9 January 2015 at para. 6.
[218] CE, No. 400074, 13 July 2016 (implicitly).
[219] CE, No. 392191, 11 May 2016. The Council decided that, in principle, the denial of a social grant in such cases was not contrary to article 8 of the ECHR and article 3(1) of the CRC, but a failure to ascertain if the circumstances of the case were special (with

consequences for the children would be severe an exceptional obligation to assist them arises from article 3(1). Except for abduction cases, the Court has been less inclined to shield children from the consequences of their parents' illegal conduct by relying on article 3(1). It refused, for example, to recognise the filiation with the commissioning parents of children born through surrogacy, even when one of the parents was the biological parent,[220] or to recognise filiation established through fraud.[221]

Article 3(1) and Matters That Concern Children Indirectly Article 3(1) has prompted the consideration of the best interests of the child beyond matters that *involve* children to those that *affect* them. Most often, these are measures against their parents, such as deportation and extradition. Initially, the Council considered that such decisions do not concern children and thus do not fall within the ambit of article 3(1).[222] Subsequently, however, it decided that article 3(1) 'is not applicable only to decisions whose object is to address the personal situation of minor children but also to those decisions which can affect them in a manner sufficiently direct and certain'.[223]

The invocation of article 3(1) in matters concerning children indirectly before the Court has been less successful. For example, reliance on article 8 of the ECHR (rather than article 3(1) of the CRC) led to the Court's refusal to execute a European arrest warrant against the sole carer of a five-year-old child.[224] There have been unsuccessful attempts to rely on article 3(1) in the sentencing of parents,[225] lifting the prohibition to remain on French territory after the execution of criminal

regard to, inter alia, the state of health of the applicant and the children) and if state support was indispensable may lead to a violation of those articles.

[220] Civ 1, No. 09-66486, 6 April 2011; Civ 1, No. 09-17130, 6 April 2011; Civ 1, No. 12-18315, 13 September 2013, discussed in Section 3.6.2.

[221] That is, a birth certificate obtained fraudulently: Civ 1, No. 09-68399, 17 November 2010.

[222] For example, the Council decided that a parent's extradition was beyond the scope of article 3(1) because 'the extradition is not, in itself, a measure which concerns the children': CE, No. 317125, 19 January 2009.

[223] CE, No. 359359, 25 June 2014 at para. 1. In a subsequent case, it decided that authorities must consider article 3(1) when deciding on the extradition of the primary carer of a severely disabled child, although this could not prevent the extradition if public safety grounds required it: CE, No. 385927, 9 December 2015 at paras. 6–7.

[224] Crim, No. 10-86237, 22 September 2010.

[225] Crim, No. 09-83032, 18 May 2010 (argued that the custodial sentence breached article 8 of the ECHR and article 3(1) of the CRC).

punishment,[226] and the confiscation of the family home of convicted drug offenders.[227] Nonetheless, the Court did not explicitly reject the in-principle relevance of the article for such cases. Arguably, much depends on the facts of each case, including the balancing of the interests at stake, and whether article 3(1) is genuinely invoked for the benefit of the concerned child rather than that of the parent.

3.6 Factors with Impact on the Direct Application of the CRC

With direct application being central to the effect of the CRC in France, it is useful to consider the factors that have influenced it. Some of these factors are intrinsic to the CRC while others are external to it.

3.6.1 Intrinsic CRC Factors

Two CRC-related factors have historically been acknowledged as obstacles to its direct application: article 4 (by the Court) and some norms being addressed to the states (primarily by the Council). Ironically, a presumptive strength of direct application – the assimilation of the CRC with domestic law – resulted in the restrictive approach to interpretation used in relation to domestic statutes being imported into the Convention, to the detriment of its direct application. To the factors explicitly mentioned by the courts, the literature added the absence of a complaint mechanism and the vagueness of its provisions. Eventually, the historical, judicially sanctioned obstacles to direct application were abandoned in 2005 and 2012, respectively,[228] or self-eliminated with the Optional Protocol on individual communications in 2011.[229] These developments mark the end of the denial of direct application based on a limited consideration of the substance of the CRC and, theoretically, the beginning of a new phase of closer engagement with the substance of a wider range of provisions.

However, the change in legal approach did not lead to a significant increase in the number of provisions applied directly. The litigation

[226] Crim, No. 09-83351, 9 December 2009.

[227] Crim, No. 10-87811, 3 November 2011; Crim, No. 09-81239, 16 December 2009; Crim, No. 09-81710, 18 November 2009.

[228] See the May and June 2005 judgments of the Court (discussed in Section 3.3) and the 2012 *GISTI and FAPIL* decision of the Council (discussed in Section 3.4).

[229] UN Human Rights Council, Optional Protocol to the Convention on the Rights of the Child on a Communications Procedure, 14 July 2011, A/HRC/RES/17/18.

comfort zone created around article 3(1) may have acted as a disincentive to exploring the direct application of many other CRC provisions. Further, the courts did not completely distance themselves from their historical views[230] and did not scale up the transparency of their reasoning in relation to the clarity and precision of CRC norms. After 2005, the Court has not explicitly denied direct application to specific CRC provisions[231] and it remains unclear what norms it considers without direct effect and why.[232] Similarly, the Council has offered little insight into its approach to direct application after the demise of its staple rejection justification. It remains difficult, therefore, to identify a complete set of principles that inform the approach of the courts to the direct application of the Convention.

Change may be unfolding slowly, however, with the Council recently denying direct effect to article 6 on account of its 'imprecision'.[233] While no explanation is given for the sweeping conclusion in relation to this normatively rich article, its spelling out by the Council is important. It makes clear that the change operated in *GISTI and FAPIL* applies to the CRC and it gives an opportunity to the Council and commentators to tease out the meaning of 'imprecision' in a CRC context. This may even lead to some judicial introspection in relation to article 3(1), which remains a darling of the courts regardless of its much-criticised imprecision. Article 3(1) would depart from a position of strength. Unlike the Committee and other courts,[234] French courts do not refer to article 3(1) as a right. Further, some authors have argued that the courts find the article easy to apply because it is 'not an obligation for the State' but rather a '*principle* which is of direct application'.[235] These factors may suggest that the courts' expectation of precision is more limited in

230 The Court stated that although some articles have been recognised as having direct effect, most create obligations only between states: Cour de cassation, *Rapport annuel 2005*, 416. See also Schwartz, 'La jurisprudence', 37–38; Vassallo, 'La Convention', 25.

231 Monéger, 'Rapport'.

232 Articles 6 and 14, which invite an assessment of precision, were raised by litigants but were bypassed by the Court: Crim, No. 05-86947, 27 June 2006; Ass, No. 13-28369, 25 June 2014.

233 CE, No. 440154, 1 February 2022 (see the text accompanying note 112).

234 CRC Committee, *General Comment No. 14 (2013) on the right of the child to have his or her best interests taken as a primary consideration (art. 3, para. 1)*, 29 May 2013, CRC/C/GC/14, para. 6. For the approach of the South African courts, see Chapter 5.

235 Schwartz, 'La jurisprudence', 38 (emphasis added; footnote omitted). Neirinck makes a similar suggestion that it is the flexibility and generality of article 3(1) as a principle that has facilitated its direct application: Neirinck, 'L'application'.

relation to article 3(1) when compared with more specific CRC provisions.

Overall, despite much criticism that the CRC 'contains the seeds of its own non-application',[236] its intrinsic features do not overwhelmingly account for the tribulations of its direct application. On the contrary, some of its powerful features (i.e., the general principles, represented in the French case law by article 3(1)) have substantially facilitated its direct application. What emerges from the cases, however, is that the successes and the wobbles of the CRC's direct application do not lie exclusively at its feet and are instead affected by extraneous factors.

3.6.2 CRC-Independent Factors

3.6.2.1 The Litigation Context

The type of case, the remedy sought, the relevance of the CRC provision invoked, and the potential impact of direct application have influenced the application of the CRC by the courts. Thus, many cases decided by the Council deal with immigration, a sensitive political issue that may have prompted a reserved attitude towards the CRC – especially by the Council.[237] Courts may react differently to requests for abstract and concrete application, respectively. Challenges to statutes or decrees for reasons of incompatibility with the CRC involve a more abstract application, for which the standard of completeness, for example, may be less stringent than in disputes concerning individual rights. For instance, articles 21 and 22 were used by the Council to assess the lawfulness of a decree that implemented a statute recognising same-sex marriages,[238] but it is unlikely that the Court would rely on the same articles to approve an adoption by a same-sex couple if this was not recognised by the domestic law.[239] Invoking the CRC when only superficially

[236] Khaïat, 'La défense', 22.

[237] Rongé, 'La Convention', 10.

[238] CE, No. 370459, 18 December 2015.

[239] For a further example of how abstract and concrete applications of the CRC may lead to different conclusions, compare CE, No. 282275, 12 June 2006 with *Popov* v. *France*. The Council decided that the decree authorising the detention of families with children awaiting deportation was not contrary to the CRC, while the ECtHR decided that the ECHR was violated upon finding that the applicants' conditions of detention were not adapted to children's needs. The ECtHR even referred to articles 2, 3, and 37(b) and (c) of the CRC, which were found not to have been breached by the Council in the above decision: *Popov v. France* at paras. 52, 90–91.

relevant has deterred its application,[240] but seeking its application when useful to a concrete dispute has resulted in its application.[241] Direct application may be deterred by practical challenges in some cases but not in others. It was feared, for example, that the direct application of article 7 (and article 9) would result in an 'absence of legal security'[242] in the exercise of joint parental authority because there were no domestic rules to guide it. However, in a different legal context – that is, birth *sous X* – article 7 was applied with no hesitation, as discussed above.

Provisions that converge rather than conflict with the domestic law,[243] or to which national law has given effect to some extent, are more amenable to direct application – even when they do not perfectly satisfy the direct application criteria. For example, the application of article 12(2) by the Court was facilitated by it being given some domestic effect in civil procedures.[244] Article 3(1) is not formulated as a right and thus does not theoretically meet the criteria for direct application discussed in Section 3.2, but it being 'sufficiently general and flexible so that [it does] not challenge profoundly the domestic law'[245] has enabled its application.

Judicial policy rather than legal reasons has at times determined direct application. Thus, the Court rejected the direct application of the CRC en bloc, influenced by the politico-legal controversies concerning its direct effect.[246] In 2005, it changed its position – not because this was required by the case before it, but for, inter alia, another policy reason: promoting harmony with the Council's approach.[247] The Council also makes policy-driven decisions. For judicial policy reasons, it denied direct application to CRC provisions that are similar to those in other treaties that it did apply directly.[248] The decision that only norms of direct effect can be used to invalidate administrative acts reflected a 'choice of judicial policy'.[249] The Council sought, for example, to prevent a dramatic

[240] For example, in *GISTI and FAPIL*, the *commissaire du gouvernement* dismissed the relevance of article 3(1), arguing that it was just part of a 'litany' of norms invoked by the applicants: Dumortier, 'L'effet direct'.
[241] Taxil, 'Les critères', 166.
[242] Dekeuwer-Défossez, 'La convention relative aux droits de l'enfant'.
[243] Boulanger, 'Applicabilité directe', 7; Latty, 'Observations', 694; Neirinck, 'L'application', in relation to article 3(1).
[244] Rongé, 'La Convention'.
[245] Neirinck, 'L'application'.
[246] Bonnet, 'Le Conseil d'État'.
[247] Cour de cassation, *Rapport annuel 2005*, 416.
[248] Rongé, 'La Convention', 15.
[249] Chauvaux and Girardot, 'Les clauses'.

increase in the number of international documents invocable before courts and was concerned that international instruments would be simplistically assimilated with domestic statutes.[250]

3.6.2.2 Multiple Jurisdictions and the Interaction with Supra-National Courts

The lack of uniformity between the approaches taken by the Court and the Council is a puzzling aspect of the French jurisprudence on direct application. It has created confusion and legal insecurity, leading to the marginalisation of the CRC in favour of more established legal instruments.[251] While some alignment took place in May 2005, when the Court returned to an article-by-article approach, differences persist. For example, since 2005, the Court has not excluded, as a matter of principle, the direct effect of any article,[252] while until 2012 the Council denied direct application to norms addressed to the states. Currently, only six CRC articles are directly applied by both courts.[253]

The distinct jurisdiction of the courts explains, to a certain extent, the differences.[254] The Court resolves unfolding disputes between individuals or concerning individual rights and thus needs norms that can clarify the rights of the parties.[255] Setting aside domestic statutes is only viable for the Court if the international norm can be applied instead to resolve the dispute. By contrast, the Council can engage in an objective control of legality,[256] for which it is sufficient for the norm to have *some* constraining power rather than the maximum normative power needed to resolve a dispute concerning individual rights.[257] Further, the implications concerning the separation of powers raised by assertions of CRC supremacy

[250] Chauvaux and Girardot, 'Les clauses'.

[251] Monéger, 'La Convention'; Laurent-Boutot, 'La Cour de cassation'.

[252] Monéger, 'Rapport'.

[253] Articles 1, 3, 7, 9, 12 and 16: Défenseur des droits, *Rapport du Défenseur des droits au Comité des droits de l'enfant des Nations-Unies* (2020) 9.

[254] Bordry, 'Le Conseil d'État', 17.

[255] Laurent-Boutot, 'La Cour de cassation', 122; Akandji-Kombé, 'De l'invocabilité', part III. b.2.

[256] Dumortier, 'L'effet direct'. Laurent-Boutot refers to administrative courts checking the legality of norms (*contentieux objectif*), wherein the main objective is the protection not of individual interests but of the general interest: Laurent-Boutot, 'La Cour de cassation', 121.

[257] Dumortier, 'L'effet direct'; Akandji-Kombé, 'De l'invocabilité', part III.b.2. To clarify, when the Council invalidates an administrative act, it is the issuing body, rather than the Council, that must decide how to bring its conduct into line with the CRC: Bordry, 'Le Conseil d'État', 17.

are different for the two courts: the Court only assesses the conformity of statutes with treaties, potentially opposing the CRC to the will of the democratically elected legislature. The Council, however, also assesses the legality of decrees emanating from the executive, which have a lower legal status than the CRC, according to the Constitution. However, while it is plausible that distinct jurisdictions prompt different courts to extract different normative meanings from a treaty, there can be no justification for incoherence: at different points, either the Court or the Council has reasoned that the Convention or certain of its articles created *exclusively international* obligations, while the other has given them *domestic* effect.

The shifts in the jurisprudence of both supreme courts raise questions about their mutual influence. There are examples that suggest that the two courts influence one another, without, however, striving for harmonisation. Thus, the Court acknowledged that the significant shift in its jurisprudence in May 2005 was influenced by the Council,[258] and the Council eventually accepted the direct application of articles that were already applied directly by the Court (such as articles 12(2), 7(1), and 9 (3)). However, the Council continued its reliance on the literal criterion, despite this not being explicitly embraced by the Court, and it still refuses to apply certain articles that are directly applied by the Court (such as article 8). For a long time, the two courts diverged on the application of article 3(1) to surrogacy cases. The Court's position was that because surrogacy agreements are illegal under French law,[259] it could not recognise the filiation of children born via surrogacy with their commissioning parents. According to the Court, *l'état du droit positif*[260] was not contrary to the best interests of children *in general* as, inter alia, it protected them and society from the ills of surrogacy. This *in abstracto* application of article 3(1) differed markedly from the position of the Council, which decided that the illegality of surrogacy agreements does not absolve the state of its obligation to act in the best interests of *each child* under article 3(1) and issue the children with the travel documents needed to join their commissioning parents in France.[261] When, eventually, the Court aligned

[258] Cour de cassation, *Rapport annuel 2005*, 416.

[259] Surrogacy agreements entered by French nationals overseas (even if lawful in the jurisdiction where the child is born) are void under French law because they are contrary to public order (article 16-7 read with article 16-9 of the Civil Code).

[260] Civ 1, No. 09-66486, 6 April 2011; Civ 1, No. 10-19053, 6 April 2011; Civ 1, No. 12-18315, 13 September 2013.

[261] CE, No. 348778, 4 May 2011. The Council was, nonetheless, careful to state that its position did not concern the children's French nationality or the transcription of their

itself with an *in concreto* application of article 3(1), it did so not because it found the Council's position persuasive but rather as a result of several ECtHR developments.[262] Overall, the courts are aware of each other's jurisprudence and, because *GISTI and FAPIL* reflects their common position on direct application,[263] a better alignment of the case law may occur in the future.

The jurisprudential context with impact on the direct application of the Convention goes beyond the two courts to include the Constitutional Council, the ECtHR, and the ECJ. As mentioned in Section 3.2, the Constitutional Council does not apply the CRC but makes decisions with relevance to the courts' engagement with the Convention.[264] The Constitutional Council has been criticised for its deference to the parliament in certain child-related matters.[265] It endorsed, for example, legislation potentially contrary to the CRC, such as regressive changes to the juvenile justice legislation,[266] the legal framework for births *sous X*,[267] and the stricter requirements for accessing child benefits for the children of legal migrants.[268] Such decisions may remove the incentives for judicial and administrative courts to enquire into the conformity of domestic

birth certificates, both of which are under the jurisdiction of the judicial courts (i.e., the Court).

262 See the discussion below accompanying footnotes 278–280.

263 Akandji-Kombé, 'De l'invocabilité'. On the potential for further jurisprudential alignment of the two courts, see Cour de cassation, 'Conseil d'État: rencontre à la Cour de cassation' (26 January 2015), www.courdecassation.fr; Cour de cassation, 'Lancement des travaux de groupes de reflexion visant à développer les relations institutionnelles de la Cour' (10 October 2014), www.courdecassation.fr.

264 See generally Adeline Gouttenoire, 'Cohérence des contrôles de conventionnalité et de constitutionnalité en matière de droit des personnes et de la famille' (2013) 2 *Les nouveaux Cahiers du Conseil constitutionnel* 63; Régis de Gouttes, 'Le dialogue des juges' (paper presented at the Colloque du Cinquantenaire du Conseil Constitutionnel, 3 November 2008).

265 For example, it considered births *sous X* and adoption by same-sex couples to be 'social questions' best left to the legislature: François Chénedé and Pascale Deumier, 'L'oeuvre du Parlement, la part du Conseil constitutionnel en droit des personnes et de la famille' (2013) 39 *Les nouveaux Cahiers du Conseil constitutionnel* (online).

266 For example, the introduction of minimum sentences for child offenders and adult sentences for juveniles in certain situations (Decision No. 2007-554 DC, 9 August 2007); the creation of correctional tribunals for children with only one judge specialising in juvenile matters (Decision No. 2011-635 DC, 4 August 2011); and fast-track procedures for juvenile offenders, at the risk of insufficient information about the child (Decision No. 2012-272 QPC, 21 September 2012).

267 Decision No. 2012-248 QPC, 16 May 2012; CRC Committee, *Concluding observations: France*, 2009, para. 43.

268 Decision No. 2005-528 DC, 15 December 2005 at paras. 16–18.

law with the Convention and assert the latter's supremacy, considering that its domestic status is lower than that of the Constitution.

Occasionally, there has been divergence between the constitutional and ordinary jurisprudence. Courts have sometimes differed from the Constitutional Council and delivered child-focused decisions with reliance on the CRC by using the gaps in the constitutional jurisprudence.[269] Recently, the Constitutional Council recognised the constitutional value of the best interests of the child and began to apply it in the constitutional review of legislation concerning the determination of age through radiological tests,[270] the protection of personal data,[271] juvenile justice,[272] and filiation.[273] The thrust of the Council's reasoning is that the Constitution gives rise to a requirement to protect the best interests of the child by ensuring a legal protection commensurate with the child's age.[274] It is difficult to ascertain to what extent the popularity of article 3(1) with the courts has influenced the Council, but there is now an increasing chance of interaction between the CRC-informed approach to the best interests taken by the courts, on the one hand, and the constitutional best interests as contoured by the Constitutional Council, on the other. Whether these approaches will clash or converge remains to be seen in subsequent cases.[275]

The jurisprudence of the ECJ and the ECtHR and the pressure of their more effective implementation mechanisms have directly or indirectly encouraged the direct application of international treaties, or their application more generally.[276] This powerful institutional support is absent in

[269] See the discussion of *Benjamin* and *L'Association Aides* in Section 3.5.

[270] *Adama S.*

[271] Decision No. 2019-797 QPC, 26 July 2019, *Unicef France* (creation of a file of foreign nationals who declare themselves as unaccompanied minors).

[272] Decision No. 2019-778 DC, *Loi de programmation 2018–2022 et de réforme pour la justice.*

[273] Decision No. 2019-826 QPC, 7 February 2020 at para. 5.

[274] *Adama S* at para. 6; *Unicef France* at para. 3.

[275] There are some prima facie differences. For example, the constitutional best interests seem dominated by a protection paradigm (Antonin Gelblat and Robert Medard Inghilterra, 'L'intérêt supérieur de l'enfant: radiographie d'une exigence constitutionnelle' (2019) 16 *Revue des droits de l'homme* 1) and, unlike article 3(1), the constitutional best interests are not a primary consideration.

[276] This is well documented. See, for example, Carole Nivard, 'L'effet direct de la Charte sociale européenne devant les juridictions suprêmes françaises' (2012) 28 *Revue des droits et libertés fondamentaux* (online); Dubouis, 'Droit international', para. 5; Abdelgawad and Weber, 'The Reception Process', 139–140; El Boudouhi, 'The National Judge', 29. References to international (or domestic) cases are rare, but their

the CRC context, but at times the Convention has benefited directly or indirectly from the jurisprudence of these supranational courts. Thus, concerns about France being found in breach of the ECHR have contributed to the Court accepting the direct application of the CRC in May 2005.[277] The longstanding denial of recognition of filiation[278] between French commissioning parents and children born through surrogacy overseas was reversed gradually and only after successive ECtHR judgments.[279] Following a 2019 ECtHR advisory opinion, the Court finally accepted an *in concreto*, as opposed to an *in abstracto*, application of the best interests of the child to surrogacy cases.[280] The reasoning in *GISTI and FAPIL* is 'manifestly'[281] influenced by the practice of the ECJ, which 'nourishes and is a useful reference point regarding this common notion [direct application]'.[282] This has moved the Council away from the literal approach that disadvantaged the CRC. Regrettably, the CRC Committee is absent from this influential bloc that has helped move the discourse on direct application in a positive direction.[283]

influence can be deduced from the similarity of reasoning and outcome, and from the written submissions by the reporting judges, *commissaires public*, and general advocates. For an explicit recognition of the binding nature of ECtHR judgments, see Ass, No. 10-17049, 15 April 2011.

277 Laurent-Boutot, 'La Cour de cassation', 71–72; Maynial, 'Observations', 38.

278 For representative cases, see Civ 1, No. 09-66486, 6 April 2011; Civ 1, No. 09-17130, 6 April 2011; Civ 1, No. 12-18315, 13 September 2013. See generally Béatrice Weiss-Gout, 'Trois décisions, une même deception' (2011) 146 *Gazette du Palais* 7; François Chénedé, 'Les arrêts Mennesson et Labassée ou l'instrumentalisation des droits de l'homme' (2014) *Recueil Dalloz* 1797; Adeline Gouttenoire, 'Surrogacy Agreements: At Last, the Primacy of the Child's Interests' (2015) 1 *Montesquieu Law Review* 103.

279 See *Mennesson v. France* (Application No. 65192/11, 26 June 2014) and *Labassée v. France* (Application No. 65941/11, 26 June 2014); Ass, No. 14-21323, 3 July 2015; Ass No. 15-50002, 3 July 2015; Civ 1, No. 16-16455, 5 July 2017.

280 *Advisory Opinion concerning the recognition in domestic law of a legal parent–child relationship between a child born through a gestational surrogacy arrangement abroad and the intended mother* (Request No. P16–2018-001, 10 April 2019); followed by Ass, No. 10-19053, 4 October 2019 (acknowledging the state's discretion to decide the means to recognise legally the parent–child relationship with the non-biological commissioning parent).

281 Slama, 'Adoption'. See also Latty, 'Observations', 685.

282 Dumortier, 'L'effet direct'; Taxil, 'Les critères', 165.

283 Reports presented to the courts by reporting judges may refer to its work: see, for example, Coutou and Vassallo, 'Rapport'. A search on Legifrance (12 September 2022) shows that the Court and the Council have not considered the Committee's views in their judgments. However, some lower courts have considered general comments but only to conclude that they cannot be effectively invoked by litigants (CAA de Marseille,

The positive impact of other institutions on the application of the CRC cannot be taken for granted, as their jurisprudence may circumscribe its effects. This is reflected especially in the endorsement of births *sous X* by the Constitutional Council and the ECtHR, which contributed to maintaining a practice that is problematic from a children's rights perspective.[284] Similar effects have arisen from the convergence of the Court and ECtHR practice in relation to the denial of access to social grants to children who joined their parents in France without following the procedure of family reunification.[285] In both matters, the Committee found the domestic law and practice inconsistent with the CRC,[286] but its position was not taken into consideration. Thus, over-reliance on the jurisprudential leadership of the ECtHR may be detrimental to the development of children's rights, especially their socio-economic rights.

While the CRC operates in a busy legal space, the monopoly of the courts over its direct application has enabled them to develop a distinctive child-focused jurisprudential voice that may differ from that of the Constitutional Council and the ECtHR. At times, the courts have protected this privileged position. The Court, for example, made clear that the interpretation and application of the CRC is under its jurisdiction and not that of the Constitutional Council.[287] Further, when the Court changed its jurisprudence on surrogacy, it did so by applying article 8 of the ECHR rather than article 3(1), which it had previously applied in surrogacy cases. For a parsimonious court, this looks less like an oversight and more like a careful defence of one's turf: the Court deferred to the view of the ECtHR in terms of article 8 of the ECHR, but it held onto its own in relation to article 3(1) of the CRC. That this is not accidental is confirmed by other instances where both the Court and the Council kept their reasoning distinct in relation to the ECHR and the CRC,

No. 19MA01938, 28 November 2019 at para. 6; CAA de Marseille, No. 18MA00471, 27 November 2018 at para. 7).

284 *Odièvre*; Decision No. 2012-248 QPC, 16 May 2012 at paras. 6, 8.

285 See *Osungu and Lokongo v. France* (note 92).

286 CRC Committee, *Concluding observations: France*, 2009, para. 43 (births *sous X*); CRC Committee, *Concluding observations: France*, 30 June 2004, CRC/C/15/Add.240, paras. 46–47 (access to allocations should not be subject to the modality of children entering France).

287 In 2012, the Court refused to send to the Constitutional Council a QPC in which it was argued that certain statutory provisions were contrary to article 3(1), reasoning that the mentioned article 'was not part of the rights and freedoms guaranteed by the Constitution': Soc., No. 11-40090, 25 January 2012.

respectively.[288] What this shows is that the courts are both aware of their privileged relationship with the CRC and are willing to defend it and capitalise on it.

To conclude, numerous factors have influenced the direct application of the CRC, some inherent to it and some not. Many of these factors are ambivalent, as they are able to either facilitate or obstruct direct application. This strengthens the call for a careful consideration of the domestic context in which the CRC operates and dissuades analyses that focus solely on its intrinsic features.

3.7 Conclusion

The complex picture of direct application that emerges from the French case law contrasts sharply with the oversimplified approach to direct application taken by the CRC Committee and discussed in Chapter 2. Although direct application is existential for the judicial effect of the CRC in France, it has not been a silver bullet. The stringent criteria of direct application and cautious courts have combined to result in an uneven direct application of the Convention. The initially dominant view that the CRC contains 'the seeds of its own non-application'[289] was gradually abandoned and exposed as policy-driven rather than founded in strong legal reasons, rooted in the domestic law or the Convention itself. The jurisprudential shifts in 2005 and 2012 showed that the legal vulnerabilities of the CRC have been overstated, while extraneous factors – such as context, policy, and the jurisprudence of other institutions – that have a bearing on its direct application have been neglected.

The impact of the application of the CRC is mixed but not negligible. In the absence of an extensive consolidated legal protection for children's rights, the CRC's vocation to be applied directly and its supra-legislative status have raised hopes of high impact. 'High-end' returns – that is, operating as an autonomous source of rights and duties not recognised by the domestic law, setting aside inconsistent statutes, or controlling the validity of administrative acts and delegated legislation – are seldom

[288] CE, No. 249369, 24 March 2004; CE, No. 220434, 24 March 2004 (*kafala*: see Section 3.5.1.2); Ass, No. 09-69052, 3 June 2011 (family grant: see the text accompanying note 92).

[289] Khaïat, 'La défense', 22. These seeds would include the reference to implementation measures in article 4, the alleged lack of precision and clarity of its provisions, and the fact that many provisions are addressed to the states.

obtained but are accepted in principle by both courts. A limited number of provisions have been applied directly and there is over-reliance on article 3(1), but this is mitigated to some extent by the diversity of matters in which the Convention is invoked and by this article's use as a protective normative umbrella for rights that are otherwise unlikely to be directly applied by the courts. Problematically, nonetheless, article 3(1) has created a comfort zone for the courts, which allows them to avoid engaging with the direct application of other CRC provisions. Undeniably, however, the courts have transformed article 3(1) into an effective repository of legal devices that enable child-centred decisions.

The CRC has added value to the judicial protection of children's rights by enabling the courts to make child-focused decisions that are not supported by other legal instruments. The Convention has made the rights and interests of children more visible in judicial decisions, prompting courts and parties to conceptualise legal issues in a manner that considers them. This may perhaps explain the focus on article 3(1), which the courts have come to approach as *the* provision that legally justifies considering the rights of children and giving them a distinct legal treatment.

All in all, after a rocky start, French judges seem accustomed to using the Convention, which is no longer the Cinderella of direct application. The case law has now stabilised on a cautiously positive trajectory. In time, this may be bolstered by an evolving individual communications jurisprudence of the Committee, which may offer the courts an alternative child-centred jurisprudential framework to that of the ECtHR, the ECJ, and the Constitutional Council.

4

Australia

4.1 Introduction

The Australian case study shifts the attention in this book towards dualist jurisdictions and the indirect application of the CRC. Unlike in France, where the CRC is part of the domestic law and can be applied directly by the courts, in Australia (which was also one of the early ratifiers of the CRC[1]) the CRC cannot operate as domestic law in the absence of incorporation or transformation. As the Convention has not been fully incorporated or transformed domestically, its judicial application is uneven. There have been marked differences between the courts, depending on their jurisdiction.

An Australian case study is relevant for this book for several reasons. First, it illustrates the complex interaction between an unincorporated CRC and the domestic law in a dualist legal system with multiple governance levels (i.e., federal and state), where the Parliament is supreme. While highlighting the challenges to the judicial application of the CRC resulting from that vulnerable legal position, the Australian case law also demonstrates that, even in the absence of unequivocal political and legislative support for children's rights, courts can creatively use the domestic law to give the CRC judicial effect – especially when convergence between the two can be found. Second, it shows the effect on judicial engagement with the CRC of a human rights protection system, even without its legislative incorporation. In the absence of comprehensive legislative protection of human rights at the federal level, the federal case law (aside from family law) is significantly less open to the influence of the CRC than the case law emanating from other Australian (Victorian, in this book) or foreign (South African and United Kingdom, in this book) courts whose work is informed by human rights

[1] Australia ratified the CRC on 17 December 1990: 'Status of Treaties: Convention on the Rights of the Child', *United Nations Treaty Collection*, https://treaties.un.org/Pages/ViewDetails.aspx?src=IND&mtdsg_no=IV-11&chapter=4.

legislation. Ultimately, the Australian case study shows the relevance of the structure of reception for an effective engagement with the Convention and encourages analyses that look beyond the formal rules of reception, as advocated in this book.

The jurisprudence of three superior courts[2] – the High Court of Australia (HCA), the Full Court of the Family Court (the Family Court),[3] and the Supreme Court of Victoria (the VSC) – is analysed. The High Court is the highest Australian court in all matters (including constitutional) and the ultimate decision-maker concerning the relationship between treaties and the domestic law. The Family Court and the VSC have jurisdictions informed by special statutes (family law legislation and a human rights statute, respectively), enabling them to engage with the Convention in a distinct way that warrants separate consideration.

The chapter proceeds with a general presentation of the relationship between international law, including the CRC, and Australian domestic law. Section 4.4 presents the case law and is followed by analysis and the conclusions.

4.2 International Human Rights Treaties and the Australian Law

Australia is a common law system of Anglo-American tradition, with a structure consisting of the Commonwealth (the federal state) and the States and Territories. Treaties are entered into by the Commonwealth executive, with limited involvement of the Commonwealth Parliament (the Parliament) or the States and Territories.[4] Australia follows a 'clear cut dualism'[5] in the relationship between national law and international treaties, wherein ratified treaties do not become domestically binding unless given effect by domestic legislation[6] or transformed by judicial decisions into the common law.

[2] The cases have been sourced from the Australasian Legal Information Institute (AustLII) database at www.austlii.edu.au. Cases up to 1 November 2022 have been considered.

[3] On 21 September 2021, the Family Court was replaced by the Federal Circuit and Family Court of Australia.

[4] Section 61 of the Commonwealth of Australia Constitution Act 1900 (Cth) (the Constitution). For details, see Anne Devereux and Sarah McCosker, 'International Law and Australian Law' in Donald Rothwell and Emily Crawford (eds.), *International Law in Australia* (Sydney: Thomson Reuters, 2017) 23, 26.

[5] Robert French, 'Oil and Water?: International Law and Domestic Law in Australia' (The Brennan Lecture, Bond University, 26 June 2009) 30.

[6] Devereux and McCosker, 'International Law and Australian Law', 27; *Dietrich v. R* [1992] HCA 57 at para. 17 (Mason CJ and McHugh J).

Domestic human rights protection is limited. The Parliament has not enacted most human rights treaties, allegedly because domestic law already complies with them[7] or to avoid trespassing into the legislative powers of the States.[8] Core human rights instruments, including the CRC, are declared instruments under the Australian Human Rights Commission Act 1986 (Cth) (AHRCA), to which they are appended, but this does not amount to legislative incorporation.[9] Although there is no federal Bill of Rights, the Australian Capital Territory and the States of Victoria and Queensland have passed human rights statutes applicable within their jurisdictions.[10] The federal Constitution protects a limited number of rights that embody freedoms developed at common law, rather than rights of wide scope akin to those in human rights instruments.[11] Federal statutes and the common law provide some human rights protection that overlaps with international treaties, but there are differences in the scope and the nature of that protection.[12] None of the rights recognised at common law are, for example, socio-economic or child-specific. Further, common law or treaty rights can be superseded by statutes.[13]

Although unincorporated, ratified treaties may have an indirect effect on judicial reasoning by informing the interpretation, development, and

[7] This view is strongly contested. See, for example, Gillian Triggs, 'Human Rights Across the Tasman: A Widening Gulf' (Hotung Fellowship Public Lecture, 6 April 2016); Diane Otto, 'From "Reluctance" to "Exceptionalism": The Australian Approach to Domestic Implementation of Human Rights' (2001) 26(5) *Alternative Law Journal* 219, 221.

[8] Hilary Charlesworth and Gillian Triggs, 'Australia and the International Protection of Human Rights' in Donald Rothwell and Emily Crawford (eds.), *International Law in Australia* (Sydney: Thomson Reuters, 2017) 117, 128–129; Hilary Charlesworth, 'The UN and Mandatory Sentencing' (2000) 25 *Australian Children's Rights News* 1, 4.

[9] Kirsten Walker and Penelope Mathew, 'Minister for Immigration v Ah Hin Teoh' (1995) 20(1) *Melbourne University Law Review* 236, 249. According to Single, this may enhance the status of the declared instruments: Jennifer Single, 'The Status of the UN Convention on the Rights of the Child in Australian Law' (1999) 9(1) *Polemic* 36–37. However, beyond the various functions that the Australian Human Rights Commission has in relation to them, it does not appear that human rights treaties enjoy an enhanced status.

[10] Human Rights Act 2004 (ACT); Charter of Human Rights and Responsibilities Act 2006 (Vic); Human Rights Act 2019 (Qld).

[11] Peter Bailey, *The Human Rights Enterprise in Australia and Internationally* (Chatswood, NSW: LexisNexis Butterworths, 2009) 239, 269–271.

[12] Australian Human Rights Commission, 'Common Law Rights, Human Rights Scrutiny and the Rule of Law', https://humanrights.gov.au/our-work/rights-and-freedoms/common-law-rights-human-rights-scrutiny-and-rule-law; Australian Law Reform Commission, *Traditional Rights and Freedoms: Encroachments by Commonwealth Laws* (ALRC Report 129, 2016) paras. 2.45–2.46.

[13] Triggs, 'Human Rights Across the Tasman'.

application of the law.[14] The influence of unincorporated human rights treaties on the common law is controversial,[15] and these treaties are most often given effect in the statutory interpretation process.

Two presumptions channel the use of international treaties during statutory interpretation. The presumption of consistent interpretation entails that statutes enacted to give effect to a treaty, or enacted after a treaty, are to be interpreted, as far as their language permits (i.e., if there is ambiguity in a statute), in conformity with that treaty.[16] Some judges support a wide definition of 'ambiguity', which is said to exist '[i]f the language of the legislation is susceptible of a construction which is consistent with the terms of the international instrument and the obligations which it imposes on Australia'.[17] Other judges have rejected this choice-of-meaning approach, which they contrast with legislation that is 'genuinely ambiguous'.[18] The second presumption is the principle of legality, which states that the Parliament is presumed not to intend to limit fundamental human rights unless that intention is clearly and unequivocally expressed.[19] This presumption essentially applies to fundamental rights recognised at common law and is controversial in relation to unincorporated human rights.[20] The caveat to both interpretive presumptions, however generously construed, is that they may be inoperative when legislation is very detailed (and thus not ambiguous) or when the Parliament clearly intends to legislate contrary to international law.

The Acts Interpretation Act 1901 (Cth) creates opportunities to rely on international law as extrinsic statutory interpretation material by authorising reliance on an international treaty 'referred to' in a statute in order to confirm the ordinary meaning or resolve an

14 See generally Devereux and McCosker, 'International Law and Australian Law', 36–44.

15 Devereux and McCosker, 'International Law and Australian Law', 38.

16 Perry Herzfeld and Thomas Prince, *Statutory Interpretation Principles* (Sydney: Thomson Reuters, 2014) 179–180.

17 *Teoh* at para. 27 (Mason CJ and Deane J) (footnote omitted). To paraphrase French CJ in *Momcilovic v. The Queen* [2011] HCA 34 (*Momcilovic*), the *Teoh* ambiguity does not have 'negative connotations': at para. 50.

18 *Western Australia v. Ward* [2002] HCA 28 (*Ward*) at para. 956 (Callinan J).

19 Michelle Sanson, *Statutory Interpretation* (Melbourne: Oxford University Press, 2012) 207; Dan Meagher, 'The Common Law Presumption of Consistency with International Law: Some Observations from Australia (and Comparisons with New Zealand)' (2012) 3 *New Zealand Law Review* 465. See also *Momcilovic* at para. 43 (French CJ).

20 David Dyzenhaus, Murray Hunt, and Michael Taggart, 'The Principle of Legality in Administrative Law: Internationalisation as Constitutionalisation' (2001) 1(1) *Oxford University Commonwealth Journal* 5–6; French, 'Oil and Water?', 37; *Momcilovic* at para. 43 (French CJ).

ambiguity.[21] When there is no ambiguity, the treaty may be relied on if the meaning of the statute is manifestly absurd or unreasonable.[22]

Unincorporated treaties may also influence the exercise of executive discretion,[23] and their influence on the exercise of *judicial* discretion is emerging as a new form of engaging with international law.[24] Thus, some judges have taken unincorporated treaties into account as a relevant factor without being obliged to do so.[25] Very detailed legislation may curtail administrative and judicial discretions that accommodate individualised justice or consideration of international human rights.[26]

Judicial attitudes towards international law are ambivalent,[27] ranging from enthusiasm to caution,[28] to strong opposition.[29] International treaties are often ignored by judges,[30] who tend to apply the law even

[21] Section 15AB(1)(a) and (b)(i) read with section 15AB(2)(d). See also Devereux and McCosker, 'International Law and Australian Law', 39.

[22] Section 15AB(1)(b)(ii) read with section 15AB(2)(d).

[23] Historically, this occurred through the doctrine of legitimate expectation, which is now seldom applied for this purpose. See Matthew Groves, 'Treaties and Legitimate Expectations: The Rise and Fall of *Teoh* in Australia' (2010) 15 (4) *Judicial Review* 323; Wendy Lacey, 'In the Wake of *Teoh*: Finding an Appropriate Government Response' (2001) 29(2) *Federal Law Review* 219, 232; Michael Taggart, '"Australian Exceptionalism" in Judicial Review' (2008) 36(1) *Federal Law Review* 1, 17. Nonetheless, unincorporated treaties may be considered in the exercise of executive discretion when authorised by specific statutes. See Andrew Edgar and Rayner Thwaites, 'Implementing Treaties in Domestic Law: Translation, Enforcement and Administrative Law' (2018) 19(1) *Melbourne Journal of International Law* 24.

[24] Wendy Lacey, 'Judicial Discretion and Human Rights: Expanding the Role of International Law in the Domestic Sphere' (2004) 5(1) *Melbourne Journal of International Law* 108, 123–124; Wendy Lacey, 'A Prelude to the Demise of *Teoh*: The High Court Decision in *Re Minister for Immigration and Multicultural Affairs, Ex parte Lam*' (2004) 26(1) *Sydney Law Review* 130.

[25] *Kioa v. West* [1985] HCA 81 at paras. 40 (Brennan J); 21 (Gibbs CJ).

[26] Bailey, *The Human Rights Enterprise*, 218.

[27] Hilary Charlesworth, 'The High Court and Human Rights' in Peter Cane (ed.), *Centenary Essays for the High Court of Australia* (Chatswood, NSW: LexisNexis Butterworths, 2004) 356, 368.

[28] For enthusiastic supporters, see Justices Kirby and Nicholson, formerly of the High Court and the Family Court, respectively. Former Chief Justice French has been more cautious, referring to international law as 'an 'elusive' concept that faces 'taxonomical challenges': French, 'Oil and Water?', 6–7.

[29] Justice Callinan refers to international norms as 'often ambiguous' or 'often vague and conflicting': *Ward* at paras. 956, 958.

[30] Alastair Nicholson, 'Australian Judicial Approaches to International Human Rights Conventions and "Family Law"' (Miller Du Toit Conference, Cape Town, 26 March 2002) 15.

when it results in a serious breach of human rights.[31] The judges' underlying concern is with the legitimacy of providing judicial protection to unincorporated rights.[32] This is perhaps not surprising, considering the often-politicised domestic context in which human rights operate and the absence of legislative support for a human rights culture.[33] There is a 'legacy of exceptionalism and isolation from global human rights jurisprudence',[34] with 'a sense of self-sufficiency [being] promoted within domestic legal discourse'.[35] It is in this context that the CRC interacts with domestic law.

4.3 The CRC and the Australian Law

Australia has not enacted the CRC post-ratification, allegedly because the government ensured prior to ratification that domestic law complied with the Convention.[36] Australia's record before the CRC Committee proves differently, with the state routinely criticised on matters such as juvenile justice and child protection, immigration, and First Nations children.[37] The Committee has expressed concerns in relation to the absence of national legislation incorporating the CRC[38] and to the Convention being overridden by domestic law.[39]

Matters covered by the CRC fall under the legislative and executive powers of States Territories and the Commonwealth.[40] For example, marriage and parental rights are governed by Commonwealth legislation,

31 Triggs, 'Human Rights Across the Tasman'.

32 Meagher, 'The Common Law Presumption', 478.

33 Triggs, 'Human Rights Across the Tasman'. See also Charlesworth and Triggs, 'Australia', 118.

34 Triggs, 'Human Rights Across the Tasman'. See also Otto, 'From "Reluctance"', 221.

35 John Tobin, 'Finding Rights in the "Wrongs" of Our Law: Bringing International Law Home' (2005) 30(4) *Alternative Law Journal* 164.

36 Attorney-General's Department, *Australia's Report Under the Convention on the Rights of the Child* (1995) para. 6; CRC Committee, *Summary Record of the 1054th Meeting*, 22 September 2005, CRC/C/SR.1054 para. 30.

37 The CRC Committee has issued concluding observations in relation to Australia in 1997, 2005, 2012, and 2019. For the latest, see CRC Committee, *Concluding observations on the combined fifth and sixth periodic reports of Australia*, 1 November 2019, CRC/C/AUS/CO/5-6, especially paras. 22–23, 44–45, 48.

38 CRC Committee *Concluding Observations: Australia*, 2019, para. 7.

39 CRC Committee *Concluding Observations: Australia*, 20 October 2005, CRC/C/15/Add.268, para. 9. See also paras. 18–19, 58.

40 Rita Shackel, 'The UN Convention on the Rights of the Child: Tracing Australia's Implementation of the Provisions Relating to Family Relations' in Olga Cvejić Jančić (ed.), *The Rights of the Child in a Changing World* (Cham: Springer, 2016) 37, 41.

while public law issues such as child protection and juvenile justice are governed by State and Territory laws. The Commonwealth can rely on its external affairs power[41] enlivened by the ratification of the CRC to legislate on child-related issues that are otherwise under State and Territory competence. However, it has been reluctant to do so even when State legislation conflicts with the Convention.[42]

The CRC has influenced some federal statutes and policies – including, for example, the import into the Family Law Act 1975 (Cth) (FLA) of the notion of the best interests of the child[43] and the formulation of some provisions in a rights language.[44] In 2011, section 60B(4) was introduced into Part VII of the Act (titled 'Children'), which deals, inter alia, with the relationship between children and parents.[45] It reads:

> (4) An additional object of this Part is to give effect to the Convention on the Rights of the Child done at New York on 20 November 1989.

The amendment does not incorporate the Convention, which remains an interpretation aid to ambiguities in Part VII, with the Act prevailing in the event of inconsistency.[46] Other federal statutes have been influenced by the CRC, but the statutory protection for children's rights remains fragmented in the absence of a children's rights statute at the federal level.[47]

[41] Section 51(xxix) of the Constitution. The Parliament may only legislate if it has the power to do so under section 51 of the Constitution.

[42] Moira Rayner, 'The State of Children's Rights in Australia' in Bob Franklin (ed.), *The New Handbook of Children's Rights: Comparative Policy and Practice* (London: Routledge, 2002) 345, 350; Alastair Nicholson, 'The United Nations Convention on the Rights of the Child and the Need for Its Incorporation into a Bill of Rights' (2006) 44(1) *Family Court Review* 5, 10. An example is the failure of the Commonwealth Parliament to raise the minimum age of criminal responsibility from 10 to 14, consistently with the CRC.

[43] Single, 'The Status', 37. See also Anthony Dickey, *Family Law* (Sydney: Thomson Reuters 2014) 305.

[44] Frank Bates, '"Out of Everywhere into Here": The Disparate Bases of Childrens' [sic] Rights in Australia' (2007) 15(2) *Asia Pacific Law Review* 235, 250; Adiva Sifris, 'Children in Immigration Detention: The Bakhtiyari Family in the Family Court' (2004) 29(5) *Alternative Law Journal* 212, 216. See sections 60(2)(b), (c) and 60B(2)(a) of the FLA.

[45] Family Law Legislation Amendment (Family Violence and Other Measures) Act 2011 (Cth) (effective June 2012).

[46] See The Parliament of the Commonwealth of Australia *Replacement explanatory memorandum to the Family Law Legislation Amendment (Family Violence and Other Measures) Bill 2011 (Cth)* para. 24.

[47] Shackel, 'The UN Convention', 42; John Tobin, 'The Development of Children's Rights' in Lisa Young, Mary Anne Kenny and Geoffrey Monahan (eds.), *Children and the Law in Australia*, 2nd ed. (Chatswood, NSW: LexisNexis Butterworths, 2016) 25–26.

The Convention has not enjoyed political and popular support. It has been plagued by misconceptions concerning its potential effects on state sovereignty, federal balance, and parent–child relationships,[48] as well as an overall apprehension about its vagueness, its generality, and the qualified wording of many of its articles.[49]

This downcast perspective is borne by much of the case law of the High Court, which engages with the CRC under the traditional reception rules discussed in Section 4.2. However, a glimmer of hope is offered by the judgments of the Family Court and the VSC, whose ability to apply the CRC is enhanced, in the case of the Family Court, by its jurisdiction over statutes that give partial effect to the Convention, and, in the case of the VSC, by applying human rights legislation. These aspects are discussed in Sections 4.4 and 4.5, which present the case law of the federal courts (the High Court and the Family Court) and of the VSC, respectively.

4.4 The CRC and the Federal Courts

The engagement of the federal courts with the CRC is governed by the traditional common law rules of reception, which are used as a framework for the presentation of the case law below. This engagement is characterised by a tight control by the Parliament over the domestic effect of the CRC, but it is also peppered with examples of judicial creativity and willingness to use the available domestic framework to its maximum to give judicial effect to the Convention.

4.4.1 The Legal Status of the CRC

The common wisdom is that the CRC is not an autonomous source of domestic law because it is an unincorporated treaty. However, more nuance is needed in discussing these issues. First, when the CRC enlivens the exercise of external affairs power, it has some autonomous constitutional effect; and second, judicial views have been expressed that the Convention is incorporated by the FLA. These two issues are discussed below.

48 Of the submissions to the Joint Standing Committee on Treaties, 51 per cent were disapproving of the CRC: Joint Standing Committee on Treaties, Parliament of the Commonwealth of Australia, *United Nations Convention on the Rights of the Child* (1998) ix.

49 Bates, 'Out of Everywhere', 245.

In enlivening the external affairs power, the CRC has some limited direct constitutional effect. This direct effect concerns not the substance of the Convention but rather the activation of the Parliament's power to pass federal legislation to give it domestic effect. The legislation so passed would be constitutionally invalid if it was so substantially inconsistent with the CRC that it lost the character of a law implementing it.[50] This gives the CRC a powerful role in the constitutional review of legislation, provided that the legislation was passed under the external affairs power.[51]

There is little judicial engagement with the CRC as a trigger of external affairs power. Courts have not yet used the CRC as a standard in the constitutional review of legislation in an external affairs power context. There is some judicial debate about whether the CRC meets the requirements to enliven the external affairs power and thus be relevant for such review.[52] For some judges, the CRC is sufficiently specific and normative for this purpose;[53] for others, it may be too aspirational.[54] With no explicit judicial precedent, the judicial scrutiny of legislation under the external affairs power remains of uncertain value as a CRC vehicle.

The Family Court engaged with the CRC and the external affairs power – although not to assess the validity of legislation, but to interpret the FLA in a way that extended that court's protective jurisdiction to matters normally under the jurisdiction of State and Territory courts (i.e., child protection) or beyond the scope of the Act (i.e., the relationship between parents and children). In essence, the Court's view was that because certain provisions in the FLA were amended or introduced after

[50] *Victoria v. Commonwealth* [1996] HCA 56 at para. 38 (not a CRC case).

[51] This is not inevitable even when legislation is passed to give effect to the CRC. This is because the Commonwealth Parliament can make laws concerning children under its other powers in section 51 of the Constitution.

[52] For the criteria, see Devereux and McCosker, 'International Law and Australian Law', 29; *Commonwealth v. Tasmania* [1983] HCA 21; *Victoria v. Commonwealth*.

[53] *B v. MIMIA* [2003] FamCA 4 at para. 267 (Nicholson CJ and O'Ryan J) (article 3); *Re Minister for Immigration and Multicultural and Indigenous Affairs; Ex parte Lam* [2003] HCA 6 (*Ex parte Lam*) at paras. 98–99 (McHugh and Gummow JJ) (article 3); *Purvis v. New South Wales (Department of Education and Training)* [2003] HCA 62 at para. 6 (Gleeson CJ) (articles 3 and 19); *XYZ v. Commonwealth* [2006] HCA 25 at paras. 62–63 (Kirby J) (articles 19 and 34 of the CRC can enliven the external affairs power).

[54] *AMS v. AIF* [1999] HCA 26 at para. 50 (Gleeson CJ, McHugh, and Gummow JJ). For Callinan J, there is a 'strong possibility' that the CRC is aspirational only: *Minister for Immigration and Multicultural and Indigenous Affairs v. B* [2004] HCA 20 (*MIMIA v. B*) at para. 222 (Callinan J).

the ratification of the CRC, they were passed in the exercise of external affairs power,[55] which justified construing them in line with the CRC.

Thus, in *Re Z*,[56] a majority of the Family Court suggested ('it may be that') that the external affairs power enlivened by the CRC enabled the Commonwealth to make a law such as the FLA to cover the *overall* welfare of children,[57] because the welfare of children cannot be compartmentalised between federal and State matters (i.e., family law and child protection, respectively).[58] The welfare jurisdiction of the Family Court articulated post-CRC[59] was a 'separate jurisdiction' that extended beyond the parent–child relationship to include public law matters, such as child protection issues.[60] Subsequently, in *B v. MIMIA*,[61] the Family Court similarly relied on the external affairs power to hold that its welfare jurisdiction extended beyond the FLA to cover the immigration detention of children.[62] This was because the welfare jurisdiction under the Act was not 'simply a re-enactment of the original welfare jurisdiction'.[63] On appeal, a unanimous High Court held that the welfare jurisdiction of the Family Court did not extend to immigration detention. Had the Family Court's view been endorsed, it would have considerably widened the scope of the best interests provisions in the FLA and contributed to the mainstreaming of the best interests of the child to *all decisions* concerning children, as envisaged by article 3(1) of the CRC.

55 This was controversial because the FLA was in fact passed under the constitutional heads of marriage, divorce, and matrimonial causes (sections 51(xxi) and (xxii) of the Constitution). See Dickey, *Family Law*, 13–15; Sifris, 'Children in Immigration Detention', 214–215.

56 [1996] FamCA 89.

57 *Re Z* at para. 317 (Nicholson CJ and Frederico J).

58 *Re Z* at para. 325 (Nicholson CJ and Frederico J).

59 Section 67ZC(1) of the FLA reads: 'In addition to the jurisdiction that a court has under this Part in relation to children, the court also has jurisdiction to make orders relating to the welfare of children'. The Family Court exercised welfare jurisdiction prior to section 67ZC but did so under the common law rather than statute. The Court has exercised its welfare powers on matters such as the sterilisation of a child for non-therapeutic purposes; the authorisation of treatment for transgender children; the disclosure of parentage; relocation; obtaining a child's passport; and child abduction: Dickey, *Family Law*, 301–302.

60 *Re Z* at paras. 323–324 (Nicholson CJ and Frederico J).

61 *B v. Minister for Immigration & Multicultural & Indigenous Affairs* [2003] FamCA 451 (*B v. MIMIA*).

62 *B v. MIMIA* at paras. 272–273, 276–278, 281 (Nicholson CJ and O'Ryan J).

63 *B v. MIMIA* at para. 283 (Nicholson CJ and O'Ryan J).

The second issue that requires consideration is the unincorporated status of the CRC. The general view is that the CRC does not create domestic rights in the absence of legislative intervention[64] and that when domestic law conflicts with the CRC, the courts must apply the domestic law, which they cannot overrule in order to give effect to the Convention.[65] A majority of the Family Court held, however, that the CRC was partially incorporated by the FLA. The Court's view is now of historical significance only, as it gathered no support, but it is relevant to canvass as an illustration of the diverse ways in which judges have used the available legal framework – sometimes pushing its boundaries – to accommodate the CRC.

The incorporation views were the high point of the Family Court's attempts (under the leadership of its former Chief Justice, Nicholson CJ) to extract some legal capital from the influence that the CRC has had on the Family Law Reform Act 1995 (Cth) (the Reform Act), which amended the FLA. It was in that context that the Court aired a variety of contentious views, including in relation to the incorporation of the CRC.[66]

Thus, in *B v. MIMIA*,[67] the Court held that the CRC was incorporated through the welfare jurisdiction of the Family Court in section 67ZC introduced by the Reform Act in 1995. The applicants (an undocumented immigrant family with three minor children) approached the Family Court, urging it to exercise its discretion under the welfare jurisdiction and free the children from mandatory immigration detention under the Migration Act 1958 (Cth) (Migration Act). Although reliance on the CRC was deemed 'not essential',[68] the majority of Nicholson CJ and O'Ryan J held that the post-CRC amendments to the FLA extended the welfare jurisdiction beyond its traditional boundaries to include making orders against the Minister for Immigration to release children from detention that was harmful to them.[69] The wording of the Reform

[64] *Teoh* at paras. 25 (Mason CJ and Deane J); 35, 37 (McHugh J).

[65] *Murray v. Director, Family Services, ACT* [1993] FamCA 103 (*Murray*) at paras. 153, 160 (Nicholson CJ and Fogarty J); *H v. W* [1995] FamCA 30 at para. 64 (Fogarty and Kay JJ) (the paramountcy of a child's interests cannot be disregarded in favour of article 12 of the CRC); *MIMIA v. B* at paras. 155, 171 (Kirby J).

[66] The others concerned its ability to fill lacunae in the domestic law and the protection of its rights under the principle of legality.

[67] For comments, see Lara Ruddle and Sally Nicholes, '*B & B and Minister for Immigration and Multicultural and Indigenous Affairs*: Can International Treaties Release Children from Immigration Detention Centres?' (2004) 5(1) *Melbourne Journal of International Law* 256.

[68] *B v. MIMIA* at para. 249 (Nicholson CJ and O'Ryan J).

[69] *B v. MIMIA* at para. 287 (Nicholson CJ and O'Ryan J).

Act and domestic and international political statements[70] were 'strongly supportive of the proposition that the 1995 amendments to Part VII did intentionally incorporate certain articles of UNCROC into municipal law',[71] and the introduction of section 67ZC 'has implemented the relevant parts of UNCROC'.[72] These views were not considered by the High Court on appeal, albeit Callinan J opined that the influence of the CRC on law reform did not amount to incorporation because the Parliament gave no indication that it wanted to implement the CRC 'by, in some way enlarging or creating an all-embracing welfare jurisdiction'.[73]

Nicholson CJ and O'Ryan J reiterated their incorporation reasons in *KN & SD & Secretary, Department of Immigration and Multicultural and Indigenous Affairs*,[74] a case heard at the same time as *B v. MIMIA* but not appealed to the High Court. The mother of an Australian child born in Australia entered the country illegally prior to the child's birth. She was placed in mandatory immigration detention and was awaiting deportation.[75] The issue was whether section 60B(2) of the FLA[76] could be used to interpret an alleged ambiguity in the Migration Act in a way that prevented the mother's deportation. Nicholson CJ and O'Ryan J held that the CRC was 'sufficiently incorporated'[77] into the domestic law 'by (inter alia) s.60B of the [Reform] Act'[78] for the reasons stated in *B v. MIMIA*, to which they added the almost universal ratification of the Convention and it being a declared instrument under the AHRCA.[79] The incorporation finding contributed thereafter to the majority view that the CRC rights are protected by the principle of legality, as discussed in Section 4.4.3.

The incorporation views of the Family Court were considered 'controversial and less capable of immediate justification'[80] and have clear vulnerabilities. Thus, the Court overlooked Australian statements made

[70] *B v. MIMIA* at paras. 272–278, 281 (Nicholson CJ and O'Ryan J).
[71] *B v. MIMIA* at para. 275 (Nicholson CJ and O'Ryan J).
[72] *B v. MIMIA* at para. 288 (Nicholson CJ and O'Ryan J); Ellis J dissented (see at para. 423).
[73] *MIMIA v. B* at paras. 220–222 (Callinan J).
[74] [2003] FamCA 610 (*KN & SD*).
[75] The case differed from *B v. MIMIA* because it did not involve the welfare jurisdiction, as only the mother (and not the child) was detained.
[76] Section 60B(1) contains the objects of Part VII, while section 60B(2) contains the principles underlying those objects. The latter provides that children have the right to know and be cared for by their parents, and to have regular contact with them.
[77] *KN & SD* at para. 67.
[78] *KN & SD* at para. 68.
[79] *KN & SD* at para. 68.
[80] Bates, 'Out of Everywhere', 239.

to the CRC Committee that it had no intention of enacting the CRC as domestic law.[81] It made far-reaching statements about incorporation but did not spell out which CRC rights were incorporated – something unlikely for the Parliament to have done. Further, the incorporation *locus* oscillated between section 67ZC (the welfare jurisdiction) and section 60B (the objects and principles of Part VII of the FLA) in an approach too pliant to be persuasive. However, the Court used 'incorporation' not to import self-standing norms with no domestic correspondent, but rather to justify an interpretation of the FLA that extended its scope and elevated the protection of values already recognised in the domestic law to bring them closer to compliance with the CRC.

Section 60B(4), introduced into the FLA in 2011,[82] revived incorporation arguments because of its explicit reference to the CRC. These arguments were dismissed in *Langmeil & Grange*,[83] but the Court suggested that this section could be interpreted either as requiring that the Court gives effect to the CRC as an *additional consideration* or as simply requiring that it be used to interpret the Act in case of ambiguity.[84] In some cases, the Court allowed the parties to rely directly on the CRC despite its unincorporated status.[85] This came to an end in *Ralton & Ralton*, where the Court said that

> the contents of the Convention are not enshrined as operative principles of law. ... [T]he Convention is applicable only to the extent that it has been incorporated by specific provisions of the *Family Law Act*. Accordingly, the Court applies the *Family Law Act* and not the Convention.[86]

In *Oram & Lambert*[87] and *Badeni & Dangerfield*,[88] the Court confirmed that the CRC is to be given effect through the interpretation of the FLA

[81] *B and B: Family Law Reform Act 1995* [1997] FamCA 33 at para. 10.12 (*B and B: Family Law Reform Act*).

[82] See Section 4.3. See generally Michelle Fernando, 'Express Recognition of the UN Convention on the Rights of the Child in the Family Law Act: What Impact for Children's Participation?' (2013) 36(1) *UNSW Law Journal* 88.

[83] *Langmeil & Grange* [2013] FamCAFC 31.

[84] *Langmeil & Grange* [2013] FamCAFC 31 at para. 25.

[85] *Langmeil & Grange* [2012] FamCAFC 39 at paras. 136–137 (decided that articles 34 and 19 of the CRC were not breached by the primary court). See also *Zlotnik & Gerasimov* [2015] FamCAFC 174; *Rilak & Tsokas* [2017] FamCAFC 26.

[86] [2017] FamCAFC 182 at para. 18. See also *Barrett & Barrett* [2017] FamCAFC 4 at paras. 112–113.

[87] [2019] FamCAFC 4 at para. 156.

[88] [2020] FamCAFC 133 at para. 13.

and not as a separate consideration. It seems therefore that the incorporation argument has been put definitively to rest by its own maker.

To conclude, the domestic legal status of the CRC is largely under the control of the Parliament, which decides whether and how to give it domestic effect. The fervent belief of an early majority of the Family Court that statutory recognition of the CRC should boost its status and thus judicial effectiveness was not shared by the High Court or by other Family Court judges, suggesting that most judges are unlikely to go beyond the typical effect of unincorporated treaties (i.e., as interpretation aids) in the absence of unequivocal statutory authorisation.

4.4.2 The CRC and Statutory Interpretation

This is the most widely accepted method of engaging with unincorporated treaties, but it is unevenly applied in relation to the CRC. Thus, it has not been extensively used by the High Court, where the Convention primarily appears in the dissenting or concurring judgments of one former justice, Kirby J. In fact, in no case thus far has a majority of the Court given a statute an interpretation that is consistent with the CRC so as to avoid inconsistency with the Convention.[89]

The reserved attitude of the High Court in relation to the Convention is particularly stark when compared with that of the Family Court, which at times has put forward alternative interpretations of domestic statutes in which it has sought to accommodate the CRC. Illustrative are the cases in which a majority of the Family Court relied on the CRC to extend the scope of the best interests provisions in the FLA beyond the parent–child relationship. This was rejected by the High Court, as discussed below.

In *Northern Territory of Australia v. GPAO*,[90] the relevant issue was whether certain best interests provisions in the FLA (a Commonwealth statute)[91] informed the validity of child protection legislation in the

[89] In a recent case concerning female genital mutilation, Kiefel CJ and Keane J stated that an interpretation of the statutory term 'mutilate' to include any injury to the child was consistent with article 24(3) of the CRC: *R v. A2* [2019] HCA 35 at para. 56. No further attention is paid to the CRC, and the reference is so fleeting that it is not meaningful.

[90] [1999] HCA 8 (*GPAO*).

[91] Section 43 provided that the Family Court exercised jurisdiction under that Act by having regard to the need to protect the rights of children and their welfare. Section 64 (later replaced with sections 65E and 67ZC(2)) provided that in custody, guardianship, welfare, and access applications, the welfare of the child must be regarded as the paramount consideration.

Northern Territory.[92] The case came before the Family Court as *Re Z*,[93] a parental rights dispute in which Northern Territory authorities refused to provide information to the Court because a Territory child protection statute prevented them from doing so. The applicants argued that the Territory statute prevented the Court from giving paramount importance to the interests of children and was therefore inconsistent with the FLA. Nicholson CJ and Frederico J (the majority) agreed. The Court reasoned that the change in the terminology of the FLA from the traditionally used 'welfare' to the 'best interests' of the child reflects the wording of the Convention.[94] This justified an interpretation of the best interests provisions in the Act to recognise them as extending the scope beyond the traditional 'welfare'.[95] Fogarty J (dissenting) opposed the use of the CRC, which in the circumstances would amount to 'interference with . . . clear words, rather than an interpretation of an uncertainty or ambiguity'.[96]

A majority of the High Court upheld the appeal against the majority decision in *Re Z* and gave a narrow scope to the relevant best interests provisions (i.e., the merits of parenting orders rather than preliminary orders relating to evidence) in judgments that overlooked the CRC. Dissenting, Kirby J identified as an issue:

> the extent to which ambiguities in the meaning of that federal law, concerning its ambit and operation, should be resolved in a way compatible with international law and so as to ensure that Australian law conforms, as far as it properly can, to international law.[97]

Like the majority of the Family Court, Kirby J agreed that the change in terminology from 'welfare' to 'best interests' implies a wider scope for the FLA provisions that refer to the latter.[98] Kirby J stressed that Part VII of the FLA was enacted to give effect to the CRC and thus ambiguities in

[92] It is worth remembering that child-related matters are addressed by both State/Territory and Commonwealth legislation and that, in the event of inconsistency, the latter prevails under section 109 of the Constitution.

[93] [1996] FamCA 89.

[94] *Re Z* at para. 307 (Nicholson CJ and Frederico J), where the majority refers to articles 9 (1), 3, and 18(1) and (2) but without further discussion. An additional reason was the Parliament's exercise of its external affairs power enlivened by the CRC when articulating the welfare jurisdiction in section 67ZC of the FLA, as discussed above: *Re Z* at paras. 317–325 (Nicholson CJ and Frederico J).

[95] Which was limited to decisions on guardianship, custody, and contact.

[96] *Re Z* at para. 183 (Fogarty J).

[97] *GPAO* at para. 203 (Kirby J) (footnote omitted).

[98] *GPAO* at para. 230 (Kirby J) (footnote omitted).

relation to its *scope* (not only its substance) should be interpreted so as to uphold international law.[99] The Convention makes no distinction between interim decisions on evidence and decisions on merits, requiring instead that the best interests of the child be considered throughout the judicial process.[100]

While in *GPAO* there was misalignment between domestic law and the CRC, immigration cases confront the courts with legislation that is in clear conflict with the Convention. Approaches differ, with a majority of the Family Court again relying on the CRC to capitalise on the decisional discretion it enjoys under the FLA[101] and extend its protective jurisdiction to limit the application to children of the inflexible migration legislation. In *B v. MIMIA*, upon deciding that it had welfare jurisdiction over children's mandatory immigration detention, the Court considered the lawfulness of the detention. Applying the presumption of consistent interpretation,[102] the majority held that the Migration Act under which the children were detained could not be interpreted as authorising their indefinite detention because such interpretation would be inconsistent with article 37 of the CRC and a 'serious breach' of Australia's obligations under the Convention.[103] The detention was therefore unlawful and not authorised by the Migration Act correctly interpreted in conformity with the CRC.[104]

The appeal against the majority decision of the Family Court was upheld by the High Court. Only Kirby J addressed the use of the CRC for interpretation purposes. While noting the Family Court's view that the indefinite detention of children is contrary to article 37 of the CRC,[105] Kirby J observed that the courts are entitled to note the breach, but they must still apply the domestic law.[106] When statutory language is clear, the courts have no option but to give effect to a constitutionally

[99] *GPAO* at para. 232 (Kirby J).
[100] *GPAO* at para. 231 (Kirby J).
[101] Sifris, 'Children in Immigration Detention', 213.
[102] *B v. MIMIA* at para. 363 (Nicholson CJ and O'Ryan J).
[103] *B v. MIMIA* at para. 388 (Nicholson CJ and O'Ryan J).
[104] *B v. MIMIA* at para. 381 (Nicholson CJ and O'Ryan J). On the litigation following the decision of the Family Court, see Ruddle and Nicholes, '*B & B*', 261–262. See also *Bakhtiyari v. Australia*, Communication No. 1069/2002, 6 November 2003, CCPR/C/79/D/1069/2002, in which the Human Rights Committee found Australia in breach of several provisions of the ICCPR.
[105] *MIMIA v. B* at paras. 152–153 (Kirby J).
[106] *MIMIA v. B* at para. 155 (Kirby J).

valid statute.[107] The Parliament did not differentiate between the immigration detention of children and adults; thus, 'the requirements of international law . . . cannot be given effect'[108] by Australian courts.

In *B v. MIMIA*, the High Court thwarted hopes that reliance on the favourable triad of the FLA, the welfare jurisdiction, and the CRC could secure a differentiated treatment for children in immigration detention. Thus, in *Re Woolley; Ex parte M276/2003*,[109] litigants turned to the *parens patriae* jurisdiction,[110] a common law near-equivalent to the welfare jurisdiction. The case concerned four children aged 7 to 15 who entered Australia illegally with their parents in 2001 and were detained under the mandatory detention provisions of the Migration Act. The applicants argued that the provisions of the Act were constitutionally invalid if and to the extent that they authorised the prolonged detention of children.[111] The High Court unanimously dismissed the application.

The CRC was mentioned generically by some judges;[112] only Kirby J identified a specific provision (i.e., article 37) as relevant.[113] The judges unanimously decided that the CRC could not be relied on to exclude children from a detention that is clearly mandated by the Migration Act. The Act did not distinguish between adults and children[114] and it was 'impossible' to read down the statutory provisions so as to allow for an 'individual assessment of particular unlawful non-citizens'.[115] Further, the constitutional validity of the Migration Act was not affected by its inconsistency with the CRC,[116] which could not justify a refusal by the Court to apply the Act.[117] Thus, '[i]f the law is clear and constitutionally

107 *MIMIA v. B* at paras. 155ff (Kirby J).

108 *MIMIA v. B* at para. 171 (Kirby J) (footnote omitted).

109 [2004] HCA 49 (*Re Woolley*).

110 *Parens patriae* jurisdiction is a protective common law jurisdiction that entitles the Supreme Courts of States and Territories to make decisions for the care, protection, and welfare of children: Dickey, *Family Law*, 299. The *parens patriae* jurisdiction is wide; its limits have not been and cannot be established: *AMS v. AIF* at paras. 85–89 (Gaudron J); 213 (Hayne J).

111 *Re Woolley* at para. 3 (Gleeson CJ).

112 *Re Woolley* at paras. 7, 11, 31 (Gleeson CJ); 107, 114 (McHugh J); 221 (Hayne J). Callinan J and Heydon J do not refer to the CRC.

113 *Re Woolley* at para. 199 (Kirby J).

114 *Re Woolley* at paras. 7 (Gleeson CJ); 46 (McHugh J); 129 (Gummow J).

115 *Re Woolley* at para. 10 (Gleeson CJ).

116 *Re Woolley* at para. 115 (McHugh J).

117 *Re Woolley* at para. 11 (Gleeson CJ). Other judges shared the view that the task of the Court is to assess the validity of legislation against the Constitution and not against international treaties: at paras. 115 (McHugh J); 122 (Hayne J); 201 (Kirby J).

valid, it is the duty of Australian courts to apply its terms. This is so whatever judges or others may think about the content and effect of such law',[118] and 'whatever views might be urged about the wisdom, humanity and justice of that policy'.[119]

Re Woolley was another attempt to make the courts responsive to children's unique vulnerabilities in the application of the Migration Act. As the protection-minded Family Court was not involved,[120] legislative intransigence dominates the reasoning in *Re Woolley*, with judges rejecting all arguments that children's inherent vulnerability should result in a special treatment in the absence of legislative authorisation. Judges refused to see the children as having a legal position distinct from that of their parents.[121] They held that children's vulnerability did not determine the constitutionality of the Act[122] and that an argument about children's special status, interests, and vulnerabilities 'wrongly fixes upon the nature of the person detained'[123] instead of considering the purpose of the detention (which was not punitive). The detention does not become punitive (and thus unconstitutional) because the applicants are children[124] or because the state owes them protection.[125]

Re Woolley is the ultimate confirmation that legislative intransigence can deprive the CRC of any judicial effect, either independently or in association with aligned domestic concepts such as *parens patriae*. Interestingly, several judges made *obiter* statements about *parens patriae* jurisdiction and its potential relevance in assessing the constitutionality of statutes.[126] Clearly, the judges felt comfortable to speculate about how a domestic legal institution can further develop to protect children, while completely overlooking the CRC as an instrument that provided some support in doing so. This suggests that without legislation, judicial

[118] *Re Woolley* at para. 173 (Kirby J).
[119] *Re Woolley* at para. 198 (Kirby J) (footnote omitted).
[120] The case was not argued under the FLA, so the Family Court did not have jurisdiction.
[121] *Re Woolley* at paras. 103 (McHugh J); 153, 157 (Gummow J); 266 (Callinan J). Cf. *B v. MIMIA*, where the majority of the Family Court responded to the argument that children's immigration detention can be ended if their parents seek the return of the family to the country of origin, as equating to 'treating the children as the chattels of their parents' (para. 282).
[122] *Re Woolley* at para. 29 (Gleeson CJ).
[123] *Re Woolley* at paras. 162–163 (Gummow J).
[124] *Re Woolley* at para. 99 (McHugh J).
[125] *Re Woolley* at para. 100 (McHugh J).
[126] *Re Woolley* at paras. 193 (Kirby J); 101 (McHugh J); 168 (Gummow J).

innovation in protecting CRC values is likely to occur only if it is based upon close synergies with the domestic law.

Cases such as *B v. MIMIA* and *Re Woolley* are notoriously contentious because restrictive immigration legislation sometimes conflicts with individual liberties under international law. However, the tension between domestic law and the CRC occurs in other areas of law, where the CRC also yields even at the hands of receptive judges. In an abduction case, *De L v. Director-General, Department of Community Services (NSW)*,[127] the courts had to interpret the phrase 'child objects to being returned'.[128] The question was whether an objection entailed a strong opposition to return, as per the Hague Convention, or simply giving weight to a child's views, however strongly expressed, according to their age and maturity, as required by article 12 of the CRC. Kirby J (dissenting) noted the tension between the two legal standards and preferred the narrower interpretation supported by the Hague Convention, the standards of which were domestically incorporated and thus binding. Regardless of the ultimate rejection of article 12, Kirby J engaged carefully with it primarily to acknowledge the factors that may prevent children from expressing views that amount to what adults perceive as 'objections' (e.g., differences in capacity and culture, loyalty conflicts, and lack of familiarity with those eliciting their views). Where the conventional use of article 12 was powerless, Kirby J used this article as a reflection tool to highlight the complexities of child participation in fraught family law disputes. What is distinctive in Kirby J's judgments in *De L*, and subsequently in *B v. MIMIA* and *Re Woolley*, is his refraining from summary dismissals of the CRC, which were open therein. His reflective engagements with the CRC had no major consequences for the outcomes but have educational merits that are absent from other judgments.

In the family law context, the FLA offers more opportunities to use the CRC for interpretation purposes because of the latter's influence in law reform and their common protective ethos. In *B and B: Family Law*

[127] [1996] HCA 5 (*De L*).

[128] Regulation 16(3) of the Family Law (Child Abduction Convention) Regulations 1986 (which made the Hague Convention a part of the domestic law) had a formulation identical with article 13(2) of the Hague Convention. This formula is part of an exception that permits a court to refuse to order the return of an abducted child to the country of habitual residence.

Reform Act 1995,[129] wishing to prevent the relocation of his ex-wife and children, a father argued that the newly introduced section 60B(2) of the FLA recognised his children's right to know and have regular contact with him.[130] The Family Court strongly affirmed the interpretive role of the CRC in relation to Part VII of the Act and rejected the view that the CRC 'was only of general origin'[131] and could not be used as an interpretive aid. Indeed, '[i]t is difficult … to imagine a better starting point'[132] than the CRC, which influenced the Reform Act and was scheduled to the AHRCA. The Convention 'must be given special significance because it is an almost universally accepted human rights instrument and thus has much greater significance for the purposes of domestic law'[133] than other treaties. The Court recognised that the two rights in section 60B(2) reflected several CRC articles,[134] but noted that the wording of that section indicated that they were *principles* that informed the application of Part VII of the Act rather than enforceable rights,[135] as argued by the applicant. Further, section 60B did 'not represent anything like the full quotient of rights of children provided by UNCROC'[136] and it was not possible to use the CRC *as a whole* for its interpretation.

B and B: Family Law Reform Act[137] illustrates that the interpretive influence of the CRC is limited by the scope of the interpreted legislation and the way the Parliament decided to give it effect therein. Thus, if the Parliament gives partial legislative effect to the CRC in a statutory provision, the entire CRC cannot be used for its interpretation. As the overall scope of the FLA is limited to parent–child relationships, many CRC provisions could be excluded from the interpretation process under

129 [1997] FamCA 33 (*B and B: Family Law Reform Act*). For a comment, see Lisa Young, '*B and B: Family Law Reform Act* 1995 (Cth): Relocating the Rights Debate' (1997) 21(2) *Melbourne University Law Review* 722.

130 *B and B: Family Law Reform Act* at paras. 6.2–6.3.

131 *B and B: Family Law Reform Act* at para. 6.35.

132 *B and B: Family Law Reform Act* at para. 10.14.

133 *B and B: Family Law Reform Act* at para. 10.19. The significant role of the CRC was also stressed in *Murray* at para. 149 (Nicholson CJ and Fogarty J).

134 The Court identified as the 'more directly relevant' articles 2(1), 3(1), 3(2), 7(1), 9(3), 18 (1), and 5, 9, and 12: *B and B: Family Law Reform Act* at paras. 3.28–3.32.

135 *B and B: Family Law Reform Act* at paras. 10.26, 10.57. In *KN & SD* (discussed in Section 4.4.1), however, the Court retreated from this view and decided that the section contained enforceable human rights.

136 *B and B: Family Law Reform Act* at para. 10.25. Section 60B referred only to children's rights to know and be cared for by their parents and to have regular contact with them.

137 [1997] FamCA 33.

this reasoning. Further, if the Parliament gives effect to the CRC through principles enshrined in the legislation, the Convention or the relevant rights are applied as principles and not as enforceable rights. This approach was also used in *AS v. Minister for Immigration and Border Protection*,[138] which, although not a federal case, speaks to the same issue. Thus, section 4AA(1) of the Migration Act states that '[t]he Parliament affirms as a *principle* that a minor shall only be detained as a measure of last resort' (emphasis added). This language corresponds with article 37(b) of the CRC. It was argued that, consequently, the section gave rise to justiciable domestic rights.[139] The Court agreed that the Parliament enacted 'the proposition that the Parliament affirmed as a principle "that a minor shall only be detained as a measure of last resort" ',[140] but the section mentioned was not independently justiciable and operated instead as a legal principle.[141] Thus, the role of the CRC in statutory interpretation can be capped by the Parliament.

In other cases, especially where the synergy between the FLA and the CRC was clearer, the Family Court engaged with the latter generously. In *Re Jamie*,[142] Bryant CJ noted that as the CRC and the FLA 'share an underlying common purpose or object, namely a concern that decisions are made in a child's best interests, in an application under s 67ZC [the welfare jurisdiction], it is appropriate for the court to have regard to the relevant provisions of the Convention on the Rights of the Child'.[143] The Act did not prescribe the issues to be taken into account when exercising the welfare jurisdiction and it was useful for the Court to turn to the CRC, which 'makes it clear that it is important that children have input into decisions that affect them and that parents have special responsibility for assisting their children in making these decisions'.[144] Thus, in the case of a competent child who considers stage 2 treatment for gender dysphoria, the authorisation of the Family Court is not required. The views of the child should be given weight according to the child's age and

[138] [2016] VSCA 206 (*AS v. MIBP*).
[139] *AS v. MIBP* at para. 18.
[140] *AS v. MIBP* at para. 29, referring to the wording of article 37(b).
[141] *AS v. MIBP* at para. 29.
[142] [2013] FamCAFC 110. This judgment is now superseded by *Re: Kelvin* [2017] FamCAFC 258 (which makes no reference to the CRC).
[143] *Re Jamie* at para. 120.
[144] *Re Jamie* at para. 122.

maturity, and the state should respect the guidance given by the parents, as required by articles 12 and 5 of the CRC.[145]

B and B: Family Law Reform Act and *Re Jamie* took the traditional path of using the CRC to interpret ambiguous statutory provisions. In *obiter*, however, the Nicholson Court took the opportunity to make further-reaching statements. In *Murray*,[146] for example, a majority of the Full Court (Nicholson CJ and Fogarty J) rejected as 'too restrictive'[147] the ambiguity-driven approach to interpretation and stated that the CRC 'can also be used to fill lacunae in such legislation and to resolve ambiguities and lacunae in the common law'.[148] In *B and B: Family Law Reform Act*, the Court opined that the courts should not be 'too restrictive' in their use of the Convention, as they could use it to fill lacunae in legislation[149] and to interpret the mandatory direction in section 43(c) of the FLA for the Court to consider the rights and welfare of children when exercising jurisdiction under the Act.[150] The Court saw the latter section as a domestic gateway for the CRC rights that aligned with the scope of the Act.[151] These comments are far-reaching and challenge the dualist position in that they come close to treating the CRC as an autonomous legal source. The filling-of-lacunae view was seen as controversial[152] and was not widely embraced. Nonetheless, these attempts were an early manifestation of a trend that permeates the CRC case law of the Nicholson Court: a determination to use whatever legal mechanisms were available to maximise the impact of the CRC and improve outcomes for children.

145 *Re Jamie* at paras. 129, 134.

146 It was argued that, by ordering the immediate return under the 1980 Hague Convention on the Civil Aspects of International Child Abduction, the trial judge erred by not considering and applying article 3 of the CRC: *Murray* at para. 80. To the argument that there was a conflict between the Hague Convention and the CRC, the Court responded in the negative and referred to articles 11 and 35 as an indication of the Convention's stance against abduction: *Murray* at paras. 156, 159.

147 *Murray* at para. 147.

148 *Murray* at para. 149 (Nicholson CJ and Fogarty J).

149 *B and B: Family Law Reform Act* at para. 10.5.

150 *B and B: Family Law Reform Act* at para. 10.7.

151 *B and B: Family Law Reform Act* at para. 10.25. Section 43 of the FLA is titled 'Principles to be applied by courts' and, although the Court does not clarify this, consistently with the reasoning in relation to section 60B, relying on the CRC in the context of that section would lead to its rights being treated as 'principles' rather than enforceable rights.

152 Michael Kirby, 'Chief Justice Nicholson, Australian Family Law and International Human Rights' (2004) 5(1) *Melbourne Journal of International Law* 221, 232.

In conclusion, absence of incorporation, legislative intransigence, and the lack of an obligation to consider international law have diminished the ability of the CRC to influence statutory interpretation. Legislative techniques, such as confining the effects of the CRC to sectoral laws or relegating the Convention to a purpose or principle, have further limited the ability of the courts to give effect to the CRC. Remarkably, in the High Court, the only instance of statutory interpretation consistent with the CRC is in a dissenting judgment.[153] By contrast, the Family Court sought to use the FLA as a domestic gateway for the Convention, although some of its judgments were set aside by the High Court for reasons that strike at the exceptionalism mentioned in Section 4.2.

The methods of engagement discussed below are less widely accepted in terms of their application to the CRC or their recognition as a legitimate way to consider international treaties. Engagement with the CRC under the principle of legality and in the exercise of administrative discretion has stagnated, but the canvassing of these approaches gives a sense of their historical evolution, including opportunities and obstacles. More promising is the use of the CRC in the exercise of judicial discretion, a method that still strives for full recognition.

4.4.3 *The CRC and the Principle of Legality*

As discussed in Section 4.2, the application of the principle of legality to unincorporated rights is contentious because its habitual protective scope is common law rights. Only the Family Court has used this principle in connection with CRC rights, and its view has not been endorsed by the High Court. In *KN & SD*,[154] the relevant issue was whether the rights in section 60B(2) of the FLA (i.e., the child's rights to know and be cared for by their parents and to have regular contact with them) were *fundamental* rights that were protected by the presumption that the Parliament (through the Migration Act) would not intentionally limit fundamental rights unless it clearly indicated that intention.[155] A majority of the Family Court (Nicholson CJ and O'Ryan J) decided that the rights

[153] *GPAO* (Kirby J) (see Section 4.4.2).

[154] For the facts, see Section 4.4.1.

[155] It is relevant that in *B and B: Family Law Reform Act*, the Family Court decided that the rights mentioned were not enforceable but served as principles of the FLA. See Section 4.4.2.

mentioned were fundamental and thus protected by the principle of legality,[156] but went further and extended that protection to the CRC rights:

> We reject the proposition that fundamental rights are limited to those conferred by the common law. We are of the view that the terms of s.60B itself confers fundamental rights on a child. We also think that fundamental rights and freedoms are also grounded in international law and in Instruments such as . . . UNCROC . . .[157]

It is not clear what made the statutory and CRC rights *fundamental* in the sense of the principle of legality, but the majority stressed the importance of the CRC for the domestic law, so it is possible that the weight of the statutory rights was enhanced by their international significance. The majority decided, however, that the principle of legality was not operative because the Migration Act was clear and precise in authorising the deportation of the mother, thus negating the fundamental rights arising from the FLA and the CRC.[158] Ellis J (dissenting) disagreed with the extension of the principle of legality, taking the traditional view that a right is fundamental only if it has common law recognition and not simply because it is 'important'.[159] As the judgment was not appealed to the High Court, the application of the principle of legality to the CRC remains doubtful.

4.4.4 The CRC and the Exercise of Administrative Discretion

Minister of State for Immigration and Ethnic Affairs v. Teoh[160] is an iconic case in which the High Court innovatively extended the possible effects of unincorporated treaties to creating a legitimate expectation that the executive complies with them domestically. In a CRC context, *Teoh* remains the only High Court case in which the entire bench engaged with the Convention and positive results arose from the engagement of the majority.[161]

[156] Nicholson CJ and O'Ryan J abandoned as 'incorrect' their *obiter* view in *B and B: Family Law Reform Act* that section 60B contains only broad general principles and not enforceable rights: *KN & SD* at para. 70.

[157] *KN & SD* at para. 69 (Nicholson CJ and O'Ryan J).

[158] *KN & SD* at para. 76 (Nicholson CJ and O'Ryan J).

[159] *KN & SD* at para. 133 (Ellis J).

[160] [1995] HCA 20 (*Teoh*).

[161] For comments, see Margaret Allars, 'One Small Step for Legal Doctrine, One Giant Leap towards Integrity in Government: *Teoh's* Case and the Internationalisation of Administrative Law' (1995) 17(2) *Sydney Law Review* 204; Groves, 'Treaties and

Mr Teoh, a Malaysian citizen, was granted a temporary entry permit to Australia. He married an Australian citizen and they had three children. Pending the approval of his permanent residency application, Mr Teoh was convicted of drug trafficking. Mr Teoh was then denied residency, which made him liable to deportation. He challenged the denial of residency, arguing that his deportation would severely affect his family, but, given the seriousness of the crime, the internal appeal was rejected. On appeal, the High Court had to decide what role an unincorporated treaty such as the CRC could play in the making of administrative decisions where the decision-makers enjoyed some discretion and the outcome was not imposed by a statute.

Mason CJ and Deane J wrote the leading judgment, with which Toohey J largely agreed. The judges observed that none of the traditional avenues applied but decided that the Convention was relevant for the discharge of statutory discretion by administrative decision-makers,[162] who were entitled, although not obliged, to consider it.[163] The 'crucial question' for the relevance of the CRC was whether the visa decision was an action 'concerning children' in the sense of article 3(1) of the CRC.[164] The two justices favoured the ordinary wide meaning of 'concerning'[165] and rejected a narrow construction according to which although the decision affected children, it did 'not touch or relate to them'.[166] In relation to the weight attached to the interests of the child, Mason CJ and Deane J stressed that they need not be automatically prioritised:

> The article is careful to avoid putting the best interests of the child as the primary consideration; it does no more than give those interests first importance along with such other considerations as may, in the circumstances of a given case, require equal, but not paramount, weight.[167]

Upon establishing the relevance of the CRC, Mason CJ and Deane J held that its ratification gives rise to a legitimate expectation that 'absent statutory or executive indications to the contrary, administrative decision-makers will act in conformity with the Convention and treat

Legitimate Expectations' ; Lacey, 'In the Wake of *Teoh*'; Anne Twomey, 'Minister for Immigration and Ethnic Affairs v Teoh' (1995) 23(2) *Federal Law Review* 348.

162 *Teoh* at para. 22 (Mason CJ and Deane J).

163 *Teoh* at paras. 22 (Mason CJ and Deane J); 36 (McHugh J agreeing).

164 *Teoh* at para. 30 (Mason CJ and Deane J).

165 *Teoh* at para. 30 (Mason CJ and Deane J) (footnote omitted); see also par. 31 (Toohey J).

166 *Teoh* at para. 30 (Mason CJ and Deane J).

167 *Teoh* at para. 31 (Mason CJ and Deane J).

the best interests of the children as "a primary consideration"'.[168] Further, a legitimate expectation did not compel a decision-maker to act according to a treaty,[169] but if a contrary decision was envisaged, those affected should be given an opportunity to be heard.[170] Mason CJ and Deane J found that the decision-maker took the interests of the children into account, but did not treat them as a primary consideration. For this, it was necessary for the decision-maker to ask themselves 'whether the force of any other consideration outweighed it'.[171] Instead, the decision-maker treated

> the policy requirement as paramount unless it can be displaced by other considerations ... A decision-maker with an eye to the principle enshrined in the Convention would be looking to the best interests of the children as a primary consideration, asking whether the force of any other consideration outweighed it.[172]

Gaudron J, concurring, took the view that the CRC was only of 'subsidiary significance' and more important were the facts that the children were Australian citizens and the state had protective obligations towards them.[173] *Obiter*, Gaudron J said that

> it is arguable that citizenship carries with it a common law right on the part of children and their parents to have a child's best interests taken into account, at least as a primary consideration, in all discretionary decisions by governments and government agencies which directly affect that child's individual welfare.[174]

This was a 'novel'[175] right sourced to the *parens patriae* jurisdiction. For Gaudron J, the CRC simply 'gives expression to a fundamental human right which is taken for granted by Australian society'[176] and arises from the 'special vulnerability of children'.[177] Should the existence of such domestic right be doubted, 'ratification [of the CRC] would tend to

[168] *Teoh* at para. 34 (Mason CJ and Deane J) (footnote omitted); see also at para. 29 (Toohey J).
[169] *Teoh* at para. 36 (Mason CJ and Deane J).
[170] *Teoh* at para. 37 (Mason CJ and Deane J); see also at para. 32 (Toohey J).
[171] *Teoh* at para. 39 (Mason CJ and Deane J).
[172] *Teoh* at para. 39 (Mason CJ and Deane J).
[173] *Teoh* at para. 3 (Gaudron J).
[174] *Teoh* at para. 4 (Gaudron J).
[175] Allars, 'One Small Step', 225.
[176] *Teoh* at para. 6 (Gaudron J).
[177] *Teoh* at para. 5 (Gaudron J).

confirm the significance of the right within our society'.[178] As the CRC gives expression to 'an important right valued by the Australian community, it is reasonable to speak of an expectation that the Convention would be given effect'.[179] Put differently, the CRC *gives effect* to an Australian expectation, rather than *creates* one.

McHugh J, in dissent, disagreed with the application of the legitimate expectation doctrine to international treaties. In a judgment reflecting a strict dualism, he held that a breach of a ratified treaty should be sanctioned in the international sphere, including by recourse to relevant treaty bodies such as the CRC Committee.[180] It is the role not of the courts but of the Parliament to give effect to international treaties,[181] and the Parliament fulfilled that role by scheduling the CRC to the AHRCA and by making available the latter's remedial mechanisms to address breaches of the former.[182] McHugh J also questioned the relevance of the CRC to immigration decisions against parents, cautioning that casting the article 3 net so wide 'will have enormous consequences for decision-making in this country if it applies to actions that are not directed at but merely have consequences for children'.[183]

Teoh innovatively used the doctrine of legitimate expectation to give *some* domestic effect to international treaties, but it did not guarantee a CRC-compatible outcome[184] and preserved the possibility of making contrary decisions.[185] The decision was narrow and applied only to federal decision-makers who enjoyed statutory discretion. Subsequent domestic developments have limited *Teoh*'s relevance. In *Ex parte Lam*,[186] the High Court retreated from (but did not overrule[187]) *Teoh* in a case concerning a permanent resident parent of two Australian children whose residency was cancelled because of his criminal activity.

178 *Teoh* at para. 6 (Gaudron J).
179 *Teoh* at para. 6 (Gaudron J).
180 *Teoh* at para. 37 (McHugh J).
181 *Teoh* at para. 37 (McHugh J).
182 *Teoh* at paras. 40–41 (McHugh J).
183 *Teoh* at para. 43 (McHugh J). McHugh J questioned whether article 3 ought to be a primary consideration when sentencing a parent, repossessing the property of a parent, or exercising powers relating to taxation issues. Similar concerns were also raised by Callinan J in *Ex parte Lam* at para. 147.
184 Allars, 'One Small Step', 231–232.
185 Lacey, 'A Prelude'; 135. Allars, 'One Small Step', 233.
186 *Minister for Immigration and Multicultural and Indigenous Affairs, Re; Ex parte Lam* [2003] HCA 6 (*Ex parte Lam*).
187 Groves, 'Treaties and Legitimate Expectations'; Lacey, 'A Prelude', 156.

Only Callinan J considered the CRC, noting that its 'non-enactment ... could well indicate parliamentary resistance to it'.[188] This resistance was possibly generated by a concern with the wide scope of the CRC, which might 'distort the fine balance in criminal sentencing' of adult offenders who have children and might not sufficiently deter crimes by migrants.[189] Other administrative law developments have accentuated *Teoh*'s loss of relevance,[190] but the case is historically important and the judgments remain rich repositories of CRC interpretation, as further discussed in Section 4.6.

4.4.5 *The CRC and the Exercise of Judicial Discretion*

The use of the CRC to inform the exercise of judicial discretion (common law or statutory) has not been endorsed by the HCA but can be found in cases from the Family Court and the VSC. The latter's case law is of persuasive value throughout Australia to the extent that it applies common law, rather than statutory principles.

In *B and B: Family Law Reform Act*, for example, the Family Court said that 'regard may be had to a convention or treaty in the exercise of a discretion, which the Family Court clearly exercises in determining matters of parenting responsibility and the best interests of children'.[191] In *Re Jamie*, the same Court relied on articles 5 and 12 as relevant factors in the exercise of its welfare jurisdiction,[192] and, in *Re K*[193] it issued discretionary guidelines for the appointment of separate legal representatives for children, upon considering articles 9 and 12 of the CRC.

The Family Court has not formulated a set of principles to guide the use of the CRC in the exercise of judicial discretion, but Bell J of the VSC held that the CRC (and other treaties) can be so used

> if the subject matter of the case before the court comes within its [the Convention's] scope, which is a test of relevance; if taking the human right into account is not inconsistent with any applicable legislation, the operation of which such a convention obviously does not impair; and if

188 *Ex parte Lam* at para. 147 (Callinan J).
189 *Ex parte Lam* at para. 14 (Callinan J).
190 See Naomi Sharp, 'Procedural Fairness: The Age of Legitimate Expectation Is Over' (2016) 90(11) *Australian Law Journal* 797; Edgar and Thwaites, 'Implementing Treaties'.
191 *B and B: Family Law Reform Act* at para. 10.18.
192 See Section 4.4.2.
193 [1994] FamCA 21 at para. 11.

> doing so is not inconsistent with the common law (broadly defined), the content of which, equally obviously, such a convention does not alter.[194]

In *Director of Public Prosecutions (Vic) v. TY (No. 3)*, when sentencing a juvenile offender for murder, Bell J noted the relevance of article 40(1) of the CRC.[195] The Court used the CRC to reinforce existing domestic principles which stressed the importance of factors such as youth and rehabilitation in sentencing young offenders.[196] The Court pointed out that 'the Convention runs with the grain of the Court's sentencing discretion, not against it',[197] and 'the exercise of the sentencing discretion will be the better for it [if the CRC is relied on]'.[198]

In *In re TLB*, the father of a seven-month-old baby, a mentally impaired man who had committed a violent crime, applied for an extension of his leave to remain in the community.[199] The statutory framework allowed the Court to consider, alongside listed factors concerning the applicant's medical condition and community safety, any other relevant matters. Bell J found that the best interests of the child in not being separated from his father were a relevant matter,[200] a finding consistent with the terms of the statute and the CRC. Although the CRC was not domestically incorporated, it was a relevant consideration for the exercise of judicial powers because granting the extended leave would prevent the separation of the child from his father, which, according to article 9(1), was only permissible if in the best interests of the child.[201] The father was a good parent and it was not in the child's best interests to be separated from him. Although the Court referred to the CRC as 'an additional basis on which the best interests of the applicant's son should be taken into account',[202] the Convention helped identify the child's interests in not being separated from his father as a relevant factor for the decision.

In brief, the unevenness that has characterised the use of the CRC for statutory interpretation purposes permeates the other methods of

194 *Director of Public Prosecutions (Vic) v. TY (No. 3)* [2007] VSC 489 (*DPP v. TY*) at para. 49.
195 *DPP v. TY* at para. 50.
196 *DPP v. TY* at para. 51.
197 *DPP v. TY* at para. 50.
198 *DPP v. TY* at para. 51.
199 *In re TLB* [2007] VSC 439 at paras. 5–6.
200 *In re TLB* at para. 18.
201 *In re TLB* at para. 20.
202 *In re TLB* at para. 20.

engagement. There has been little exploration of the relationship between the principle of legality and the CRC, and the use of the CRC in the exercise of administrative discretion has lost momentum. There are, however, encouraging developments in relation to the use of the CRC in the exercise of judicial discretion under the common law or statutes, especially by the VSC. Equally encouraging is the body of case law that the VSC has built under the human rights statute of the State of Victoria, as discussed in the following section.

4.5 The CRC and Human Rights Statutes: A Victorian Case Study

4.5.1 Introduction

In contrast to the limited legislative scaffold for the application of the CRC in the federal courts, the Charter of Human Rights and Responsibilities Act 2006 (Vic) (the Charter)[203] has facilitated its application. Although the Charter has a limited scope and applies only in Victoria and only to matters governed by State law, it is relevant for significant child-related matters such as juvenile justice, child protection, and education.

As a human rights statute in the tradition of the UK Human Rights Act 1998, the Charter requires public authorities not to act contrary to it and not to make decisions without giving proper consideration to relevant human rights.[204] Should a court find that a human right is engaged (i.e., potentially affected), the interference must be reasonably justifiable in order to pass Charter muster.[205] Courts must apply the Charter when exercising functions under it[206] and must interpret statutes in accordance

[203] The Charter provisions concerning the interpretation of laws and the obligations of public authorities under the Charter came into force in January 2008, with the balance of provisions coming into force in January 2007 (section 2).

[204] Section 38(1).

[205] There are two steps in assessing lawfulness under the Charter. First, it must be established that a right is 'engaged' and, for this purpose, rights are to be construed as widely as possible: *Certain Children v. Minister for Families and Children* [2016] VSC 796 (*Certain Children*) at para. 143. Second, if a right is engaged, the decision is lawful only if the interference with the right can be justified under section 7(2). That section reads, in part, '[a] human right may be subject under law only to such reasonable limits as can be demonstrably justified in a free and democratic society based on human dignity, equality and freedom, and taking into account all relevant factors'. Those factors are listed in the section.

[206] Section 6(2)(b).

with the human rights in the Charter '[s]o far as it is possible to do so consistently with their purpose'.[207] This requires a court to favour a meaning that aligns to the Charter if, according to ordinary techniques, a provision is capable of more than one meaning.[208] According to French CJ, '[s]ection 32(1) applies to the interpretation of statutes in the same way as the principle of legality but with a wider field of application'.[209] Indeed, the Charter yields to other statutes or law more generally.[210] Further:

> It operates upon constructional choices which the language of the statutory provision permits. Constructional choice subsumes the concept of ambiguity but lacks its negative connotation. It reflects the plasticity and shades of meaning and nuance that are the natural attributes of language and the legal indeterminacy that is avoided only with difficulty in statutory drafting.[211]

The VSC cannot invalidate legislation that is not open to an interpretation that is consistent with human rights.[212] Instead, it 'may make' a declaration of inconsistent interpretation,[213] which can thereafter be acted upon by the political branches of the State (i.e., Victoria).

The Charter enhances the capacity of the courts to engage with unincorporated treaties such as the CRC by legitimising their use in the interpretation of statutes, including the Charter. Thus, section 32(2) states that, inter alia, international law relevant to a human right in the Charter 'may be considered' in the interpretation of statutory provisions.[214]

The Charter has a limited number of sections explicitly referring to children. Section 17(2) provides that '[e]very child has the right, without discrimination, to such protection as is in the child's best interests and is needed by the child by reason of being a child'. Section 23 addresses the

[207] Section 31(2).

[208] *ZD v. Secretary to the Department of Health and Human Services* [2017] VSC 806 at paras. 103–105.

[209] *Momcilovic* at paras. 51 (French CJ); 565–566, 684 (Crennan and Kiefel JJ). This approach adheres to 'orthodox principles of statutory construction', with the Charter yielding to statutory provisions: Stephen Tully, 'Momcilovic v The Queen (2011) 245 CLR 1' (2012) 19(1) *Australian International Law Journal* 279, 281.

[210] Section 38(2) of the Charter.

[211] *Momcilovic* at para. 50 (French CJ).

[212] Section 36(5).

[213] Section 36(2).

[214] *Momcilovic* at para. 18. For comments, see Tully, 'Momcilovic v The Queen'.

rights of children in the criminal process, while section 25(3) provides for a right to a criminal law procedure that considers a child's age and promotes rehabilitation. These rights were inspired by the ICCPR rather than the CRC,[215] but a recommendation to introduce some of the latter's rights into the Charter was rejected.[216]

With this background in mind, the following sections present the Charter case law of the VSC. Although the cases discussed are not exhaustive, they demonstrate that legislative support for judicial protection of human rights in general and permissive rules for the application of international law can result in a positive engagement with the CRC.

4.5.2 *The CRC and the Exercise of Judicial Functions Under the Charter*

Under section 6(2)(b), the Charter binds courts and tribunals to the extent that they have functions under its substantive provisions and also in the interpretation of laws. Although, under that section, the CRC can assist in the interpretation of the Charter, the Convention is being used autonomously of the Charter and applied in the traditional methods of engagement (i.e., the interpretation of statutes and the development of the common law).

Thus, in *ZZ v. Secretary, Department of Justice*,[217] the Court had to interpret the statutory phrase 'unjustifiable risk' to children or the public, which was relied on by the Secretary to deny employment clearance to a person wanting to become a bus driver.[218] The Secretary found that the applicant posed a risk to children due to his criminal record, which consisted of serious offences that were unrelated to children and were not sexual offences. Bell J used both the Charter (under section 32(1)) and, inter alia, the CRC (under the common law presumption of consistent interpretation) to interpret 'unjustifiable risk',[219] finding the CRC and the Charter mutually reinforcing as they spelled out a positive State

[215] Explanatory memorandum to the Charter of Human Rights and Responsibilities Bill 2006 (Vic) at 1, 14, 17–18.

[216] See Scrutiny of Acts and Regulations Committee, Parliament of Victoria, *Review of the Charter of Human Rights and Responsibilities Act 2006* (2011), Recommendation 2 at 52; see also at paras. 236–249.

[217] [2013] VSC 267 (*ZZ*).

[218] The presumption of consistency applies also to state legislation: *Director of Public Prosecutions v. Kaba* [2014] VSC 52 at para. 144 (Bell J).

[219] *ZZ* at para. 67.

obligation to protect children against harm.[220] Nonetheless, neither justified a severe limitation of the right to work when no *real* risk to children exists, as in the current case.[221]

In two subsequent cases, Bell J issued judicial directions informed by the CRC for child-friendly proceedings in the VSC. Criminal proceedings in children's courts had been adapted to children's needs by statute,[222] but the proceedings against children charged with more serious offences in the VSC had not. Bell J issued directions in relation to proceedings in the VSC concerning the hearing and determination of criminal charges against, and the sentencing of, children in *Director of Public Prosecutions v. SL*,[223] and in relation to bail applications by children in *Director of Public Prosecutions v. SE*.[224] The Court directed that, inter alia, a child should be separated from adults when at court and should not be handcuffed; a more child-friendly and less intimidating courtroom should be used; the judge and counsel should not wear robes; and a child should not sit in the dock.[225] The Court gave special attention to securing the effective participation of the child in the sentencing process. It rested its reasoning on sections 8(3) (equal protection under the law) and 25(3) (the right to procedures that take into account a child's age and the desirability of rehabilitation) of the Charter and, in relation to the latter, 'its counterparts in the ICCPR and [the CRC]',[226] including the views of the CRC Committee on ensuring the effective participation by children in legal processes.[227]

Although well aligned and founded on the observation that the Charter reflects the standards of the ICCPR and the CRC,[228] Bell J deliberately maintained a distinction between the Charter and the international law strands of reasoning:

[220] *ZZ* at paras. 63–66, referring to articles 3, 19, 34, and 36 of the CRC. Under the Charter, Bell J relied primarily on section 17(2), which he calls 'the human right to protection' (para. 71).

[221] *ZZ* at para. 68 in relation to the CRC; at paras. 70–71 in relation to section 17(2) of the Charter.

[222] Through the Children, Youth and Families Act 2005 (Vic) (CYFA).

[223] [2016] VSC 714 (*DPP v. SL*).

[224] [2017] VSC 13 (*DPP v. SE*).

[225] For the full set of directions, see *DPP v. SL* at para. 25. Similar directions were given in relation to bail hearings in *DPP v. SE* at paras. 16–17.

[226] *DPP v. SL* at para. 11 (footnote omitted). The reference to the CRC is to article 40(1).

[227] *DPP v. SL* at para. 11.

[228] *DPP v. SL* at para. 7.

> These requirements [enabling a more child-friendly process] arise as a matter of human rights under the Charter and, on a discretionary basis, under certain international obligations. They especially arise under the fundamental principle of the best interests of the child.[229]

Bell J consistently stressed that the directions were issued as an *obligation* under the Charter and arose from taking the CRC and the ICCPR into consideration as *discretionary considerations*.[230] This two-pronged reasoning is important. First, it preserves the autonomous normative relevance of the CRC and safeguards its consideration, even where its complementarity with the Charter is not obvious.[231] Second, it boosts support for reliance on the CRC in the exercise of courts' discretion by providing persuasive authority for judges in other Australian jurisdictions with or without human rights legislation. Third, the comprehensiveness of Bell J's directions in *DPP v. SL* and *DPP v. SE* suggests that the Charter functioned as a legitimising medium for the CRC. It is doubtful that the Court would have drawn so extensively from the CRC had it been relying on it only as a discretionary consideration.

4.5.3 *The CRC and the Interpretation of the Charter*

The cases discussed above presented traditional common-law uses of the CRC emboldened by the Charter. The cases discussed below, however, illustrate an interpretive integration that is more typical under a human rights statute, whereby the CRC is used to interpret the Charter.

On 12–13 November 2016, riots occurred at a detention facility for children in Melbourne, resulting in significant damage and loss of accommodation. Subsequently, children were held in inadequate conditions. Later that month, an executive order excised part (the Grevillea Unit) of an adult prison (Barwon Prison), with Grevillea being declared a youth detention facility. Young offenders (aged 15–18) were

[229] *DPP v. SE* at para. 11 (footnotes omitted), endorsing *DPP v. SL* (see, for example, at para. 10). The Court acknowledged that its reasoning in *DPP v. SL* was based on 'ss 6(2)(b), 8(3), 17(2), 23(1), (2) and (3) and 25(3) of the Charter, arts 10(2)(b), 14(4) and 24(1) of the ICCPR and arts 37(c) and 40(1) and (2) of CROC' (*DPP v. SE* at fn 10).

[230] *DPP v. SL* at paras. 9–16; *DPP v. SE* at paras. 12–13.

[231] In *Tomasevic v. Travaglini* [2007] VSC 337 (*Tomasevic*), Bell J said in relation to the ICCPR that it has 'an independent and ongoing legal significance' that 'is not diminished, but can only be enhanced, by the enactment of the Charter': at para. 72.

transferred to Grevillea, despite the unit being unsuitable for accommodating children.[232]

In *Certain Children v. Minister for Families and Children*,[233] the plaintiff children challenged, inter alia, the lawfulness under the Charter of the orders that established Grevillea. Referring to section 32 (2) of the Charter, Garde J determined that the CRC and other UN materials inform the scope of the rights protected by section 17(2)[234] and provide a framework by which to give them substance.[235] Articles 3, 6(2), 12, and 40(1) of the CRC were found to be relevant for this purpose. Article 3(1) creates special protective obligations 'because "children differ from adults in their physical and psychological development, and their emotional and educational needs"'.[236] Article 6(2), as interpreted by the CRC Committee, goes against the incarceration of children, which has negative effects on their development.[237] Article 40(1) requires a treatment that is consistent with children's vulnerability and that respects and promotes their dignity and rehabilitation.[238] Garde J determined that section 17(2) was engaged because the orders to establish Grevillea directly affected the children in various ways, contrary to guidance derived from the CRC and the Beijing Rules.[239]

Thereafter, the Court found that the decision-makers did not properly consider the rights of the affected children, as required by section 38 of the Charter, and that the ensuing decisions were inconsistent with the rights of the detained children.[240] Moving to the justification analysis under section 7(2), Garde J found that the orders did not reasonably limit the rights of children. When the decision was made to establish Grevillea, no consideration was given to children's rights, to the nature and extent

[232] *Certain Children* at paras. 57–92, 108, 121–125 (e.g., lengthy lockdown periods, limited outdoor time, poor education services, reduced opportunities for family visits, harsh treatment by staff, and an absence of adequate medical and psychosocial support).

[233] [2016] VSC 796 (*Certain Children*).

[234] *Certain Children* at para. 146. The UN materials to which the Court refers include CRC Committee, *General Comment No. 10 (2007): Children's rights in juvenile justice*, 9 February 2007, CRC/C/GC/10; and the Beijing Rules: at paras. 152–153.

[235] *Certain Children* at para. 154.

[236] *Certain Children* at para. 149, quoting *General Comment No. 10*, para. 10.

[237] *Certain Children* at para. 149, quoting *General Comment No. 10*, para. 11.

[238] *Certain Children* at para. 151, referring to *General Comment No. 10*, para. 13.

[239] *Certain Children* at 157–158; cf. para. 155, which refers to guidance from *General Comment No. 10*; *United Nations Standard Minimum Rules for the Administration of Juvenile Justice ('The Beijing Rules')*, 29 November 1985, A/RES/40/33 (Beijing Rules).

[240] *Certain Children* at paras. 197–203, 223.

of their limitation, or to the existence of alternative means to pursue the objective sought by authorities.[241] The orders were therefore declared unlawful.[242]

Pending the appeal, new executive orders were made once more establishing, inter alia, Grevillea as a juvenile detention centre.[243] An additional order authorised the use of oleoresin capsicum spray (OC spray) and extendable batons at Grevillea to ensure security, good order, and the safety of children and staff.[244] The children detained in Grevillea challenged the validity of the new orders, including their transfer to the unit. Under section 38(1), the orders to re-establish Grevillea (and some transfer orders) were again found unlawful. Dixon J determined that the rights in sections 17(2) and 22(1) (humane treatment when deprived of liberty) of the Charter were limited by children being placed in a maximum security adult prison unit, which had a demoralising and dehumanising effect on them,[245] and by authorising the use of OC spray at Grevillea, with negative consequences for the children.[246] Dixon J found these limitations not to be proportionate with the important values protected by sections 17(2) and 22(1).[247]

It was once more in giving content to section 17(2) that the Court turned to the CRC. Dixon J noted the similarity between article 24(1) of the ICCPR, article 3 of the CRC, and section 17(2) of the Charter.[248] In relation to the content of section 17(2), Dixon J found that the best interests of the child require hearing and giving due weight to the views of the child in a wide range of matters, including the making of transfer decisions. The Court referred to General Comment No. 12[249] of the CRC Committee to support its wide approach to matters that require giving

241 *Certain Children* at paras. 221–222.

242 The decision was largely maintained in appeal in *Minister for Families and Children v. Arthur* [2016] VSCA 343.

243 *Certain Children v. Minister for Families and Children (No. 2)* [2017] VSC 251 (*Certain Children (No. 2)*) at para. 9.

244 *Certain Children (No. 2)* at para. 11.

245 *Certain Children (No. 2)* at para. 424.

246 *Certain Children (No. 2)* at para. 433.

247 *Certain Children (No. 2)* at para. 455.

248 *Certain Children (No. 2)* at para. 260. Dixon J endorsed Garde J's reliance on the ICCPR, the CRC, and the Beijing Rules in giving content to section 17(2) of the Charter: *Certain Children (No. 2)* at para. 262.

249 CRC Committee, *General Comment No. 12 (2009): The right of the child to be heard*, 20 July 2009, CRC/C/GC/12.

due weight to the views of the concerned child.[250] For Dixon J, the international instruments stressed that children require a different treatment in the criminal justice process for reasons of their age and continuing development.[251] In the administration of juvenile justice, article 3 requires that the best interests should be a paramount consideration, because, as the Committee stressed, children differ from adults in their development and needs.[252] Dixon J endorsed the views of Garde J in terms of various requirements arising from the CRC in relation to the detention of children that informed the content of section 17(2) of the Charter, such as maintaining family contact, the quality of the physical environment, education opportunities, securing children's developmental needs, medical care, and disciplinary measures consistent with the dignity of the child.[253] It is not surprising, therefore, that the limitations identified by Dixon J in relation to section 17(2)[254] largely constitute contraventions of the CRC standards as interpreted by the Committee, which Garde J and Dixon J have embraced in defining the content of the section.[255]

The *Certain Children* cases highlight the influence of the Victorian Charter on the application of the CRC. There is deep engagement with the substance of its standards and the general comments of the CRC Committee, which the judges found useful in giving content to section 17 (2). In *DPP v. SL* and *DPP v. SE*, Bell J associated his CRC reasoning with the aligned provisions of the Children, Youth and Families Act 2005 (Vic) (CYFA), but in the *Certain Children* cases the CYFA was ineffective because the impugned orders were excluded from the application of the best interests provisions in the Act. Nonetheless, the decision-makers had to comply with the best interests obligations arising from section 17(2)[256] and thus the Charter and the CRC in tandem led to an outcome favourable to children.

In brief, the Charter has facilitated the judicial engagement with the CRC by legitimising reliance on it and thus freeing judges to engage with its standards. The Charter has reassured judges of the value of the

[250] *Certain Children (No. 2)* at para. 262 (fn 179).
[251] *Certain Children (No. 2)* at para. 265.
[252] *Certain Children (No. 2)* at para. 262 (fn 181). The Court also referred to articles 6(2) and 40(1) of the CRC.
[253] *Certain Children (No. 2)* at para. 263.
[254] *Certain Children (No. 2)* at paras. 424, 453.
[255] *Certain Children (No. 2)* at para. 263.
[256] *Certain Children* at para. 145; *Certain Children (No. 2)* at para. 259.

Convention and has enabled them to detect and capitalise on its harmony with the Charter, including by pursuing a bolder application of the CRC under the common law methods of engagement.

4.6 The Impact of the Judicial Engagement with the CRC

Although unevenly and hesitantly, Australian courts have engaged with the CRC. How the rules of reception have informed that engagement (Section 4.6.1) and, within those engagement paths, what impact the CRC has had on judicial reasoning (Section 4.6.2) are discussed below.

4.6.1 *Methods of Engagement: Tradition, Innovation, and* Sui Generis

As an unincorporated treaty in a legal system that does not mandate the consideration of international law, the CRC is in a vulnerable position before the Australian courts. While human rights statutes in selected States have made an important step forward in legitimising reliance on the CRC,[257] they do not compel it and do not enhance its status when in conflict with domestic law. Legislatures (Commonwealth and State, when relevant) control the domestic judicial effect of the Convention through various legislative devices. Thus, at Commonwealth level, it is the Parliament that decides whether to give legislative effect to the CRC or not. The Parliament also decides whether it relies on its external affairs power to pass laws giving effect to the CRC, and thus exposes itself to the scrutiny enlivened by the Convention (discussed in Section 4.4.1), or whether it relies on other powers in order to avoid that scrutiny.

Further, even when some legislative effect is given to the CRC, the Parliament controls the role that it assigns to the Convention. Embedding a statutory principle or objective, as opposed to a rule, as exemplified in *B and B: Family Law Reform Act* and *AS v. MIBP*,[258] deprives the domestic provision that reflects the CRC of self-standing justiciability. Encasing the CRC in sectoral laws such as the FLA, child protection laws, or other field-specific legislation limits the scope of CRC-aligned interpretations to the ambit of the interpreted statute. Human rights statutes, despite their wider scope, may limit the catalogue

[257] Section 31(2) of the Charter; section 31(2) of the Human Rights Act 2004 (ACT); section 48(3) of the Human Rights Act 2019 (Qld).

[258] See Section 4.4.2.

of rights they protect and indirectly narrow the opportunities for the application of the CRC.[259] Lastly, passing legislation that is clearly inconsistent with the CRC prevents the application of interpretive presumptions that can accommodate it, as demonstrated in the immigration cases discussed above in Section 4.4.2. Positive developments are not, however, excluded, even in this less-than-ideal context, and so a mixed picture of engagement emerges, as discussed below.

With the judicial consideration of the CRC largely discretionary,[260] its usage by judges is erratic.[261] Many variables contribute to courts deciding to use the CRC, including whether it is raised in argument, its relevance and usefulness, and avoiding outcomes that are contrary to the domestic law. At times, cursory statements are made that a particular statutory interpretation or the domestic law itself is consistent with the CRC,[262] but this type of use rarely has analytical merits and amounts to little more than a statement of fact. In the High Court, closer engagement with the CRC comes mostly from Kirby J's judgments, which are often dissenting – although Callinan J has sometimes given attention to the CRC, but only to reject its use. High Court judgments rarely move beyond discussing the legitimacy of relying on the CRC in a particular case. When the CRC is rejected at this early stage of judicial reasoning, it has no opportunity to interact with domestic law and create links on which its further application can develop. Thus, albeit not ideal, even judgments in which the CRC is considered but not followed (e.g., Kirby J in *De L* and *Minister for Immigration and Multicultural and Indigenous Affairs v. B*,[263] McHugh J in *Teoh*, or Callinan J in *MIMIA v. B*) are important for the analytical value arising from their identification of the similarities

[259] The Victorian Charter, for example, protects only civil and political rights (section 3).

[260] Two recent major cases concerning children, both with favourable outcomes, make no mention of the CRC, although it was arguably relevant. In *VYZ v. Chief Executive Officer of the Department of Justice* [2022] WASC 274, the Supreme Court of Western Australia (Tottle J) declared that prolonged periods of solitary detention of a child were unlawful. In *Sharma v. Minister for the Environment* [2021] FCA 560 (*Sharma*), Bromberg J decided that the state had a duty of care in relation to children to prevent the risk of personal harm arising from climate change. That decision was overturned in appeal.

[261] Sometimes, the absence of engagement with the CRC is justified on procedural grounds, such as the CRC-relevant issue not being appealed or the CRC being used only in *obiter* by the trial court or as an additional reasoning (e.g., *B v. MIMIA*, *Re Z*).

[262] For illustrations, see *CDJ v. VAJ (No. 1)* [1998] HCA 67 (in relation to the paramountcy principle, at fn 182 (Kirby J)); *Cattanach v. Melchior* [2003] HCA 38 (article 18, at para. 35 (Gleeson CJ)); *R v. A2* at para. 56.

[263] [2004] HCA 20 (*MIMIA v. B*).

and differences between the CRC and domestic law, or for offering a glimpse into what judges see as the obstacles to the application of the Convention.

The Victorian case law illustrates that where the Charter permits the use of the CRC, judges are more likely to progress to a stage where they engage with its substance. It may be that, as put by French CJ in *Momcilovic*,[264] section 32(2) of the Charter 'does not authorise a court to do anything which it cannot already do',[265] but by giving courts the authority to use international law it alleviates concerns about its legitimate use. This emboldened the VSC to make use not only of the CRC but also of the Committee's general comments,[266] thereby widening the interpretive reference framework for the Charter and the sources that can assist in the development of domestic law.

As noted in Section 4.5.2 above, in cases such as *DPP v. SL* and *DPP v. SE*, the Charter played a facilitating role even when the VSC engaged with the CRC under the traditional methods, in parallel to the Charter rather than for its interpretation. To paraphrase Bell J, the Charter seems to have increased the autonomous value of the CRC,[267] or rather the judicial perception of that value. The Charter's enabling approach to the judicial use of international law is based on an explicit legislative acceptance of its domestic value. This contrasts with the defensive use of common law methods by the High Court, which often seems to use the reception rules to protect domestic law against the CRC. This defensiveness arguably arises from the ambiguous federal support for the CRC, which, in the words of Callinan J, 'could well indicate parliamentary resistance to it'.[268] In a system of parliamentary supremacy, this resistance is not taken lightly by the courts.

Further illustrating the inconsistent use of the CRC is the contrast between certain judgments emanating from the Family Court and from the High Court. In cases such as *Re Z, B and B: Family Law Reform Act* and *B v. MIMIA*, the Family Court, led by Nicholson CJ, created opportunities to consider the Convention (even when that was not strictly required for the resolution of the matter[269]) and to draw domestic legal

[264] *Momcilovic v. The Queen* [2011] HCA 34 (*Momcilovic*).

[265] *Momcilovic* at para. 18 (French CJ).

[266] See *DPP v. SE*, *DPP v. SL* and the *Certain Children* cases.

[267] *Tomasevic* at para. 76.

[268] *Ex parte Lam* at para. 147 (Callinan J).

[269] In *Re Z*, Nicholson CJ and Frederico J referred to the CRC, coupled with the external affairs power, as 'another source of power' (para. 317) and placed the CRC in an add-on

benefits from its ratification. By contrast, the CRC was marginalised by a majority of judges when those cases reached the High Court on appeal. Such vastly differing judgments are reminiscent of Bates's view that an effective and genuine dialogue between CRC promoters and detractors is unlikely in the absence of a solid domestic foundation for children's rights.[270]

The lack of uniformity in supporting the CRC exists not only between courts but also among judges of the same court. In the High Court, the CRC often makes its appearances in Kirby J's dissenting or concurring judgments. Some judges of the High Court have been mindful of a conflict between domestic legislation and the CRC, while others have held strong views that the latter's breach is to be sanctioned internationally and not by domestic judges.[271] The maximalist views in relation to the incorporation of the CRC or its impact on the jurisdiction of the Family Court spearheaded by Nicholson CJ were not unanimously supported by other judges of that court and eventually faded with their promoter's retirement from the bench. In Victoria, Bell J's judgments are strongly supportive of the CRC, but – perhaps understanding that support for international law is not uniform – that justice felt a need to defend his reliance on international law.[272]

Judges are weary of treating the CRC as an autonomous source of domestic law, as clearly illustrated by the demise of *Teoh* and the lack of traction for the incorporation theory formulated by the Family Court. The Family Court itself (under new leadership) has clearly rejected that theory, although the statutory framework has become more supportive of it.[273] As suggested in Section 4.4.1, exceptionally, the CRC may play a semi-autonomous role in the constitutional review of legislation passed by the Parliament in the exercise of its external affairs power. The activation of such a role is conditioned by several factors[274] and judicial

role in the reasoning. In *B and B: Family Law Reform Act*, the views on the CRC were not considered relevant for the outcome of the appeal: at para. 10.1 (Nicholson CJ and Fogarty J). In *B v. MIMIA*, the external affairs reasoning linked to the CRC was not 'an essential aspect' of the majority reasoning: at para. 249 (Nicholson CJ and O'Ryan J).

270 Bates, 'Out of Everywhere', 244.

271 Cf. *Teoh* at para. 34 (Mason CJ and Deane J) and *Teoh* at para. 37 (McHugh J) and *Ex parte Lam* at para. 98 (McHugh and Gummow JJ).

272 *Tomasevic* at para. 76.

273 See Section 4.4.1.

274 For example, the Parliament exercising the power, or a court finding that the CRC provision concerned has the legal qualities needed to enliven the power. See Section 4.4.1.

review of the exercise of the external affairs power is not an effective tool to give judicial effect to the CRC. First, the open-ended nature of many CRC provisions may make it difficult for the courts to establish a *substantial* inconsistency with the Convention.[275] Second, the Parliament can avoid CRC-informed judicial scrutiny by legislating under another power. Third, the external affairs power is an inward-facing mechanism that is primarily concerned with the distribution of legislative powers between the States and the Commonwealth, and only indirectly a CRC-supportive tool. At a minimum, nonetheless, when the external affairs power is activated, a potential review can be a deterrent against laws that are *substantially* inconsistent with the CRC. Apart from this narrow context, the CRC has no leverage in constitutional issues relevant to children.[276]

The most widely and openly accepted method to give judicial effect to the CRC is in the interpretation of statutes, federal or State, with the proviso that this is not open where there is conflict between the CRC and the domestic law. In *AMS v. AIF*,[277] Gleeson CJ, Gummow, and McHugh JJ questioned the interpretive value of the Convention, suggesting (without elaborating) that the CRC contains 'aspirational rather than normative' provisions that might not have interpretive value because they are not 'established *rules* of international law'.[278] In *Re Woolley*, however, some of the same judges seemed prepared to accept the CRC as an interpretive aid.[279] Nonetheless, there is no case in which the HCA comprehensively engages with the CRC to give a consistent interpretation to a domestic statute. The Family Court and the VSC have, nonetheless, used the CRC for statutory interpretation purposes with ease. The former capitalised on the convergence between the FLA and the CRC, including its role in reforming family laws in Australia, while the VSC used the interpretive opportunities created by the 2006 Charter.

Different approaches to ambiguity as a prerequisite for consistent interpretation and the scope of the interpreted statute emerge as factors of relevance in the deployment of the presumption of consistent interpretation. The High Court has supported a concept of ambiguity understood as the existence of a choice of meanings (i.e., ambiguity as a

275 A condition of successful review, as discussed in Section 4.4.1.
276 Illustrative cases are *GPAO*, *AMS v. AIF*, *B v. MIMIA* and *Re Woolley*.
277 [1999] HCA 26.
278 *AMS v. AIF* at para. 50 (Gleeson CJ, McHugh, and Gummow JJ) (my emphasis).
279 See the separate judgments of Gleeson CJ and McHugh J.

'constructional choice'[280]), as formulated in *Teoh*,[281] but has not acted on it in relation to the CRC. Some judges are mindful of spelling out the ambiguity they seek to clarify[282] and, when they do so, they present ambiguity as something that has 'negative connotations'[283] and needs fixing. Statutory interpretation and the CRC are then approached as remedial tools.

The case law of the Family Court and the VSC reflects a different interpretive paradigm – namely, the constructional choice approach. Judges do not always spell out the ambiguity they address, which seems often to arise from the underdevelopment of the domestic law rather than from the intrinsic language of the text. The clearest illustration is in the *Certain Children* cases, where the limited domestic children's rights case law prompted the judges to turn to international law.[284] Here, judges use the CRC to develop domestic law and they deploy the presumption and the CRC constructively rather than remedially. It may be that, when the presumption is used remedially, judges are weary of defining the will of a supreme Parliament in alignment with extra-national sources of law, while, when it is used constructively, judges have more flexibility to navigate a space unoccupied by the will of the Parliament.

The scope of the statute that requires interpretation also impacts the operation of the presumption and thus of the CRC. As the Family Court recognised in *B and B: Family Law Reform Act*, it is only the CRC provisions with relevance for the object and purpose of the FLA that can be used for its interpretation.[285] Under section 31(1) and (2) of the Victorian Charter, only international law 'relevant to a human right' under the Charter (read as civil and political rights, according to its section 3) may be relied on. It is uncertain what interpretive function socio-economic rights in the CRC can play, although it is encouraging

280 To borrow from French CJ in *Momcilovic* at para. 50 (see Section 4.5.1).

281 *Teoh* at para. 27 (Mason CJ and Deane J); *AMS v. AIF* at para. 50 (Gleeson CJ, McHugh and Gummow JJ); *GPAO* at para. 232 (Kirby J).

282 *AMS v. AIF* at paras. 280–281 (Callinan J); *Re Z* at para. 183 (Fogarty J); *MIMIA v. B* at para. 171 (Kirby J); *GPAO* at para. 203 (Kirby J).

283 The phrase used by French CJ in *Momcilovic* at para. 50.

284 *B v. MIMIA* is another example. The boundaries of the welfare jurisdiction were defined by the common law but the consideration of the CRC revealed to the majority of the Family Court that the wording of the FLA supported an extension of that jurisdiction beyond its traditional boundaries.

285 See Section 4.4.2. Encouragingly, nonetheless, the Family Court has occasionally considered provisions that are not strictly related to parent–child relationships (article 37 in *B v. MIMIA*, or articles 19 and 34 in *Langmeil*).

that the VSC has referred to articles 6(2) and 12, the nature of which extends beyond civil or political rights.[286]

What is being interpreted, or *where* the CRC is located within the judicial reasoning, emerges as an issue that requires further attention. Human rights protection involves not only defining the substance of rights but also deciding when they can be limited. The VSC human rights case law, like that in South Africa and the United Kingdom, raises the issue of interpretive location. The VSC has used the CRC to define the scope and legal content of Charter rights at the 'engagement' stage. This is advantageous for the Convention because, in that phase, Charter rights are to be construed in the 'broadest possible way',[287] including with reliance on international treaties. Further, the absorption of the CRC standards in relevant Charter rights enhances the former's protection in that the rights can be limited only if the stringent test in section 7(2) is satisfied. However, at this point, it is uncertain what role, if any, the CRC will play in the justification enquiry under section 7(2),[288] and this may lead to situations where a breach of rights is justifiable under the Charter but may not be under the CRC. Further, an exclusion of the CRC from the limitation enquiry could lead to a lack of focus on child-specific issues when deciding whether a trespassing on rights is reasonably justifiable under the Charter.

Among the other methods of engagement discussed in Section 4.2 above, the use of the CRC in the exercise of judicial discretion is gathering some pace in the case law, especially of the VSC but also of the Family Court. Once more, judges have used the decisional space unregulated by legislation to apply the CRC and safeguard its values in matters such as child representation and juvenile justice.[289] The principle of legality was purportedly extended to the CRC by the Family Court in *KN & SD*, but the departure by the Court from the habitual scope of the principle and the fact that its view has not been tested in the High Court leave this issue hanging. Notably, the CRC has not been used to develop the common law, although this may be a consequence of many child-relevant issues now being regulated by statutes.

[286] *Certain Children* at paras. 147–149; *Certain Children (No. 2)* at para. 262.

[287] *Certain Children* at para. 143; *Certain Children (No. 2)* at para. 221 (footnotes omitted).

[288] This is unlike South Africa (see Chapter 5 below) and the United Kingdom (see Chapter 6).

[289] *Re K*; *DPP v. TY*; *DPP v. SL*; *DPP v. SE*.

Common law methods of engaging with the CRC do not fully capture the techniques used by courts. Courts have related to the Convention in ways that are not formally recognised as distinct and that are difficult to capture in the conventional language currently used to conceptualise the interaction between international and domestic law. These methods do not fit into the formal categories of engagement and are therefore informal and diffuse – or, in other words, *sui generis*.

Thus, the CRC has been used as a reference framework to throw new light on the domestic law. In this way, the Convention enhances the courts' understanding and application of domestic law, or enables the courts to 'discover' correspondent domestic concepts that are able to act as carriers for Convention rights. Therefore, unincorporated treaties may be 'an often useful context for the exposition of what Australian law requires',[290] and international law 'may also sometimes assist a judge to exercise the applicable statutory powers'.[291] International instruments may 'reveal but do not resolve the conflicting interests',[292] and they may 'help to put . . . controversies into a conceptual context and express the basic values which must be taken into account'.[293] In *Teoh*, prompted by article 3(1), Gaudron J discovered the possible common law right to give a primary consideration to the best interests of the citizen child.[294] In *Re Z* and *B v. MIMIA*, the wider scope of the best interests of the child under article 3(1) inspired the Family Court to seek convergent domestic norms that would enable it to extend its protective jurisdiction. In *DPP v. TY*, article 40 enabled Bell J to identify common law rules that emphasise youth and rehabilitation as sentencing factors.[295]

These approaches may avoid the difficult question concerning the relationship between the international and domestic law,[296] and may arguably preserve an undesirable status quo, but they deserve some

[290] *Koroitamana v. Commonwealth of Australia* [2006] HCA 28 at para. 66 (Kirby J), referring to articles 7 and 8 of the CRC.

[291] *AMS v. AIF* at para. 169 (Kirby J) (footnote omitted).

[292] *AMS v. AIF* at paras. 50 (Gleeson CJ, McHugh and Gummow JJ); 169 (Kirby J).

[293] *AMS v. AIF* at para. 169 (Kirby J).

[294] In *DJL v. The Central Authority* [2000] HCA 17, Kirby J embraced Gaudron J's view (para. 135), which was also supported in *Sharma* (paras. 306–311) but without reference to the CRC.

[295] *DPP v. TY* at para. 50.

[296] In relation to using international law 'to discover' rights in the common law, Dyzenhaus, Hunt, and Taggart argue that it prevents a careful consideration of international law under the pretence that it overlaps with the common law: Dyzenhaus, Hunt, and Taggart, 'The Principle of Legality', 18.

attention. One feature that distinguishes them from being simple consolation prizes or a cop-out from difficult questions is their analytical qualities and their purposeful deployment. Gaudron J's judgment in *Teoh* is again illustrative. It describes the CRC as being of only 'subsidiary significance', but this is doubtful considering the liberal use of article 3(1) formulas such as 'the best interests of the child' and 'a primary consideration'[297] to give contour to a purported domestic right. Admittedly, a better understanding of these techniques is needed, but it is useful to canvass them and invite further analysis.

4.6.2 *What Did Reliance on the CRC Achieve?*

As suggested above, the impact of the judicial application of the CRC is mixed. In the early years post-ratification, 'big questions' came before the courts that proposed significant changes to the status quo: incorporation, legitimate expectation, the principle of legality, and the mainstreaming of some CRC rights through the expansion of the Family Court jurisdiction. None of these questions received a final positive answer, but they testify to the Convention having inspired some judges to develop the domestic law to protect the rights of children and respond to their unique needs more effectively. In engaging with these questions, judges who questioned the status quo respected the boundaries of the domestic law but teased their extension, encouraged by what they saw as a special relationship between the CRC and the domestic law.

In *Teoh*, the majority developed a new avenue to engage with an unincorporated treaty because the treaty aligned with domestic values[298] and contained 'internationally accepted standards to be applied by courts and administrative authorities in dealing with basic human rights affecting the family and children'.[299] The incorporation views of the Family Court sought to boost the protection of children under the domestic law rather than to import self-standing norms with no domestic equivalent. These views came on the back of the Family Court making a strong case about the 'special significance' of the CRC, which is domestically of 'much greater significance' than any other 'ordinary bilateral or

[297] *Teoh* at paras. 3–4 (Gaudron J).

[298] *Teoh* at para. 6 (Gaudron J).

[299] *Teoh* at para. 34 (Mason CJ and Deane J). The wide ratification of the CRC as a justification for it creating a legitimate expectation is also mentioned by Toohey J at para. 29.

multilateral treaty'.[300] *B v. MIMIA* and *Re Z* saw the Family Court using best interests provisions in the FLA to extend the Court's protective jurisdiction beyond its traditional reach, and better align it with the CRC. If upheld by the High Court, the consequences would have been significant: the CRC could be approached as a source of domestic law; the standard of the best interests of the child would provide a unified thread through the fragmented legislation concerning children at the federal and State levels; and the best interests of the child standard would be relevant for assessing State and Territory legislation. The setbacks in these cases, however, signalled that judicial application of the CRC is unlikely to lead to systemic change by itself, suggesting that incremental change built on domestic norms that accommodate the Convention is a more feasible aspiration.

Several cases developed around article 3(1). Of the rich content of that article, it is its scope and its promise of a special legal treatment for children that have enticed the courts. In *Teoh*, article 3(1) enabled the majority to extract the best interests of the child from its traditional field (i.e., family law and child protection, and matters involving the child) and support its application to *all* actions concerning *or affecting* children. But such wide application of best interests provisions (article 3 and domestic norms) was not universally supported, with several judges expressing concerns about their potential impact in sensitive areas, including taxation, national security, and the sentencing of parents.[301] Despite criticism,[302] the significance of *Teoh* endures. *Teoh* compensated for the absence of a comprehensive domestic children's rights framework by legitimising recourse to the CRC to make such rights visible in litigation. It showed that children's rights can be relevant in areas of law that are not traditionally associated with them. Although *Teoh* did not create an obligation to consider the CRC, it did result in the Convention being regarded 'in a practical sense'[303] by requiring

[300] *B and B: Family Law Reform Act* at para. 10.19.

[301] *Teoh* at para. 43 (McHugh J); *Re Z* at para. 29 (Fogarty J); *Ex parte Lam* at para. 147 (Callinan J).

[302] Among the criticisms are that *Teoh* promoted a procedural protection of rights (Jonathan Todres, 'Emerging Limitations on the Rights of the Child: The U.N. Convention on the Rights of the Child and Its Early Case Law' (1998) 30 *Columbia Human Rights Law Review* 159) and that it simply enabled the identification of interests protected by procedural fairness rules (Lacey, 'A Prelude', 155).

[303] Allars, 'One Small Step', 229.

decision-makers to direct '[s]ome sort of mental activity'[304] towards the rights of children.

In a similar vein are the judgments of the majority of the Family Court in *Re Z* and Kirby J in *GPAO*, where judges held that the change in the terminology of the FLA from 'welfare' to 'best interests' under the influence of the CRC gave the Family Court a wider welfare jurisdiction. *B v. MIMIA* similarly relies on the CRC (articles 3 and 19) to extend the ambit of the Family Court's welfare jurisdiction to migration decisions, which were traditionally outside its scope.

The CRC prompted the courts to give attention to children as holders of rights and interests independent of those of their parents. *Teoh* pioneered this approach, while in *B v. MIMIA* the Family Court envisaged the exercise of the welfare jurisdiction to distinguish between the legal protection of children and that of their parents.

The CRC, and especially article 3, has provided the courts with a framework that is capable of giving legal significance to children's special vulnerability and justifying their special protection. In *Teoh*, article 3(1) prompted Gaudron J to identify children's special vulnerability as citizens and the state's duty of protection independent of that provided by and to their parents.[305] Legal issues have been conceptualised in a child-sensitive way,[306] with legal protections being adapted and enhanced to respond to children's vulnerability in the criminal justice process where the law permitted.[307] Ultimately, however, the ability of courts to respond to children's distinct vulnerabilities can be thwarted by legislation to the contrary, as illustrated by *MIMIA v. B* and *Re Woolley*.

Domestic institutions associated with the best interests of the child and convergent with article 3(1), such as the welfare of the child and *parens patriae* jurisdictions, were used as a gateway for the CRC in response to its vulnerability as an unincorporated treaty. In *Re Jamie*, the Family Court used articles 5 and 12 to give guidance in the exercise of the welfare jurisdiction. In *B v. MIMIA*, the Family Court invoked articles 3 and 19 to support its argument that the state was fulfilling its duty to protect children against harm by vesting a wide welfare jurisdiction in the Court.

304 Allars, 'One Small Step', 229.

305 *Teoh* at paras. 3–5 (Gaudron J).

306 As done by Kirby J in *De L* in relation to a child's objection to returning to the country of habitual residence in abduction cases.

307 See the adaptation of procedures in relation to sentencing in *DPP v. SL* and bail in *DPP v. SE*, discussed in Section 4.5.2.

In the *Certain Children* cases, the VSC made a finding of Charter unlawfulness in relation to the best interests provision in the Victorian Charter, interpreted with reference to article 3(1) but also articles 6, 12, 37, and 40 and general comments of the CRC Committee.[308]

The reliance on articles beyond article 3(1) is important. First, the *Certain Children* cases articulate a rights-based approach to a cross-cutting best interests provision (i.e., one that is not confined to a specific area of law). This balances the protection-oriented wording of section 17(2) of the Charter and gives it a rights-informed content. *Re Jamie* can be commended for a similar approach. Second, a best-interests-of-the-child provision has been used as a gateway for the protection of rights that are not explicitly recognised domestically.[309]

The partial overlap with domestic standards and the influence of other sources make it at times difficult to establish the independent legal impact of the CRC.[310] However, the momentum for judicially generated radical change that might have inspired cases such as *Teoh*, *B v. MIMIA* and *Re Z* has passed, and the attention must shift to finer details and subtler effects that, to paraphrase Bell J, go with the grain of the domestic law and not against it.[311] It is often in the space not occupied by the legislator's will that these effects occur. In *Re Jamie*, for example, CRC articles guided the exercise of welfare jurisdiction in the absence of statutory direction. In *DPP v. SL*, Bell J used language akin to that of the CRC Committee, and the practice directions His Honour gave respond specifically to the issues raised by the latter in its general comments. Further, the Victorian Charter does not define 'protection in the best interests of the child' in section 17(2), so the VSC used article 12 to interpret it as requiring a consideration of the views of the child.[312] Further, in the *Certain Children* cases, the VSC defined the lawful detention conditions for children relying on the CRC and the general comments of the Committee.

Sometimes, the benefits of engaging with the CRC are abstract and may consist of creating a pattern of reasoning that is supportive of its use. The disciplined reliance on the CRC independently of the Victorian

[308] See Section 4.5.3.

[309] *Certain Children* cases (Section 4.5.3).

[310] In cases such as *DPP v. TY*, *In re TLB*, *DPP v. SL*, *DPP v. SE* and *ZZ* (discussed in Section 4.5), the CRC reasoning was additional to or reinforced the domestic law. In *DPP v. SL*, for example, ideas were also drawn from other sources, such as ECtHR decisions, the CYFA, and practice directions from the United Kingdom (paras. 12–16).

[311] *DPP v. TY* at para. 50.

[312] *Certain Children (No. 2)* at para. 262.

Charter by Bell J in *ZZ*, *DPP v. SL* and *DPP v. SE* are such examples. Reliance on the CRC in these cases was not strictly needed, which could perhaps question the meaningfulness of such engagement when the same outcome was justifiable by simply applying the domestic law. In *Tomasevic*, Bell J addressed this concern, holding that international law may strengthen the application of domestic law and enhance its capacity to evolve. Thus, domestic law

> always remains the source of the binding law, but its nature is better understood, its function in the law is strengthened, its application is more penetrating and its capacity to evolve is enhanced once it is appreciated that its performance has an international dimension.[313]

Or, put differently, decision-making 'will be the better for it'.[314] If more widely shared, this approach could help develop a judicial culture of willingness to consider the Convention – a good premise for identifying domestic standards that can accommodate its values.

It is relevant to point to some obstacles to the effect of the CRC beyond legislative intractability and judicial weariness regarding international law. The CRC is difficult to use in the absence of domestic legal hooks that facilitate its insertion into legal argument. As Bates observed, the lack of a solid and uncontested domestic children's rights foundation contributes to those rights having little effect on the application of the law.[315] In the absence of a national children's rights statute, Convention arguments must fit into or be accommodated by domestic legal concepts, which is challenging in itself because of the lack of a comprehensive transformation of the law to receive the values of the CRC. When convergence exists, courts such as the Family Court and the VSC have identified common grounds on which they built their engagement with the Convention. Issues connected to constitutional design, such as the fragmentation of child-related legislation between States/Territories and the Commonwealth and between different legal regimes (such as family law child protection and juvenile justice) are unlikely to be addressed using the CRC. The unsuccessful attempts made by the Family Court in *Re Z* to overcome the compartmentalisation of the best interests of the child along jurisdictional lines,[316] or to extend its jurisdiction over a

313 *Tomasevic* at para. 76.
314 *DPP v. TY* at para. 51.
315 Bates, 'Out of Everywhere', 255, 258.
316 *Re Z* at para. 325 (Nicholson CJ and Frederico J).

cabinet minister in *MIMIA v. B*, are a clear illustration that constitutionally endorsed arrangements cannot be altered by the CRC.

4.7 Conclusions

The Australian case study illustrates the vulnerabilities of the judicial application of the CRC in a dualist legal system of parliamentary supremacy where the Convention is unincorporated. Because the CRC has no autonomous domestic power as an unincorporated treaty, the courts can apply it only indirectly and provided they do not go against the will of the Parliament. Thus, when the CRC conflicted with the domestic law, the latter prevailed; and interpretive presumptions that could accommodate the CRC have at times been superseded by legislation. When the legislatures have endorsed the domestic value of the CRC in sectoral laws or human rights legislation, even short of incorporating it, the courts have shown more openness towards the Convention and have engaged more meaningfully with it. Thus, beyond the domestic legal status of the Convention, the structure of reception or the legal context in which it operates affects its judicial application. The federal structure of the state is part of that structure of reception and has had an ambivalent effect on the judicial application of the CRC. On the one hand, it has generated a fragmented child-related case law that the CRC was unable to unify. On the other hand, it has created opportunities for States and the relevant courts to engage more generously with the CRC within the limits of their powers, as illustrated in the VSC cases.

While challenges remain, the Australian law has strengths on which the application of the CRC can continue to be built. Unlike in France, for example, where the quasi-totality of the case law concerned the direct application of the CRC, in Australia the methods of judicial engagement with the Convention are more diverse and so are the opportunities for the courts to interact with it. State human rights legislation gives courts many possibilities to engage with the CRC, although it remains to be seen whether the application of such legislation may prompt a warmer reception for the CRC in the High Court once relevant cases reach it. The use of the CRC to guide judicial discretion and the *sui generis* techniques developed by the courts accommodate a non-antagonistic relationship with the domestic law and may facilitate engagement with the Convention in the future.

5

South Africa

5.1 Introduction

South Africa, a party to the CRC since 1995,[1] is a jurisdiction that is well known for its progressive jurisprudence on children's rights. It is relevant for this study for two reasons. First, the Constitution of the Republic of South Africa, 1996 (the Constitution)[2] creates a hybrid reception system for international treaties, which allows for their direct application (or self-execution) but also for their use in the interpretation of the Constitution and statutes. This unusual blending of monist- and dualist-specific methods of engagement with international treaties presents unique opportunities to analyse the strengths and weaknesses of various approaches to using the CRC. Second, the Convention has been given domestic effect through section 28 of the Constitution, which is titled 'Children', as well as child protection and child justice statutes.[3] Observing the operation of the CRC within such a strong reception framework elicits insights into the independent role that the Convention can still play in a system that is well endowed to protect children's rights.

This case study ultimately shows that the constitutional infrastructure, from substantive provisions to the formal rules of reception, has had an overwhelmingly positive effect in supporting the application of the Convention by the courts. In a legal space that is crowded with standards and comprises many overlapping instruments, the CRC has continued to

[1] 'Status of Treaties: Convention on the Rights of the Child', *United Nations Treaty Collection*, https://treaties.un.org/Pages/ViewDetails.aspx?src=IND&mtdsg_no=IV-11&chapter=4. South Africa ratified the CRC on the symbolic day of 16 June 1995, a date that commemorates the 1976 student uprising in Soweto, which was met with gunfire by the apartheid government. See South African History Online, 'The June 16 Soweto Youth Uprising' (2013), https://www.sahistory.org.za/article/june-16-soweto-youth-uprising.

[2] Constitution of South Africa Act 200 of 1993.

[3] The most important are the Children's Act 38 of 2005 (entered into force partially on 1 July 2007 and the balance on 1 April 2010) (Children's Act) and the Child Justice Act 75 of 2008 (in force 1 April 2010) (Child Justice Act).

demonstrate its value. Like those in France and the United Kingdom, however, the South African courts have developed an application 'comfort zone' and gravitate towards using the CRC in the interpretation of section 28 of the Constitution, leaving unexplored other means of engagement (i.e., self-execution and statutory interpretation). The case law shows that a constitutional and statutory framework receptive to the CRC influences not only the formal development of the law, but also judicial attitudes and thus the long-term sustainability of the Convention's usage.

The case study focuses on the case law of the Constitutional Court with references to the case law of the Supreme Court of Appeal (the SCA) when that complements the former's case law.[4] The chapter contains an overview of the reception rules as they apply to treaties, followed by an introduction to the relationship between the CRC and the South African law, a presentation of the case law, and an analysis of the forms of engagement and the impact of the CRC.

5.2 The International Treaties and the South African Law

South Africa is a system of common law tradition with strong English law influences in relation to international public law.[5] After a long period of racial segregation, the country engaged in democratic reform, which culminated in the drafting of the Constitution. The Constitution is supreme and justiciable; all law or conduct inconsistent with it can be invalidated by the higher courts (the High Court, the SCA, and the Constitutional Court) to the extent of the inconsistency.[6] The Constitution contains a comprehensive Bill of Rights that 'applies to all law, and binds the legislature, the executive, the judiciary and all organs of state'.[7] When interpreting legislation or developing the common law, the courts must promote 'the spirit, purport and objects of the Bill of Rights'.[8]

[4] The SCA was initially included in this study because, until 2013, it was the court of final appeal in non-constitutional matters. On 1 February 2013, the Constitutional Court became the court of final appeal in all matters, both constitutional and non-constitutional. No meaningful distinctions in the usage of the CRC by the two courts have been detected on account of their historically distinct jurisdictions.

[5] John Dugard, *International Law: A South African Perspective* (Lansdowne: Juta, 2005) 50.

[6] Section 2 read with section 172(1)(a) of the Constitution.

[7] Section 8(1) of the Constitution.

[8] Section 39(2) of the Constitution.

South Africa used international law to shape its new identity as a democratic state.[9] It constitutionalised the courts' obligation to consider international law in interpreting the Bill of Rights,[10] opening the door for the courts to play a role in the process of constitutional transformation.[11] However generous the reception of international law, giving it domestic effect must not conflict with the Constitution.[12] Human rights treaties have not been enacted into law. While some rights are given effect through the Constitution, statutes, or the common law, others lack explicit domestic recognition (e.g., the right to play in a children's rights context). When domestically incorporated, international standards do not become constitutional rights and obligations,[13] which means that constitutional review is conducted against the Constitution and not against the international standards.[14] Nonetheless, treaties remain relevant for the interpretation of the constitutional standards against which constitutional review takes place, as discussed below.

5.2.1 *The Status of International Treaties in the South African Law*

South Africa combines features of both dualist and monist approaches to treaties.[15] Section 231(1) and (2) of the Constitution reflect a dualist

[9] John Dugard, 'International Law and the South African Constitution' (1997) 8(1) *European Journal of International Law* 77; John Dugard, 'International Law and the "Final" Constitution' (1995) 11(2) *South African Journal on Human Rights* 241.

[10] Graham Hudson, 'Neither Here nor There: The (Non-) Impact of International Law on Judicial Reasoning in Canada and South Africa' (2008) 21(2) *Canadian Journal of Law & Jurisprudence* 321, 336. See generally John Dugard, 'The Role of International Law in Interpreting the Bill of Rights' (1994) 10(2) *South African Journal on Human Rights* 208; Michèle Olivier, 'International Human Rights Agreements in South African Law: Procedure, Policy and Practice (Part 2)' (2003) 3 *Tydskrif vir die Suid Afrikaanse Reg* 490–492.

[11] Devika Hovell and George Williams, 'A Tale of Two Systems: The Use of International Law in Constitutional Interpretation in Australia and South Africa' (2005) 29(1) *Melbourne University Law Review* 95, 121, 128. Far-reaching consequences arose sometimes from the engagement with international law. For example, in *S v. Makwanyane* 1995 (3) SA 391 (CC) (*Makwanyane*), the death penalty was declared unconstitutional and, in *S v. Williams* 1995 (3) SA 632 (CC), corporal punishment as a sentencing option for juveniles was declared unconstitutional.

[12] *Glenister v. President of the Republic of South Africa* 2011 (7) BCLR 651 (CC) (*Glenister II*) at para. 205 (Moseneke DCJ and Cameron J).

[13] *Glenister II* at paras. 100–102 (Ngcobo CJ); 181–183 (Moseneke DCJ and Cameron J).

[14] *Azanian Peoples Organization (AZAPO) v. President of the Republic of South Africa* 1996 (8) BCLR 1015 at para. 26.

[15] Views differ on whether South Africa is monist or dualist. Some consider it dualist (Julia Sloth-Nielsen, 'Children's Rights in the South African Courts: An Overview since

approach by providing that an international agreement signed by the executive and approved by the Parliament is not part of the South African law unless enacted into law by national legislation. Section 231 (4) reads:

> Any international agreement becomes law in the Republic when it is enacted into law by national legislation; but a self-executing provision of an agreement that has been approved by Parliament is law in the Republic unless it is inconsistent with the Constitution or an Act of Parliament.

Thus, exceptionally, self-executing treaty provisions are automatically law in the Republic and acquire a sub-constitutional and sub-statutory status.[16] The notion of self-execution is a post-apartheid novelty that has attracted mixed reactions.[17] The courts have generally been reluctant to engage with it or have done so superficially.[18] An 'autochthonous meaning'[19] of self-execution is thus absent and, unless unavoidable, its

Ratification of the UN Convention on the Rights of the Child' (2002) 10(2) *International Journal of Children's Rights* 137, 153n8) and some consider it monist (Ann Skelton, 'South Africa' in Ton Liefaard and Jaap E. Doek (eds.), *Litigating the Rights of the Child: The UN Convention on the Rights of the Child in Domestic and International Jurisprudence* (Dordrecht: Springer, 2015) 13, 15). Others consider it a hybrid system (David Sloss, 'Treaty Enforcement in Domestic Courts: A Comparative Analysis' in David Sloss (ed.), *The Role of Domestic Courts in Treaty Enforcement: A Comparative Study* (New York: Cambridge University Press, 2009) 1, 7), or one that 'cut[s] across the well-known debate' between monism and dualism: Edwin Cameron, 'Constitutionalism, Rights, and International Law: The *Glenister* Decision' (2013) 23 *Duke Journal of Comparative & International Law* 389, 391.

16 According to section 231(4), to be deemed self-executing a treaty norm must be consistent with the Constitution and national statutes.

17 Neville Botha and Michèle Olivier, 'Ten Years of International Law in the South African Courts: Reviewing the Past and Assessing the Future' (2004) 29(1) *South African Yearbook of International Law* 65, 76; Dugard, *International Law*, 62.

18 See generally Neville Botha, 'Public International Law' (2010) *Annual Survey of South African Law* 1269; Neville Botha, 'Justice Sachs and the Use of International Law by the Constitutional Court: Equity or Expediency?' (2010) 25(1) *South African Public Law* 235. For a case in which the self-execution of article 9(5) of the ICCPR is discussed and rejected, see *Claassen v. Minister of Justice and Constitutional Development* 2010 (6) SA 399 (WCC). For critical comments, see Magnus Killander, 'Judicial Immunity, Compensation for Unlawful Detention and the Elusive Self-Executing Treaty Provision: *Claassen v Minister of Justice and Constitutional Development* 2010 (6) SA 399 (WCC)' (2010) 26(2) *South African Journal on Human Rights* 386.

19 Gerrit Ferreira and Werner Scholtz, 'Has the Constitutional Court Found the Lost Ball in the High Weeds? The Interpretation of Section 231 of the South African Constitution' (2009) 42(2) *Comparative and International Law of Southern Africa* 264, 271.

inherent difficulties and judicial ambivalence are likely to usher the courts towards the less controversial interpretive injunctions.[20]

5.2.2 *International Treaties and the Interpretation of the Domestic Law*

The most significant judicial tools to give effect to international treaties are the provisions that enjoin the courts to consider them in the interpretation of the Bill of Rights and of statutes.

'A jewel in the Constitution',[21] section 39(1)(b) states that, when interpreting the Bill of Rights, courts 'must consider international law'. Much of the application of international law has taken place under this section, which allows for the domestic law to develop in harmony with international law.[22] The term 'must' in section 39(1)(b) mandates the consideration of international law, even when the same outcome can be obtained through applying domestic law only.[23] The term 'consider' accommodates engagements of variable depth, from cursory attention to acting in accordance with international law.

The phrase 'must consider' does not indicate the weight to be attached to international law in the interpretive process.[24] Unlike section 233, which encourages an alignment of statutory interpretation with international law, no such requirement appears in section 39(1)(b).[25] Nonetheless, while courts 'are not bound to follow' international law, neither can they 'ignore it'.[26] Arguably, to give consideration in a

[20] Killander, 'Judicial Immunity', 389.

[21] Dugard, 'International Law and the "Final" Constitution', 242. For a detailed analysis of the application of section 39(1) and (2) of the Constitution, see Iain Currie and Johan de Waal, *The Bill of Rights Handbook*, 6th ed. (Cape Town: Juta, 2013) ch. 6.

[22] Dugard, 'International Law and the "Final" Constitution', 242. See also Cameron, 'Constitutionalism', 390.

[23] This is to 'respect the careful way in which the Constitution itself creates concordance and unity between the Republic's external obligations under international law, and their domestic legal impact': *Glenister II* at para. 201 (Moseneke DCJ and Cameron J).

[24] See Andreas O'Shea, 'International Law and the Bill of Rights', paras. 7A2–7A4 (last updated October 2004, SI 15) in *Bill of Rights Compendium* (loose-leaf publication; LexisNexis Butterworths, South Africa).

[25] Hudson also argues that section 233 is the 'weightier section' because it requires compliance with international law: Hudson, 'Neither Here nor There', 348.

[26] *S v. Williams* 1995 (3) SA 632 (CC) at para. 50. In the same vein is *Government of the Republic of South Africa v. Grootboom* 2001 (1) SA 46 (CC) (*Grootboom*), in which the Court acknowledged but did not adopt the concept of minimum core obligations coined by the Committee on Economic and Social Rights: at paras. 29–33.

constitutional interpretive context means 'to look at and evaluate' international law and 'to give reasons either for adopting or rejecting the solution proposed' by it.[27] The Constitution preserves for the courts space to depart from international law in order to develop an interpretation of the Bill of Rights that takes account of South Africa's own history, values, and realities,[28] or even to develop higher protection standards.[29] Generally, the courts have largely applied section 39(1)(b) as if a conformity requirement is implied therein.[30] Occasionally, they have pushed the boundaries of interpretation. In *Glenister II*,[31] a majority of the Constitutional Court gave international law a role of authority[32] by allowing it to define not the content of substantive constitutional rights (which is the habitual practice) but the state's general obligations in relation to human rights under section 7(2) of the Constitution.[33] By doing so, the majority engaged 'arguably [in] a process of translation, rather than interpretation',[34] a transgression that has attracted criticism but also praise.[35]

[27] Juha Tuovinen, 'The Role of International Law in Constitutional Adjudication: *Glenister v President of the Republic of South Africa*' (2013) 130(4) *South African Law Journal* 661, 669.

[28] *S v. Williams* at para. 50. In *Makwanyane*, Mokgoro J (para. 304) stated that the constitutional requirement to consider international law in interpreting the Bill of Rights is an acknowledgement of the lack of relevant domestic jurisprudence; see similarly Chaskalson P (para. 37).

[29] In *Makwanyane*, Chaskalson P (para. 39) did not follow the international law (which did not prohibit the death penalty) and instead engaged in an interpretation of the Interim Constitution that was more protective of individual rights.

[30] See *Glenister II* at para. 97 (Ngcobo J); 178 (Moseneke DCJ and Cameron J); O'Shea, 'International Law', para. 7A2.

[31] *Glenister v. President of the Republic of South Africa* 2011 (7) BCLR 651 (CC) (*Glenister II*).

[32] See generally Tuovinen, 'The Role of International Law', 663, 666. In effect, the relevant constitutional provisions were the starting point for the majority, but the concrete constraints on the Parliament stemmed from international law.

[33] *Glenister II* at paras. 189–190, 194 (Moseneke DCJ and Cameron J). For comment, see Christin Gowar, 'The Status of International Treaties in the South African Domestic Legal System: Small Steps towards Harmony in Light of *Glenister*?' (2011) 36(1) *South African Yearbook of International Law* 307.

[34] Michael Bishop and Jason Brickhill, 'Constitutional Law' (2011) 1 *Annual Survey of South African Law* 188, 237.

[35] For critical opinions, see Gowar, 'The Status', 322; Tuovinen, 'The Role of International Law'. For supporting opinions, see Neville Botha, 'Public International Law' (2011) *Annual Survey of South African Law* 1174, 1184; Pierre de Vos, '*Glenister*: A Monumental Judgment in Defence of the Poor', *Constitutionally Speaking* (blog, 18 March 2011), https://constitutionallyspeaking.co.za/glenister-a-monumental-judgment-in-defence-of-the-poor/.

The second interpretive mechanism is the constitutional entrenchment of the common law presumption that statutes should be interpreted consistently with international law. Section 233 of the Constitution requires:

> When interpreting any legislation, every court must prefer any reasonable interpretation of the legislation that is consistent with international law over any alternative interpretation that is inconsistent with international law.

Unlike in other jurisdictions where similar presumptions apply (e.g., Australia and the United Kingdom), there is no explicit requirement for ambiguity in legislation for this presumption to be activated.

As discussed above, therefore, the reception framework for international law is generous in South Africa, the Constitution itself mandating the consideration of international law and creating numerous opportunities for its application. Nonetheless, as also illustrated in this study, international law is not always consistently and coherently applied.[36] Uncertain about how to apply international law,[37] courts end up not always using it for analytical purposes and sometimes depriving it of influence on their reasoning.[38] This often relegates international law to a position of simply supporting decisions that are made on domestic grounds.[39]

With that said, this chapter now turns to looking into the relationship between the CRC and the South African law, followed by its judicial application.

[36] Hovell and Williams, 'A Tale of Two Systems', 115; Hudson, 'Neither Here nor There', 348.

[37] The uncertainty can have various causes. Hovell and Williams suggest the level of abstraction and the limited international case law, as well as the doubtful usefulness of international law for the cases at hand: Hovell and Williams, 'A Tale of Two Systems', 118, 120, 128. The absence of usefulness of international law may have been Sachs J's point in *Coetzee v. Government of the Republic of South Africa v. Commanding Officer Port Elizabeth Prison* 1995 (10) BCLR 1382 (*Coetzee*), where he noted that international law did not elucidate the problem brought to the court: at paras. 52–54.

[38] Botha and Olivier, 'Ten Years', 65. For similar concerns, see Dugard, 'International Law and the South African Constitution', 90–91; Olivier, 'International Human Rights Agreements', 502; Hudson, 'Neither Here nor There', 349.

[39] Hudson, 'Neither Here nor There', 352. Hovell and Williams refer to the Court approaching international law 'as a source of normative guidance on basic principles': Hovell and Williams, 'A Tale of Two Systems', 118.

5.3 The CRC and the South African Law

The Convention has influenced the drafting of children's rights clauses in the Interim and Final Constitutions,[40] with section 28 of the Constitution responding in an 'expansive way'[41] to South Africa's obligations under the CRC.

Section 28 reads:

(1) Every child has the right –

(a) to a name and a nationality from birth;
(b) to family care or parental care, or to appropriate alternative care when removed from the family environment;
(c) to basic nutrition, shelter, basic health care services and social services;
(d) to be protected from maltreatment, neglect, abuse or degradation;
(e) to be protected from exploitative labour practices;
(f) not to be required or permitted to perform work or provide services that –

(i) are inappropriate for a person of that child's age; or
(ii) place at risk the child's well-being, education, physical or mental health or spiritual, moral or social development;

(g) not to be detained except as a measure of last resort, in which case, in addition to the rights a child enjoys under sections 12 and 35, the child may be detained only for the shortest appropriate period of time, and has the right to be –

(i) kept separately from detained persons over the age of 18 years; and
(ii) treated in a manner, and kept in conditions, that take account of the child's age;

[40] Constitutional Assembly, Constitutional Committee, *Supplementary Memorandum on Bill of Rights and Party Submissions* (not dated), http://www.justice.gov.za/legislation/constitution/history/REPORTS/tc4-SUPPL.PDF; Panel of Constitutional Experts, 'Memorandum, Re: Children' (5 February 1996), http://www.justice.gov.za/legislation/constitution/history/LEGAL/CP005026.PDF, especially paras. 3.3–3.4. See also Julia Sloth-Nielsen, 'Ratification of the United Nations Convention on the Rights of the Child: Some Implications for South African Law' (1995) 11(3) *South African Journal of Human Rights* 401.

[41] *M v. S (Centre for Child Law Amicus Curiae)* 2007 (12) BCLR 1312 (CC) (*M v. S*) at para. 16. Sloth-Nielsen argues that this amounts to a constitutionalisation of the 'major features of the Convention': Sloth-Nielsen, 'Children's Rights', 139.

(h) to have a legal practitioner assigned to the child by the state, and at state expense, in civil proceedings affecting the child, if substantial injustice would otherwise result; and
(i) not to be used directly in armed conflict, and to be protected in times of armed conflict.

(2) A child's best interests are of paramount importance in every matter concerning the child.
(3) In this section 'child' means a person under the age of 18 years.

Many rights in section 28 responded to the plight of children during apartheid – including arbitrary detention, the denial of nationality, the deprivation of basic necessities, and separation from parents[42] – but some were included as a result of successful advocacy campaigns based on the CRC by the South African children's rights movement.[43]

Later, the CRC influenced the drafting of comprehensive child-focused statutes, such as the Children's Act and the Child Justice Act. Although some aspects of the existing law still fall short of the CRC,[44] overall, the Convention operates in South Africa from a position of strength. It is informed by a constitutional framework that is accommodating of international law, a comprehensive children's rights clause in the Constitution, and equally comprehensive child-focused legislation.

Previous studies have often commended the judicial application of the CRC by the South African courts.[45] According to Sloth-Nielsen and

[42] Julia Sloth-Nielsen, 'The Role of International Human Rights Law in the Development of South Africa's Legislation on Juvenile Justice' (2001) 5(1) *Law, Democracy & Development* 59. More generally, see Julia Sloth-Nielsen, 'Chicken Soup or Chainsaws: Some Implications of the Constitutionalisation of Children's Rights in South Africa' (1996) 27 *Acta Juridica* 6; Tshepo L. Mosikatsana, 'Children's Rights and Family Autonomy in the South African Context: A Comment on Children's Rights under the Final Constitution' (1998) 3(2) *Michigan Journal or Race and Law* 341.

[43] Skelton, 'South Africa', 14; Sloth-Nielsen, 'The Role', 71.

[44] For example, the right to life does not include a right to survival and development, and the parents' status is not an unlawful ground of discrimination: Sloth-Nielsen, 'Ratification', 417–418. For further criticism, see CRC Committee, *Concluding observations: South Africa*, 27 October 2016, CRC/C/ZAF/CO/2, paras. 21, 35, 39–40, 71.

[45] Sloth-Nielsen, 'Children's Rights'; Julia Sloth-Nielsen and Benyam D. Mezmur, '2 + 2 = 5? Exploring the Domestication of the CRC in South African Jurisprudence (2002–2006)' (2008) 16(1) *International Journal of Children's Rights* 1; Julia Sloth-Nielsen and Helen Kruuse, 'A Maturing Manifesto: The Constitutionalisation of Children's Rights in South African Jurisprudence 2007–2012' (2013) 21(4) *International Journal of Children's Rights* 646; Ann Skelton, 'Child Justice in South Africa: Application of International Instruments in the Constitutional Court' (2018) 26(3) *International Journal of Children's Rights* 391; Karabo Ngidi, 'The Role of International Law in the Development of Children's Rights in

Kruuse, the CRC 'punches beyond [its] weight' in terms of its effect on constitutional jurisprudence.[46] The Committee itself has been complimentary about the progressive judicial application of the CRC[47] and 'the excellent jurisprudence'[48] on the application of the best interests of the child. Courts are seldom criticised for how they engage with the CRC – although, occasionally, some authors have questioned the 'narrow, legalistic'[49] approach of judges, or their failure to engage with the substance of the Convention when giving content to children's socio-economic rights.[50]

Authors have seldom closely considered the formal reception framework discussed above. Section 39(1)(b) of the Constitution is internalised as legitimising the judicial engagement with the CRC, but its deployment receives scant critical scrutiny. Other possible engagement methods receive limited attention, owing perhaps to the courts' own preference for the formal framework. With some exceptions,[51] the self-execution of the CRC is hardly acknowledged, even when far-reaching statements are made that South Africa 'has crossed the line from dualism to monism'[52] in relation to the CRC because section 28 is 'merely an entry point into a whole gamut of other sources at the international level, which then become directly applicable domestically'.[53] Skelton has suggested that the Constitutional Court has directly applied the CRC owing to the intensity of the latter's impact in some cases.[54] These statements are not accompanied by references to, or a discussion of, section 231(4) of

South Africa: A Children's Rights Litigator's Perspective' in Magnus Killander (ed.), *International Law and Domestic Human Rights Litigation in Africa* (Pretoria: Pretoria University Law Press, 2010) 173.

46 Sloth-Nielsen and Kruuse, 'A Maturing Manifesto', 677.

47 CRC Committee, *Concluding observations: South Africa*, 2016, para. 5.

48 CRC Committee, *Concluding observations: South Africa*, 2016, para. 25.

49 Skelton criticising Jafta J's position in *C v. Department of Health and Social Development, Gauteng* 2012 (4) BCLR 329 (CC): Skelton, 'South Africa', 23.

50 Solange Rosa and Mira Dutschke, 'Child Rights at the Core: The Use of International Law in South African Cases on Children's Socio-Economic Rights' (2006) 22(2) *South African Journal on Human Rights* 224; Linda Stewart, 'The Grootboom Judgment, Interpretative Manoeuvring and Depoliticising Children's Rights' (2011) 26(1) *South African Public Law* 97, 101.

51 Rosa and Dutschke, for example, argue that a 'binding international law agreement like the UNCRC should in principle be directly applicable in the Court': Rosa and Dutschke, 'Child Rights at the Core', 244.

52 Sloth-Nielsen and Kruuse, 'A Maturing Manifesto', 671.

53 Sloth-Nielsen and Kruuse, 'A Maturing Manifesto', 677.

54 Skelton, 'Child Justice', 405, 414.

the Constitution, which is *the* section under which courts are able to apply the CRC directly if they wish to do so.[55]

The terminology used to describe the courts' engagement with the CRC shows the difficulty of capturing what the courts are doing with the Convention. Thus, Constitutional Court jurisprudence is 'rooted'[56] in international law and the Convention is a 'backdrop'[57] for decisions. Courts 'mention', 'highlight', or 'quote verbatim' the CRC, or use it 'to support the ... reasoning'.[58] These terms do not communicate whether the courts do what is expected of them under sections 39(1)(b) and 233 – namely, interpret constitutional or statutory provisions upon considering the CRC. This terminological uncertainty mirrors the courts' own lack of clarity in using the Convention, as discussed below.

Thus, despite extensive academic engagement with the judicial application of the CRC, there is scope for a closer consideration of how the reception rules have been used and to what effect. Consistent with the methodology of this book, the focus is on cases that contain a meaningful engagement with the CRC. Cases in which the CRC is referred to generically, or in which the engagement is marginal, are not analysed but may be referred to for analytical purposes.[59] The cases are grouped according to the relevant method of engagement: self-execution, constitutional interpretation, statutory interpretation, and a *sui generis* category containing cases that do not easily fit under the framework discussed in Section 5.2.

5.4 The CRC Case Law of the South African Courts

5.4.1 The Self-Execution of the CRC

As discussed above, section 231(4) of the Constitution recognises the possibility of the self-execution of international treaties. This powerful domestic tool remains a utopia for the CRC. Courts have avoided it even when the opportunity presented itself when a lacuna was established in

[55] It is therefore not clear whether these authors use the phrase 'directly applicable' with the technical meaning of 'self-executing', or as a metaphor for the impact of the CRC.

[56] Skelton, 'South Africa', 15.

[57] Sloth-Nielsen and Kruuse, 'A Maturing Manifesto', 657.

[58] Sloth-Nielsen and Mezmur, '2 + 2 = 5?', 8, 12.

[59] Examples include *Grootboom* at para. 75; *Raduvha v. Minister of Safety and Security* 2016 (10) BCLR 1326 (CC) at para. 20, fn 13; *Governing Body of the Juma Musjid Primary School v. Essay NO* 2011 (8) BCLR 761 (CC) at paras. 40, 43.

the domestic law. In *Minister for Welfare and Population Development v. Fitzpatrick*[60] and *AD v. DW*,[61] two intercountry adoption cases, the courts integrated into their reasoning the subsidiarity principle, which at that stage was not explicit in the domestic law. Instead of applying article 21 of the CRC directly, the courts interpreted section 28(2) – the best interests provision in the Bill of Rights – so as to include the principle.

The strongest acknowledgement of a potential direct application of the CRC is the oblique statement of Jafta J in his dissenting judgment in *C v. Department of Health and Social Development, Gauteng*,[62] according to which '[i]nternational law may form part of our law if it is not inconsistent with the Constitution or an Act of Parliament'.[63] The comment was made in relation to article 9 of the CRC, which Skweyiya J relied on to support an automatic judicial review of the emergency removal of children from their family environment, in the presence of the affected parties. However, because such review was not provided by the domestic law, Jafta J considered that the CRC could not be a part of the South African law as it was inconsistent with the Constitution and the relevant statute.

Occasionally, the courts appear to apply the CRC openly and directly without finding a need to justify it. For example, in *F v. F*,[64] a father relied exclusively on article 12 of the CRC to ask the SCA to listen to his child directly in a relocation matter. The Court agreed that a court must consider the child's wishes 'where the child is old enough to articulate his or her preferences'[65] and only mentioned article 12 as a possible support for this conclusion. In *R v. H*,[66] the High Court raised *mero motu* the desirability of appointing a legal representative for a child involved in an acrimonious divorce. The Court relied on section 28(1)(h) of the Constitution, but then indicated that the *court itself* has an obligation arising from article 12 'to afford a child ... the right to express those views' and to give them 'due weight according to the age and maturity of the child'.[67]

60 2000 (7) BCLR 713 (CC) (*Fitzpatrick*).
61 2008 (4) BCLR 359 (CC) (*AD v. DW*).
62 2012 (4) BCLR 329 (CC) (*C v. Department of Health*).
63 *C v. Department of Health* at para. 109 (Jafta J).
64 [2006] 1 All SA 571 (SCA) (*F v. F*), especially at para. 24.
65 *F v. F* at para. 25.
66 2005 (6) SA 535 (C) (*R v. H*).
67 *R v. H* at para. 6.

In the last two cases, the statements of principle in support of child participation drew directly and exclusively from the CRC, as the domestic law at the time did not contain an explicit recognition of a child's right to be heard.[68] However, the technique used in these cases is problematic because the courts gave no consideration to the domestic status of article 12 and engaged with it as if it was domestic law. Courts have avoided the intricacies of section 231(4) of the Constitution, although this is the very section that would enable them to justify how they engaged with the CRC.

5.4.2 *The CRC and the Interpretation of the Bill of Rights*

Undoubtedly, the CRC has been most often considered for the purposes of interpreting the Bill of Rights, as mandated by section 39(1)(b) of the Constitution. It is in the context of the constitutional best interests provision that the CRC has proved most popular, as shown below, although it has also been used to interpret the right to parental care and rights concerning the administration of justice, as discussed thereafter.

5.4.2.1 The CRC and the Best Interests of the Child

The CRC has been relied on to interpret section 28(2) in many contexts, such as intercountry adoptions, the sentencing of parents, the treatment of child victims and witnesses, and torts/delict. Compared to the other jurisdictions studied in this book, article 3(1) is less dominant in South Africa. Instead, the courts have considered other substantive provisions in the CRC to interpret and develop the autochthonous best interests provision. Under the auspices of section 28(2), the courts have used the CRC to cover gaps in the domestic law and to clarify the weight of the best interests of the child in decision-making and the courts' duties to protect children in relevant proceedings. Often, the courts have used the CRC together with section 28(2) to strengthen the justification of a special legal treatment for children. These issues are illustrated below.

The generous ambit of section 28(2) enabled the Constitutional Court (and the SCA) to rely on the CRC to read into the section the subsidiarity principle[69] in intercountry adoptions and the right of children to be heard in matters affecting them.

[68] This was rectified in 2007 with the entry into force of section 10 of the Children's Act.

[69] The principle requires that domestic arrangements for the alternative care of a child are to be preferred over placing a child with an adoptive family overseas.

In *Fitzpatrick*, an English family residing in South Africa wished to adopt a South African toddler whom they fostered, but were unable to do so because the applicable statute (now repealed) prohibited the adoption of a South African child by foreign nationals in the applicants' position.[70] The Court declared the relevant statutory provision inconsistent with section 28(2) because it prevented a best interests assessment in relation to each individual child.[71] The Court made the far-reaching statement that section 28(2) is a right independent of the more specific children's rights in section 28(1),[72] but this does not seem to have been prompted by the consideration of the CRC.[73] Instead, the Court quoted, inter alia, article 3(1)[74] to point out that the best interests standard has not been given exhaustive content[75] – an indication that the standard should remain flexible, 'as individual circumstances will determine which factors secure the best interests of a particular child'.[76] The Court also acknowledged the CRC when it considered whether to suspend the declaration of invalidity of the statute on the grounds that the existing law was not adequately equipped to deal with intercountry adoption, including, inter alia, respect for the principle of subsidiarity contained in article 21(b) of the CRC.[77] The Court found that the existing legal framework accommodated the principle of subsidiarity, which was part of the best interests enquiry via section 39(1)(b). The Court noted that

> [a]lthough no express provision is made for the principle of subsidiarity in our law, courts would nevertheless be obliged to take the principle into account when assessing the 'best interests of the child', as it is enshrined in international law, and specifically article 21(b) of the Children's Convention. This obligation flows from the imperative in s 39(1)(b) of

[70] For the text, see fn 2 in *Fitzpatrick*.

[71] *Fitzpatrick* at para. 20.

[72] The Court pioneered this approach well ahead of the CRC Committee, which took a similar position in 2013: CRC Committee, *General Comment No. 14 (2013) on the right of the child to have his or her best interests taken as a primary consideration (art. 3, para. 1)*, 29 May 2013, CRC/C/GC/14.

[73] Article 3(1) of the CRC possibly strengthened the Court's view that the best interests of the child must remain a flexible standard adaptable to individual circumstances. This may have supported its decision that section 28(2) contained an independent *individual* right. See *Fitzpatrick* at para. 18.

[74] In fn 11, alongside the ACRWC and relevant literature.

[75] *Fitzpatrick* at para. 18.

[76] *Fitzpatrick* at para. 18 (footnote omitted).

[77] *Fitzpatrick* at para. 23. The principle is also contained in article 4(b) of the Hague Convention on the Protection of Children and Co-operation in Respect of Intercountry Adoption, 29 May 1993, in force 1 May 1995 (1993 Hague Convention).

the Constitution that '[w]hen interpreting the Bill of Rights, a court, tribunal or forum ... must consider international law'.

The individual-focused approach to the best interests in *Fitzpatrick* was somewhat challenged by the collective-focused approach employed by the SCA in a subsequent intercountry adoption case. In *De Gree v. Webb*,[78] which was later heard on appeal by the Constitutional Court as *AD v. DW*, an American couple wished to adopt a South African toddler. They sought a custody and sole guardianship order that would have enabled them to adopt the child in the United States, a procedure resorted to because of the uncertainties in intercountry adoption procedures in South Africa at the time. The High Court held that this was in fact an application for intercountry adoption and ought to have followed that path.

A narrow majority (3:2) of the SCA decided that the principle of subsidiarity – as provided by, inter alia, the CRC – was not complied with.[79] Theron AJA (as she then was), writing for the majority, agreed with *Fitzpatrick* that section 39(1)(b) of the Constitution requires the principle of subsidiarity to be considered when assessing the best interests of the child, despite it not being explicitly reflected in the domestic law at the time.[80] Citing articles 3(1) and 21 of the CRC (and the 1993 Hague Convention),[81] the majority decided that it was in the interests of children *generally* that all intercountry adoptions be concluded according to the principles and the protective mechanisms – including the subsidiarity principle – provided in international instruments.[82] The principle of subsidiarity was clearly central to the majority position, with Theron AJA emphasising that a court should not approve intercountry adoptions that conflict with international procedures accepted by South Africa and aimed at protecting the best interests of a child.[83]

78 2007 (5) SA 184 (SCA) (*De Gree*).

79 The 1993 Hague Convention was in the process of being incorporated into the Children's Act (see chapter 16 and Schedule 1, effective 1 July 2010). The minority accepted the relevance of the principle of subsidiarity but considered that it was not breached: *De Gree* at paras. 48–55 (Heher JA). Hancke AJA, dissenting, indirectly referred to the issues raised by the principle of subsidiarity as 'legal niceties': at para. 99.

80 *De Gree* at para. 12 (Theron AJA).

81 *De Gree* at paras. 17 (Theron AJA); 85–86, 94 (Ponnan JA).

82 *De Gree* at para. 17 (Theron AJA). Ponnan JA also referred to it as 'foundational' to intercountry adoptions: at para. 96.

83 *De Gree* at para. 27 (Theron AJA); see also at para. 92 (Ponnan JA).

In the prospective parents' appeal to the Constitutional Court, Sachs J (for a unanimous court) noted that the lacuna in the domestic law was to be covered by the subsidiarity principle found in international law.[84] Sachs J softened the 'too bald'[85] approach to the subsidiarity principle taken by the SCA, arguing that the guarantees introduced by the 1993 Hague Convention 'reduce the relatively autonomous effect of the subsidiarity principle as expressed in the CRC',[86] inter alia. Given its protective function, the principle of subsidiarity remained a 'core factor'[87] but one that 'must be seen as subsidiary to the paramountcy principle',[88] as required by the Constitution. The Court referred to articles 3 and 21 of the CRC, noting that in the context of adoption they gave the best interests of the child more weight than in other legal matters.[89] Sachs J backed, therefore, the prioritisation of *individual* best interests by referring to the CRC, inter alia, and reoriented the interpretation of section 28(2) towards the best interests of the individual child who is subject to an intercountry adoption application.

Notably, both courts have interpreted *into* the permissive section 28(2) a principle (i.e., subsidiarity) that was not spelled out in the domestic law but was nonetheless accommodated by it. The principle was clearly important, as Theron AJA refused to make an order that she considered contrary to it and Sachs J held that it filled the gap in the domestic law. Despite its undeniable weight, none of the judges considered the self-execution of the principle, firmly grounding their reasoning as an interpretation exercise under section 39(1)(b). The interplay between the CRC (and other cited international instruments) and section 28(2) of the Constitution prompted the courts to reflect on the relationship between individual and collective best interests. Although the issue has not yet received comprehensive attention from the courts, the intercountry adoption cases are early precedents for a matter that is likely to come to the courts in a jurisdiction (i.e., South Africa) where courts can invalidate legislation that is inconsistent with the constitutional provision that protects the best interests of the child.

[84] *AD v. DW* at para. 36.
[85] *AD v. DW* at para. 54.
[86] *AD v. DW* at para. 47.
[87] *AD v. DW* at para. 49.
[88] *AD v. DW* at para. 55.
[89] *AD v. DW* at fn 47. The Court also referred to corresponding provisions of the ACRWC.

Perhaps the most distinctive contribution of the CRC to the interpretation of section 28(2) has been to enable a reading in of a child's right to be heard – a right that is without explicit constitutional recognition. *J v. National Director of Public Prosecutions*[90] concerned the constitutional validity of a statutory provision requiring that, upon sentencing a person for a sexual offence against a child or a disabled person, a court must order that the particulars of the offender be entered into a National Register for Sex Offenders. Several adverse consequences arose from registration, including that the particulars so entered could never be removed. The applicant, a fourteen-year-old child at the time of the offences, was sentenced for rapes against younger children. A court ordered that the child's details be entered (for perpetuity) onto the Register. The High Court, however, decided that the rights of the child were violated by the relevant section and declared it unconstitutional.

In the Constitutional Court, Skweyiya ADCJ (for a unanimous court) found that the mandatory registration was contrary to section 28(2) because, inter alia, it prevented a consideration of the representations made by the child.[91] Skweyiya ADCJ noted that section 28(2) requires, among other things, that the child or their representative be given the opportunity to make representations and to be heard at all stages of the criminal proceedings,[92] including post-sentencing procedures. This requirement was anchored in the domestic statutes and precedent, as well as in article 12 of the CRC and General Comments Nos. 10 and 12 of the CRC Committee.[93] Prima facie, the engagement with the CRC is minimal and limited to a mention in a footnote (i.e., footnote 45). It was, however, consequential because, alongside the general comments, it justified the Court's position that section 28(2) requires that the child's views be heard at *all stages* of *all criminal proceedings*. None of the domestic sources provided such wide protection. Section 3(c) of the Child Justice Act, for example, makes child participation a guiding principle of that Act, but the current proceedings did not fall under its purview. Section 10 of the Children's Act, while supportive of child participation in all proceedings, has an uncertain application to criminal

[90] 2014 (7) BCLR 764 (CC) (*J v. NDPP*).

[91] *J v. NDPP* at para. 42.

[92] *J v. NDPP* at para. 40.

[93] See *J v. NDPP* at para. 40, fn 45; CRC Committee, *General Comment No. 12 (2009): The right of the child to be heard*, 20 July 2009, CRC/C/GC/12; CRC Committee, *General Comment No. 10 (2007): Children's rights in Juvenile Justice*, 9 February 2007, CRC/C/GC/10.

proceedings because it is a *sensu lato* child protection statute. Article 12 of the CRC, however, has a distinctly wide scope that extends to *all proceedings*, and the general comments explicitly supported child participation in juvenile justice processes.

The (partial) constitutionalisation *via* the CRC of children's right to be heard as a component of section 28(2) was further cemented in *AB v. Pridwin Preparatory School.*[94] That case concerned the exclusion of two young boys from a private primary school following the unilateral termination of the contract by the school because of the parents' toxic behaviour. Theron J's majority judgment decided, in the relevant parts, that section 28(2) required that the school give the parents an opportunity to make representations on the best interests of their children.[95] The CRC was briefly mentioned by Theron J but featured prominently in Khampepe J's concurring judgment, which was endorsed by a majority of judges.

Khampepe J differs from Theron J by strongly supporting listening to children's *own* views.[96] Theron J, and the minority, agreed that representations on the best interests of the child ought to have been made prior to the termination of the contract, but their reasoning is fairly process-oriented and can be satisfied by the parents making the relevant representations.[97] Khampepe J, however, takes the view that the procedural right aspect of the best interests of the child is 'first and foremost a right given to the *child*, which may be exercised by a representative where children are not of sufficient age or maturity to make these representations themselves'.[98] To support the primacy of children's *own* voices, Khampepe J relies on domestic precedent,[99] 'buttressed'[100] by international instruments and domestic statutes. Article 12 of the CRC,

[94] [2020] ZACC 12 (*Pridwin Preparatory School*).

[95] *Pridwin Preparatory School* at paras. 153, 209 (Theron J).

[96] Both Theron J (at para. 187) and Khampepe J (at para. 226) are careful to stress that their judgments do not deal with child participation in *all* contractual contexts. In this case, however, the matter (i.e., education) was so important to the children that child participation was necessary.

[97] *Pridwin Preparatory School* at para. 223 (Khampepe J).

[98] *Pridwin Preparatory School* at para. 226 (Khampepe J) (emphasis in original).

[99] *Pridwin Preparatory School* at para. 234 (Khampepe J).

[100] *Pridwin Preparatory School* at para. 235 (Khampepe J). Arguably, international law was the most cogent support for Khampepe J's position because the reliance on the Children's Act and its provisions on child participation is debatable. Arguably, the school's decision is not within the ambit of that Act (see section 6(1)). Further, Khampepe J (like Skweyiya ADCJ in *J v. NDPP*) used the Children's Act to give meaning to the Constitution, which is the reverse of what section 39(2) of the Constitution provides.

General Comment No. 12[101] (including its support for child participation in disciplinary procedures at school), and article 4 of the African Charter on the Rights and Welfare of the Child[102] (ACRWC) determined Khampepe J's conclusion that children must be given an opportunity to speak for themselves: '[i]nternational law enjoins us to give due regard to the views and wishes of the child and to allow them to participate in matters that affect them. This is a right held by children themselves, as independent rights-holders'.[103] Thus, *Pridwin Preparatory School* firmly entrenches a child's right to be heard as an element of the legal content of section 28(2) of the Constitution, creating something akin to a presumption that a child should be listened to directly when of sufficient age and maturity.

Another category of relevant cases includes those where courts have used the CRC to develop or strengthen the ability of section 28(2) to guarantee special legal protection to children in cases involving or simply affecting them. In *M v. S*,[104] a core children's rights case in South Africa,[105] the Court had to determine if judicial officers who sentence primary caregivers have obligations arising directly from section 28(2). The accused was the single mother of three children (aged 8, 12, and 16) who was convicted of fraud and sentenced to a short period of imprisonment. She argued that the sentencing court did not sufficiently consider the rights of her children, an argument agreed with by the Court. Writing for the majority, Sachs J applied sections 28(1)(b) and 28(2) and gave guidance to courts on how to give effect to children's rights when sentencing primary caregivers.[106] Sachs J did not use the Convention extensively, but acknowledged that section 28 responded in 'an expansive way' to the state's obligations under a treaty that has become 'the international standard against which to measure legislation and policies'.[107] The CRC and the Constitution have introduced a 'change in mindset',[108] which requires regard

[101] CRC Committee, *General Comment No. 12 (2009): The right of the child to be heard*, 20 July 2009, CRC/C/GC/12.

[102] African Charter on the Rights and Welfare of the Child, 11 July 1990, CAB/LEG/24.9/49 (1990).

[103] *Pridwin Preparatory School* at para. 241 (Khampepe J).

[104] 2007 (12) BCLR 1312 (CC) (*M v. S*).

[105] See the comment by Jacqui Gallinetti, '2kul2Btru: What Children Would Say about the Jurisprudence of Albie Sachs' (2010) 25(1) *South African Public Law* 108.

[106] *M v. S* at paras. 33, 36 (Sachs J).

[107] *M v. S* at para. 16 (Sachs J) (footnotes omitted).

[108] *M v. S* at para. 16 (Sachs J).

> to be paid to the import of the principles of the CRC as they inform the provisions of section 28 in relation to the sentencing of a primary caregiver. The four great principles of the CRC which have become international currency, and as such guide all policy in South Africa in relation to children, are said to be survival, development, protection and participation. What unites these principles, and lies at the heart of section 28, I believe, is the right of a child to be a child and enjoy special care.[109]

No further attention is given to the CRC and, apart from article 3(1), the Court does not identify other relevant provisions despite mentioning its 'four great principles'. In a footnote, Sachs J notes the distinction between article 3(1) and section 28(2), pointing out that the latter 'is notably stronger than the phrase "primary consideration"' in the former,[110] but does not explore the distinction further. Thus, the blending of the CRC in Sachs J's reasoning is subtle and muted.

In *Director of Public Prosecutions, Transvaal v. Minister for Justice and Constitutional Development*,[111] international law is more prominent. The case considered the compatibility of several statutory provisions concerning child witnesses and complainants with section 28(2). The impugned provisions established the conditions under which child victims and/or child witnesses in sexual offence cases could testify through intermediaries or be heard in camera or through closed-circuit television.[112] The High Court found the provisions inconsistent with section 28(2) because the use of the specified protective methods was a matter of judicial discretion rather than a positive obligation for the courts. The Constitutional Court, however, decided that the impugned provisions could be given an interpretation consistent with section 28(2), which minimises risks to children's development and well-being arising from the application of the law.[113]

The Court relied on article 3(1) of the CRC and extensively on the detailed 2005 UN Guidelines on Justice in Matters Involving Child Victims and Witnesses of Crime (the Guidelines) to interpret section 28(2).[114] The Court stressed that international instruments were 'relevant considerations' under section 39(1)(b)[115] and that

[109] *M v. S* at para. 17 (Sachs J) (footnotes omitted).
[110] *M v. S* at fn 31 (Sachs J).
[111] 2009 (7) BCLR 637 (CC) (*DPP Transvaal*).
[112] *DPP Transvaal* at para. 3 (Ngcobo J).
[113] *DPP Transvaal* at para. 84.
[114] *DPP Transvaal* at para. 70ff; Economic and Social Council (ECOSOC), *UN Economic and Social Council 2005/20: Guidelines on Justice in Matters Involving Child Victims and Witnesses of Crime*, 22 July 2005, E/RES/2005/20.
[115] *DPP Transvaal* at para. 75.

> [t]he international and regional instruments on the rights of the child therefore provide a framework within which section 28(2), and ultimately the invalidated provisions, can be evaluated and understood.[116]

Upon noting the similarity between section 28(2) and article 3(1),[117] Ngcobo J referred to the latter and to general comments of the CRC Committee to stress *the courts'* obligation to ensure that children's best interests are protected. Accordingly, General Comment No. 7 of the Committee stressed that article 3(1) was introduced into the CRC to recognise that children's immaturity makes them reliant on authorities for their protection.[118] Courts are among such authorities and article 3(1) and General Comment No. 5[119] recognise their responsibility to protect the best interests of the child in the exercise of their judicial functions, including by considering the impact of their decisions on children[120] and by avoiding trauma that may arise from children giving evidence in criminal proceedings.[121] Therefore, the statutory provisions concerning the appointment of intermediaries must be interpreted and applied in a manner consistent with section 28(2), understood in light of article 3(1) and the Guidelines, so as to avoid potential trauma arising from a child testifying in court.[122]

Notably, the Court did not use article 3(1) as an autonomous interpretive aid in relation to statutes,[123] opting instead for a mediated interpretive influence through section 28(2). Article 3(1) and the general comments relied on by the Court were used primarily to stress the direct responsibility of the *courts* to ensure that, when exercising their judicial functions, they give paramount importance to the best interests of the child.[124] Admittedly, it was the Guidelines rather than the CRC that the Court engaged with, probably because of their detailed and practical standards for dealing with child witnesses. Surprising is the Court's shunning of article 12 of the CRC, despite it referring repeatedly to the

[116] *DPP Transvaal* at para. 75.

[117] *DPP Transvaal* at para. 76. Article 4 of the ACRWC was also mentioned.

[118] *DPP Transvaal* at para. 77; CRC Committee, *General Comment No. 7 (2005): Implementing child rights in early childhood*, 1 November 2005, CRC/C/GC/7, para. 13.

[119] CRC Committee, *General Comment No. 5 (2003): General measures of implementation of the Convention on the Rights of the Child (arts. 4, 42 and 44, para. 6)*, 27 November 2003, CRC/GC/2003/5.

[120] *DPP Transvaal* at para. 77.

[121] *DPP Transvaal* at para. 79.

[122] *DPP Transvaal* at paras. 98, 110–113.

[123] Which it could have done under section 233, as discussed in Section 5.2.2.

[124] See especially *DPP Transvaal* at paras. 95, 113.

importance of respecting the wishes and feelings of child witnesses and complainants.[125] It preferred instead to treat the issue as an aspect of the best interests provision.

Contrasting with the receptiveness to the CRC in the above cases is *Le Roux v. Dey*.[126] Here, three teenagers (aged 15 to 17) played a prank on the principal and deputy principal of the school they attended. They superimposed the heads of their two teachers on a picture of two men depicted in a sexually suggestive position. The deputy principal successfully sued the children for defamation and the case reached the Constitutional Court in the children's appeal. The appeal was rejected by the majority, who struggled to integrate children's constitutional rights into their reasoning and differentiate the tortious liability of children from that of adults. Yacoob J and Skweyiya J dissented, concluding that the image, properly interpreted in light of section 28 of the Constitution, was not defamatory. Yacoob J's judgment (with which Skweyiya J concurred) is distinctly child-focused and reaches its conclusion by applying section 28 exclusively.

Skweyiya J – the only judge to mention the CRC – focused on the role of section 28(2) in civil claims against children for incidents occurring at school. He turned to article 3, which he found 'appealing'[127] because of the 'interesting difference' with section 28(2) – namely, article 3 refers to the best interests of the child as 'a primary consideration' and section 28 (2) refers to it as of 'paramount importance'.[128] Skweyiya J approached these texts as complementary, in effect blending their normative contents. Article 3(1), read with section 28(2),

> would mean that . . . the best interests of the child consideration is not artificially elevated above all others; rather, it forms the basis and starting point from which the matter is to be considered. Once the considerations relevant to this foundation are clearly cemented, one can then begin to examine the other rights that enter the balance, without losing sight of the fact that the best interests of the child remain 'of paramount importance'.[129]

The balance of Skweyiya J's judgment is an attempt to give children's interests a primary consideration by focusing on the reasons for them being treated differently from adults. While this judgment highlights the

[125] See, for example, *DPP Transvaal* at paras. 124–127.
[126] 2011 (6) BCLR 577 (CC) (*Le Roux*).
[127] *Le Roux* at para. 211 (Skweyiya J).
[128] *Le Roux* at para. 211 (Skweyiya J).
[129] *Le Roux* at para. 211 (Skweyiya J).

marginalisation of children's rights by the majority, it is regrettable that, as a concurring dissent, it does not independently and more completely grapple with its own legal implications for *Le Roux* and similar cases.

To conclude this part, aspects of the CRC have made a rich contribution to developing the legal content of the autochthonous constitutional protection of the best interests of the child, albeit cases exist where the Convention is shunned although potentially relevant.

5.4.2.2 The Right to Parental and Family Care

C v. Department of Health concerned the constitutional validity of two sections of the newly enacted Children's Act, which allowed the emergency removal of children from their family environment to temporary safe care without an automatic judicial review conducted in the presence of the children and their carers.[130] Relying on the impugned provisions, social workers removed three children from the care of two parents found working or begging on the streets with their children.[131] Three judgments were written. Yacoob J's majority judgment decided that the impugned statutory provisions were unconstitutional but did not mention the CRC.

The two minority judgments refer to the CRC but in starkly different terms. Skweyiya J (Froneman J concurring) found that the emergency removal of a child was an interference with the right to parental and family care in section 28(1)(b) of the Constitution.[132] Although the section recognises the right to alternative care, that right was secondary to the right to parental and family care[133] – a conclusion reached by relying on the ACRWC and articles 7(1) and 8(1) of the CRC.[134] Turning to the reasonableness and justification of interference with the constitutional right, Skweyiya J found it 'helpful to consider the applicable international law'[135] – including article 9 of the CRC, which contains specific requirements for the removal of children from their families (i.e., judicial review and the participation of interested parties).[136] Skweyiyaj

130 Sections 151 and 152 of the Children's Act.

131 One of the children accompanied her shoe-making father on the street because her mother was in the hospital giving birth; the other two children were together with their blind mother, who was begging for a living.

132 *C v. Department of Health* at para. 24 (Skweyiya J).

133 *C v. Department of Health* at para. 24 (Skweyiya J).

134 *C v. Department of Health* at para. 25 (Skweyiya J).

135 *C v. Department of Health* at para. 32 (Skweyiya J).

136 *C v. Department of Health* at para. 32 (Skweyiya J).

acknowledged the CRC's 'interpretive influence ... on section 28 of the Constitution'[137] and stated:

> The right to parental care or family care requires that the removal of children from the family environment must be mitigated in the manner described in the UNCRC, in order to satisfy the standard set for the limitation of rights in section 36(1) of the Constitution. The requirements that the removal be subject to automatic review and that all interested parties, including the child concerned, be given an opportunity to be heard, in my view, stand as essential safeguards of the best interests of the child.[138]

Jafta J (joined by Mogoeng CJ) took the view that the CRC had no role in the constitutional review. Section 28 did not provide for a judicial review and, consequently, such requirement could not be incorporated into the section by way of judicial interpretation. Thus:

> Section 28 does not refer to automatic review at all. Therefore, the requirement for judicial review in the Convention does not form part of the section. Nor can it be incorporated into the section. Consequently, it cannot be used as a constitutional standard for determining the validity of legislation. This is so despite the fact that the Convention and the Charter were ratified and are binding on South Africa. International law may form part of our law if it is not inconsistent with the Constitution or an Act of Parliament. This illustrates that where there is an inconsistency between international law and an Act of Parliament, the latter prevails.[139]

This indeed 'gives rise to some concern with regard to international law'.[140] Fortunately, such blunt rejection of the CRC by South African judges is rare but, for reasons discussed later, should be considered more carefully.

The contribution of the CRC to Skweyiya J's reasoning, on the other hand, is nuanced yet significant. First, articles 7(1) and 8(1) were used to clarify the scope of section 28(1)(b) of the Constitution and to conclude that parental and family care are the primary forms of care protected by it, with alternative care as their subsidiary. Second, section 28(1)(b) does not spell out the conditions to be fulfilled when separating children from their families, but Skweyiya J filled the gap by relying on article 9 to conclude that automatic judicial review and the participation of those

137 *C v. Department of Health* at para. 33 (Skweyiya J).
138 *C v. Department of Health* at para. 34 (Skweyiya J).
139 *C v. Department of Health* at para. 109 (Jafta J) (footnote omitted).
140 Skelton, 'South Africa', 23.

affected were necessary.[141] Arguably, article 9 is used not to interpret the substance of a constitutional right,[142] but rather to inform an assessment of the legitimacy of its limitation. Third, reliance on the CRC gives Skweyiya J's reasoning a better justification. Yacoob J (for the majority) does not explain why *automatic judicial* review (and no other measure) satisfies the best interests of the child.[143] Skweyiya J, however, clearly locates the requirement for judicial review in the CRC, giving a sounder foundation to his judgment.

5.4.2.3 Children as Victims and Offenders

This is a well-represented category, containing cases concerning the sentencing of juvenile offenders and cases concerning child victims and witnesses. In these cases, the CRC is relied on primarily to strengthen the principle that children must be treated differently from adults when in contact with the justice system.

Brandt v. S[144] concerned the mandatory sentencing of children aged 16–18 who committed certain serious offences. Under the mandatory sentencing regime, the accused was sentenced to life imprisonment for murder, which he committed when he was 17 years and 7 months old. On appeal, the SCA interpreted the minimum sentencing legislation in light of the Constitution[145] and decided that, in the case of children aged 16–18, the application of the minimum sentence was a matter of discretion for the sentencing court.[146] The Constitution and international instruments constituted the backdrop for the Court's approach.[147] Citing academic commentators, the Court remarked that international instruments, including the CRC, have revolutionised juvenile justice and their principles have been articulated in the Constitution.[148] International instruments provided guidelines on how to achieve this new approach to juvenile justice, with the CRC having become an 'international benchmark against which legislation and policies can be

141 *C v. Department of Health* at para. 34 (Skweyiya J).

142 This can be approached differently. Skweyiya J may have drawn into the *substantive* content of the right to parental and family care the *procedural* safeguards provided for in article 9(1) and (2) of the CRC: at para. 34.

143 See, for example, *C v. Department of Health* at para. 77 (Yacoob J).

144 [2005] 2 All SA 1 (SCA) (*Brandt*).

145 *Brandt* at para. 9.

146 *Brandt* at para. 12.

147 *Brandt* at para. 13.

148 *Brandt* at para. 16.

measured'.[149] The 'overriding message'[150] of the international instruments (article 37(b) of the CRC and Beijing Rule 17.1) and the Constitution concerned the use of deprivation of liberty as a last resort, the individualisation of sentencing, and the preparation of the child for their release into society. Should the minimum sentencing apply to children automatically, imprisonment would be a first rather than a last resort and would conflict with the principles of proportionality and individualisation.[151]

In *Brandt*, the SCA read sections 28(2) and 28(1)(g) of the Constitution with international instruments, which the Court found useful because of their 'detailed and ... specific suggestions' for the realisation of constitutional goals.[152] The Court relied on the CRC (and other instruments, including section 28(2) of the Constitution) to stress the need to interpret the minimum sentencing legislation in a way that treated child offenders differently from adult offenders, as opposed to following an interpretation that would obscure such differences.

To reverse the effects of *Brandt*, the Parliament passed legislation that restricted the sentencing discretion of the courts by providing that, in relation to 16- to 18-year-olds, courts could only depart from mandatory minimum sentences if substantial and compelling circumstances existed. The constitutionality of these statutory amendments was challenged in *Centre for Child Law v. Minister for Justice and Constitutional Development*[153] (*CCL*), where the Court declared the amended statutory provisions inconsistent with section 28(1)(g).[154] Cameron J's majority judgment is child-focused,[155] but the references to the CRC are limited to the observations that section 28 'draws upon and reflects'[156] the Convention and that the latter rejects the application of minimum sentencing to children, requires that children be incarcerated as a last resort and for the shortest period of time, and requires that children are treated differently from adults.[157] Thereafter, however, Cameron J pulls

[149] *Brandt* at para. 17 (footnote omitted).
[150] *Brandt* at para. 19.
[151] *Brandt* at para. 22.
[152] *Brandt* at para. 17.
[153] 2009 (11) BCLR 1105 (CC) (*CCL*).
[154] *CCL* at paras. 46–48, 64 (Cameron J).
[155] See especially *CCL* at paras. 26–32.
[156] *CCL* at para. 25 (footnote omitted). Cameron J quotes articles 37(b) and 40(1) of the CRC (see fnn 62–63).
[157] *CCL* at para. 61, referring to, inter alia, articles 37(b) and 40(1) of the CRC.

the discussion firmly under the Constitution, the provisions of which 'merely need to be given their intended effect' as they 'amply embod[y] these internationally accepted principles'.[158]

The outcome of the application of the constitutional principles is no doubt compatible with the CRC, but the reasoning is strongly rooted in the domestic law. Cameron J's technique is interesting in that the CRC is relied on not to establish the content of section 28(1)(g), but to decide if its limitation was reasonable and justifiable. The Court stressed that the interference with the rights in this section must be justified in relation to the group whose rights were limited (i.e., 16- to 18-year-olds). This group has special rights under international instruments and, when deciding if the interference with constitutional rights is reasonable and justifiable under the Constitution, the international instruments that give recognition to those special rights are relevant. As the Court remarked, in this instance, these instruments were fully reflected in the Constitution, so their role was not extensive, but the technique is noteworthy for looking beyond the traditional use of international law (i.e., to interpret the substance of constitutional rights) to a role in controlling or guiding their application.[159]

Du Toit v. Ntshinghila[160] concerned an adult charged with possession of child pornography, who argued that his right to a fair trial under section 35 of the Constitution was breached because he was not provided with copies of the images alleged to constitute child pornography. The Court held that while the normal practice was to give the accused copies of the relevant materials, countervailing interests may justify the accused having the materials disclosed in an alternative way (i.e., a private viewing).[161] In determining the countervailing interests, the Court noted that sections 39 and 233 of the Constitution enjoined it to consider international law.[162] The interests of children (i.e., to have their dignity and privacy protected) were established in relation to a range of domestic and international norms,[163] including article 3(1) of the CRC and the

[158] *CCL* at para. 63.

[159] A similar technique was used in *Christian Education South Africa v. Minister of Education* 2000 (10) BCLR 1051 (CC) (*Christian Education*), discussed in Section 5.5.1.

[160] [2016] 2 All SA 328 (SCA) (*Ntshinghila*).

[161] *Ntshinghila* at paras. 8–9.

[162] *Ntshinghila* at paras. 10–11, fn 7. It is not clear, however, what statute was to be interpreted in a manner consistent with international obligations.

[163] Including article 4 of the ACRWC, section 28(2) of the Constitution, relevant jurisprudence, and the Children's Act. The domestic sources were especially noted for their protection of a child's dignity.

Optional Protocol to the Convention on the Rights of the Child on the Sale of Children, Child Prostitution and Pornography.[164] Upon balancing the rights of the accused with children's interests, the Court decided that not providing copies to the accused reached the correct balance. The reliance on the CRC in this case was limited, but the Convention was used as part of a web of norms that enabled the Court to frame children's interests in a way that justified their consideration in the legal enquiry.

In sum, courts use the CRC primarily to interpret section 28 and this has sometimes resulted in the expansion of the scope of the constitutional protection for the rights of children or strengthened children's protection as a special class of human rights holders. Judges are seldom explicitly reluctant to consider the Convention, but this has not led to its consistent or comprehensive application, as further discussed in Section 5.5.

5.4.3 *The CRC and Statutory Interpretation*

As discussed in Section 5.2.2, the CRC can also be used in the interpretation of domestic statutes. None of the Constitutional Court or SCA cases considered in this research apply the CRC as an autonomous interpretive device for a domestic statute under section 233 of the Constitution. In *DPP Transvaal*, an opportunity arose to do so. The Court acknowledged the possibility of using section 233 to justify reliance on the CRC to interpret the impugned statute,[165] but it resorted instead to a statutory interpretation in light of section 28(2), which the Court construed relying on, inter alia, article 3(1).[166] The CRC's interpretive influence was therefore filtered through section 28(2). This was possibly the result of context rather than a reluctance to apply the CRC autonomously, because the question put to the Court was one of *constitutional* compatibility, which had to be decided in relation to constitutional standards rather than international instruments.

Brandt offered another opportunity to apply the CRC autonomously under section 233 because the Court considered minimum sentencing inconsistent with the Convention. Once more, the Court gave the CRC a

[164] *Ntshinghila* at para. 11; Optional Protocol to the Convention on the Rights of the Child on the Sale of Children, Child Prostitution and Child Pornography, New York, 25 May 2000, in force 18 January 2002, 2171 UNTS 227.

[165] *DPP Transvaal* at para. 75.

[166] See the discussion of the case in Section 5.4.2.1.

mediated effect and interpreted the relevant statute in accordance with section 28(1)(g) construed with reference to the Convention.

5.4.4 Sui Generis *Forms of Application*

There are cases in which it is difficult to place the method of engagement in one of the constitutionally recognised methods discussed above. This is because courts do not always refer to the constitutional sections that justify their reliance on the CRC or because they sometimes use techniques that do not fit neatly into the formal engagement categories discussed in Section 5.2.

In *Geldenhuys v. The State*,[167] the accused challenged the constitutionality of the age of consent to sexual intercourse set by the legislature,[168] arguing that some children below that age may be competent to make decisions regarding sexual activity.[169] The Court decided that setting a minimum age was aimed at protecting children and was consistent with section 28(1)(d) and (2) of the Constitution and with South Africa's international protection obligations, including under article 34 of the CRC.[170] It is not clear how the Court used the CRC. It can, perhaps, be argued that article 34 was used to interpret section 28(1)(d). The constitutional standard is general and refers to protection against maltreatment, neglect, abuse, or degradation, while the CRC provision is explicit in relation to protection against sexual exploitation. This may be why the Court found it of 'particular importance'.[171] The absence of reference to section 39(1)(b), or at least some indication of the purpose for which the CRC is used, combined with comments about the compatibility of the statute with the state's international obligations, creates the impression that the Convention was used as an autonomous standard to assess the legislation.

Similar uncertainty about how the Court used the CRC is present in *Centre for Child Law v. Governing Body of Hoërskool Fochville*.[172] The case concerned a dispute between a public school and education

[167] 2009 (1) SACR 1 (SCA) (*Geldenhuys*).
[168] That is, 16 for heterosexual intercourse and 19 for same-sex intercourse.
[169] *Geldenhuys* at para. 57. See section 14(1)(b) of the Sexual Offences Act, 1957.
[170] *Geldenhuys* at paras. 58–59, 63. The Court found that the statutory framework was inconsistent with the Constitution in that it provided different ages of consent in relation to homosexual and heterosexual acts.
[171] *Geldenhuys* at para. 59.
[172] [2015] 4 All SA 571 (SCA) (*Hoërskool*).

authorities, whereby the former disagreed with the latter's instruction to admit children beyond the school's numeric capacity. The parents of the children so admitted were joined as parties on account of their own interests and as representatives of their children. The children were not cited as respondents. The Centre for Child Law (the Centre) applied to intervene as a third party representing the children themselves. It submitted an affidavit containing information obtained through discussions with the children, which was critical of the school. The school sought to compel the Centre to disclose the questionnaires it used to collect information from the children, which the Centre refused to do on grounds, inter alia, that maintaining confidentiality protected the interests of the children, who feared victimisation at school. The SCA decided that courts had the discretion to decide on the disclosure sought by balancing the relevant interests, which in this case included the interests of the children.[173]

The SCA identified the children's right to separate representation as one of the relevant interests to be balanced in deciding on the disclosure, which flows from the children's right to participate as recognised internationally and domestically.[174] Children's separate representation by the Centre was contested by the school, which argued that the affected children were already represented by their parents joined as respondents. The Court relied on articles 12 of the CRC and 4(2) of the ACRWC,[175] section 28(1)(h) of the Constitution,[176] and various participation rights in the Children's Act[177] to demonstrate the recognition of children's right to participate in matters affecting them through their *own representatives* rather than through their guardians. According to the Court, children had the right to be heard in a manner that would not damage their best interests[178] and this was best secured by having the Centre represent them and maintain their confidentiality.[179]

It is difficult to ascertain how the Court uses the CRC, but it appears to be doing so in the exercise of discretion as a tool to identify one of the

[173] *Hoërskool* at para. 19.
[174] *Hoërskool* at para. 19.
[175] *Hoërskool* at para. 20.
[176] *Hoërskool* at para. 22. However, this section was not directly relevant because this was not a case where children were represented at the state's expense.
[177] See sections 10 (the general right to participate), 14 (the right to access the courts, including being assisted by others), and 15 (a reiteration of the standing criteria in the Constitution).
[178] *Hoërskool* at paras. 25–26.
[179] Especially *Hoërskool* at para. 27.

relevant interests to be balanced by the courts. The Court deduced children's right to separate legal representation from a blending of domestic and international norms: the Constitution contained a right to legal representation paid for by the state if injustice would otherwise occur; the international standards recognised a right to participate through a representative (a lawyer or otherwise) in all matters affecting the child; and the Children's Act was sufficiently wide to accommodate a combination thereof: a right to participate through a legal representative. These standards were amalgamated with little distinction in terms of their legal status and each contributed something to clarifying the right at stake. The CRC was not used to interpret section 28(1)(h), the content of which is much narrower than that of article 12 and was not directly relevant to the case save to support, in principle, the idea that children can express their views through a representative. It does seem, therefore, that the CRC was used as an autonomous factor in the exercise of the courts' discretion. Section 8(1) of the Constitution covers situations where courts use the Bill of Rights interpreted with consideration of the CRC in the exercise of discretion, but not explicitly its autonomous use in guiding the exercise of judicial discretion.

Reliance on the CRC in the exercise of judicial discretion is arguably present in other cases. In *S v. P*,[180] the SCA endorsed a 10-year imprisonment sentence imposed on a grandfather for the rape of his grandson. The Court mentioned the CRC generically and stated that, in addition to the constitutional obligations to protect children against maltreatment, abuse, neglect, and degradation,

> in terms of our constitutional mandate to consider international law (see ss 231, 232, 233 and 234 of the Constitution), the United Nations Convention on the Rights of the Child, 1989, places an obligation on the Republic to eradicate violence against children.[181]

The relevant CRC provisions are not identified, and it is not clear if the Convention is used to interpret section 28(1)(d) or as an independent factor guiding sentencing discretion when sexual crimes are committed against children. Whether the Court would have invoked the CRC in the absence of a convergent constitutional provision is uncertain, but the wording of the judgment is open to be read as an autonomous use, *in addition to* rather than *as part of* the constitutional reasoning.

[180] 2000 (2) SA 656 (SCA) (*S v. P*).

[181] *S v. P* at para. 13.

Director of Public Prosecutions, KZN v. P[182] (*DPP v. P*) concerned the sentencing of a fourteen-year-old girl who, when aged twelve years and five months, instigated two persons to kill her grandmother. On appeal, the SCA overturned the sentence of the High Court (a postponement of the sentence for 36 months under correctional supervision) and imposed a suspended sentence coupled with correctional supervision. The SCA largely used the CRC and soft law instruments to stress their convergence with section 28(1)(g)[183] and their joint effect of widening the scope of sentencing to permit a court to use detention as a last resort and for the shortest appropriate time.[184] The Court remarked that article 37(b) was a 'replica' of section 28(1)(g), but then noted that article 40(1) promoted the child's dignity and worth in the sentencing process and the desirability of promoting the child's reintegration.[185] It is difficult to ascertain the purpose of relying on the CRC, which does not seem to be directly used in interpreting section 28(1)(g). Instead, it appears that together they informed the Court's exercise of sentencing discretion.[186]

In addition, there are cases discussed above where the CRC is used in the limitation enquiry under section 36 of the Constitution, rather than in the interpretation of the substance of rights.[187] *Geldenhuys* follows a limitation reasoning but does not formally rely on section 36. The implications of this type of use are analysed in the following part.

Thus, even in a legal system where the courts are well equipped to engage with the CRC, they have departed from the constitutional script. Links with the constitutional reception rules are not completely absent, but the techniques used constitute a different enough category to be highlighted as distinct and in need of further analysis – in this work but also more generally.

[182] [2006] 1 All SA 446 (SCA) (*DPP v. P*).

[183] *DPP v. P* at paras. 11, 15. In addition to the CRC, the Court also referred to the Beijing Rules: see at para. 16.

[184] *DPP v. P* at para. 18.

[185] It nonetheless considered that imprisonment was called for in this case, given the gravity of offence: *DPP v. P* at para. 22.

[186] See especially *DPP v. P* at para. 11, where the Court states: 'This issue [sentencing] must of course now be considered not only with reference to the so-called traditional approach to sentencing but also with due regard to the sentencing regime foreshadowed in section 28(1)(g) of the Constitution of the Republic of South Africa Act 1996 and international developments as reflected in, for instance, instruments issued under the aegis of the United Nations'.

[187] *Christian Education*, *CCL* and Skweyiya J's judgment in *C v. Department of Health.*

5.5 The Impact of Judicial Engagement with the CRC

5.5.1 *The Methods of Engagement: Formal and* Sui Generis

There is no doubt that South African courts have been receptive to the CRC, encouraged by a constitutional framework that requires them to consider the Convention alongside soft-law instruments, such as general comments of the Committee and other UN documents. Courts do not always give the CRC close attention, but – apart from Jafta J's rejection in *C v. Department of Health* – the legitimacy of reliance on the Convention has not been contested.

This may not necessarily indicate an unreserved embracing of the CRC. The Convention has generally been invoked to ends that are also supported by the Constitution. In some cases, the courts' openness to the CRC was not tested, with the state itself referring to the CRC to defend its legislation[188] or to support a solution consistent with the CRC even when that questioned the validity of domestic law.[189] Further, there are cases where the Convention has been glossed over or where it appears only in minority or separate judgments.[190] This inconsistent application of the Convention questions the commitment of the courts to the interpretive injunction in section 39(1)(b), but also raises the pragmatic question of a need to consider the CRC when it overlaps with the domestic standards or when domestic law and jurisprudence are more developed.

The wording of section 39(1)(b) compels courts to consider international law. The majority in *Glenister II* opined that this injunction applies regardless of the comprehensiveness of the domestic law.[191] In *Makwanyane*,[192] however, Mokgoro J pointed out that this injunction sought to provide interpretive assistance at a time when the domestic jurisprudence was underdeveloped. A pragmatic approach contiguous with the latter view may be reflected in some judgments, showing that if courts do not find the CRC useful, they lack the incentive to engage with it. As previous commentators have noted,[193] in socio-economic rights

188 See, for example, *Christian Education* (note 159) and *Fitzpatrick*.

189 In *Director of Public Prosecutions, YG v. S* [2017] ZAGPJHC 290, confirmed in *Freedom of Religion South Africa v. Minister of Justice and Constitutional Development* [2019] ZACC 34, the reasonable chastisement defence was declared unconstitutional.

190 For example, *C v. Department of Health* and *Le Roux*, where only Skweyiya J used the CRC.

191 *Glenister II* at para. 201 (Moseneke DCJ and Cameron J).

192 *S v. Makwanyane* 1995 (3) SA 391 (CC) (*Makwanyane*).

193 Rosa and Dutschke, 'Child Rights at the Core'; Stewart, 'The Grootboom Judgment'.

cases the Convention is little utilised. This may be because the domestic jurisprudence is, or is perceived to be, more developed. For example, in *Governing Body of the Juma Musjid Primary School v. Essay NO*[194] and *Pridwin Preparatory School*, the CRC is minimally or not at all used in relation to the right to education, arguably because the horizontal application of this right is little developed in a CRC context. By contrast, at other times, judges have engaged with the Convention when they found it 'helpful',[195] 'appealing',[196] able to act as 'a useful starting point',[197] or containing standards that 'are detailed and provide specific suggestions'.[198] Thus, the value that the CRC is perceived to be adding to the domestic law may be an incentive for its consideration by the courts.

Courts should articulate some guidance for a more predictable application of the CRC. The *Glenister II* approach is not inconsistent with a pragmatic approach, given the wide meaning of the phrase 'must consider' in section 39(1)(b). Arguably, the CRC must be considered whenever relevant, but if an overlap with the Constitution is established through a careful, as opposed to a casual, consideration of the Convention, limited attention to the latter should suffice. If differences (e.g., tensions, different wording or a different scope) are detected, closer attention should be given to its standards because the CRC is likely to be able to contribute something concrete to the reasoning (e.g., by serving as an analytical lens, proposing a new or different perspective, or influencing the content of the right).

Most judicial engagement with the CRC has occurred in the interpretation of section 28 under section 39(1)(b).[199] Despite the latter not requiring a consistent interpretation, one that is in harmony with the CRC is most often pursued – a process no doubt facilitated by the general convergence between the two sets of norms. In this way, aspects of the CRC become 'constitutionalised by proxy' through their influence on the interpretation of constitutional rights. This is a double gain for children's rights: first, the scope of section 28 has been enlarged through the cooptation of certain aspects of the CRC; and second, CRC aspects not explicitly covered by the letter of section 28 have been given

[194] 2011 (8) BCLR 761 (CC).
[195] *C v. Department of Health* at para. 32 (Skweyiya J).
[196] *Le Roux* at para. 211 (Skweyiya J).
[197] *Hoërskool* at para. 19.
[198] *Brandt* at para. 17.
[199] But see its use in *Ntshinghila* in the context of the right to a fair trial in section 35 of the Constitution.

constitutional protection. The clearest illustration is in cases such as *J v. NDPP* and *Pridwin Preparatory School*, where article 12 was used to give content to section 28(2)[200] and, in the process, it acquired constitutional protection.

No case acknowledges an explicit conflict between constitutional norms and the CRC,[201] although some courts have noted some differences between them. In *AD v. DW*, for example, Sachs J compared the paramountcy requirement in section 28(2) with the weaker formulation in article 3(1) ('a primary consideration') but reconciled them by noting that the CRC itself recognised the best interests as 'the' primary consideration in the adoption context.[202] In *Le Roux*, also relying on the difference in wording between section 28(2) and article 3(1), Skweyiya J made useful remarks in relation to treating the best interests of the child as a paramount consideration.[203] Reconciliation may not always be pursued, however. For example, in *Grootboom*,[204] Yacoob J refused to adopt the minimum core obligations concept in relation to socio-economic rights.[205] More recently, in *Raduvha v. Minister of Safety and Security*,[206] it was open to the Court to interpret section 28(1)(g) – child *detention* as a last resort – to include *arrest* (as a last resort), with reliance on article 37(b) of the CRC. Although the Court refused on the ground that detention and arrest are two distinct processes, it nonetheless interpreted *into* section 28(2) the requirement that a child's *arrest* be of last resort. The CRC played no explicit role in this process, although it is not excluded that it gave the Court a nudge to address the under-inclusiveness of section 28(1)(g).

The Constitutional Court and the SCA have not used the CRC autonomously to give statutes an interpretation consistent therewith under section 233, although the possibility is occasionally acknowledged.

200 Similar observations can, however, be made in relation to *Fitzpatrick*, which absorbed the subsidiarity principle into section 28(2), or Skweyiya J's position in *C v. Department of Health*, which absorbed aspects of article 9 (review of child removals) into section 28 (1)(b).

201 But see Jafta J (dissenting) in *C v. Department of Health*. The view is problematic because it is difficult, without more, simply to argue that an inconsistency exists when the Constitution has omitted things provided for in the CRC.

202 See the discussion in Section 5.4.2.

203 See the discussion in Section 5.4.2.

204 *Government of the Republic of South Africa v. Grootboom* 2001 (1) SA 46 (CC) (*Grootboom*).

205 *Grootboom* at paras. 30–33.

206 2016 (10) BCLR 1326 (CC) (*Raduvha*).

The interpretive influence of the CRC on statutes has been filtered through section 28, which the two courts have interpreted with reference to the Convention. This approach obscures the dual autonomous control over the interpretation of statutes, which can be exercised through the Constitution and the CRC respectively. These control processes are technically distinct and not identical as to their outcome. Thus, possible tensions may appear within this dual control space. So far, inconsistency with the CRC equated to constitutional inconsistency, but this cannot be taken for granted. The mechanics of this dual control have not yet been clarified, and the dexterity with which courts interpret domestic statutes in line with the Constitution under section 39(2) makes it unlikely that they will, without more, routinely engage with the CRC under section 233.

It is not clear why the Constitutional Court and the SCA have not applied the CRC under section 233, but this is unlikely to have been caused by reservations in relation to an autonomous use of the CRC. Cases that reach these highest courts possibly raise the constitutionality of a statute for which, prima facie, section 233 is irrelevant. This section is also ineffective when the Parliament deliberately legislates against the CRC. This is illustrated by the tandem cases of *Brandt* and *CCL*. In *Brandt*, the SCA read down the minimum sentencing provisions in light of the Constitution interpreted with reference to the CRC. The *Brandt* interpretation was subsequently reversed through legislation. Consequently, the courts were no longer able to rely on the CRC to interpret the amended legislation under section 233 because the will of the Parliament was clearly opposed to the CRC. Thus, the only option left to the Constitutional Court to use the CRC was under section 39(1)(b), which it did by striking down the new legislation as inconsistent with the Constitution, interpreted upon considering the CRC. Thus, it is apposite to see sections 39(1)(b) and 233 as part of a web of legal support for the CRC, where engagement mechanisms act as mutual safety nets.

Reliance on section 233 can be boosted if litigants argue that interpreting a statute in line with the CRC avoids constitutional invalidation. The latter may be a sound litigation strategy because the courts are bound to give statutes a meaning that does not conflict with the Constitution, to the extent reasonably possible. It can be argued that if the spirit of the CRC is respected, the exact procedural avenue used – under section 39(2) or section 233 – is of little consequence. Litigants will likely rely on whatever mechanism is more likely to deliver a successful outcome, as they have little interest in what may ultimately be an academic endeavour to stimulate the use of an underdeveloped constitutional provision. Nonetheless, section 233 should be kept alive as a mechanism to give effect to the CRC because it is difficult to anticipate all the issues that arise from its interaction with the domestic law and thus to predict the ways in which the Convention can be utilised most effectively.

Similar underutilisation with section 233 is experienced by section 231(4), which leaves unutilised perhaps the furthest-reaching constitutional tool to give effect to the CRC – namely, self-execution. This was a lost opportunity, especially when lacunae existed in the domestic law prior to the enactment of the Children's Act and the Child Justice Act.[207] Nonetheless, judges have used language that resonates with direct application. In *C v. Department of Health,* Skweyiya J stated that article 9 of the CRC 'sets the specific requirements in respect of the removal of children from their families',[208] and that the effect of the removal must be mitigated as required by the CRC.[209] In *J v. NDPP*, Skweyiya ADCJ noted that article 12 'obliges state parties' to ensure child participation and that General Comment No. 12 requires child participation throughout the juvenile justice process.[210] These are *international state obligations*, but Justice Skweyiya makes them appear domestically binding.[211] In *F v. F*, the Court sourced the right of the child to be heard in a custody battle to article 12 of the CRC.[212] The use of such strong normative language places the CRC in a 'relationship of authority'[213] with the domestic law, which arguably goes beyond a typical constitutional interpretation and borders on direct application if not supremacy. The intensity of the CRC influence in some cases and the amalgamation of its norms with constitutional or statutory norms without questioning the former's domestic status may indicate a de facto direct application of the Convention.

207 See, for example, the principle of subsidiarity in intercountry adoptions in cases such as *Fitzpatrick* and *AD v. DW*, as well as child participation.

208 *C v. Department of Health* at para. 32 (Skweyiya J).

209 *C v. Department of Health* at para. 34.

210 *J v. NDPP* at para. 40, fn 45.

211 Similar is *R v. H*, discussed in Section 5.4.1.

212 See Section 5.4.1. Notably, this case precedes the Children's Act and the precedents where courts have interpreted the right to be heard into section 28(2).

213 The expression used by Tuovinen in a comment on *Glenister II*: Tuovinen, 'The Role of International Law', 663.

All these factors may validate Sloth-Nielsen and Kruuse's view that South Africa 'has crossed the invisible line from dualism to monism'[214] in relation to the rights of children. While the CRC has sometimes had a profound effect, this may be reading too much into the judgments and indirectly suggesting a children's rights exceptionalism – a surreptitious and unprecedented judicial acceptance of the self-execution of *one* treaty *only*. The deliberate avoidance of engaging with the potentially taxing requirements in section 231(4) is hardly worth celebrating when the courts knowingly walk a tightrope between direct application and interpretation while they claim to guard against incorporating international standards 'by the back door'.[215] To the extent that the courts do not engage with section 231(4) when seeking to give direct effect to the CRC, they are incorrect and do not create good law. De facto direct application may promote the CRC but does not result in legal principles cemented in binding precedent that cannot be easily displaced.

Worth remembering is that even if a provision is declared self-executing, it does not benefit from the highly prized legal status enjoyed by similar norms in France (i.e., directly applicable and also prevailing over domestic law). The legal status bestowed on self-executing international norms in South Africa is under-constitutional and under-statutory, which gives these provisions a legal clout that is considerably weaker than what they enjoy as interpretive aids under section 39(1)(b). However, a CRC norm recognised as self-executing would, as a *whole*, be part of the domestic law, while the interpretation process under section 39(1)(b) leads to an à la carte co-optation into the domestic law of only those aspects of a CRC norm relevant to a particular case.

The reasons for overlooking self-execution are a matter of speculation and are most likely contextual rather than connected to a mistrust of the legal qualities of the CRC of the kind experienced in France. In some cases, courts may have lacked an incentive to do so because an alternative reasoning was available. As Killander also noted, the difficulties of self-execution are likely to push the courts towards using international treaties under sections 39 and 233.[216] In most cases, the Convention

[214] Sloth-Nielsen and Kruuse, 'A Maturing Manifesto', 671. Skelton also advances the idea that, in some cases (*CCL* and *J v. NDPP*), the Constitutional Court has applied the CRC directly: Skelton, 'Child Justice', 414.

[215] *Glenister II* at para. 112 (Ngcobo CJ) and the position of Jafta J in *C v. Department of Health*.

[216] Killander, 'Judicial Immunity'.

was applied alongside a supporting constitutional provision that made possible the link with section 39(1)(b). In *Fitzpatrick*, for example, the wide interpretation given by the Court to section 28(2) absorbed the principle of subsidiarity and alleviated the need to decide on its self-execution. Where there was some overlap with the Constitution, the CRC made only small (yet important) contributions to defining the normative power of constitutional norms. Thus, when the CRC only complemented the Constitution, a wholesale importation of a Convention provision through a taxing self-execution enquiry may not have been advisable. Pragmatic reasons may also be at play. In *AD v. DW*, for example, a self-execution argument in relation to the subsidiarity principle was not made. Further, self-execution may have been questionable because the SCA highlighted a possible tension between the principle of subsidiarity in the CRC (appearing to favour a collective best interests of children) and the focus on the best interests of the individual child under section 28(2) as interpreted in *Fitzpatrick*. Lastly, the impending entry into force of the Children's Act, which introduced the principle into the domestic law, made unnecessary a likely complicated discussion of self-execution.

It can therefore be said that self-execution has played no explicit role in giving effect to the CRC, albeit some cases may reflect de facto self-execution. Legal clarity would be welcome in relevant cases and – although it is unlikely that self-execution will have a major contribution to giving domestic effect to the CRC in the context of comprehensive legislative reform and a generously interpreted section 28 of the Constitution – opportunities for its use should not be foreclosed.

The methods of engagement explicitly authorised by the Constitution do not fully capture how the courts relate to the CRC, giving rise to instances of *sui generis* engagement. Such instances are not a cohesive or coherent category. Their identification is not infallible and is brought about not by the clarity with which such methods are reflected in judgments, but by the analytical challenges experienced when trying to fit them into the formal engagement framework. The *sui generis* methods are embryonic and uncertain as to their actual existence, legitimacy, normative boundaries, and potential to give domestic effect to the CRC.

One of the reasons that drew this author's attention to *sui generis* methods is the difficulty of identifying the method of engagement when courts omit reference to the constitutional provisions that justified their consideration of the CRC.[217] In some cases, the grounds for engagement can be implied, but this is difficult in other cases.[218] By omitting the enabling constitutional provision, courts avoid self-reflection (and outside scrutiny) in relation to the operation they perform – namely, whether they engage in constitutional or statutory interpretation, or something else. They also create analytical difficulties by inhibiting the identification and conceptualisation of innovative ways to engage with the CRC and debate their constitutional legitimacy.

Another reason that prompted attention to *sui generis* methods is that courts have extended the interpretation process beyond defining the content of the constitutional rights concerned, which is the typical use of international law for interpretation purposes. This 'interpretation beyond substance' has occurred in at least three ways. First is the use of the CRC as a reference framework[219] for the assessment of domestic law. In *Christian Education*[220] and *Geldenhuys*, for example, the courts affirmed the constitutional validity of two statutes by referring in parallel and seemingly autonomously to constitutional and international obligations, including those arising from the CRC. Judges have also pointed out that the CRC has become 'an international standard against which to measure legislation and policies',[221] or an 'international benchmark against which legislation and policies can be measured'.[222] The second method of interpretation beyond substance appears when courts rely on the CRC to guide their judicial discretion, as happened in cases concerning the disclosure of documents during litigation[223] and sentencing (of child offenders or of adults whose victims are children).[224] The third method is using the CRC in limitation analyses under section 36 in relation to children's rights or the rights of others. Examples include *Geldenhuys*, *CCL*, Skweyiya J's approach in *C v. Department of Health*, and *Christian Education*. In *Christian Education*, the Court decided that statutory provisions that prohibited corporal punishment in independent schools at the behest of the parents justifiably limited the parents' religious rights in order to protect the dignity and physical integrity of the

[217] *Hoërskool*; *Brandt*; *DPP v. P*; *M v. S* (in some aspects of reasoning); *J v. NDPP*.
[218] *Ntshinghila*; *S v. P*; *J v. NDPP*.
[219] Also noted by Sloth-Nielsen and Mezmur, '2 + 2 = 5?', 27.
[220] *Christian Education South Africa v. Minister of Education* 2000 (10) BCLR 1051 (CC).
[221] *M v. S* at para. 16 (Sachs J).
[222] *Brandt* at para. 17 (footnote omitted).
[223] *Ntshinghila*; *Hoërskool*. See Section 5.4.4.
[224] *DPP v. P*; *S v. P*. See Section 5.4.4.

children. Children's rights are addressed only when the Court assessed whether the interference with parental rights was justifiable. The Court accepted as a legitimate purpose of, inter alia, interfering with parental rights the state's compliance with its international obligations to protect children against violence including under articles 4, 19, and 34 of the CRC.[225] The Court's reference to the CRC is limited to acknowledging the protective obligations above.

How do these *sui generis* methods fare in relation to the formal engagement framework spelled out in the Constitution? It is not clear where the 'reference framework' usage fits therein because although it resembles interpretation, it is arguably distinct. The interpretation process requires that the interpreted norm and the interpretive aid are identified, but in some cases the courts do not identify a specific constitutional provision that they interpret in light of a specific CRC provision. The absence of an ambiguity requirement as a justification for considering international law under the generous section 39(1)(b) may have facilitated the development of this method. An ambiguity requirement would normally channel the courts towards identifying the ambiguity they seek to clarify, but, in its absence, courts do not always spell out the aspects of the rights they interpret with reliance on the CRC. An example is *M v. S*, where the Court relied on the CRC not to interpret an identified constitutional provision but rather to distil therefrom the right to be treated as a child and thus differently from adults. This resonates with Sachs J's view in *Coetzee*, which enjoined recourse to international instruments 'with a view to finding principles rather than to extracting rigid formulae, and to look for rationales rather than rules'.[226]

It is also uncertain how using the CRC as a reference framework articulates with *AZAPO*,[227] which affirms that the constitutionality assessment is conducted against the Constitution and not international instruments. It remains puzzling that courts amalgamate international obligations and domestic law, bypassing explanations about how (or whether) an international obligation is brought down into the domestic sphere to serve a domestic purpose. Made in a safe space where law and precedent are largely consistent with the Convention, such statements do not seem to have been controversial, but questions linger about how the

[225] *Christian Education* at fn 44.

[226] *Coetzee* at para. 57.

[227] *Azanian Peoples Organization (AZAPO) v. President of the Republic of South Africa* 1996 (8) BCLR 1015.

courts will handle situations where domestic law appears consistent with the Constitution but not with the CRC.[228] One can only hope that the courts will not turn their back to the CRC, as the majority of the Constitutional Court did in *Le Roux*.

The other two 'beyond substance' interpretation techniques have a stronger constitutional footing. That footing is grounded in the idea that section 39(1)(b) of the Constitution mandates the consideration of international law in the interpretation of the *entire* Bill of Rights – substantive rights, as well as operative provisions concerning the application and limitation of rights (sections 7, 8, and 36 of the Constitution). Thus, courts can justify reliance on the CRC in the exercise of judicial discretion because section 8(1) – the exercise of judicial function in conformity with the Bill of Rights – as part of the Bill of Rights can legitimately be interpreted in light of the CRC under section 39(1)(b). Further, section 36 is also part of the Bill of Rights and thus can be interpreted upon considering the CRC on the same grounds.

The use of treaties to interpret operative provisions in the Constitution has not yet received a great deal of attention and raises some questions. It remains to be determined to what extent such interpretive operations differ materially from the interpretation of substantive rights, but some issues can be highlighted. It may be that they place the CRC too closely to directly controlling the exercise of judicial power, which is antithetical to the primarily dualist approach to treaties reflected in the Constitution. This was contentious in *Glenister II*, where the majority interpreted the *domestic* human rights obligations of state organs, rather than the content of the rights themselves, in accordance with international treaties. However, the distinction between the majority and minority judgments concerned not the legitimacy of the use of international law to interpret operative provisions of the Bill of Rights, which was agreed to by all judges,[229] but the intensity of its influence in the majority judgment.[230]

[228] Such cases cannot be excluded. For example, virginity testing is condemned by the CRC Committee as contrary to the Convention (CRC Committee, *Concluding observations: South Africa*, 2016, paras. 39–40), but the practice is recognised (with limits and safeguards) in section 12 of the Children's Act.

[229] *Glenister II* at paras. 193–194 (Moseneke DCJ and Cameron J); 106 (Ngcobo CJ).

[230] Bishop and Brickhill point out that the majority and the minority differ in relation to the '*intensity* of the interpretive influence of international law': this is 'great' for the majority, but less so for the minority: Bishop and Brickhill, 'Constitutional Law', 236 (emphasis in original).

It can also raise concerns that courts seek to extend their power by expanding on the constitutionally recognised engagement methods. When the CRC is used in the exercise of judicial discretion or in a limitation enquiry, technically, it is not used to elucidate the meaning of sections 8 and 36 but rather to guide their application. The depth of engagement with the CRC may vary, depending on the purpose of its use. For example, under section 36, attention to the CRC could legitimately be limited to pointing out that to give it effect is a legitimate aim that may justify a limitation of rights. However, using the CRC to interpret a substantive right, especially when the development of the domestic law is envisaged, may require a more in-depth examination of the Convention.[231]

It is fair to say that the *sui generis* uses of the CRC retain sufficient proximity to the constitutionally recognised engagement methods so as not to undermine their legitimacy. Such proximity is facilitated by the wide scope of section 39(1)(b), which makes it unlikely that they will be recognised anytime soon as distinct methods of engagement with the Convention. Be that as it may, the difficulty of conceptualising these categories calls, at a minimum, for a diversification of how we understand the interpretive enterprise that involves the CRC. The CRC has been used for purposes such as to define the scope, content, and limits of rights, and to inform the exercise of judicial power. Highlighting this multi-layered interpretation process should prompt attention to possible differences in the interpretation process depending on the purpose for which the Convention is used.

To conclude, the highest South African courts have clearly engaged with the CRC, although it is not always clear *how* they utilise the constitutional framework that legitimises their recourse to the Convention. Paradoxically, the formal reception framework is concomitantly underutilised, in that self-execution is overlooked and section 233 is seldom relied on, and insufficient to capture the courts' relationship with the CRC as the courts give effect to the Convention in ways that go beyond the formal framework and require further conceptualisation.

5.5.2 *What Did Reliance on the CRC Achieve?*

The South African legal framework accommodates impact of different degrees, from self-execution to a benign 'consideration' and consistent

[231] Good examples are Skweyiya J in *C v. Department of Health* and Khampepe J in *Pridwin Preparatory School.*

statutory interpretation. Overall, the CRC has not revolutionised domestic adjudication, but its consistent presence and weaving into judgments have contributed to the development of domestic children's rights jurisprudence. As a high-impact method of engagement, explicit self-execution has had no impact, and much the same can be said about CRC-consistent statutory interpretation – at least in the case law of the courts discussed here. Most significant effects have occurred under the interpretive injunction in section 39(1)(b), which mandates the consideration of the CRC in the interpretation of the Bill of Rights. As indicated previously, although that section does not mandate a constitutional interpretation consistent with the CRC, the courts have preferred interpretations that are in harmony with it.

The Constitutional Court and the SCA mention the Convention often, but they seldom analyse its content in detail. As indicated in Chapter 1, this work has sought to base its analysis on cases where there is meaningful engagement with the CRC. Such engagement exists when the Convention is used with a purpose, and its content and domestic implications are carefully thought out, even if the CRC is not followed. In most cases, courts favour a constitutional interpretation that is consistent with the CRC. The only contrary example is in *C v. Department of Health*, where Jafta J refused to follow the Convention because of its unincorporated status. Ironically, Jafta J's engagement with the CRC, despite its shortcomings, is more meaningful than its use in cases where it is paid lip service.

The South African case law shows that meaningful engagement need not be lengthy to be effective. The key to this effectiveness is for the courts to extract from the CRC what is necessary or useful in the context, if they respect the normative integrity of the Convention. *DPP Transvaal* is an example of effective use, wherein Ngcobo J selected from the rich normative content of article 3(1) its explicit recognition of the role of the courts in safeguarding the best interests of the child. Additionally, in *Hoërskool*, the SCA relied on aspects of article 12 that supported child participation in proceedings through a representative, while, in *Pridwin Preparatory School*, Khampepe J relied on the same article to support direct child participation. The courts have thus selected what they needed from the CRC and then grafted it onto a structure built of domestic legal bricks. This does not diminish the value of the CRC because, as courts operate in the domestic legal space, their reasoning is inevitably dominated by domestic law.

One form of effective engagement has been, perhaps counter-intuitively, identifying the *differences* between section 28 and the CRC.

Much of the South African CRC jurisprudence is built around the overall alignment between section 28 and the CRC, which no doubt has contributed to the openness of the courts towards the latter. However, their similarities do not exclude certain differences and, to the extent that they do not amount to a conflict that is irreconcilable through interpretation, these differences are important for prompting constitutional interpretations that enhance the protection of children's rights. For example, in *M v. S*, Sachs J implied a stronger domestic protection upon noting the distinction between the 'paramount consideration' under section 28(2) and 'a primary consideration' under article 3(1).[232] In *Le Roux*, differences between the wording of section 28(2) and article 3(1) prompted Skweyiya J to combine the two and develop some practical guidance on the application of the former when the interests of children conflict with other legitimate interests. Arguably, in identifying differences, the courts have used the CRC as a reference framework – one that does not determine the validity of the law (which is constitutionally impermissible) but enables the courts to imagine an interpretation that they might not have reached by considering exclusively the domestic law.

Cases where the engagement with the CRC is quantitatively limited should not be easily dismissed as irrelevant for assessing its domestic effect because forensic measurements may not always give an accurate picture of impact. In *M v. S*, Sachs J did not discuss the CRC extensively; only one article is mentioned and there are inaccuracies in the reference to the 'four great principles of the CRC'.[233] The Convention is then approached as an overarching standard that is irreducible to the mathematical sum of its articles, and the philosophy of which is reflected in section 28. The normative value of specific CRC provisions is muted in favour of the general tenor of the Convention, as distilled from its principles. Sachs J's 'right to childhood'[234] is then crafted with support from the spirit of the general principles of the CRC.[235]

[232] *M v. S* at para. 25 (also fn 31).

[233] Sachs J identifies the four CRC principles (survival, development, protection, and participation) in the work of the South African Law Commission (*The Review of the Child Care Act: First Issue Paper* (Project 110, 18 April 1998) para. 2.1), rather than that of the CRC Committee, according to which the principles are non-discrimination, the best interests of the child, the right to survival and development, and the right to be heard.

[234] *M v. S* at para. 19 (Sachs J).

[235] *M v. S* at paras. 18–20 (Sachs J).

Courts may consider a cursory attention to the Convention sufficient, given its use to support positions that are grounded primarily in constitutional provisions. This 'additional ballast'[236] approach to engaging with the Convention prevents a clear distinction between its independent effect and that of the Constitution.[237] The independent impact of the CRC can sometimes be ascertained by comparing majority and minority judgments. In *De Gree*, for example, the principle of subsidiarity in the CRC and the 1993 Hague Convention prompted a majority of the SCA to consider the best interests of children as a class, an aspect overlooked by minority judges who focused exclusively on the interests of the individual child.[238] In *C v. Department of Health*, Skweyiya J developed the content of a right seldom applied by the Constitutional Court – the right to parental care in section 28(1)(b) – by relying on articles 7–9 of the CRC, which was eschewed by Yacoob J (in the majority), whose judgment focused only on the Constitution. In *Pridwin Preparatory School*, Khampepe J's close consideration of article 12 and General Comment No. 12 of the CRC Committee enabled her to support the primacy of children's direct/own participation in matters affecting them. This went beyond Theron J's majority judgment, which equated the procedural aspect of section 28(2) with procedural fairness (i.e., representations on children's best interests, regardless of who makes them). Thus, engagement with the CRC can bring to the decision-making considerations that are otherwise overlooked, generating child-friendly developments in the domestic law.

The similarity between the constitutional and CRC standards questions the value of engaging with the latter when the same outcome can be obtained by simply applying the Constitution. There are constitutional judgments that are clearly advancing the rights of children in which the CRC was not even mentioned.[239] Nonetheless, two arguments support a consistent consideration of the CRC.

236 Sloth-Nielsen and Mezmur, '2 + 2 = 5?', 27.

237 See similarly Skelton, 'Child Justice', 401.

238 Compare, for example, *De Gree* at para. 33 (Heher JA) and at paras. 13, 17 (Theron AJA).

239 For example, *MEC for Education: Kwazulu-Natal v. Pillay* 2008 (1) SA 474 (CC) (religious and cultural rights of children in schools); *Minister of Health v. Treatment Action Campaign* 2002 (10) BCLR 1033 (CC) (the right to access to health services by pregnant women and their newborn babies to prevent the transmission of HIV); *Khosa v. Minister of Social Development* 2004 (6) SA 505 (CC) (access to social grants by permanent residents and their children); and *Teddy Bear Clinic for Abused Children*

First, it must not be assumed that domestic and CRC standards overlap based on a perfunctory analysis of their wording. Although comprehensive, the scope of section 28 pales in comparison with the gamut of Convention provisions. This is implicitly acknowledged by courts that refer to the CRC when needed detail is absent from section 28. For example, in *DPP v. P*, the court referred to article 40 to stress the importance of rehabilitation and social reintegration in sentencing children. In *C v. Department of Health*, Skweyiya J referred to the CRC to determine the legal parameters for the separation of children from their parents. A clear illustration is provided in *Raduvha*. When comparing section 28(1)(g) of the Constitution with article 37(b) of the CRC, a cursory analysis could conclude that both standards support detention (broadly defined) as a last resort. It took *Raduvha* to acknowledge that section 28(1)(g) was under-inclusive because it did not refer to 'arrest as a last resort' and for the Court to fill the gap by reading this requirement into the best interests of the child in section 28(2). There must, therefore, be alertness to gaps in protection and inconsistencies with the CRC in the domestic law, some of which are difficult to anticipate in the abstract and may only be discovered when a relevant case arises. The expanding jurisprudence (domestic and international) on the rights of children requires an ongoing appraisal of the relationship between the Convention and the domestic law. International and domestic children's rights jurisprudence is dynamic. It is likely that some differences will always exist between them, which, if capitalised on, could prompt progressive developments in children's rights.

A second reason for a consistent engagement by courts with the CRC is that identifying differences with the domestic law is essential for revealing the unique contribution the Convention can make to the judicial reasoning, or its added value.

Effective engagement with the CRC has often resulted in ascertainable positive consequences. Thus, the CRC has helped courts justify a differential legal treatment for children when compared to adults,[240] or confirm the constitutionality of legislation restricting the rights of adults in order to protect children.[241] The Convention has occasionally been relied

v. Minister of Justice and Constitutional Development 2014 (2) SA 168 (CC) (the constitutional validity of legislation that criminalised consensual sexual penetration and other non-penetrative forms of sexual interaction between children aged 12–16).

240 *Brandt*; *J v. NDPP*; *Le Roux* per Skweyiya J.

241 *Christian Education*; *Geldenhuys*.

on to fill gaps in the domestic law. In *Fitzpatrick* and *AD v. DW*, the courts interpreted section 28(2) of the Constitution to include considerations that informed the subsidiarity principle in the CRC (and the 1993 Hague Convention) as it applies to intercountry adoptions. In *J v. NDPP* and *Pridwin Preparatory School*, judges have relied on article 12 to interpret section 28(2) in a way that requires the views of the affected children to be considered. In *C v. Department of Health*, Skweyiya J developed the sparse content of section 28(1)(b) by relying on the CRC and established a hierarchy of forms of care and legal parameters for the lawfulness of separation of children from their families.

The judicial consideration of the CRC has not revolutionised the domestic law, but, through smaller or larger contributions and a steady presence, it has assisted in its development by revealing problems with the domestic framework, by assisting with discovering domestic norms that can address those problems, or by guiding the development of the law. In many cases, the incentive for the application of the CRC has been the courts considering it to be useful. Article 12 cases are perhaps the best illustration, as the CRC responded clearly and precisely to the absence of constitutional recognition for the right to be heard. At the opposite end is the absence or limited consideration of the CRC in socio-economic rights cases, wherein the domestic jurisprudence is arguably better developed. This suggests the need for a conscious effort to identify the added value of the CRC, both generally and in specific cases. In a legal system that is well endowed with a progressive Constitution and comprehensive child-related statutes and case law, the sustainability of the use of the CRC may depend on persuading the courts of its continued value.

Whether judicial engagement with the CRC amounts to a *significant* impact on the South African law may be a matter of contention and, perhaps, subjective evaluation. Doubts about the intensity of impact aside, the CRC has clearly influenced judicial reasoning. Sometimes, its influence has been subtle and diffuse, or difficult to conceptualise. However, mere coexistence of the CRC with child-friendly outcomes in specific judgments does not prove its impact. Identifying the independent effect of the CRC may be difficult if the task is approached in a syllogistic fashion because, inter alia, the influence of the Convention cannot be explained solely through micro-analysis.[242] Arguably, the CRC has also exercised 'less tangible'[243] influences, including by 'changing hearts and

[242] That is, by looking at individual cases: Sloth-Nielsen and Mezmur, '2 + 2 = 5?', 27.
[243] Sloth-Nielsen, 'The Role', 79.

minds over time'.[244] Despite their nebulous normative significance, these less tangible influences strengthen the legitimacy of the CRC presence in the judicial discourse. They show that the Convention 'has become an essential frame of reference in the South African legal system'.[245] While in concrete cases the impact of the CRC may seem minimal, its acceptance by the judiciary suggests that it has a well-established place in judicial reasoning. Although the Convention appears at times as a set of norms 'in abeyance', courts know that it is available to prevent a straying from the values it protects.

5.6 Conclusion

As a hybrid legal system, South African law offers the courts a range of methods of engaging with the CRC. However, the monist method of self-execution is absent in the case law, with the heavy lifting being done by the indirect application of the CRC primarily as a constitutional interpretation tool. The largely uncontested and successful indirect application of the Convention in South Africa is the result of a favourable reception framework. The framework is dominated by an enabling Constitution, which contains a children's rights section and several provisions that enjoin the judiciary to consider the CRC, but also contains comprehensive child justice and child protection statutes – both giving effect to the CRC. This strong reception framework sends a message of political commitment to Convention values and signals to the courts that giving effect to the CRC aligns with the political will. Regardless, meaningful engagement with the CRC is not consistent and the case law is dominated by courts using it to interpret the children's rights clause in the Constitution. Paradoxically, while sidelining other constitutionally endorsed engagement methods, courts have applied the CRC in *sui generis* ways, which, although not completely detached from the formal constitutional framework, are sufficiently distinct to note.

The use of the CRC alongside section 28 of the Constitution makes it difficult to discern its independent impact in specific cases. No major overhaul of domestic jurisprudence can be unreservedly associated with the application of the CRC in individual cases, and, in some of the

244 Sloth-Nielsen, 'The Role', 79. In a similar vein is Skelton's observation that the *Teddy Bear Clinic* judgment 'is arguably imbued' with the principles derived from, inter alia, the CRC, despite the judgment not referring to it: Skelton, 'Child Justice', 410.

245 Sloth-Nielsen and Mezmur, '2 + 2 = 5?', 27.

leading children's rights cases, its impact has been limited. Overall, the engagement with the CRC is not extensive, but, as this chapter demonstrates, what matters is an effective engagement in which the relevant aspects of the CRC are considered for a specific purpose, as required by the case at hand. Meaningful engagement with the CRC has contributed to the development of the domestic law by justifying, orienting, or facilitating the development of the law in a child-focused direction.

Underpinning the impact of the CRC on the judicial reasoning in South Africa is the overall compatibility between the CRC and the domestic law, combined with the capacity and willingness of the courts to find relevant distinctions between the two sets of norms, which then enables them to move beyond what is achievable exclusively under the domestic framework. Ultimately, the South African case study shows that the CRC continues to have a meaningful role, even in a legal system in which children's rights and relevant case law are well developed, and that its added value evolves as the domestic and international jurisprudence develops.

6

The United Kingdom

6.1 Introduction

The United Kingdom of Great Britain and Northern Ireland (UK) ratified the CRC in 1991[1] and has not incorporated it domestically, which means that the courts can apply the Convention only indirectly. The UK experience of judicial application of the CRC is relevant to this project for several reasons.

The UK case law shows that even in the absence of full legislative incorporation in a dualist, multi-jurisdictional legal system, opportunities exist to give judicial effect to the CRC. It provides a counter-exemplar to the application of the CRC by the High Court of Australia, another dualist court that operates with similar rules of reception and within a similar legal tradition. The comparison strengthens one of the arguments made in this book: that, alongside the formal rules of reception, the structure of reception plays an important role in whether and how domestic courts engage with the CRC. As illustrated in the UK study, a legislative framework that is protective of human rights, boosted by membership to a regional system of human rights protection, facilitates the application of the CRC by domestic courts. Further, like the South African cases, the UK cases prompt attention to the overlap between the CRC and other normative frameworks, and its implications for the sustainability of judicial engagement with the Convention. The UK case study strengthens the argument for a more consistent application of the CRC unmediated by other domestic or international instruments and for uncovering the added value of the CRC for each judicial system.

The UK has a common law legal system with an unwritten constitution. Since 1999, the legislative power has been shared between

[1] The UK signed the CRC on 19 April 1990 and ratified it on 16 December 1991, 'Ratification Status for CRC: Convention on the Rights of the Child', *UN Treaty Body Database*, https://tbinternet.ohchr.org/_layouts/15/TreatyBodyExternal/Treaty.aspx?Treaty=CRC&Lang=en.

the devolved jurisdictions (Wales, Scotland, and Northern Ireland) and the Union (the central UK government).[2] Legislation made by devolved parliaments must fall within their devolved powers and must be in conformity with the ECHR.[3] By contrast, the central UK Parliament may pass laws contrary to the ECHR on account of its sovereignty. The UK was a member of the European Union, with all the consequences that membership entails, until 31 January 2020.[4] It remains a party to the ECHR (which it ratified in 1950), the rights of which it incorporated into the Human Rights Act 1998 (HRA) (effective October 2000).

The highest domestic court in all matters (including constitutional issues) is the Supreme Court, which replaced the House of Lords as the judicial apex in 2009. The case law of both courts is considered in this chapter.

The chapter is structured as follows. The next two sections describe the relationship between international treaties and the CRC, on the one hand, and the UK law, on the other. They are followed by presentations of the cases in which the two courts have engaged with the CRC through the traditional methods of engagement (Section 6.4), the HRA-created methods (Section 6.5), and *sui generis* methods (Section 6.6). The analysis and conclusion follow thereafter.

6.2 The International Treaties and the UK Law

The UK takes a 'fundamentally dualist view'[5] of the relationship between domestic and international law. Treaties ratified by the executive become part of the domestic law only through legislation passed by the UK Parliament or devolved legislatures acting within their devolved powers, or through reception by judges into the common law.[6] This dualism is a

[2] David Hoffman and John Rowe, *Human Rights in the UK: An Introduction to the Human Rights Act 1998*, 4th ed. (Harlow: Pearson, 2013) 50.

[3] Jane Williams, 'England and Wales' in Ton Liefaard and Jaap E. Doek (eds.), *Litigating the Rights of the Child: The UN Convention on the Rights of the Child in Domestic and International Jurisprudence* (Dordrecht: Springer, 2015) 53–54. Hoffman and Rowe, *Human Rights in the UK*, 50.

[4] See European Union (Withdrawal) Act 2018.

[5] Jonathan Mance, 'International Law in the UK Supreme Court' (speech, King's College, London, 13 February 2017) 1, www.supremecourt.uk/news/speeches.html.

[6] See generally Anthony Aust, 'United Kingdom' in David Sloss (ed.), *The Role of Domestic Courts in Treaty Enforcement: A Comparative Study* (New York: Cambridge University Press, 2009) 476; Shaheed Fatima, *Using International Law in Domestic Courts* (Oxford: Hart Publishing, 2005); Malcolm N. Shaw, *International Law*, 8th ed. (Cambridge: Cambridge University Press, 2017) 105–119.

consequence of the separation of powers: ratified treaties are not directly applicable because this would endorse law-making by the executive.[7] Consequently, unincorporated treaties cannot prevail over statutes, and breaches of treaty obligations unincorporated in the UK have no domestic consequences.[8] The ECHR has a privileged status in that, unlike other human rights treaties, its rights have been domestically incorporated through the HRA. As discussed in Section 6.5, the HRA has played an important facilitating role in the application of the CRC.

The principles that inform the relationship between unincorporated international treaties, such as the CRC, and the UK law are the principle of non-justiciability (i.e., matters under the prerogative of the Crown cannot be litigated) and the principle of the absence of direct effect (i.e., an unincorporated treaty cannot by itself create enforceable domestic rights or deprive individuals of existing rights).[9] Unincorporated treaties can, however, be used in the interpretation of domestic legislation or in the development of the common law.[10]

In relation to statutory interpretation, a presumption of compatibility with international treaties operates, enabling judges to interpret ambiguities in legislation to avoid a breach of obligations under international treaties.[11] The presumption can be displaced by clear statutory words.[12] Ambiguity is defined generously and is deemed to exist when legislation is reasonably capable of a meaning compatible with a treaty.[13] In the absence of ambiguity, courts must give effect to domestic legislation even if it is contrary to international treaty obligations.[14] As discussed in Section 6.5, more generous interpretation rules apply in relation to the ECHR. With regard to the common law, unincorporated treaties have been used to resolve its uncertainties, to develop it in new directions, or to cause its reappraisal.[15]

7 Shaw, *International Law*, 113.

8 James Crawford, *Brownlie's Principles of Public International Law*, 9th ed. (Oxford: Oxford University Press, 2019) 60.

9 Fatima, *Using International Law*, 8.8; Crawford, *Brownlie's Principles*, 60, 68; Shaw, *International Law*, 114.

10 Treaties may also inform the exercise of discretion by executive and courts: Fatima, *Using International Law*, 11.4.2; Mance, 'International Law', 4–5. More controversially, treaties may form the basis of a legitimate expectation.

11 Fatima, *Using International Law*, 9.2.

12 Fatima, *Using International Law*, 9.15.

13 Fatima, *Using International Law*, 9.14; Shaw, *International Law*, 116.

14 Shaw, *International Law*, 116.

15 Fatima, *Using International Law*, 10.1, 10.6.

Beyond these traditional and well-accepted modes of interaction, UK authors have identified a 'hazily defined – and ever expanding – penumbra where unincorporated treaties are used freely and creatively subject to the restraining effect of the principles of non-justiciability and no direct effect'.[16] In that 'penumbra', unincorporated treaties may be used to interpret unambiguous legislation, to provide background and context for the operation of domestic law, or for comparison and analogy.[17] The penumbra is 'elusive and def[ies] rigid description', being 'marked with both creativity and common sense'.[18]

With this context in mind, the discussion moves to the relationship between the CRC and the UK legal system.

6.3 The Status of the CRC in the UK Legal System

The Union has not fully incorporated the CRC, in a context of lack of political enthusiasm for a treaty that is perceived as aspirational[19] and a climate of negative public attitudes towards children, especially adolescents.[20] Consequently, the CRC does not create domestic children's rights and corresponding duties, although it may be applied by courts indirectly, as discussed above.[21] Williams has argued, however, that the existing judicial culture may permit an incremental absorption of the CRC into the domestic law.[22]

The UK law is broadly, although not entirely, aligned with the CRC.[23] The multilevel governance system in the UK has resulted in an

[16] Fatima, *Using International Law*, 9.4.

[17] Fatima, *Using International Law*, 9.4.

[18] Fatima, *Using International Law*, 9.18.

[19] Jane Fortin, *Children's Rights and the Developing Law*, 3rd ed. (Cambridge: Cambridge University Press, 2009) 50n128.

[20] CRC Committee, *Concluding Observations: United Kingdom of Great Britain and Northern Ireland*, 20 October 2008, CRC/C/GBR/CO/4, para. 24.

[21] For a judicial endorsement, see *R (on the application of SG (previously JS)) v. Secretary of State for Work and Pensions* [2015] UKSC 16 (*SG*) at para. 137 (Lord Hughes).

[22] Williams, 'England and Wales', 67.

[23] For example, the Children Act 1989 does not mention children's rights, focusing instead on the powers and duties of relevant institutions: Williams, 'England and Wales', 59. The paramountcy principle enshrined in section 1 of the Act extends only to decisions concerning the child's upbringing and property, rather than '*all* decisions concerning the child' under article 3(1). Further, according to the CRC Committee, there is insufficient attention to children's views in policymaking, the endorsement of reasonable corporal punishment at home, and a mental health legislation insufficiently protective of children's freedoms, to name but a few: CRC Committee, *Concluding Observations on*

'asymmetrical'[24] evolution of children's rights. Within the limits of their distinct devolved powers,[25] Wales and Scotland have been more pro-active than the Union government in giving legislative effect to the CRC.[26] Wales introduced a duty for administrative decision-makers to have due regard to CRC rights in the exercise of their functions,[27] but stopped short of incorporating the Convention. The Children and Young People (Scotland) Act 2014 introduced a similar statutory ministerial duty and, in March 2021, the Scottish Parliament went a step further and sought to incorporate the CRC into the Scottish law. The UK government challenged the validity of the incorporating Bill, and in October 2021, the Supreme Court decided that some of its provisions went beyond the powers of the Scottish Parliament.[28] The impugned Bill was thereafter adjusted, and in December 2023, the Scottish Parliament approved the United Nations Convention on the Rights of the Child (Incorporation) (Scotland) Bill, which became an Act on 16 January 2024.

The CRC can play an indirect role in the judicial review of devolved legislation, as it is beyond the power of devolved Parliaments to legislate contrary to the ECHR[29] – which is often interpreted with reliance on the Convention. Regrettably, only one case reflects this important role of the

the Fifth Periodic Report of the United Kingdom of Great Britain and Northern Ireland, 12 July 2016, CRC/C/GBR/CO/5.

24 Williams, 'England and Wales', 55.

25 For devolved and reserved powers, see Jane Williams, 'Multi-Level Governance and CRC Implementation' in Antonella Invernizzi and Jane Williams (eds.), *The Human Rights of Children: From Visions to Implementation* (Burlington, VT: Ashgate, 2011) 239.

26 See, for example, Children (Equal Protection from Assault) (Scotland) Act 2019 (effective 7 November 2020) and Children (Abolition of Defence of Reasonable Punishment) (Wales) Act 2020 (effective 20 March 2022) (prohibition of corporal punishment); Age of Criminal Responsibility (Scotland) Act 2019 (effective 17 December 2021), which raised the minimum age of criminal responsibility to 12.

27 Rights of Children and Young Persons (Wales) Measure 2011 (effective May 2014). Simon Hoffman and Sean O'Neil, *The Impact of Legal Integration of the UN Convention on the Rights of the Child in Wales* (Equality and Human Rights Commission, August 2018) 8; Rachel Taylor, 'Putting Children First?: Children's Interests as a Primary Consideration in Public Law' (2016) 28(1) *Child and Family Law Quarterly* 45, 49.

28 *Reference by the Attorney General and the Advocate General for Scotland: United Nations Convention on the Rights of the Child (Incorporation) (Scotland) Bill* [2021] UKSC 42.

29 Jane Williams, 'Incorporating Children's Rights: The Divergence in Law and Policy' (2007) 27(2) *Legal Studies* 261, 276; Hoffman and O'Neil, 'The Impact', 17. See section 29(1) and (2) of the Scotland Act 1998; Wales Act 2017, especially Schedule 7A, section 10.

Convention. In *Christian Institute v. Lord Advocate (Scotland)*,[30] the Supreme Court decided that the provisions of the Children and Young People (Scotland) Act that enabled certain officials to share information about a child without the consent of the child or the child's parents were outside the powers of the Scottish Parliament, because they were contrary to article 8 of the ECHR interpreted with reference to the CRC provisions that protect children's privacy and their relationship with their parents.[31]

The unincorporated status of the CRC has not prevented the courts from engaging with it, but it makes it necessary for judges to justify their reliance on the Convention. As Lord Wilson observed, unincorporated treaties 'are not part of our law so our courts will not ordinarily reach for them'.[32] However, the application of a strong dualist approach in relation to the CRC has been challenged. Lord Kerr's dissenting judgment in *R (on the application of SG (previously JS)) v. Secretary of State for Work and Pensions*[33] (discussed in more detail in Section 6.5.2) suggested that the rejection of direct application – premised on the protection of individuals against executive law-making – should not apply to human rights treaties, which protect rather than curtail individual rights.[34] In his Lordship's view, a direct application was 'particularly' fitting in the case of the CRC, which is the most widely ratified treaty in the world.[35]

This 'constitutionally unorthodox position'[36] has generated mixed reactions. Lord Kerr did not subsequently pursue it on account of its lack of support by other judges, but his view was significant enough to be neutrally acknowledged by Lord Wilson in the main judgment in a subsequent case.[37] Other judges were less open to Lord Kerr's innovation. In *SG*, it was argued that the cap on welfare payments to non-working families was contrary to article 3(1) of the CRC and thus unjustifiably discriminated against women, who were most often the heads of single-parent families. Lord Reed rejected this argument, which in his view

30 [2016] UKSC 51 (*Christian Institute*).

31 *Christian Institute* at paras. 83–84. See references to the Preamble of the CRC and to articles 3(2), 5, 14(2), 16, 27 and 18, and 19: at para. 72.

32 *Mathieson, a deceased child v. Secretary of State for Work and Pensions* [2015] UKSC 47 at para. 38 (Lord Wilson).

33 [2015] UKSC 16 (*SG*).

34 *SG* at paras. 247, 256 (Lord Kerr).

35 *SG* at para. 256 (Lord Kerr).

36 Stephen Gilmore, 'Use of the UNCRC in Family Law Cases in England and Wales' (2017) 25(2) *International Journal of Children's Rights* 500–501.

37 *R (on the application of DA) v. Secretary of State for Work and Pensions* [2019] UKSC 21 (*DA*) at para. 67 (Lord Wilson).

sought to replace the test of 'manifestly without reasonable foundation' that applied in the context of socio-economic measures with 'a test of compliance with article 3(1)'.[38] In the same case, Lord Hughes also objected to the minority judgments that appeared to give this article 'the force of domestic English law'.[39] In relation to an argument relying on Lord Kerr's view in *SG*, Laws J in the Court of Appeal said:

> The rule of law's strength in this jurisdiction depends at least in part on the fact that our law flows only from two principal foundations: Parliament and the judges. I do not think that the benign nature of this or that international treaty, including the UNCRC, should begin to license the government to make law.[40]

While methods of engaging with the CRC that may resemble direct application have been rebuked by some judges, there is some incongruity between the rejection of direct application and the central role of the CRC in some cases. All judges in *SG* assessed the benefit cap policy against article 3(1) of the CRC, regardless of its unincorporated status.[41] Lord Kerr even suggested that there was a violation of the ECHR because the policy breached article 3 of the CRC.[42] Lord Wilson came close to the same view in *DA*,[43] when he said that 'a foundation for the decision not made in substantial compliance with article 3.1 might well be manifestly unreasonable',[44] and thus breach the ECHR. In *Mathieson, a deceased child v. Secretary of State for Work and Pensions*,[45] Lord Wilson assessed official conduct against article 3(1) and concluded that it breached the procedural rule contained therein.[46] Although these views must be seen in a context in which inconsistency with the CRC *in itself* does not equate to domestic unlawfulness,[47] the CRC was so central to the reasoning that the boundaries between direct and indirect application appear blurred.

[38] *SG* at para. 81 (Lord Reed).
[39] *SG* at para. 140 (Lord Hughes).
[40] *Public Law Project v. Lord Chancellor* [2015] EWCA Civ 1193 at para. 27.
[41] *SG* at paras. 88 (Lord Reed); 105–112, 122–128 (Lord Carnwath); 148–155 (Lord Hughes).
[42] Claire Fenton-Glynn, 'Austerity and the Benefit Cap: In Whose Best Interests?' (2015) 37 (4) *Journal of Social Welfare and Family Law* 467, 469.
[43] *R (on the application of DA) v. Secretary of State for Work and Pensions* [2019] UKSC 21 (*DA*).
[44] *DA* at para. 78 (Lord Wilson).
[45] [2015] UKSC 47 (*Mathieson*). The case is discussed more fully in Section 6.6.
[46] *Mathieson* at para. 41 (Lord Wilson).
[47] *R v. Durham Constabulary* [2005] UKHL 21 at para. 44 (Lady Hale); *SG* at para. 133 (Lord Carnwath).

However, the limited explicit support for forms of application that come close to direct effect makes it unlikely that any change in legal principles will occur soon. It rests, therefore, on the indirect forms of application to enable the courts to engage with the Convention.

6.4 The CRC, the Development of the Common Law, and Statutory Interpretation

These common law techniques involve an independent usage of the CRC that takes place outside of the HRA context. Most cases in which the CRC has been applied independently are from the House of Lords, although the Supreme Court has supported it in principle.[48] In *ANS v. ML (AP) (Scotland)*,[49] for example, Lord Reed (with Lady Hale and Lord Wilson) reinforced the normative autonomy of the CRC by deciding that courts ought first to interpret legislation according to the presumption that the Parliament did not intend to breach international treaty obligations, including under the CRC, before relying on the specific HRA interpretive mechanisms.[50]

The only case identified in this research in which the CRC was used to suggest the development of the common law is *Hunter v. Canary Wharf Ltd*,[51] where Lord Cooke (dissenting) argued that article 16 of the CRC, the right to privacy, 'may be taken into account in shaping the common law' of private nuisance so that the affected children are recognised as having standing to sue independently of their parents. The scarcity of cases in which the CRC was used to develop the common law may be due to many child-related issues being now regulated by statute, but Lord Cooke's view in *Hunter* is encouraging because it sought to develop the law in a legal field where the rights of children are often absent – that is, torts. The technique continues to have in-principle support[52] and should not be discounted as the common law permeates the fabric of the UK legal system. The application of the CRC in the development of the common law could influence, for example, traditionally entrenched and potentially untransformed aspects of the domestic law, including procedural and evidence law.

48 *SG* at paras. 137 (Lord Hughes); 238 (Lord Kerr).
49 [2012] UKSC 30 (*ANS v. ML*).
50 *ANS v. ML* at paras. 16–17.
51 [1997] UKHL 14 (*Hunter*) (Lord Cooke).
52 *SG* at paras. 137 (Lord Hughes); 238 (Lord Kerr).

The application of the CRC as an interpretive tool for the domestic legislation is more frequent than its use to develop the common law, but remains somewhat uncertain.[53] As discussed in Section 6.2, the Convention can be used if there is some ambiguity in domestic legislation – that is, when a legal provision *can* be interpreted consistently with it or, put differently, when there is a choice of meanings, one of which is consistent with the CRC. In *Sanderson v. McManus*,[54] for example, Lord Clyde (concurring) relied on article 9(3) of the CRC to interpret a domestic provision that required contact decisions to be made in the interests of the child so as to also permit a court to *deny* contact if required by the child's best interests. In *Venables and Thompson*,[55] Lord Browne-Wilkinson concluded that it was legitimate 'to assume that Parliament has not maintained on the statute book a power capable of being exercised in a manner inconsistent with the treaty obligations of this country'. Upon citing from articles 3(1) and 40(1), his Lordship decided that the policy that enabled the Secretary of State to detain convicted children throughout their childhood, without considering their welfare and the progress made towards rehabilitation, would infringe upon the treaty obligations of the UK and would be unlawful.

A robust take on the 'ambiguity as choice' approach is reflected in *R v. G*,[56] which concerned two children convicted of arson. There was no technical ambiguity in the word 'reckless' in section 1 of the Criminal Damage Act 1971, which was clarified by precedent. However, Lord Steyn (concurring) decided that the ratification of the CRC 'on its own justified a reappraisal' of its meaning, which was previously interpreted from the point of view of the 'ordinary prudent adult individual'[57] with 'no allowance . . . for the youth or lack of mental capacity of the defendant'.[58] Similar is *In re D (a child)*,[59] where an abducted child strenuously opposed the return to the country of habitual residence under the Hague

[53] Fiona Donson, 'Commentary on *R (on the Application of Castle) v Commissioner of Police for the Metropolis*' in Helen Stalford, Kathryn Hollingsworth, and Stephen Gilmore (eds.), *Rewriting Children's Rights Judgments: From Academic Vision to New Practice* (Oxford: Hart Publishing, 2017) 275, 277.

[54] [1997] UKHL 1 (*Sanderson*).

[55] *R v. Secretary of State for the Home Department ex parte Venables and Thompson* [1997] UKHL 25 (*Venables and Thompson*) (Lords Browne-Wilkinson and Steyn).

[56] [2003] UKHL 50 (*R v. G*).

[57] *R v. G* at para. 44 (Lord Steyn).

[58] *R v. G* at para. 44 (Lord Steyn).

[59] [2006] UKHL 51 (*D (a child)*).

Convention (incorporated domestically). Baroness Hale (for the Court) held that children should be listened to more frequently in Hague Convention cases, even when this is not strictly required.[60] Her Ladyship relied on article 12 of the CRC to create a presumption in favour of listening to children in most Hague Convention cases:

> [T]he principle is in my view of universal application and consistent with our international obligations under article 12 of the United Nations Convention on the Rights of the Child. . . . It erects a presumption that the child will be heard unless this appears inappropriate. Hearing the child is, as already stated, not to be confused with giving effect to his views.[61]

There is no inherent ambiguity in the wording of the legislation discussed in *R v. G* and *D (a child)*.[62] On the contrary, in *R v. G*, the meaning of legislation was clarified in the case law, and in *D (a child)*, the incorporated Hague Convention clearly required listening to children in some cases but not in others. The ambiguity in the law, and consequently the available interpretive choices, became available upon the Court's engagement with the CRC.

This flexible approach to interpretation blurs the lines between an ambiguity-justified reliance on the CRC and the ambiguity-independent interpretation techniques under the HRA, but has not encouraged an increased independent use of the CRC in statutory interpretation. In *Smith v. Secretary of State for Work and Pensions*,[63] the House of Lords had an opportunity to interpret consistently with the CRC legislation that was clearly ambiguous. The phrase 'total taxable profits' – relevant for the calculation of child maintenance – required interpretation. Baroness Hale noted that article 8 of the ECHR did not create a right to receive maintenance but that the ECtHR 'looks to other international instruments when interpreting its own Convention'.[64] Thereafter, Baroness Hale quoted from article 27(2) and (4) of the CRC and said:

> When two interpretations of these regulations are possible, the interpretation chosen should be that which better complies with the commitment

[60] *D (a child)* at paras. 58–59.
[61] *D (a child)* at para. 58.
[62] It is possible to see both of these cases as instances of *sui generis* application, meaning a statutory interpretation with reliance on an unincorporated treaty in the absence of ambiguity: Fatima, *Using International Law*, 9.4; see Section 6.2.
[63] [2006] UKHL 35 (*Smith*).
[64] *Smith* at para. 77 (Baroness Hale).

> to the welfare of children which this country has made by ratifying the United Nations Convention on the Rights of the Child.[65]

Notably, instead of interpreting the ambiguities in legislation with direct reliance on the CRC, Baroness Hale resorted to doing so through the mediation of article 8 of the ECHR.

Further illustrating the reluctance of judges to consider the presumption of compatibility to the CRC applied independently is *Nzolameso v. City of Westminster*,[66] where a single mother of five children challenged the decision of a local government to stop offering social housing to the family. The local government was bound by section 11(2)(a) of the Children Act 1989 to discharge its functions by giving consideration to the welfare of children, but the section did not require that the children's welfare be the paramount or even a primary consideration.[67] No ECHR article was invoked in that case, and Lady Hale left 'for another day' the 'interesting question of whether, even where no Convention [ECHR] right is involved, section 11 should nevertheless be construed consistently with the international obligations of the United Kingdom under article 3 of the UNCRC'.[68] Thus, the independent application of the CRC when an ECHR right is not argued, and the extension to the CRC of an HRA-style interpretive approach freed of the ambiguity requirement, remain in limbo.

Apart from its dependency on ambiguity (however generously approached), consistent interpretation has other limits. When domestic legislation is inconsistent with, or less protective than, the CRC, the Convention's independent interpretive role is limited. In *R v. Durham Constabulary*,[69] the applicant sexually assaulted several schoolmates when he was 14 and was given a warning. It was argued that the warning was contrary to article 6 of the ECHR because the child and one of his parents accepted it without being fully informed of its consequences. Upon quoting from articles 3(1), 37, and 40 of the CRC, Baroness Hale (concurring) concluded that, although some CRC provisions might have been breached, there was no breach of the ECHR, which contains fair trial rights that are more limited than the corresponding CRC rights.[70]

65 *Smith* at para. 78.
66 [2015] UKSC 22 (*Nzolameso*).
67 *Nzolameso* at para. 28 (Lady Hale).
68 *Nzolameso* at para. 29 (Lady Hale).
69 [2005] UKHL 21 (*R v. Durham Constabulary*).
70 *R v. Durham Constabulary* at para. 44 (Baroness Hale).

This suggests that consistent interpretation with the CRC might be difficult to achieve where there is some tension with the ECHR standards, especially in the absence of authority from the ECtHR to harmonise the two standards.

Although, ultimately, the number of cases in which the CRC was applied independently of the ECHR is not high, those cases testify to the autonomous value of the CRC as a legal instrument. *Hunter, Sanderson*, and *Venables and Thompson* were decided before the legislative incorporation of the ECHR and suggest that when the two conventions had an equivalent domestic legal status, the Court preferred to apply the CRC because of its direct relevance for child-related matters. The independent application of the CRC after the enactment of the HRA points to a tendency to apply the Convention to support reasoning that is not directly justified by the ECHR in issues such as juvenile justice, socio-economic rights, and child participation. Thus, in a post-HRA era, the distinct added value of the CRC has become more important.

6.5 The CRC and the HRA

The CRC has been applied most often within the context of the HRA, which has had a major impact on human rights protection in the UK in general.[71] The HRA has created a legislative context where the synergy between the ECHR and the CRC could be capitalised on, to the benefit of the latter. Thus, section 2 of the HRA requires courts to consider the ECtHR jurisprudence, which they usually follow although they are not bound to do so.[72] Section 3 requires legislation to be interpreted consistently with the ECHR 'so far as it is possible to do so', unless this is inconsistent with the fundamental nature of the legislation.[73] Section 3 has two important features: first, it establishes an interpretive 'power and ... duty' that is different from the discretionary compatibility

[71] See Tom Hickman, *Public Law after the Human Rights Act* (Oxford: Hart Publishing, 2010); Merris Amos, *Human Rights Law* (Oxford: Hart Publishing, 2006); Nicolas Kang-Riou, Jo Milner, and Suryia Nayak (eds.), *Confronting the Human Rights Act: Contemporary Themes and Perspectives* (London: Routledge, 2012); Hoffman and Rowe, *Human Rights in the UK*.

[72] Amos, *Human Rights Law*, 18; Hoffman and Rowe, *Human Rights in the UK*, 64. Shaw, *International Law*, 119.

[73] Amos, *Human Rights Law*, 123.

presumption that applies to international law more generally;[74] and second, its application is not dependent on ambiguities in the legislation.[75] If a compatible interpretation is not possible, section 4 enables the courts to make a declaration of incompatibility, but not to invalidate the legislation. Section 6 has the 'most practical force'[76] and requires all public authorities, including the courts, to act consistently with the ECHR.[77]

As suggested above, the HRA has facilitated judicial engagement with the CRC. Thus, the Convention is applied to interpret the ECHR (see Section 6.5.1), with article 3(1) of the CRC dominating the interaction between the CRC, the HRA, the ECHR, and the courts (see Section 6.5.2). These two aspects are discussed in Sections 6.5.1 and 6.5.2, respectively.

6.5.1 *The CRC and the Interpretation of the ECHR*

It is often in the context of sections 2, 3, and 6 of the HRA that the CRC is applied, although in some cases it informed the courts' reasoning when a declaration of the incompatibility of domestic law with the ECHR was sought under section 4 of the HRA. This gave the CRC an indirect role in assessing the quality of domestic legislation. In *In the matter of an application by McLaughlin for Judicial Review (Northern Ireland)*,[78] for example, the Supreme Court declared incompatible with the ECHR, reinforced by articles 2, 3(1), and 26 of the CRC, legislation that disqualified an unmarried parent from receiving the widowed parent benefit.[79] In *R (on the application of MM (Lebanon)) v. Secretary of State for the Home Department*,[80] the Court found that the highly prescriptive nature

[74] Brenda Hale, 'High Points and Low Points in the First Ten Years: A View from the Bench' in Nicolas Kang-Riou, Jo Milner, and Suryia Nayak (eds.), *Confronting the Human Rights Act: Contemporary Themes and Perspectives* (London: Routledge, 2012) 49, 55; Amos, *Human Rights Law*, 120.

[75] Amos, *Human Rights Law*, 122; Hoffman and Rowe, *Human Rights in the UK*, 71, discussing *Ghaidan v. Godin-Mendoza* [2004] UKHL 30, especially the speech of Lord Nicholls. The courts can adopt an ECHR-compatible interpretation that departs from the ordinary meaning of the law, even when the law is clear.

[76] Hoffman and Rowe, *Human Rights in the UK*, 81.

[77] It is said that the HRA has created 'a new type of illegality in domestic public law': Hickman, *Public Law*, 27 (references omitted). However, under section 6(2), public authorities can act contrary to the ECHR if the primary legislation prevents them from acting in line with it.

[78] [2018] UKSC 48 (*McLaughlin*).

[79] *McLaughlin* at para. 40 (Lady Hale).

[80] [2017] UKSC 10 (*MM*).

of immigration rules on family reunification made them contrary to article 8 of the ECHR interpreted with reference to article 3(1) of the CRC.[81]

When ECHR rights are engaged under the HRA, 'it is well established that they have to be interpreted and applied consistently with international human right standards, including the UNCRC'.[82] The mandatory consideration of the ECtHR jurisprudence under section 2 of the HRA has been a frequent justification for the use of the CRC. British judges cite the likely reliance on the Convention by the Strasbourg court[83] and the scrutiny by that court of potential breaches of the CRC[84] as a justification for considering it.

There are instances where the CRC was used to interpret the ECHR without Strasbourg guidance, with the British judges operating an original CRC-aligned interpretation of the ECHR. In *T v. Secretary of State*,[85] for example, the Supreme Court had to decide whether the compulsory disclosure to potential employers, in perpetuity, of warnings received as a child for minor offences was a lawful interference with the applicant's right to private life under article 8 of the ECHR. In the absence of directly relevant ECtHR authority,[86] Lord Reed's justification assessment under article 8(2) of the ECHR was set against, inter alia, article 40 of the CRC and Rule 21 of the Beijing Rules,[87] which made rehabilitation the main purpose of juvenile justice and which would be defeated if there was an obligation of permanent disclosure.

81 *MM* at paras. 88–92.

82 *Nzolameso* at para. 29 (Lady Hale); see similarly *DA* at para. 217 (Lady Hale). For further precedent, see *In the matter of an application by JR38 for Judicial Review (Northern Ireland)* [2015] UKSC 42 (*JR38*) at para. 49 (Lord Kerr) (discussed below); *DA* at para. 71 (Lord Wilson); *SG* at paras. 83 (Lord Reed); 141 (Lord Hughes).

83 This so-called predictive reasoning (Hickman, *Public Law*, 41–42) is present in, for example, *R v. Durham Constabulary* at paras. 26, 44 (Lady Hale); *Smith* at para. 77 (Baroness Hale); *ZH (Tanzania) v. Secretary of State for the Home Department* [2011] UKSC 4 (*ZH*) at paras. 23–26 (Lady Hale); *HH v. Deputy Prosecutor of the Italian Republic, Genoa* [2012] UKSC 25 (*HH*) at paras. 30, 33 (Lady Hale); 89 (Lord Hope agreeing); *MM* at para. 44 (Lady Hale and Lord Carnwath); *McLaughlin* at para. 34 (Lady Hale); *R (on the application of T) v. Secretary of State for the Home Department* [2014] UKSC 35 (*T v. Secretary of State*) at para. 128 (Lord Reed); *Makhlouf v. Secretary of State for the Home Department (Northern Ireland)* [2016] UKSC 59 (*Makhlouf*) at para. 47 (Lady Hale).

84 *SG* at para. 218 (Lady Hale).

85 [2014] UKSC 35 (*T v. Secretary of State*).

86 *T v. Secretary of State* at paras. 128, 137 (Lord Reed).

87 *T v. Secretary of State* at para. 142 (Lord Reed).

Any relevant CRC right can be used to interpret the scope and content of ECHR rights, and potentially give the entitlements and obligations therein a child-rights focus. In *Smith*, for example, reliance on article 27 of the CRC enabled Baroness Hale to support a positive obligation, arising from article 8 of the ECHR, for the state to devise alternative mechanisms for the payment of child maintenance where the law precluded the primary carer from claiming maintenance from the other parent in court.[88] *In re E (a child) (Northern Ireland)*,[89] a mother and her child argued that police breached their rights under article 3 of the ECHR by failing to protect them against ill-treatment by unlawful protesters. Lord Carswell suggested that consideration of article 3(1) of the CRC could give rise to child-specific obligations under article 3 of the ECHR.[90]

The most comprehensive illustration of this technique is the separate judgment of Lord Kerr (joined by Lord Wilson) in *In the matter of an application by JR38 for Judicial Review (Northern Ireland)*.[91] It was argued that by publishing, without the permission of the child or his family, the picture of a fourteen-year-old child who was involved in street rioting in Northern Ireland, the police breached the rights of the child under article 8 of the ECHR. The majority decided that those rights were not engaged because a child involved in criminal activity in public does not have a reasonable expectation of privacy. Lord Kerr used a 'more nuanced approach'[92] and stressed that the reasonable expectation of respect for privacy was 'to be approached with some caution . . . particularly in the case of children'[93] because there is 'at the least, a possible tension between the application of a reasonable expectation of privacy test and the well-established principle that any decision affecting a child should give prominence to his or her best interests'.[94] Lord Kerr pointed out that 'as is common case, the nature and content of a child's right under article 8 must be informed by relevant international treaty provisions'.[95] Upon citing articles 3(1) and 40(2)(b)(vii) of the CRC, the

[88] *Smith* at para. 77 (Lady Hale).
[89] [2008] UKHL 66 (*E (a child)*).
[90] *E (a child)* at para. 60.
[91] [2015] UKSC 42 (*JR38*).
[92] *JR38* at paras. 55, 62 (Lord Kerr).
[93] *JR38* at para. 36.
[94] *JR38* at para. 37.
[95] *JR38* at para. 49.

Beijing Rules and, extensively, General Comment No. 14,[96] Lord Kerr concluded that it would be 'out of step with the philosophy which underpins article 3(1) of UNCRC'[97] to decide that a child involved in criminal activity in public falls outside the protection of article 8 of the ECHR. Thus, '[t]he ambit of article 8 of ECHR must be seen as including within its embrace the need to protect a child from exposure as a criminal'[98] because '[a] child's need for protection can go beyond what, if he was an adult, he would be reasonably entitled to expect'.[99] Although this powerful judgment articulated the need for the development of a child-focused interpretation of ECHR rights, it did not sway the majority, who refused to modify the adult-centred legal test that applied to the protection of privacy.[100]

JR38 is not the only case where the majority has eschewed a CRC-informed, child-focused interpretation of ECHR standards. In *In re S (a child),*[101] the six-year-old applicant sought a 'no publication order' in relation to the surname and pictures of his mother (who was standing trial for killing the applicant's brother) and of the deceased. A balance had to be struck between the applicant's rights under article 8 and the media's rights under article 10 of the ECHR. Lord Steyn held that the CRC protected the privacy of children *directly* involved in criminal proceedings, but an injunction protecting the privacy of children *indirectly affected* by a criminal trial would be 'a step too far'[102] and would likely open the door for other exceptions to media freedom.[103] Regrettably, Lord Steyn approached articles 17 and 40(2)(b)(vii) of the CRC in isolation, without considering article 3(1), which could have justified a differentiated treatment of children without the risk of unduly extending the exceptions to freedom of expression.

While it is accepted that the CRC has an interpretive role in relation to the ECHR, what *interpretation* entails is not always clear. There are two

[96] CRC Committee, *General Comment No. 14 (2013) on the right of the child to have his or her best interests taken as a primary consideration (art. 3, para. 1)*, 29 May 2013, CRC/C/GC/14.

[97] *JR38* at para. 50.

[98] *JR38* at para. 53.

[99] *JR38* at para. 65. Lord Kerr found, however, that the interference with article 8 of the ECHR was justified.

[100] *JR38* at paras. 95 (Lord Toulson); 113 (Lord Clarke).

[101] [2004] UKHL 47 (*S (a child)*).

[102] *S (a child)* at para. 26.

[103] *S (a child)* at para. 32.

interpretive locations for the CRC: the substance of ECHR rights; and the justification of interference therewith. The classic interpretation paradigm envisages the use of unincorporated treaties to interpret the substance of rights, but the current case law transcends that usage. Judges' reliance on the CRC in the justification analysis has created additional avenues to apply the Convention in instances where the content or the scope of the right concerned does not require interpretation (e.g., *SG*, *Mathieson* and *DA*), or when the rights of children are not directly the object of litigation but are nonetheless affected (e.g., *ZH*[104] and *HH*[105]). In some cases, however, the interpretive location has been contentious, with judges disagreeing on the legitimacy of using the CRC in the justification analysis rather than in the interpretation of a substantive right.[106] Ultimately, wherever the CRC is located within the legal enquiry, it clarifies the normative conglomerate that the ECHR provisions are – albeit in different ways.

When used in the justification analysis, the CRC informs the limitation of ECHR rights. Article 3(1) of the CRC has often assisted in the balancing of competing interests during the proportionality assessment under article 8(2) of the ECHR, and it has often served to boost parental rights.[107] Reliance on the CRC has not yet yielded a child-specific justification analysis when the children's *own* ECHR rights were subjected to interference. In *T v. Secretary of State*, this opportunity arose in relation to the disclosure of diversion measures, which interfered with the child's rights under article 8(1) of the ECHR. Lord Reed carried out the justification assessment by reference to, inter alia, article 40 of the CRC and Rule 21 of the Beijing Rules,[108] but approached these standards as part of the context without integrating them into the justification matrix under article 8(2) of the ECHR. No principle was articulated in relation to whether or why a child should be treated differently in relation to the disclosure of diversion measures, although it is apparent that the applicant's age has influenced the reasoning.[109]

[104] *ZH (Tanzania) v. Secretary of State for the Home Department* [2011] UKSC 4 (*ZH*).

[105] *HH v. Deputy Prosecutor of the Italian Republic, Genoa* [2012] UKSC 25 (*HH*).

[106] *SG* (Lord Reed and Lord Hughes); cf. at para. 220 (Lady Hale). Lady Hale disagreed that the CRC can inform the substantive content of the ECHR rights 'but not the approach to proportionality and discrimination': at para. 220.

[107] *ZH*; *HH*; *SG*; *Christian Institute*; *Zoumbas v. Secretary of State for the Home Department* [2013] UKSC 74 (*Zoumbas*) (discussed below).

[108] *T v. Secretary of State* at para. 142 (Lord Reed).

[109] *T v. Secretary of State* at para. 142 (Lord Reed); see also at para. 41 (Lord Wilson).

While the use of the CRC in the justification enquiry increases the opportunities for its application, this has some drawbacks. First, the CRC does not shape the core of the legal content of ECHR rights (i.e., the entitlements and obligations). For example, there was little (if any) effort in *ZH*, *HH*, and *DA* to give article 8 of the ECHR a child-focused content, with the legal analysis dominated by the parental equivalent right while article 3(1) of the CRC was used in the justification enquiry. Second, there is an over-representation of article 3(1) of the CRC in the justification analysis, which may discourage the utilisation of other relevant CRC provisions and stifle their judicial development. Third, the justification analysis is a context characterised by much discretion in which the review powers of the courts are more limited. This is clearly illustrated in the benefit cap cases, where a majority of the Court refrained from interfering with the balancing exercise by the government. As Lord Wilson put it:

> This court must impose on itself the discipline not, from its limited perspective, to address whether the government's evaluation of its impact was questionable; nor whether its assessment of the best interests of young children was unbalanced in favour of perceived long-term advantages for them at the expense of obvious short-term privation.[110]

Fourth, when the justification analysis pertains to the rights of others, the CRC applies only *to the extent* that it is relevant to the protection of those rights. The CRC rights are then used not as self-standing rights, but rather as relevant factors or interests in the proportionality exercise. Statements such as 'children's interests [are] part of the substantive right of the parent which is protected',[111] or views that single *parents' rights* under articles 8 and 14 of the ECHR should be construed in light of the CRC because their interests are indistinguishable from their children's interests,[112] suggest a tendency to address child-related issues as *interests* rather than rights. In this sense, children's rights remain somewhat sub-legal and benefit less from analytical attention.

The nature of the cases and the arguments presented to the courts may be such that there is little choice involved in whether to use the CRC in interpreting the content of ECHR rights or in the justification enquiry, but it is important to acknowledge that the location of the CRC in the legal analysis can have legal consequences.

[110] *DA* at para. 87 (Lord Wilson).
[111] *SG* at para. 146 (Lord Hughes).
[112] *DA* at para. 78 (Lord Wilson).

6.5.2 *Article 3(1) of the CRC, the ECHR, and the UK Case Law*

Article 3(1) of the CRC dominates the recent jurisprudence of the Supreme Court, in yet another rebuke to the well-versed doctrinal concerns about its vagueness and imprecision. On the contrary, its wide use implies that this article is not 'too broadly expressed' or 'too ambivalently stated'[113] to be judicially applied. The Court has embraced the best interests terminology in preference to the domestic mirror concept of 'child welfare' in what appears to be an acknowledgement of the changing legal nature of the best interests of the child under the influence of the CRC. This change in legal nature is reflected in two aspects of the Court's case law: first, the expansion of the scope of the best interests of the child; and second, its 'legalisation' – that is, the absorption of the concept in the human rights reasoning pattern. These are discussed in Sections 6.5.2.1 and 6.5.2.2 respectively below.

6.5.2.1 The Scope of the Best Interests of the Child

The welfare (or well-being) of the child has traditionally informed decisions concerning children's upbringing and other matters provided by statutes,[114] but there is no common law or statutory duty that primary consideration should be given to children's best interests in *all* decisions concerning them. In *ZH*,[115] the scope of the duty was judicially extended to public law matters, including those affecting children indirectly. The duty currently applies to decisions concerning, for example, the extradition of parents,[116] deportation,[117] welfare payments,[118] widowed parental allowance,[119] planning and leave from prison.[120]

[113] *SG* at para. 261 (Lord Kerr).

[114] Section 1(1) of the Children Act 1989; section 11(2) of the Children Act 2004; section 55 of the Borders, Citizenship and Immigration Act 2009.

[115] For a comment, see Jane Fortin, 'Are Children's Best Interests Really Best? *ZH (Tanzania) v Secretary of State for the Home Department*' (2011) 74(6) *Modern Law Review* 947.

[116] *HH*.

[117] *Zoumbas*. A father argued that the best interests of his children were not given a primary consideration under article 8 of the ECHR when the Secretary of State rejected his application for asylum or humanitarian protection. The appellant, his wife, and their three children (all of whom were foreign nationals) had lived in the UK since 2001. The appeal was dismissed.

[118] *SG*.

[119] *McLaughlin*.

[120] Taylor, 'Putting Children First?', 54.

In *ZH*, the Tanzanian mother and primary caregiver of two British children aged nine and twelve was liable to deportation because of her irregular immigration status. Her removal meant that the children would have to accompany her and leave their country of birth and nationality. The mother argued that the decision to remove her would disproportionately interfere with the right to respect for *her* private and family life under article 8 of the ECHR.

The best interests of the children and article 3(1) of the CRC were relevant for several reasons. The ECtHR jurisprudence recognised that family life is enjoyed with the other members of the family unit,[121] which made it necessary to consider children's interests. The Strasbourg court requires that article 8 of the ECHR is interpreted in harmony with other international treaties, including article 3(1) of the CRC.[122] Lastly, the all-encompassing formula 'in all actions concerning children' in the CRC enabled the application of the best interests to matters other than the upbringing of children, including the removal of their mother from the UK. Thus, a combination of factors in the ECHR and article 3(1) of the CRC enabled the utilisation of the latter in the proportionality assessment under article 8(2) of the ECHR. In her leading judgment, Lady Hale concluded that the interference with the mother's right was disproportionate because of the significant negative consequences that it would have on the children.

In most cases, article 3(1) of the CRC was invoked alongside the ECHR rights of the parents.[123] The wide ambit of the right to respect for family life under article 8 of the ECHR and its intersection with the traditional scope of the welfare principle have made this a safe space for the application of article 3(1). The collective nature of family life and the interconnectedness of parents' and children's interests therein have been key justifications for considering this article in cases where children were affected by measures taken against their parents.[124] The tight relationship between the two provisions suggests a certain complementarity, if not a dependency, between article 3(1) of the CRC and article 8 of the ECHR,

121 *ZH* at paras. 14–15 (Lady Hale).
122 *ZH* at para. 21 (Lady Hale).
123 For some exceptions, see *Venables and Thompson* (juvenile justice legislation); *E (a child)* (article 3 of the ECHR); *R v. Durham Constabulary* (article 6 of the ECHR); *Mathieson* (Protocol No. 1 to the Convention for the Protection of Human Rights and Fundamental Freedoms, 20 March 1952, ETS 9).
124 *SG* at paras. 86 (Lord Reed); 146 (Lord Hughes); *DA* at para. 77 (Lord Wilson).

which creates a risk that judges might sideline the former when its habitual vector norm does not apply.

This is, arguably, what happened in *SG*. Two single mothers and their children argued that regulations providing for a cap on welfare benefits payable to parents in non-working or underemployed households unjustifiably discriminated between men and women, contrary to article 14 of the ECHR (on the prohibition of discrimination) read with article 1 of Protocol No. 1 to the ECHR (A1P1) (concerning the protection of property).[125] The cap disproportionately affected single-parent households, of which most were female-headed. The application of the cap could be avoided if parents worked a certain number of hours per week, which was difficult for single parents. The appellants argued that the discrimination between women and men was not justifiable because the best interests of the children affected were not given a primary consideration, as required by article 3(1) of the CRC. A narrow majority decided that article 3(1) was not relevant for establishing that discrimination existed between women and men in relation to the enjoyment of their property because a substantive *right of children* was not alleged to have been breached.[126] Relevantly, Lord Reed and Lord Hughes also questioned the application of article 3(1) of the CRC when article 8 of the ECHR was not argued.[127]

That judges are more comfortable when article 3 of the CRC is invoked with article 8 of the ECHR is clear in *DA*. A new challenge was mounted by two five-year-old children and their single mothers to a revised benefits cap policy, which further reduced benefits for non-working families and pushed single-parent families below the poverty line. This time, the discrimination argument was made in relation to the enjoyment of the rights of single parents, regardless of gender, and their children under article 8 of the ECHR. The ability of a family to provide the necessities of life to its members was said to fall within the scope of article 8, and it was thereafter readily accepted that article 3(1) of the CRC was relevant.[128] The judges agreed that there was discrimination between single parents and other parents affected by the cap, but the

[125] Protocol No. 1 to the Convention for the Protection of Human Rights and Fundamental Freedoms, 20 March 1952, ETS 9 (A1P1). The initial argument based on article 8 was dropped in favour of A1P1.

[126] *SG* at paras. 87–88 (Lord Reed); 129, 131 (Lord Carnwath); 144–146 (Lord Hughes).

[127] Cf. *SG* at paras. 117 (Lord Carnwath); 263, 267 (Lord Kerr); 213 (Lady Hale).

[128] *DA* at paras. 72, 76 (Lord Wilson); 100–101 (Lord Carnwath, joined by Lord Reed and Lord Hughes).

majority decided that the discrimination was justified by the long-term positive effect of encouraging parents to take up work.[129] Apart from some technical aspects (i.e., the right argued and the intricacies of discrimination law), *SG* and *DA* are quasi-identical: a cut in welfare support left children in single-parent families facing severe poverty. Lord Wilson's explanation that the interests of the single mothers and their young children were 'indistinguishable' in *DA*,[130] a case under article 8 of the ECHR, but not, by implication, in *SG*, an A1P1 case, therefore appears unconvincing.

The expansion of the scope of the best interests of the child has generated some resistance, fuelled by the absence of a cross-cutting duty to give a primary consideration to the best interests of the child in all official decisions concerning children. Some statutes, for example, require consideration of children's interests but have a limited reach,[131] or do not require that such interests be a primary consideration.[132] Some judges have questioned the application of this duty to law-making processes[133] and the inclusion of socio-economic measures in the phrase 'action concerning children' in article 3(1) of the CRC.[134] The unanimous acceptance by the Court in *Mathieson* of the CRC Committee's interpretation of article 3(1) as authoritative confirms, as a matter of principle, its wide scope in the domestic law. The signs are encouraging in that the duty was applied to the designing of welfare measures[135] and the making of immigration rules and guidance.[136] This was sometimes facilitated by the complementarity between statutes that contain references to the welfare of children and the applicable statute,[137] or section 6(1) of the HRA.[138]

[129] *DA* at para. 88 (Lord Wilson).

[130] *DA* at para. 77 (Lord Wilson).

[131] The paramountcy principle in section 1(1) of the Children Act 2004 does not apply to immigration decisions because they do not concern the upbringing of children: *ZH* at para. 25 (Lady Hale).

[132] Section 11(2)(a) of the Children Act 2004; section 55 of the Borders, Citizenship and Immigration Act 2009.

[133] *SG* at para. 149 (Lord Hughes).

[134] *SG* at para. 88 (Lord Reed).

[135] *DA* at para. 75 (Lord Wilson).

[136] *MM* at para. 46 (Lady Hale and Lord Carnwath for the Court).

[137] Legislation for social housing was complemented by the Children Act 1989 (*Nzolameso*), while legislation concerning deportation in criminal matters was complemented by the Borders, Citizenship and Immigration Act (*Ali (Iraq) v. Secretary of State for the Home Department* [2016] UKSC 60 (*Ali*)).

[138] *Makhlouf* at para. 47 (Lady Hale).

A final issue relating to the scope of article 3 of the CRC is the application of the duty to give a primary consideration to the best interests of the child to decisions affecting children in general, including legislation and policies. Many judges accepted that under the influence of article 3(1) of the CRC, the best interests of the child must be considered in decisions affecting individual children, as well as children generally.[139] The potential tension between collective and individual interests came to the fore in *SG* and *DA*, which pitched the long-term general interests of *all* children to live in families that are not dependent on welfare payments against the shorter-term interests of the children directly affected by the cap in having their basic needs met.

Some judges agreed with the government that article 3(1) was not breached because, inter alia, the cap was aimed at ensuring the interests of children in general,[140] while others held that the interests of those children directly affected must be given a primary consideration.[141] As Lady Hale said, '[i]t cannot possibly be in the best interests of the children affected by the cap to deprive them of the means to provide them with adequate food, clothing, warmth and housing, the basic necessities of life'.[142] Relying on General Comment No. 14, Lord Kerr was unequivocal that 'first consideration be given to the best interests of the children directly affected by the decision'.[143] By accepting the argument that at least *some* children could benefit from the cap, some judges sent a concerning signal that the best interests of children as a class can become a shield against the judicial review of polycentric decisions. This is compounded by the low threshold for compliance with the duty to give a primary consideration to children's best interests used by the majority, as discussed in Section 6.5.2.2 below.

6.5.2.2 The Best Interests of the Child as a Primary Consideration

The phrase 'a primary consideration' has been the site of judicial discussions on two distinct issues: the weight of children's interests in public law decisions and the order in which such interests are to be considered.

[139] *SG* at paras. 108 (Lord Carnwath); 153 (Lord Hughes); 226 (Lady Hale); 268 (Lord Kerr).
[140] *SG* at paras. 153, 155 (Lord Hughes).
[141] *SG* at paras. 108–109 (Lord Carnwath); 226 (Lady Hale); 268 (Lord Kerr); *DA* at para. 178ff (Lord Kerr).
[142] *SG* at para. 226 (Lady Hale).
[143] *SG* at para. 268 (Lord Kerr). See also *DA* at paras. 178–179 (Lord Kerr).

In most public law cases, children's interests need to be balanced against other legitimate interests. The weight of children's interests has been variously described as 'substantial',[144] or not 'a factor of limitless importance' but one that 'must rank higher than any other',[145] or requiring that 'no factor should be given greater weight'.[146] The core idea of these diverse statements is that the best interests of the child cannot be the overriding consideration at all times and in all public law decisions. The expansion in scope makes it 'less possible . . . to impose the best interests . . . as a determinative or even priority factor over the frequently complex legal or socio-economic considerations'.[147] It is nonetheless accepted that no other legitimate interests are inherently more important than a child's best interests,[148] but the weight of other considerations may justify interference with relevant rights even when this has 'very severe consequences for children'.[149] However, children's interests cannot be dismissed 'with the bland statement that "these cannot be a trump card"'.[150] As put by Lady Hale:

> One thing is clear. It is not enough to dismiss these cases in a simple way – by accepting that the children's interests will always be harmed by separation from their sole or primary carer but also accepting that the public interest in extradition is almost always strong enough to outweigh it.[151]

The frequent use of article 3(1) in the justification analysis under the ECHR means that children's interests are often portrayed as being in tension with the interests of others. In *HH*, the question was whether the extradition of three parents in two separate cases (one of historical fraud and the other concerning drug offences) unjustifiably interfered with the children's right to respect for family life under article 8 of the ECHR. The applicable principle was that the public interest in extradition would prevail over the rights of family members of the person subject to extradition, unless the consequences of extradition would be

144 *HH* at paras. 155 (Lord Wilson); 15 (Lady Hale).
145 *ZH* at para. 46 (Lord Kerr).
146 *Zoumbas* at para. 12 (Lord Hodge).
147 *SG* at para. 152 (Lord Hughes).
148 *ZH* at paras. 26 (Lady Hale); 44 (Lord Hope); *HH* at para. 145 (Lord Kerr); *Zoumbas* at para. 10 (Lord Hodge).
149 *Zoumbas* at para. 13.
150 *PJS v. News Group Newspapers Ltd* [2016] UKSC 26 (*PJS*) at para. 72 (Lady Hale).
151 *HH* at para. 34 (Lady Hale); see also at para. 86. See similarly *Zoumbas* at para. 12 (Lord Hodge); *Makhlouf* at paras. 38 (Lord Kerr); 46 (Lady Hale).

exceptionally severe.[152] Applying the *ZH* principles, the Court weighed the best interests of the affected children against the public interest (including the state's obligations under an extradition treaty). The extradition was unanimously rejected in the fraud case because of the 'extraordinarily severe'[153] consequences of the mother's extradition on her two young children. In the drug-related case, however, the majority allowed the extradition of both parents, deciding that the interference with the rights of children was outweighed by the public interest.[154] Lady Hale dissented on the extradition of the father, who was the primary caregiver of the family's young children.[155] Lady Hale took a novel approach and suggested that the children's interests were not in tension with the public interest because there is a strong public interest in children's optimal upbringing and in minimising the negative impact on children of the measures taken by the state,[156] which could be achieved by extraditing only one parent.

The alignment of the best interests of the child and the public interest as a relevant issue for the courts is reflected in a limited number of subsequent judgments. It was held, for example, that the interests of the community are not contrary to those of a child offender who would benefit from undergoing a diversion process that could assist the child in reintegrating into the community,[157] and that 'the public interest is multi-faceted' and 'there is a public interest in families being kept together, [and] in the welfare of children being given primacy'.[158] These judgments invite a reassessment of the relationship between the best interests of the child and the public interest by suggesting that giving priority to children's interests may be justified not only by their vulnerability but also by the interests of the wider community. A potential risk of this approach is that the absorption of children's interests within public or community interests may detract from giving due weight to

[152] See the summary of principles in *HH* at para. 8 (Lady Hale).

[153] *HH* at paras. 44 (Lady Hale); 89 (Lord Hope); 133 (Lord Judge); 147 (Lord Kerr), referring to 'profound and irretrievable consequences'.

[154] *HH* at paras. 135–138 (Lord Judge); 94 (Lord Hope); 96 (Lord Brown); 103 (Lord Mance); 149 (Lord Kerr); 170–172 (Lord Wilson).

[155] *HH* at para. 79 (Lady Hale).

[156] *HH* at para. 33. Compare, however, *Makhlouf* at para. 46, where Lady Hale said that children's interests must be treated separately from adults' and public interests.

[157] *JR38* at para. 79 (Lord Kerr).

[158] *Ali* at para. 169 (Lord Kerr).

the interests of individual children directly affected by certain measures, as illustrated in the benefits cap cases.

The second sense in which the phrase 'a primary consideration' is discussed in the case law is whether 'primary' equates with first-in-line for consideration, or 'the starting point',[159] or to be 'considered first'.[160] Lord Kerr explains the relevance of this issue:

> This is not merely a mechanistic or slavishly technical approach to the order in which the various considerations require to be evaluated. It accords proper prominence to the matter of the children's interests. . . . [I]t seems to me that there is much to be said for considering those interests first, so that the risk that they may be undervalued in a more open-ended inquiry can be avoided.[161]

Most judges, however, opined that a prescribed analytical order is not necessary,[162] provided that the best interests of the child are adequately considered and judges ask themselves 'the right questions and in an orderly manner'.[163]

In their interpretation of the phrase 'giving a primary consideration', judges have oscillated between what could be called raw procedural, advanced procedural, and substantive approaches. Under a raw procedural approach, article 3(1) is satisfied should the state simply 'pay regard to the interests of children'.[164] This is an excessively procedural approach that is seldom explicit in judgments but is occasionally used.[165]

An advanced procedural approach emphasises transparency and accountability. Thus, article 3(1) requires a 'careful consideration'[166] of children's interests and sufficient relevant information to assess children's best interests independently of the interests of others.[167] It is Lord Carnwath's embrace of General Comment No. 14 as authoritative in *SG* that gave shape to this approach. As put by his Lordship, 'article 3 (1) is more than a restatement of the ordinary administrative law duty to

159 *ZH* at para. 44 (Lord Hope).
160 *ZH* at para. 26 (Lady Hale).
161 *HH* at para. 145 (Lord Kerr).
162 *HH* at paras. 98, 100 (Lord Mance); 126 (Lord Judge); 153, 155 (Lord Wilson). In *ZH*, Lady Hale seems to have supported such an approach: at para. 26.
163 *HH* at para. 33 (Lady Hale).
164 *E (a child)* at para. 61 (Lord Carswell).
165 *SG* at paras. 154–155 (Lord Hughes); *DA* at para. 87 (Lord Wilson).
166 *DA* at paras. 122 (Lord Carnwath, with Lord Reed and Lord Hughes); 87 (Lord Wilson); *HH* at para. 34 (Lady Hale); *Zoumbas* at para. 12 (Lord Hodge).
167 *Makhlouf* at paras. 41 (Lord Kerr); 46 (Lady Hale); *DA* at para. 194 (Lord Kerr).

have regard to material circumstances'.[168] Accordingly, article 3(1) requires the spelling out of how children's interests have been given high priority when weighed against other interests, how the conflict of interests was resolved, and what considerations overrode children's interests.[169] Following this approach, and in contrast with judges preferring a raw procedural approach, his Lordship decided that the impugned cap regulations were not compliant with article 3(1) because of the insufficient attention given to the interests of children affected by the cap, as well as the government's silence on how concerns raised about the hardship the cap caused would be addressed.[170] Government awareness of the impact of certain measures on children does not mean that 'their best interests were treated as a primary consideration'.[171] The state must show that it reached a balanced solution when considering the impact of its measures on children.[172]

The substantive approach has two dimensions: first, a reasoning that safeguards the *opportunity* for children's interests to prevail over countervailing legitimate interests by stressing their significant weight; and second, defining best interests by referring to other rights of the child. The first dimension remains centred on the procedural aspects of article 3(1) but is distinguished from the advanced procedural approach by its emphasis on the weight of the best interests, as opposed to the procedural guarantees that children's interests would be considered in the decision-making.

Lord Kerr's judgment in *ZH*, modelled on the Australian cases of *Teoh* and *Wan* and their interpretation of article 3(1),[173] is the high watermark of the first dimension. Accordingly, a decision-maker should first consider the best interests of the child and ascertain what decision would favour those interests. The best interests of the child 'should customarily dictate the outcome ... and it will require considerations of substantial moment to permit a different result'.[174] In *HH*, however, his Lordship aligned with the majority view that 'primacy' means that no interest is

[168] *SG* at para. 122 (Lord Carnwath).
[169] *SG* at paras. 108, 112 (Lord Carnwath). For similar views, see *Mathieson* at para. 39 (Lord Wilson); *DA* at paras. 68–69 (Lord Wilson); 178 (Lord Kerr).
[170] *SG* at paras. 109, 111, 123 (Lord Carnwath).
[171] *SG* at para. 225 (Lady Hale).
[172] *DA* at para. 188 (Lord Kerr).
[173] *ZH* at para. 46 (Lord Kerr); *HH* at para. 145 (Lord Kerr).
[174] *ZH* at para. 46 (Lord Kerr).

inherently superior to children's interests.[175] While this was a step backwards from Lord Kerr's view in *ZH*, its essence remains. The impact of *ZH* was consolidated by its unanimous acceptance by the Court in *Zoumbas*.[176] Another illustration of this dimension is Lady Hale's balancing of interests in *SG*, where she opined that the longer-term collective interests of children and adults should not override the interests of children directly affected by the cap to have their basic needs met.[177]

The second dimension of the substantive approach is its branching beyond the procedural aspects of article 3(1) and towards defining the interests of children with reference to other CRC rights. Thus, articles 7 and 8 of the CRC made the British nationality of 'particular importance in assessing the best interests of any child'.[178] Article 12 of the CRC requires that children's best interests are established with regard to the views of the affected children.[179] In *SG*, Lady Hale called on the 'specific obligations' in article 27 of the CRC to support her article 3(1) reasoning,[180] while in *DA*, Lord Kerr referred to articles 26 and 27 as 'an essential backdrop',[181] 'central', and 'an indispensable yardstick'[182] in balancing the interests of the community with those of the children affected by welfare cap measures.

There remains, however, a limited number of judgments where other CRC rights define the best interests under article 3(1). There is no statement of principle yet in that regard, despite this position being reflected in General Comment No. 14,[183] which was embraced by the Court. Lord Kerr comes close in *DA*, where his Lordship opposed the 'concentration on the question whether the government has *acted in breach* of article 3 of UNCRC'.[184] Instead, Lord Kerr suggested that compliance with that article should be assessed by considering the spirit of the CRC:

175 *HH* at para. 145 (Lord Kerr); *Zoumbas* at para. 10.3 (Lord Hodge for the court, including Lord Kerr).
176 *Zoumbas v. Secretary of State for the Home Department* [2013] UKSC 74 (*Zoumbas*).
177 *SG* at para. 226 (Lady Hale).
178 *ZH* at para. 30 (Lady Hale, with Lord Brown and Lord Mance). Cf. *Zoumbas*, where the children did not have British nationality.
179 *ZH* at paras. 34, 37 (Lady Hale); *HH* at paras. 85–86 (Lady Hale).
180 *SG* at para. 227 (Lady Hale).
181 *DA* at para. 180 (Lord Kerr).
182 *DA* at para. 181 (Lord Kerr).
183 CRC Committee, *General Comment No. 14*, part IV.A.3, part V.
184 *DA* at para. 183 (Lord Kerr) (emphasis in original).

> UNCRC contains a number of enjoinders to those countries which subscribe to it. Some of these are expressed in imperative terms. The duty of the state is to keep faith with the spirit of the Convention. Whether it has discharged that duty is not to be answered solely on whether it can be said to be in technical breach of its terms. The proportionality of a government measure which has an impact on the best interests of children is not to be judged by a mechanistic approach to the question whether there has been technical compliance with article 3. It must be assessed on the basis of whether, given the injunctions in UNCRC, the government's decision, taking into account where the best interests of children lie, represents a balanced reaction to those interests and the aims which a particular measure seeks to achieve.[185]

Article 3(1) has therefore attracted significant judicial attention, likely due to a combination of factors. Its generality enabled an articulation with domestic standards, including the ECHR. Its evaluative features (i.e., 'a primary consideration') have offered pragmatic assistance in the proportionality analysis under the ECHR, where competing interests are weighed against each other. Further, the partial overlap with domestic 'welfare' made the concept and its underlying philosophy familiar to the judges, and the statutory support for the welfare of the child increased its acceptability.[186]

Under the influence of article 3(1), the scope of the duty to give a primary consideration to the best interests of the child has been extended and certain safeguards have been created to ensure that they are considered and given adequate weight in public law decision-making. Article 3(1) has been applied mostly independently of other CRC rights, raising concerns about its over-proceduralisation. On the positive side, this has increased its mobility and facilitated its association with non-CRC rights, particularly ECHR rights. Although, so far, this association has been limited to article 8 of the ECHR, it has created opportunities for the cross-pollination of the legal content of associated rights and for expanding the influence of article 3(1). Often fused with article 8 of the ECHR, article 3(1) has not, however, been obliterated: it has influenced judicial thinking on the relevance of children's interests for a wide range of decisions, the official duties in relation to them, and their weight.

To conclude, the HRA has clearly enabled the judicial application of the CRC and diversified its use. The Convention, however, is not always

[185] *DA* at para. 187 (Lord Kerr).

[186] This anchor role of domestic legislation is noted in *SG* by Lord Reed (para. 82) and Lord Carnwath (para. 115). See also Taylor, 'Putting Children First?', 51.

used effectively and opportunities have been missed to interpret the ECHR in accordance with the CRC in the absence of precedent from the ECtHR. Although some socio-economic and juvenile justice-related rights have been applied, the case law is dominated by article 8 of the ECHR and article 3(1) operating in tandem. In general, this has been beneficial for article 3(1), but there is a risk that its scope would be circumscribed by that of article 8 of the ECHR and that its independent application would be undermined.

6.6 *Sui Generis* Forms of Application

In addition to the methods previously discussed, there are also methods that have not yet received explicit judicial recognition, as discussed below.

In *Mathieson*, the father of a severely disabled child in need of extensive medical care challenged the cessation, after eighty-four days of hospitalisation, of the child's disability allowance, arguing that it unjustifiably discriminated against the child on account of his disability status, contrary to article 14 of the ECHR read with article 1 of A1P1. The father argued that the state had to justify the application of the eighty-four-day rule to the child 'through the prism of international conventions', a contention that Lord Wilson (writing for the Court) accepted because the applicable law (i.e., the ECHR) 'demand[ed] reference' to unincorporated international treaties.[187] Lord Wilson assessed the state's decision directly against article 3(1) of the CRC, as interpreted by the Committee in General Comment No. 14,[188] and concluded that by not evaluating the impact of the application of the rule on the affected child,[189] the state breached article 3(1) of the CRC read with article 7(2) of the Convention on the Rights of Persons with Disabilities.[190] The breach of the CRC was relevant because the ECHR must be interpreted 'in harmony' with the general principles of international law.[191] It was in harmony with the best interests of the child and the non-discrimination norms in international law to decide that there was no justification for the application of the eighty-four-day rule.[192]

[187] *Mathieson* at para. 38 (Lord Wilson).
[188] *Mathieson* at para. 39.
[189] *Mathieson* at para. 41.
[190] Convention on the Rights of Persons with Disabilities, 13 December 2006, in force 3 May 2008, 2515 UNTS 3.
[191] *Mathieson* at paras. 42, 44.
[192] *Mathieson* at para. 44.

Lord Wilson's approach is interesting. His Lordship assessed an official act directly against article 3(1) of the CRC, despite its unincorporated status. His Lordship then established what would accord with that article and made a decision that aligned with it, but based that decision on domestic legal principles. This harmonisation approach is decidedly dualist in that the CRC is not 'brought down' and interwoven into the domestic legal standards. It is instead maintained in the international sphere and used as a mirror for the domestic decision. This is, arguably, a generous approach, but its downside is that it favours the status quo and does not embed the CRC values in the domestic law.

In other cases, the CRC was used to reinforce convergent aspects of the domestic law. Lord Browne-Wilkinson and Lord Hope, in their separate judgments in *Venables and Thompson*, referred to articles 3(1) and 40(1) of the CRC to reinforce their views that section 44(1) of the Children and Young Persons Act 1933 required the Secretary of State to consider the welfare of the child in establishing and adjusting the period that the accused children were required to spend in custody. In *In the matter of D (a child)*,[193] which concerned the placement, with parental consent, in restrictive accommodation of a sixteen-year-old who lacked capacity due to significant mental health conditions, Lady Hale decided that the placement amounted to a deprivation of liberty under article 5 of the ECHR – a decision that was 'reinforced' by its alignment with articles 2 and 37(b) and (d) of the CRC.[194]

The CRC has also been used to justify legislation that provided enhanced protection to children by restricting the rights of others. For example, the Committee's view that corporal punishment is contrary to the CRC was a strong indication that legislation barring corporal punishment in private schools was a legitimate and proportionate limitation of the religious rights of parents and teachers.[195] Articles 2(2) and 22, together with General Comment No. 6,[196] were relied on to justify domestic legislation that provided more protection to unaccompanied

193 [2019] UKSC 42 (*D (a child) 2019*).

194 *D (a child) 2019* at para. 45. *McLaughlin* is another example of the CRC (articles 2, 3, and 26) playing a reinforcing role: at para. 40.

195 *R v. Secretary of State for Education and Employment ex parte Williamson* [2005] UKHL 15 (*Williamson*) at paras. 82–84 (Baroness Hale).

196 CRC Committee, *General Comment No. 6 (2005): Treatment of unaccompanied and separated children outside their country of origin*, 1 September 2005, CRC/GC/2005/6.

children.[197] In other cases, CRC provisions provided a context for the decision. In *T v. Secretary of State*, relevant CRC articles provided a context for deciding whether the perpetual disclosure of diversion measures taken against a child unjustifiably interfered with article 8 of the ECHR. Arguably, articles 7 and 8 of the CRC in *ZH*, and articles 26 and 27 in the benefits cap cases, were contextual factors that informed the best interests of the child and the application of article 3(1) of the CRC.

Sui generis methods are difficult to define, but highlighting some of their features may contribute to their theoretical clarification in the future – both in the UK and in other legal systems where they have emerged (in this study, Australia and South Africa). First, these methods do not always perform an interpretive function, but have some analytical value. Gilmore, for example, considers them to be descriptive forms of engagement.[198] The techniques sometimes straddle two distinct aspects of the legal reasoning, which are most often conflated: the interpretation and the application of the law. If one conceives of legal interpretation widely, some *sui generis* methods could be included therein, but this would conceal the diversity of methods of engagement for the sake of doctrinal certainty. It would discourage the broadening of understanding regarding the complex interaction between the CRC and the domestic law, and the identification and conceptual clarification of these methods.

Second, the substance of the CRC is often used independently, without it being filtered through the ECHR even when it was invoked together with the latter. This indirectly affirms the normative autonomy of the CRC. Apart from *Venables and Thompson*, all other cases in which it is suggested that *sui generis* methods have been used were cases in which the CRC was accompanied by the ECHR. It may be that the legitimising effect of the duo HRA–ECHR meant that less attention was paid to the technicalities of the application of the Convention (i.e., detecting an ambiguity in the law), leading to more flexibility and ultimately innovation in how judges engaged with the Convention.

Third, these methods are used when there is general alignment between the domestic law and the CRC, or, to use the *Mathieson* terminology, when the domestic law can be applied in harmony with

[197] *AL (Serbia) v. Secretary of State for the Home Department* [2008] UKHL 42 at para. 32 (Lady Hale).

[198] Gilmore includes in this category the use of the CRC as context or support for the domestic law or a certain interpretation of it, or as an explanation for the rationale of domestic legislation: Gilmore, 'Use of the UNCRC', 518.

the CRC. The methods tend therefore to maintain the status quo. Nonetheless, although subtle and somewhat ancillary, they are not innocuous. Gilmore's designation of these methods as 'descriptive' portrays them as playing a passive or neutral role, which obscures their soft-normative influence consisting of channelling, however mildly and indirectly, the application of the domestic law towards a more CRC-friendly outcome.

Overall, it is difficult to gauge the level of judicial support for *sui generis* methods as a discrete category of engagement with the CRC. While they remain diffuse and theoretically ill-defined, they illustrate the complexity of the interaction between the CRC and domestic law, and the judicial creativity in managing it.

Having considered the CRC case law of the House of Lords and the Supreme Court in Sections 6.4 and 6.5, attention now moves to assessing the impact of judicial engagement with the CRC in light of the methods of engagement and the contribution it has made to the courts' reasoning.

6.7 The Impact of the Judicial Engagement with the CRC

6.7.1 The Methods of Engagement: Formal and Sui Generis

The CRC is regularly considered by the UK's highest courts regardless of its unincorporated status, but the multitude of dissenting and concurring judgments shows that its application is not yet settled. Lord Kerr's unsuccessful advocacy for a direct application of the CRC in *SG* reinforced the orthodox position that the Convention can only be applied indirectly. The consequences are that reliance on the Convention must be justified under the formal rules of reception, and that the Convention cannot operate as an autonomous source of law. This may sound limiting, but the infrastructure for the indirect application of the CRC in the UK is enabling. This is because the traditional common law methods of engagement (i.e., the use of the CRC to develop the common law and to interpret domestic legislation) are complemented by the use of the CRC to interpret the ECHR, either under the HRA or to inform the validity of statutes made under the devolved statutes. As already clear from Sections 6.4 and 6.5, the CRC has been most successful when applied in the HRA context and, since the latter came into force, the CRC has seldom been applied independently.

Nonetheless, there has been some innovation in the application of the presumption of compatibility in relation to the CRC used independently.

Notable is Lady Hale's reliance on article 12 of the CRC in *D (a child)* to create a presumption of listening to children in Hague Convention cases.[199] This pushed the boundaries of traditional engagement rules but was probably accepted by the Court because of the confined scope of the ruling and the convergence of article 12 of the CRC with the EU law, to which the UK adhered at the time. Interestingly, despite its popularity, article 3(1) of the CRC has not generated a similar presumption. Lord Kerr came close, but refrained from doing so:

> Where the best interests of the child clearly favour a certain course, that course should be followed unless countervailing reasons of considerable force displace them. It is not necessary to express this in terms of a presumption but the primacy of this consideration needs to be made clear in emphatic terms.[200]

An article 3(1)-inspired presumption would frame its domestic application in a procedural form familiar to the courts, which might eliminate some of the uncertainties regarding its scope and weight. However, the article's widespread use might make a presumption unnecessary, and its wide scope might create difficulties in the formulation of a presumption.

The emergence of *sui generis* forms of application, the diverging views in *SG* concerning the legitimacy of applying article 3(1) of the CRC to the justification analysis, and some judicial statements that pointed to the relevance of the CRC for the 'interpretation *and application*'[201] (emphasis added) of the ECHR indicate that there needs to be more attention to the use of the Convention beyond the interpretation of the substance of domestic norms. This would more accurately reflect the nuances of the courts' engagement with the CRC.

The under-use of common law engagement methods in relation to the CRC shows the importance of the HRA as a vector for the Convention. The prevalence of cases where the CRC has been applied in an HRA context[202] indicates that legislative endorsement, however indirect, has facilitated its judicial application. The HRA, through the prominence it gives to ECtHR judgments that customarily refer to the CRC, ensures a

[199] See Section 6.4.

[200] *ZH* at para. 46 (Lord Kerr).

[201] *R v. Durham Constabulary* at para. 26 (Lady Hale); *SG* at para. 217 (Lady Hale); *Nzolameso* at para. 29 (Lady Hale).

[202] Prior to 2 October 2000, the CRC was referred to by the House of Lords in only four cases.

minimum engagement by the courts with the Convention. As put by Lady Hale, the CRC

> is not only binding in international law; it is reflected in the interpretation and application by the European Court of Human Rights of the rights guaranteed by the European Convention: ... to that extent at least, therefore, it must be taken into account in the interpretation and application of those rights in our national law.[203]

Overall, the application of the CRC in an HRA context has benefited the former by being its 'primary vehicle'[204] and by providing the rights of children with 'real and practical value'.[205] This has strengthened the legitimacy of the judicial use of the CRC and enabled its systematic application. The HRA has also smoothed the judicial application of the Convention. By requiring the consideration of ECtHR judgments, section 2 of the HRA enables the courts to adopt that Court's position developed with reference to the CRC, without navigating the more taxing requirements specific to the common law engagement methods (i.e., establishing an ambiguity in the domestic law). The inclusion of the CRC in the powerful normative radius of the ECHR has thus benefited the former.

The HRA has diversified the location of the Convention in the legal reasoning. Thus, if not deemed relevant or useful for interpreting the scope and content of ECHR rights, the CRC may be relevant for the justification/proportionality analysis. For example, the Borders, Citizenship and Immigration Act 2009 mentions children's welfare in section 55, but, in *ZH*, Lady Hale did not interpret it according to article 3(1) of the CRC.[206] Instead, she went on to use that article in the proportionality analysis under article 8(2) of the ECHR. In *T v. Secretary of State*, Lord Reed did not use the CRC to interpret the

[203] *R v. Durham Constabulary* at para. 26 (Lady Hale).

[204] Kathryn Hollingsworth, 'Commentary on *R v JTB*' in Helen Stalford, Kathryn Hollingsworth, and Stephen Gilmore (eds.), *Rewriting Children's Rights Judgments: From Academic Vision to New Practice* (Oxford: Hart Publishing, 2017) 421, 426.

[205] Jane Fortin, 'Children's Rights: Flattering to Deceive?' (2014) 26(1) *Child and Family Law Quarterly* 51, 53.

[206] Lady Hale did not explain the reason for not interpreting the Borders, Citizenship and Immigration Act in light of the CRC. It may be that she considered that the term 'welfare' had a clear domestic meaning that was difficult to align with article 3(1) through the presumption of compatibility, because of its narrower scope and it not being a primary consideration. Or, it may be the procedural explanation that such interpretation was not argued for by the parties.

substance of article 8(1) of the ECHR, for which he relied on the ECtHR jurisprudence. His Lordship instead used the Convention in the justification analysis. Further, locating the CRC in the justification analysis allowed the CRC to be used in cases where the litigated rights are the rights of adults, not those of children.[207]

Post-HRA, there has been a positive evolution in the meaningful engagement with the CRC and a rise in child rights-informed judicial reasoning. Thus, in early cases such as *Hunter, Sanderson*, and *Venables and Thompson*, the CRC was present in dissenting or concurring judgments, but, by the 2010s it was used in powerful majority and unanimous judgments such as *ZH* and *Mathieson*. Bolder usages followed, with general comments of the CRC Committee being unanimously accepted as authoritative interpretations of the Convention,[208] and powerful dissents – some going as far as suggesting a direct application of the CRC.[209]

There are, however, some drawbacks to the dominance of the joint application of the CRC with the ECHR, under the framework provided by the HRA. First, because of the administrative nature of the ECHR, most CRC cases that have reached the UK's highest courts have been public law cases. On the one hand, this is positive because it extends the application of the rights of children to areas of law where they have been generally neglected and demonstrates that children's rights are sufficiently legally mature to be capable of application to complex legal problems. On the other hand, it is problematic because it leads to much of the children's rights jurisprudence being developed in cases where these rights confront powerful public interests (i.e., immigration control and welfare policies), to which they often yield. This may not, therefore, be a context in which children's rights thrive judicially.

Second, the absence of socio-economic rights in the ECHR limits the variety of CRC rights that have been argued in courts. Although articles 26 and 27 of the CRC have been invoked in several cases,[210] their legal content is little explored as they served as interpretive tools or context for article 3(1) of the CRC or article 8 of the ECHR, in the shadow of which they remain.

[207] Baroness Hale's approach in *Williamson*.

[208] *Mathieson*.

[209] *SG* (Lord Kerr).

[210] *Smith* at paras. 77–78 (Lady Hale) (articles 27(2), 27(4)); *SG* at para. 227 (Lady Hale) (article 27); *McLaughlin* at para. 40 (Lady Hale) (article 26); *DA* at paras. 70 (Lord Wilson); 180 (Lord Kerr) (articles 26–27).

Third, the ECHR may cap the CRC and stifle its impact. Where there is tension between their standards, the ECHR prevails as an incorporated treaty even when the CRC is more protective.[211] Also, rights can be overridden by non-rights considerations (such as national security and public safety), as permitted under article 8(2) of the ECHR – despite the CRC Committee's view that children's best interests in a migration context can *only* be overridden by rights-based factors.[212] Further, unambitious ECtHR judgments can limit the prospect of domestic courts exploring more child-focused legal solutions. Thus, for Lord Judge in *HH*, it appears that the absence of ECtHR precedent to block an extradition that was in the public interest for the sake of the children of the extradited person was a nod in favour of not developing such a possibility domestically.[213] Further, the majority of the Supreme Court in cases such as *JR38*, *SG*, and *DA* was content to follow the existing ECtHR precedent, rather than develop the applicable ECHR standards in a more child-focused direction by applying the CRC.

Fourth, if the CRC is always filtered through the ECHR, it is denied its status as an independent human rights treaty that is able to make a unique contribution to the development of the UK law, as well as the opportunity to develop a direct unmediated relationship with that law. While the association with the ECHR has been beneficial to the CRC, the latter has often been somewhat ancillary and constrained by the legal algorithm of the former. As Lord Hughes stated, the CRC will not be relevant 'to every ECHR question which arises, simply because children are as a matter of fact affected by the decision or legal framework under consideration'.[214] For example, to be applied under the HRA framework, the CRC had to be 'squeezed' into the justification enquiry under article 8 (2) of the ECHR in *ZH* and *Mathieson*, or somehow be connected to the 'manifestly without reasonable foundation' test in *DA* or the 'reasonable expectation of privacy' test in *JR38*. When it did not fit into that framework, which was designed to advance the ECHR, the Convention was rejected by the majority (e.g., in *SG* and *JR38*). Collinson has rightly observed that the limited scope of article 8 of the ECHR (i.e., private and family life), with which article 3 of the CRC is most often applied, prevents a consideration of all the factors relevant under the latter for

211 *R v. Durham Constabulary* at paras. 39–40, 42 (Lady Hale).

212 *ZH* at para. 28.

213 *HH* at para. 114 (Lord Judge).

214 *SG* at para. 142 (Lord Hughes).

an assessment of the best interests.[215] A real risk of the close link between the CRC and the ECHR is that a potential abrogation of the HRA would lead to the collapse of the foundation on which most of the more recent application of the CRC has been built.[216]

6.7.2 *What Did Reliance on the CRC Achieve?*

As discussed in Section 6.7.1, there has been a positive trend in the frequency with which the CRC is applied by the Supreme Court, with the proviso that the case law is dominated by article 3(1). Overall, however, the engagement with the CRC has resulted in more child-responsive interpretations and applications of the law, with the impact of the CRC varying from limited to significant.

In some judgments the impact of the CRC is difficult to discern,[217] but in others it is clear. For example, in *Hunter*, Lord Coke would have developed the common law of nuisance with reference to article 16 of the CRC, while in *R v. G* and *Venables and Thompson* child-sensitive interpretations of relevant statutes were suggested. *ZH* has been significant in many ways, including by pioneering a rights reasoning in relation to child welfare and expanding the duty to give a primary consideration to the best interests of the child beyond decisions concerning the child's upbringing. Article 3(1) has generally justified a sharper focus on children's specific legal needs. In *MM*, the challenged immigration rules and regulations were found to be inconsistent with the HRA and section 55 of the Borders, Citizenship and Immigration Act only to the extent that they did not give a primary consideration to the best interests of the affected children.[218] The adult's claim based on the ECHR failed.

Admittedly, this wider use of the CRC has not always secured a child-responsive application of the law, especially when judges consider its relevant provisions in isolation. Illustrative is *R v. Durham Constabulary*. Lord Bingham (in the leading judgment) decided that the application of

[215] Jonathan Collinson, 'Making the Best Interests of the Child a Substantive Human Right at the Centre of National Level Expulsion Decisions' (2020) 38(3) *Netherlands Quarterly of Human Rights* 169, 172.

[216] Donson, 'Commentary'.

[217] See, for example, *R (on the application of AA) v. Secretary of State for the Home Department* [2013] UKSC 49; *TN and MA (Afghanistan) v. Secretary of State for the Home Department* [2015] UKSC 40.

[218] *MM* at paras. 91–92 (Lady Hale and Lord Carnwath). Lord Kerr's position in *Ali* is similar in this regard.

diversion measures without the consent of the child and his parents did not breach 'the spirit or the letter'[219] of the CRC because the diversion is recommended by article 40(3)(b) and (4) of the CRC.[220] By contrast, a holistic analysis with reference to articles 3(1) and 37 and to soft law instruments pertaining to juvenile justice led Baroness Hale to conclude that the endorsement of diversion in the CRC did not deprive child offenders of legal guarantees of a fair trial.[221] In *S (a child)* and *JR38*, the respective majorities declined to give children's privacy rights under the ECHR a more generous interpretation by relying on the CRC. Similarly, *HH* offered the Court the opportunity to adjust the extradition rules to give more weight to the interests of the affected children, while *T v. Secretary of State* and the benefits cap cases created opportunities to develop a child-specific approach to the limitation of ECHR rights. None of these opportunities were taken by the courts.

Judgments in which the CRC is not engaged with in depth should not be easily dismissed as lacking impact. They reinforce the legitimacy of its use and, as Gilmore suggests, they keep the Convention 'visible in domestic law' and judges 'mindful' of its availability.[222] The influence of the CRC can be subtle, although the engagement may not be extensive. In *Ali (Iraq) v. Secretary of State for the Home Department*,[223] for example, Lord Kerr's fleeting mention of article 3(1) in his dissenting judgment strengthens the domestic support for the principle that compliance with this article cannot be achieved if legislation dictates what is in a child's best interests.[224] In *Nzolameso* and *MM*, the Court reasoned in harmony with article 3(1) of the CRC and its interpretation in General Comment No. 14,[225] without formally applying either and upon a limited consideration of the Convention. Limited engagement judgments can have analytical value and may lay the foundation for future developments. For example, Lady Hale and Lord Carnwath's brief

[219] *R v. Durham Constabulary* at para. 18 (Lord Bingham).

[220] *R v. Durham Constabulary* at para. 19 (Lord Bingham).

[221] *R v. Durham Constabulary* at paras. 27, 29 (Lady Hale).

[222] Gilmore, 'Use of the UNCRC', 509. See, for example, general references to article 18 of the CRC in *R v. London Borough of Barnet ex parte G* [2003] UKHL 57 at para. 68 (Lord Hope).

[223] [2016] UKSC 60 (*Ali*).

[224] *Ali* at para. 148 (Lord Kerr).

[225] That is, failure to enquire into the impact of a decision on children and failure properly to justify the decision beyond generalities (*Nzolameso* at para. 36 (Lady Hale)); the immigration rules and guidance were unlawful because they were 'highly prescriptive' on what was in the child's best interests (*MM* at para. 91 (Lady Hale and Lord Carnwath)).

reference to article 3(1) in *MM* reinforces the significance of both the individual and the collective interests of children,[226] while, in *Nzolameso*, Lady Hale opened the discussion about the use of the CRC for statutory interpretation independently of the ECHR and in the absence of ambiguity in the domestic law.[227]

In general, reliance on the CRC has been associated with acknowledgements that children have distinct rights and interests, and with closer attention to children and their unique legal needs. This is illustrated especially in cases concerning the rights of others, usually the parents. In *R v. Secretary of State for Education and Employment ex parte Williamson*,[228] for example, Baroness Hale (writing separately) relied on the CRC to justify her focus on children's rights in a case concerning corporal punishment in schools argued on the basis that the religious rights of *parents and teachers* had been breached. In *ZH* and other subsequent immigration or extradition cases, judges focused on children's interests separately from those of their parents and agreed that children should not bear the consequences of the behaviour of their parents.[229] In *Christian Institute*, the focus was stirred away from the parent-focused argument of the parties through reference to numerous CRC provisions concerning the relationship between parents and children and the privacy rights of children.[230]

Much of the impact of the CRC has resulted from the courts' keen engagement with article 3(1). The highlight remains *ZH*, which 'radically changed'[231] the approach to children's rights in public law by requiring that the best interests of the child be given a primary consideration in official decision-making in any context. *ZH* extended the caring considerations that formerly informed judgments concerning upbringing to a wider range of public law decisions. It also demonstrated that those protective considerations can be conceptualised in a human rights framework. The approach developed in *ZH* has some commonalities with the domestic interpretation given to the welfare principle in private law, with which the judges were familiar.[232] Nonetheless, Lady Hale's reasoning

226 *MM* at paras. 45–48, 88–92 (Lady Hale and Lord Carnwath).
227 *Nzolameso* (Lady Hale).
228 [2005] UKHL 15 (*Williamson*).
229 *ZH* at paras. 33, 37 (Lady Hale).
230 *Christian Institute* at paras. 71–77.
231 Fortin, 'Children's Rights: Flattering to Deceive?', 55.
232 In *J v. C (an infant)* [1970] AC 668, Lord MacDermott interpreted the phrase 'shall regard the welfare of the infant as the first and paramount consideration' as connoting 'a

does not simply extend the private law position, which is not acknowledged, to public law cases; instead, she crafted the child-focused approach by relying on article 3(1).

The prior absorption of best interests values in the jurisprudence concerning article 8 of the ECHR, in section 55 of the Borders, Citizenship and Immigration Act, and in its implementation Guidelines may have facilitated the use of article 3(1) in *ZH*,[233] but the latter was not decorative in Lady Hale's reasons. As Collinson remarked, the cases under article 8 of the ECHR relied on in *ZH* to support the relevance of the best interests of the child to the case did not use the formula of 'a primary consideration'.[234] Section 55 of the Borders, Citizenship and Immigration Act requires the Secretary of State to consider the 'welfare of children', but does not spell out a *duty* to give a *primary* consideration to the *best interests* of the child.[235] The Guidelines, while stating the primacy of the best interests,[236] do not remedy the Act because of their subordinate legal status.

The above are not semantic matters but carry legal consequences. While the *substantive* core of the best interests concept (i.e., the child's well-being or welfare) was indeed familiar to the courts prior to the CRC, its *legal* aspects (i.e., the duty to give it a primary consideration) owe much to article 3(1). *ZH* reflects a change in the nature of the best interests of the child from a matter predominantly of *fact* into a matter of *law*: the best interests of the child were no longer simply an outcome to

process whereby, when all the relevant facts, relationships, claims and wishes of parents, risks, choices and other circumstances are taken into account and weighed, the course to be followed will be that which is most in the interests of the child's welfare as that term has now to be understood. That is the first consideration because it is of first importance and the paramount consideration because it rules upon or determines the course to be followed': at 18.

233 Fortin, 'Are Children's Best Interests Really Best?', 951. See Home Office, UK Border Agency, *Every Child Matters: Change for Children, Statutory Guidance to the UK Border Agency on Making Arrangements to Safeguard and Promote the Welfare of Children* (November 2009). Taylor also argued that the use of article 3(1) was 'least contentious' when domestic legislation required that children's welfare be considered: Taylor, 'Putting Children First?', 51.

234 Collinson, 'Making the Best Interests', 175.

235 But, see Lord Kerr's view in *Ali*: 'the obligation under section 55 of the Borders, Citizenship and Immigration Act, incorporating article 3(1) of the United Nations Convention on the Rights of the Child, to treat the child's best interests as a primary consideration' (para. 148).

236 Home Office, UK Border Agency, *Every Child Matters*, 15, at para. 2.7.

be pursued in certain decisions concerning children, but also an integral part of a rule that gives rise to entitlements and obligations, and the content of which is ascertainable through legal interpretation. This 'legalisation' of the best interests was further cemented in subsequent cases, with *SG* and *Mathieson* refining the interpretation of the duty by reference to General Comment No. 14.

The distancing from the 'welfare' terminology in *ZH* has created opportunities to develop a non-paternalistic approach to children's best interests. The numerous child-specific rights in the CRC, together with the ECHR rights, provided the tools to embark on such an approach. Thus, in some cases, children's best interests were defined in relation to the right to respect for family life in article 8 of the ECHR and to the protection of property (A1P1) in others, with consideration given to articles 12, 7, and 8 (*ZH* and *HH*), 26 and 27 (*SG* and *DA*), and 40 (*JR38* and *T v. Secretary of State*). Lady Hale, who has been a strong advocate for establishing children's best interests by considering their views,[237] relied for this purpose on article 12 of the CRC rather than the ECHR. Article 3(1) was used therefore as a gateway for other CRC rights, including socio-economic rights that otherwise have no formal legislative recognition.

The expansive meaning of the phrase 'matters concerning children' in article 3(1) of the CRC justified the extension of the duty to decisions that affect children indirectly – individually but also collectively. After *ZH*, children's interests have been engaged with even when the applicable statutes (regarding, for example, extradition, planning, and leave from prison) did not contain an obligation to consider their welfare.[238] Consideration of article 3(1) in cases involving foreign policy (extradition in *HH*) or social policies (in *SG* and *DA*) suggests that no issue, however politically or economically sensitive, is inherently beyond the scope of a duty to give a primary consideration to the best interests of the child.

It is not clear how far the duty extends in cases concerning children indirectly. Judges have been unimpressed with adult litigants using children's best interests as a passport for their own rights.[239] They were, however, amenable to applying the duty when the interests of children

[237] Lady Hale in *ZH* (paras. 34–37) and *HH* (para. 85).

[238] Taylor, 'Putting Children First?', 54. See also Fortin, 'Children's Rights: Flattering to Deceive?', 55–56.

[239] *Makhlouf* at para. 47 (Lady Hale); *MM* at para. 88 (Lady Hale and Lord Carnwath).

and parents were 'indistinguishable'[240] because of the indissolubility of those interests in the context of their common family life. The application of the duty in other contexts may therefore depend on the ability to show a similarly indissoluble link between children's interests and the subject of litigation, a restrictive test that may discourage the application of article 3(1) of the CRC to matters concerning children indirectly.

The interaction between the domestic concept of welfare and the international best interests in public law matters caused a shift from 'paramountcy' to 'primacy' as a trade-off for expanding the range of decisions in which the best interests of the child are relevant. In cases such as *ZH*, *HH*, and *Zoumbas*, the judges accepted the reality that, unlike in private law cases, children's interests cannot prevail in all public law cases, but tempered this with the caution that it was no carte blanche to ignore children's rights and interests.[241]

General Comment No. 14 gave the judges a framework by which they could articulate the idiosyncrasies of article 3(1). This interaction between domestic and international protective concepts reveals the multifaceted nature of article 3(1), which encompasses not only the traditional concept of welfare/well-being but also a rule with content ascertainable through legal interpretation. This distinction is not yet formally acknowledged by the Supreme Court, but *DA*, in which the majority concluded that article 3(1) was not breached despite the detrimental effect of welfare policies on the affected children, shows that such a distinction is being made. The distinction between welfare or best interests as a fact or outcome, and the best interests as part of a legal rule, respectively, puts the criticisms of indeterminacy and arbitrariness in a new perspective. It may be that the best interests of the child are indeterminate when approached as the potential outcome of a legal enquiry, but neither indeterminate nor arbitrary when approached as part of a legal rule the content of which has been clarified by case law and General Comment No. 14.

The flexibility of article 3(1) does not promote arbitrary decisions but ensures that children's interests are given a primary consideration, which is prevented when legal rules dictate a specific outcome irrespective of individual circumstances. Thus, rules that prescribe when the deportation of a parent is proportionate 'positively disregard[ed] the child's

[240] *DA* at paras. 77 (Lord Wilson); 182 (Lord Kerr). See similarly *SG* at para. 146 (Lord Hughes).

[241] *PJS* at para. 72 (Lady Hale). See Section 6.5.2.

interests';[242] immigration rules that 'lay down a highly prescriptive criterion'[243] for making decisions concerning family reunification were unlawful; and the application of a blanket rule to suspend disability payments without considering the best interests of the affected child was also unlawful.[244] At a minimum, article 3(1) has prevented '[t]he best interests of the children [melting] away into the background',[245] justified adapting the interpretation and application of the law to children's specific needs, and rallied judges around the view that, when relevant, no interest is inherently superior to that of children.

References to the CRC Committee's work have generally enriched UK judgments by reinforcing child-focused approaches to the interpretation and application of the law and by providing guidance when it was not available domestically or from the ECtHR.[246] For example, Lady Hale's strong support for listening to children in the determination of their best interests has been built with reliance on General Comment No. 12,[247] while Lord Kerr relied on General Comment No. 14 to support a child-friendly interpretation of article 8 of the ECHR in *JR38*.

The most significant breakthrough for the work of the Committee in the case law is the Court's unanimous acceptance of General Comment No. 14 as an authoritative interpretation of article 3(1) in *Mathieson*. The judges made it clear, however, that they did not consider it binding, either domestically or internationally.[248] This left the meaning of 'authoritative interpretation' unclear, but a solution is offered by *ZH*, where Lady Hale rejected the Committee's view but only upon considering it and explaining her divergence.[249]

The *Mathieson* unanimous recognition of a general comment as authoritative had notable consequences. First, Lord Carnwath's speech in *SG*[250] (endorsed in *Mathieson*) brought the nuances of article 3(1) into

242 *Ali* at para. 148 (Lord Kerr).
243 *MM* at para. 91 (Lady Hale and Lord Carnwath).
244 *Mathieson*.
245 *ZH* at para. 42 (Lord Hope).
246 Cases in which general comments have been quoted include *Williamson* (Lady Hale); *ZH* (Lady Hale); *HH* (Lady Hale); *SG* (Lord Carnwath); *Mathieson* (Lord Wilson); *JR38* (Lord Kerr); *Makhlouf* (Lord Kerr).
247 CRC Committee, *General Comment No. 12 (2009): The right of the child to be heard*, 20 July 2009, CRC/C/GC/12; *ZH* at para. 37 (Lady Hale); *HH* at para. 85 (Lady Hale).
248 *DA* at para. 69 (Lord Wilson). See also *SG* at para. 152 (Lord Hughes).
249 *ZH* at para. 27 (Lady Hale), citing CRC Committee, *General Comment No. 6*, para. 86.
250 *SG* at paras. 105–107 (Lord Carnwath), where *General Comment No. 14* is discussed extensively.

the domestic law, including the useful framework developed by the Committee in terms familiar to the courts and well aligned with their judicial function (i.e., article 3(1) as containing a right, a principle, and a rule of procedure). Second, the identification by the Committee of the distinct dimensions of article 3(1) provided a basis for understanding the multidimensional nature of the best interests of the child. This improved the applicability of article 3(1) because it enabled its distinct dimensions to be used independently, as relevant. In *Mathieson*, for example, the rule-of-procedure dimension of article 3(1) was relied on to decide that the official action was unlawful. The third consequence is the transparency and accountability in making decisions where the best interests ought to be a primary consideration, as discussed above. It remains regrettable that, so far, the absorption of General Comment No. 14 in judgments has been selective. Its procedural aspects are strongly represented, unlike those aspects in which the Committee stresses that children's best interests are to be defined by reference to the relevant rights in the CRC.

6.7.2.1 Added Value

As a legal instrument aimed at protecting children's rights, the CRC was intended to make a unique contribution thereto. How the uniqueness of the CRC, or its added value, manifests itself is difficult to anticipate or prescribe, but the UK case law reflects a variety of forms – most of which are associated with the use of article 3(1).

The CRC enabled the extension of the scope of the duty to give a primary consideration to the best interests of the child to decisions in which such interests were not traditionally considered, even where no ECtHR authority was available. This is important in the absence of an explicit legislative mainstreaming of such a duty. It enabled courts to adapt the interpretation and the application of the law to children's needs, and to give a primary consideration to children's interests rather than considering them only as a relevant factor. In *Smith*, article 27 of the CRC supported a positive obligation under article 8 of the ECHR, while in *D (a child)* article 12 of the CRC supported the extension of a duty to listen to children in abduction cases.

Article 3(1) legally justified giving special attention to the interests of children, independently of those of their parents. Although article 3(1) may have been found relevant in cases concerning children indirectly on the bandwagon of article 8 of the ECHR, it thereafter justified an independent analytical attention to their interests to ensure, inter alia, that children do not suffer the negative consequences of parental conduct;[251] that children's rights are prioritised over the equivalent rights of other family members;[252] and that children express their own views, especially when their interests might not overlap with those of their parents.[253] Article 3(1) also justified giving a child-focused content to general human rights, including by creating additional child-specific obligations or by safeguarding the flexibility of decision-making so as to respond to the needs of individual children. The formulation of article 3(1) (i.e., its evaluative features) has been of assistance in the proportionality enquiry under the ECHR and in the balancing of the relevant rights and interests.

In most cases, the CRC is invoked within an HRA/ECHR context, making it difficult to discern its independent impact. Where there is no Strasbourg authority, however, the influence of the CRC is easier to discern. In *T v. Secretary of State*, in the absence of Strasbourg authority, the justification assessment under article 8 of the ECHR was guided by an international law background that included article 40 of the CRC and Rule 21 of the Beijing Rules.[254] Article 12 and General Comment No. 12 have also provided support for advancing the views of the child in Lady Hale's judgments in *ZH*, *HH*, and *D (a child)*.

However, even where the CRC and the ECHR are blended in the reasoning, the Convention is not redundant. If child-focused changes to the interpretation of the law are being pursued, reliance on the ECHR might not suffice. In *Williamson*, for example, Lady Hale relied on the CRC to justify domestic legislation that prohibited all forms of corporal punishment in all schools because the ECHR standards only supported the prohibition of corporal punishment of some seriousness.[255] In *HH*, *SG*, and *DA*, judges used article 3(1) of the CRC in the ECHR justification analysis concerning extradition and social policies, which has not yet been done by the ECtHR.

The added value of the CRC can only be elicited through careful engagement with the Convention. So far, however, it is only article 3(1) that has benefited from a close analysis of its content, with the other provisions (except, perhaps, those regarding juvenile justice) often being

[251] Lady Hale in *ZH* and *HH*.
[252] *HH* at para. 33 (Lady Hale).
[253] *ZH* at para. 37 (Lady Hale); *HH* at para. 85 (Lady Hale).
[254] *T v. Secretary of State* at paras. 137, 142 (Lord Reed).
[255] *Costello-Roberts v. United Kingdom* (Application No. 13134/87, 25 March 1993) at para. 36, cited by Lord Nicholls in *Williamson* at paras. 26–27.

used as an indication of legitimate children's interests rather than rights. Opportunities to discover the added value of other provisions are therefore being missed. Another impediment to uncovering the added value of the CRC is that it has been invoked primarily in cases where adult rights were litigated.[256] This may detract attention from children's rights, leading to their 'development by ricochet', which is not conducive to their growth.

Overall, nonetheless, the CRC has left a mark on the case law by prompting judges more deliberately and carefully to consider children as bearers of rights that respond to their unique needs as a special class of rights holders.

6.8 Conclusion

The UK case law shows that the CRC can be effectively engaged with in dualist states, even if it is not legislatively incorporated, provided that the structure of reception facilitates its application. The interaction between the CRC and the reasoning of domestic courts is multifaceted, and the emergence of *sui generis* techniques shows that the traditional methods of engagement with international treaties are not able to describe in full how courts apply the Convention.

The most conducive aspect of the reception structure in the UK has been the human rights protection framework under the HRA. Although that framework was designed to advance the ECHR rather than the CRC, it served as a gateway for a more consistent and meaningful engagement with the latter. Under the framework, references to the CRC have been legitimised and normalised. In the absence of the HRA and ECHR, the application of the CRC would have been less marked and probably uncertain. Should this edifice collapse, the application of the Convention is likely to suffer. It is, therefore, stringently necessary that, in parallel with developing the CRC application under the HRA, the courts develop the independent application of the Convention under the common law methods and, perhaps, the *sui generis* methods. This is not only a survival strategy for the Convention, but also one that would better enable it to make its unique contribution to developing children's rights without being capped by the ECHR.

256 There are some exceptions, however, such as *Venables and Thompson*, *E (a child)*, *JR38* and *T v. Secretary of State*.

The macro impact of the CRC is the courts' acceptance of the Convention as a legitimate justification for developing a differential legal treatment for children and as a repository of tools that enable them to do so. The general convergence between domestic law, the ECHR, and the CRC, and proactive judges willing to engage with the standards of the CRC and its interpretation by the Committee have coalesced to facilitate such acceptance.

Article 3(1) of the CRC stands out as the article most closely considered by judges. It has produced a sophisticated domestic jurisprudence that blends normative insights from the CRC, the general comments of the CRC Committee, and the ECtHR. Article 3(1) is a special case and its success is built on a favourable reception framework and its ability to fill the gap in the domestic legal categories able to respond to children's special legal position. It remains, however, concerning that most cases reaching the highest courts that concern article 3(1) (but also other CRC rights) have involved the rights of parents. This causes an oblique development of children's rights, whereby the full potential of the CRC might not be realised.

Lastly, the contribution made by individual judges to advancing the application of the CRC should not be overlooked. Lady Hale and Lord Kerr have consistently and thoroughly engaged with the CRC in powerful judgments, occasionally pushing to tease out its potential. The children's rights legacy of these two judges provides a good foundation for further developments.

7

The Judicial Application of the CRC

From Formal Reception to Legal Effect

7.1 Setting the Scene

The CRC is an ambitious treaty that requires commitment to its implementation from states and their organs. When engaging with the Convention, courts are at the intersection between the domestic and international legal orders: they are burdened with the expectation of implementation by the promoters of the CRC, but they are embedded in the domestic law, which vests them with the power that makes them valuable as tools of implementation.

To unpack the complexity of the courts' participation in the implementation of the Convention, this book turned to those who influence it: the CRC, the CRC Committee, and the courts themselves. As discussed in Chapter 2, the CRC does not explicitly require that it be judicially applied. Article 4 omits the courts from its general implementation mechanisms and does not mention access to remedies. The article is, therefore, not prescriptive of judicial involvement in the implementation of the CRC, and it appears less supportive of judicial application than are equivalent provisions in similar treaties. Nonetheless, the CRC supports judicial application when that is the 'appropriate' mechanism of implementation, according to article 4, in relation to specific provisions. Judicial application can be the appropriate implementation mechanism in relation to, for example, articles that mention courts specifically or are related to the judicial function (e.g., juvenile justice, judicial review, and the separation of children from parents). Thus, while the CRC does not create an international obligation to apply the entire CRC judicially, the nature of certain provisions may require that if it is the appropriate implementation mechanism.

On the other hand, the CRC Committee promotes a maximalist vision of judicial application, wherein the entire Convention is justiciable and should prevail domestically, as canvassed in Chapter 2. Domestic courts will find it difficult to import that vision domestically, because they do not inherently accept the equivalence between international and domestic law without more, and they do not operate in a space where international law is the dominant paradigm. Unlike those of the Committee, their powers and functions are shaped not by the aim of maximising the effects of the CRC but by the domestic law, including the rules that divide state powers between different branches. The courts are caught, therefore, between the high international aspirations voiced by the Committee and the domestic legal realities.

The nature of judicial function (i.e., interpreting and applying the law) is such that the first question a court will consider (explicitly or implicitly) concerns the CRC's legal status, which is clarified in each legal system by the rules of reception or the rules of engagement.[1] While basic and reductionist, this perspective retains its practical and analytical merits and it continues to inform whether and how the CRC is used by the courts. In this work, the approach prompted attention towards issues such as how the courts apply the CRC in jurisdictions with diverse rules of reception, whether such application has been meaningful, and what facilitating and inhibiting factors of that engagement have been considered.

7.2 Direct and Indirect Application of the CRC: Distinct in Form but Similar in Effect

As explained in Chapter 1, the aim of this research has been to ascertain the impact of the rules of reception on the meaningful engagement of the courts with the CRC. The focus has therefore been on meaningful engagement rather than simple mentions of the Convention in judgments. As discussed in Chapter 1, meaningful engagement can be assessed based on two criteria: procedural (appropriate consideration of the relevant CRC aspects) and substantive (the added value to the reasoning of the courts).

Meaningful engagement has taken place in all four jurisdictions studied here, with courts being able to give appropriate consideration to and extract relevant meaning from the CRC according to the specific reception rules in each system. This part discusses primarily the procedural

[1] Legal status is understood, widely, to include the use of unincorporated treaties for the purposes authorised by the rules of reception. See Section 1.3.1.

side of meaningful engagement, with the substantive aspects being discussed in Section 7.4.

The use of reception rules as the main analytical tool in this work permitted a differentiation between systems where the CRC has a vocation for direct application and those where it is applied indirectly, primarily through legal interpretation. France as a monist system fits into the first category par excellence, and Australia and the UK as de jure dualist states fit into the second. South Africa straddles the two categories: a hybrid system that is rendered de facto dualist by its courts not identifying with its monist-like feature, namely the self-execution of treaties.

The four case studies confirm that distinctions based on the reception rules remain convenient, widely accepted, and useful starting points in navigating the great diversity of legal systems bound by the CRC. The reception rules remain firmly entrenched and are unlikely to change in the absence of major constitutional shifts. Attempts to do so judicially by questioning the dualist status quo and arguing that the CRC has direct effect have failed both in Australia and in the UK.[2] Even when the dualist or hybrid courts have come close to applying the CRC directly, they have not acknowledged it as such – likely aware of the contentiousness of such a position – and have used various techniques to mask it.[3]

The core yield of the distinction is, as Van Alstine has argued, that courts that can apply treaties directly engage with them differently from courts that cannot.[4] Although all courts are preoccupied with the domestic *bindingness*[5] or legal status of the Convention, they approach it from fundamentally different premises (monist or dualist) and using different lenses (reception rules). Thus, direct application courts search for provisions that can operate independently or autonomously as domestic legal rules, while indirect application courts search for provisions that can assist in the interpretation or application of domestic norms. This

[2] See Section 4.4.1 (Australia) and Section 6.3 (the UK).

[3] See Section 5.4.1 (South Africa). For the UK, see *R (on the application of SG (previously JS)) v. Secretary of State for Work and Pensions* [2015] UKSC 16 (*SG*), where Lord Reed (para. 81) and Lord Hughes (para. 180) criticised Lady Hale's and Lord Kerr's approaches, which would allegedly amount to giving the CRC the force of domestic law. See Section 6.3.

[4] Michael P. Van Alstine, 'The Role of Domestic Courts in Treaty Enforcement: Summary and Conclusions' in David Sloss (ed.), *The Role of Domestic Courts in Treaty Enforcement: A Comparative Study* (New York: Cambridge University Press, 2009) 555, 566.

[5] The term used in Karen Knop, 'Here and There: International Law in Domestic Courts' (2000) 32(2) *New York University Journal of International Law and Politics* 501.

ultimately shapes the courts' paradigmatic relationship with the CRC. For example, the French courts, which apply the CRC directly, use the Convention as a discrete legal justification or reason for their judgments, while the indirect application courts tend to weave the CRC arguments into the interpretation or application of domestic sources of law.

Before delving into the implications of different approaches to judicial engagement, two general points can be made.

First, the purpose of deploying the engagement rules may be relevant to how the courts interact with the Convention. Thus, courts can deploy the engagement rules defensively to control the flow of international law towards domestic law. This can occur regardless of the type of system, and it is associated with a restrictive application of the Convention, as seen in Australia and in France. However, the engagement rules can also be deployed constructively, to help develop the domestic law, as done in South Africa, in the UK, and by the Supreme Court of Victoria (VSC) in Australia. This deployment choice is not a legal endeavour and it is largely dictated by context, including the legislative support for the CRC and the possible tensions with the domestic law.

Second, regardless of the type of system, the judicial engagement with the CRC is not consistent. That is so even in South Africa, where courts have a constitutional obligation to consider it when interpreting the Bill of Rights, and in France, where the CRC is part of the domestic law and thus binding on courts. Thus, supportive formal rules are not sufficient to ensure a consistent application of the CRC – although they form a strong basis to achieve it,[6] as discussed in this Part below.

Direct application or self-execution involves a wholesale importation of a CRC provision, the content *and* scope of which become compulsory for the courts. The CRC provisions recognised as directly applicable in France are now mainstreamed in judicial decision-making, despite the absence of a consolidated wide-span children's rights statute. Direct application can therefore be a good antidote to the fragmentation of child rights-relevant domestic legislation. Attempts to obtain similar results through statutory interpretation in dualist Australia have failed,[7] but, in

[6] French and South African courts have sanctioned lower courts for not considering the CRC: *AB v. Pridwin Preparatory School* [2020] ZACC 12; CE, No. 375887, 10 July 2015. The French Council of State opined that the omission was 'an error of law'.

[7] See *Northern Territory of Australia v. GPAO* [1999] HCA 8 (*GPAO*); *Minister for Immigration and Multicultural and Indigenous Affairs v. B* [2004] HCA 20 (*MIMIA v. B*), discussed in Section 4.4.2.

the UK, the duo HRA and ECHR support such mainstreaming up to the normative limits of the ECHR.[8]

Direct application is a powerful tool. When directly applied, the CRC is binding on the courts and informs the lawfulness of administrative acts, as the French case law demonstrates.[9] Direct application delivers immediate effects, regardless of legislative action, and it permits the application of the CRC '*as is*',[10] rather than adulterated by legislative translation. In France, it has made it possible for the supra-legislative status of the CRC to be asserted by courts.[11] Lastly, direct application of the CRC can import new rights and cover gaps in domestic law, as shown in the *Benjamin*[12] case in France.

As if wary of unleashing such major consequences, the courts have developed strict criteria for direct application, to which the CRC is vulnerable.[13] Because a directly applicable CRC provision becomes equivalent to a domestic norm, courts evaluate it using the same logic that they apply to domestic norms. This has been detrimental to the CRC and is reflected, for example, in the initial denial of its direct effect by the French Court of Cassation and in the limited number of provisions recognised as having direct effect. The French case study shows, however, that the reluctance to apply the CRC directly may not be informed by *legal* reasons only (i.e., not meeting the requisite criteria). In France, judicial policy reasons (i.e., concerns related to the separation of powers) compounded the perceived vulnerabilities of the CRC in relation to the criteria of direct application. In South Africa, judges generally open to international law have eschewed the self-execution of the CRC, likely because section 28 of the Constitution makes it seem unnecessary. Thus, despite its deceivingly simple propositions and grand promises, direct application presents practical difficulties.

Indirect application in dualist and hybrid systems allows a flexible à la carte engagement with those aspects of the CRC that are relevant to the dispute. The high bar of direct application criteria, linked to the intrinsic legal qualities of a provision, does not apply because a self-standing operation of a CRC provision is neither envisaged nor possible (apart

[8] See Section 6.5.

[9] See especially Sections 3.4 and 3.5.1.2.

[10] André Nollkaemper, *National Courts and the International Rule of Law* (Oxford: Oxford University Press, 2011) 118.

[11] See Section 3.5.1.2.

[12] Civ 1, No. 05-11285, 7 April 2006. See Section 3.3.

[13] See Chapter 2.

from in South Africa). Therefore, courts in Australia, South Africa, and the UK have used for interpretation purposes provisions that are not recognised as directly applicable in France.[14] Some judges have also looked beyond the letter of the CRC to its spirit.[15]

Nonetheless, indirect application is subject to the vagaries of legislative will. Illustrative is the interplay between the *Brandt*[16] and *CCL*[17] cases in South Africa. The CRC-compatible interpretation of a domestic statute in *Brandt* was reversed by legislation, which was subsequently declared unconstitutional in *CCL*.[18] It was therefore the constitutional entrenchment of CRC values that protected against regressive legislation. Further, the Convention's interpretive role is limited by the ambit of the interpreted statutes. Illustrative are *GPAO*[19] and *MIMIA v. B*[20] in Australia, where the interpretive influence of the CRC was capped at the ambit of the Family Law Act 1975 (FLA),[21] and *R v. Durham Constabulary* in the UK,[22] where Lady Hale noted the more limited scope of protection under the ECHR when compared with the CRC. More importantly, courts may refuse to read down legislation made by the Parliament, deliberately seeking to depart from the Convention, as illustrated by the Australian case study. This may suggest ample powerlessness by the courts in systems of parliamentary supremacy, such as Australia and the UK.

The reality is, however, more nuanced and a closer consideration of the structure of reception shows that there are domestic mechanisms that allow some judicial input in the control of legislation against the CRC,

[14] For example, article 5 in *Re Jamie* [2013] FamCAFC 110 (Bryant CJ); article 6 in *Certain Children v. Minister for Families and Children (No. 2)* [2017] VSC 251 (*Certain Children (No. 2)*); article 19 in *Christian Education South Africa v. Minister of Education* 2000 (10) BCLR 1051 (CC) (*Christian Education*); article 34 in *Geldenhuys v. The State* 2009 (1) SACR 1 (SCA) (*Geldenhuys*); article 27 in *SG* (Lady Hale); articles 26 and 27 in *R (on the application of DA) v. Secretary of State for Work and Pensions* [2019] UKSC 21 (*DA*) (Lord Kerr).

[15] For example, *Re Jamie* at para. 120 (Bryant CJ) (Australia); *M v. S (Centre for Child Law Amicus Curiae)* 2007 (12) BCLR 1312 (CC) (*M v. S*) at paras. 18–20 (Sachs J) (South Africa); *DA* at para. 187 (Lord Kerr) (the UK).

[16] *Brandt v. S* [2005] 2 All SA 1 (SCA). See Section 5.4.2.

[17] *Centre for Child Law v. Minister for Justice and Constitutional Development* 2009 (11) BCLR 1105 (CC). See Section 5.4.2.

[18] See Section 5.4.2.

[19] *Northern Territory of Australia v. GPAO* [1999] HCA 8 (*GPAO*).

[20] *Minister for Immigration and Multicultural and Indigenous Affairs v. B* [2004] HCA 20 (*MIMIA v. B*).

[21] See Section 4.4.2.

[22] [2005] UKHL 21. See Section 6.4.

even in systems of parliamentary supremacy. Thus, in Australia, the external affairs power of the Commonwealth Parliament enables the courts to exercise some limited judicial review over legislation, with reference to the CRC, as discussed in Section 4.4.1. In the UK and the Australian State of Victoria, human rights statutes enable courts to make declarations of inconsistent interpretation, in which the CRC can play a mediated role. It is, therefore, important to look beyond the rules of reception or statutes intended to give effect to the CRC for opportunities to engage with it by using all available domestic mechanisms.

The differences between direct and indirect application show that engagement with the CRC from different judicial perspectives and using system-specific tools reveal the normative diversity of the Convention – that is, the many ways in which it can be put to legal use.

Some courts consider the domestic status or bindingness of the CRC very closely, while others do not. The type of system is not an accurate predictor in this regard. Courts in both Australia and France have taken 'all-or-nothing'[23] approaches to the Convention, rejecting it when they could not give it effect in ways formally endorsed by the rules of reception. By contrast, South African and UK courts, and, in Australia, the VSC and the Family Court, have enquired less into the domestic status of the CRC.[24] It appears that legislative ambivalence vis-à-vis the CRC dissuades the courts from applying it, with the risk of violating the Convention, by raising concerns about trespassing into the legislative domain. The unequivocal constitutional and legislative endorsement of the CRC in South Africa reflects a political and legal agreement about its value, which assures the courts that they are not at variance with the will of the legislature. The HRA, reinforced by the powerful case law of the ECtHR, has an equivalent role in the UK. Even in Australia, the more generous application of the CRC by the Family Court and the VSC, when compared to the High Court, can be explained through the legislative support for its application in the FLA and in the Victorian Charter.

Legislative endorsements of CRC values not only confirm the domestic worth of the CRC, but also create opportunities to establish convergence with domestic law or expand the methods of engagement. In Victoria, the

[23] Knop, 'Here and There', 503.

[24] Although, at times, the CRC status was raised to justify courts not giving effect to it for not being incorporated. See, for example, *C v. Department of Health and Social Development, Gauteng* 2012 (4) BCLR 329 (CC) (*C v. Department of Health*) at para. 109 (Jafta J; Mogoeng CJ concurring).

relevant interpretive rule in the Victorian Charter has not altered substantively the equivalent common law presumption, but it has muted its remedial role in favour of a constructive one. This meant that the VSC could more easily use the CRC when the domestic standards were underdeveloped. As discussed in Chapter 4, the value-confirming effect of the Victorian Charter has led to the VSC being bolder even in its use of the common law engagement methods. In the UK, the interpretive injunctions in the HRA, although directed at the use of the ECHR, have benefited the CRC, which is customarily used for the interpretation of the ECHR by the ECtHR and the domestic courts alike.

Dividing legal systems into broad categories – monist and dualist, with a hybrid in-between – is analytically useful but does not result in homogenous categories because each system operationalises the paradigm engagement methods differently. For example, direct application or self-execution is a feature nominally shared by France and South Africa, but there are differences between how it manifests itself in those two systems. A directly applicable norm has supra-legislative status in France but under-statutory status in South Africa. Direct application is existential for the CRC in France, but, in South Africa, the powerful children's rights provision in the Constitution, buttressed by various interpretive injunctions, has made self-execution de facto redundant.

The interpretive enterprise too differs in Australia, South Africa and the UK. In Australia and the UK, common law interpretive presumptions apply when there is ambiguity in the law. The rules permit, without compelling, a consideration of the CRC and enjoin a preference for consistent interpretation. In the UK, the HRA permits the use of the CRC via the ECHR, even in the absence of ambiguity in the domestic law. In South Africa, on the other hand, it is mandatory to consider the CRC in the interpretation of the Bill of Rights, whether ambiguous or not, but an interpretation that is consistent with the Convention is not formally required (albeit it is most often followed). Also, the purpose for which the CRC is used has influenced the interpretive process. Thus, when interpretation is used remedially (i.e., to address a perceived problem with the law), as by the Australian High Court, courts are more cautious about interfering with legislative power. When interpretation is used constructively (i.e., to give content to domestic law), as in South Africa, Victoria, and the UK, the use of the CRC is more generous.

The dichotomy of direct–indirect application brings to the fore further distinctions in relation to the use of the CRC. When applied directly by a monist court, the CRC serves as legal authority. It is an autonomous source of law, a rule that binds the decision-maker and constrains conduct with certain effects. Indirect application, on the other hand, gives the CRC some *legal* effect but does not transform it into a legal authority, however influential the CRC may be for the outcome. Technically, therefore, the CRC is not treated as law in the interpretive process, although it performs a legal function. This is akin to using the CRC as legislative fact.

Constitutional law literature has distinguished between adjudicative and legislative facts.[25] Briefly put, adjudicative facts relate to the dispute at hand, while non-adjudicative facts, including legislative facts, are 'more general propositions about the world'.[26] Citing work by the American scholar Kenneth Culp Davis, Carter refers to legislative facts as those that help to establish the content of law or policy or the exercise of discretion; they are general and not immediately related to the parties.[27] This fits with the position of the CRC when indirectly applied in the case studies in this book. International law analyses of domestic judicial application have not yet used the concept of legislative facts in relation to the indirect application of treaties.[28] This is not the place for a full analysis, but the issue is worthy of attention because it appears to capture the nature of the CRC in the interpretive process: not binding authority, but nonetheless relevant to establishing the content of the law and the exercise of judicial discretion. A positive answer to the question as to whether the CRC can be engaged with as a legislative fact may open new avenues to insert the CRC into domestic legal reasoning and perhaps improve the consistency of its application. The legislative facts category may also be a useful analytical tool for some structuring within the *sui generis* forms of judicial engagement, discussed in the following section.

Returning to the more general discussion of indirect application, it is common to refer to 'interpretation' as a monolithic operation, but the case law analysed here calls for some differentiations. Thus, the 'location' of interpretation (i.e., the substance of rights or the limitation enquiry) and the distinction between the arguably discrete operations of interpretation and application may be relevant. The relegation of the CRC to the

[25] Anne Carter, 'Understanding Facts' in Anne Carter, *Proportionality and Facts in Constitutional Adjudication* (Oxford: Hart Publishing, 2021) 40.

[26] Carter, 'Understanding Facts', 44.

[27] Carter, 'Understanding Facts', 45.

[28] Perhaps Knop's suggestion of approaching international law as comparative law comes close to acknowledging that the former need not always be used as legal authority to produce meaningful domestic effects. See Section 1.3.1.

latter stages of judicial reasoning (i.e., limitation enquiry and application) deprives it of a role in shaping the substance of domestic rules. While the use of the CRC in interpreting the content of domestic laws requires unpacking the legal content of the relevant CRC provision, this may not be required in the limitation enquiry. Therein, the CRC appears to be used primarily as a fact (i.e., 'a descriptive statement about the world' that gets its meaning from the concrete world rather than a rule of law[29]) – a consideration when balancing competing rights and interests.[30] For example, depending on the case, in a limitation enquiry concerning the rights of adults, it may be sufficient to point to the importance of certain children's rights or the CRC itself, without necessarily analysing and capitalising on its provisions in depth.[31] It does not contribute to the development of the substantive content of rights, but uses the CRC in a factually dependent phase of the legal reasoning, wherein the decision-makers have much discretion. Further, human rights limitation enquiries are structured and based on the factors listed in the relevant instruments. The CRC needs to be moulded into those factors, which can be constraining. Thus, there are concerns that the CRC may not be used effectively in some interpretation processes.

At the same time, the use of the CRC in the limitation enquiry increases opportunities for its application. It also reflects a diversification in the application of the CRC, which ultimately confirms its normative agility. It allows, for example, the use of the CRC when the rights of the children themselves are not the subject of litigation, or when the CRC is deemed irrelevant or not useful for interpreting the substance of rights.[32] Further, its use in the limitation enquiry may be advisable to avoid the limitation of rights that are insufficiently informed by children's special needs. A balanced approach is therefore needed to ensure an effective and varied use of the Convention that utilises its normative potential to the maximum.

[29] Carter, 'Understanding Facts', 41.

[30] Carter has suggested that proportionality reasoning does not fit neatly into either the law category or the fact category: Carter, 'Understanding Facts', 44.

[31] See, for example, *Christian Education* in South Africa; *R v. Secretary of State for Education and Employment ex parte Williamson* [2005] UKHL 15 (Baroness Hale) in the UK.

[32] As illustrated by the British cases of *ZH (Tanzania) v. Secretary of State for the Home Department* [2011] UKSC 4 (UK) (*ZH*) and *T v. Secretary of State* [2014] UKSC 35 (see Section 6.7.1); or the South African cases of *Geldenhuys* and *Du Toit v. Ntshinghila* [2016] 2 All SA 328 (SCA) (see Section 5.4.2).

To conclude, broadly dividing legal systems into monist, dualist, and hybrid – and, further, along their paradigm engagement methods – is useful as a first step in understanding the interaction between the courts and the CRC by clarifying what the courts are authorised to do under the domestic law and what can reasonably be expected of them. Beyond general features, however, it is difficult to identify a monist or dualist paradigm of judicial application of the CRC because of the numerous domestic variations in the engagement rules.

7.2.1 Sui Generis *Methods of Engagement*

The rules of reception legitimate the courts' engagement with the Convention but are also useful as tools to distinguish between engagement methods that the courts are explicitly authorised to use and those that they are not. That courts engage with the CRC outside the formal rules is surprising, considering that, in all the legal systems analysed here, these rules have been underutilised[33] upon the courts having settled into certain application 'comfort zones'. Thus, despite ample space to grow the application of the CRC *within* the existing rules of reception, courts have relied on *sui generis* methods that transcend those rules.

For example, in several South African cases, the CRC has been used as a reference norm against which domestic legislation and policy were assessed.[34] The UK Supreme Court has assessed official conduct against the CRC, or used the Convention to reinforce or justify legislation, or as part of the context in which a decision is made.[35] In Australia, courts 'can note and call attention'[36] to the inconsistency between the domestic law and the CRC. They can use international law as a 'conceptual context' or to 'express the basic values which must be taken into account',[37] while accepting that international norms 'reveal but do not resolve conflicting interests'.[38] A better understanding of domestic law[39] and a discovery in

[33] For example, the prevalence or priority of the CRC over domestic law is rarely asserted in France; South African courts have not considered self-execution; external affairs power and statutory interpretation consistent with the CRC remain unexplored by the High Court of Australia; and, in the UK, the CRC is rarely used outside of the HRA framework.

[34] See Section 5.5.1.

[35] See Sections 6.6 and 6.7.1.

[36] *MIMIA v. B* at para. 171 (Kirby J).

[37] *AMS v. AIF* [1999] HCA 26 at para. 169 (Kirby J).

[38] *AMS v. AIF* at para. 50 (Gleeson CJ, McHugh J and Gummow J).

[39] *Koroitamana v. Commonwealth of Australia* [2006] HCA 28 at para. 66 (Kirby J).

the domestic law of convergent or carrier norms for the CRC[40] are other possible *sui generis* uses. *Sui generis* methods may be emerging in France, where advocacy is growing for the use of general international treaties as aids in statutory interpretation, which is not explicitly authorised by the Constitution. Further, courts have used the CRC to recognise some discretion for decision-makers to act in children's best interests.[41] The use of the CRC in the limitation enquiry can be seen as a *sui generis* form of engagement, but this depends on how widely a legal system defines 'interpretation'.[42]

The emergence of these techniques may have different reasons and serve different purposes. What is certain is that *sui generis* methods reflect courts' acknowledgement of the relevance of the CRC, and that a desire to give the Convention some effect when engaging with it in the formally endorsed ways poses some challenges. In Australia, *sui generis* methods have been an outlet for the unincorporated CRC, the application of which through traditional engagement techniques has been made difficult by legislative intransigence. *Sui generis* methods have been used in South Africa to explore the upper limits of the constitutional protection of children's rights, and in the UK to engage with the substance of CRC provisions without the filter of the ECHR.[43]

These methods are problematic when used as means to avoid wrestling with the traditional rules of engagement.[44] However, circumventing reception rules is not inherent in these methods. Thus, *sui generis* engagement can be seen as a grey area between engagement that is explicitly authorised and engagement that is prohibited – that is, a zone of permissible engagement. Forms of *sui generis* engagement cannot thus result in a breach of domestic law. Through *sui generis* methods, courts do not overtly challenge the status quo – albeit they subtly reshape a space that is not yet occupied by the explicit rules of engagement.

[40] *Minister for Immigration and Ethnic Affairs v. Teoh* [1995] HCA 20 (*Teoh*) at paras. 4–6 (Gaudron J); *Minister for Welfare and Population Development v. Fitzpatrick* 2000 (7) BCLR 713 (CC) (*Fitzpatrick*).

[41] See Section 3.5.2.

[42] In South Africa, it is arguable that the limitation enquiry is part of the interpretation category, but this is less clear in the UK and Victoria.

[43] See Sections 6.6 and 6.7.1.

[44] David Dyzenhaus, Murray Hunt, and Michael Taggart, 'The Principle of Legality in Administrative Law: Internationalisation as Constitutionalisation' (2001) 1(1) *Oxford University Commonwealth Journal* 5, 18.

These methods have been noted by other authors,[45] and this book further confirms their existence in an increasingly complex normative environment. They should therefore be acknowledged, their legitimacy discussed, and their role and theoretical viability clarified. The methods are an outlet for judicial agency and imbue the autochthonous children's rights jurisprudence with CRC values, making them easier to accept domestically. However, they lack legal protection due to their informality, which makes them liable to discretionary abandonment by the courts.

A significant weakness is the lack of conceptual clarity and, consequently, the risk of the methods being potentially misused to avoid the stringency of formal engagement rules. Conceptual clarity in this *sui generis* space may be difficult because it contains an amorphous mix of analytical tools but also methods with some constraining (albeit mediated, rather than independent) effect. The difficulty of conceptualising *sui generis* methods is reflected in the variety of ways in which they are addressed. Knop refers to them as 'less dispositive'[46] or as akin to using international law as comparative law (i.e., 'to judge our own [law]'[47]). McCrudden notes the use of international treaties for normative purposes rather than as legal authority, giving examples of cases where treaties were used to add weight to domestic reasoning or to highlight the alignment of domestic law with the treaties.[48] Gilmore refers to *sui generis* methods as descriptive uses,[49] while Fatima calls them a 'hazily defined – and ever expanding – penumbra'.[50] None of these authors have questioned their legitimacy, pragmatically accepting them as an illustration of what the courts do in practice. McCrudden suggests that what are referred to here as *sui generis* methods have not emerged because of the moral or political authority of international treaties, but rather because they are *law*.[51] It may, therefore, be that these *sui generis* methods reflect

[45] Shaheed Fatima, *Using International Law in Domestic Courts* (Oxford: Hart Publishing, 2005) 9.4; Stephen Gilmore, 'Use of the UNCRC in Family Law Cases in England and Wales' (2017) 25(2) *International Journal of Children's Rights* 500; Christopher McCrudden, 'Why Do National Court Judges Refer to Human Rights Treaties? A Comparative International Law Analysis of CEDAW' (2015) 109(3) *American Journal of International Law* 534; Dyzenhaus, Hunt, and Taggart, 'The Principle of Legality'; Knop, 'Here and There', 511.

[46] Knop, 'Here and There', 504.

[47] Knop, 'Here and There', 507.

[48] McCrudden, 'Why Do', 534n51.

[49] Gilmore, 'Use of the UNCRC', 518.

[50] Fatima, *Using International Law*, 9.4.

[51] McCrudden, 'Why Do', 544.

a diversification of the *legal* use of the CRC, congruent with the point made in Chapter 1 that there are many ways of *being legal* or *of the law*. This empirical reality needs closer theoretical attention, including in relation to why and when the courts resort to these methods and whether their use is detrimental to the formal methods of engagement.

More precision is also needed on how to identify *sui generis* engagement. This work has used a rather rudimentary approach, which has limited analytical qualities because it defines by exclusion and not by abstracting shared features. To start the conversation, some basic features that arise from the surveyed case law can be sketched: *sui generis* methods are not formally recognised but are not prohibited; their deployment does not result in a conflict with the domestic law; they have an analytical value in that they are used for an ascertainable purpose; and they may or may not have constraining effect. Another point of reflection in conceptualising the *sui generis* space is to give closer attention to what legal *interpretation* entails, and especially whether it involves only the clarification of the wording of a domestic provision or extends to influencing the *application* of domestic norms. The implications of the distinction between the interpretation and the application of the law, respectively, should be considered in the context of the relationship between domestic law and international law. It may be that more clarity on the interpretation/application duo may absorb much of *sui generis* methods or even do away with the category altogether.

In sum, the four jurisdictions studied here reveal the existence of a remarkable range of techniques that the courts use to engage with the CRC (i.e., using it as an autonomous norm, or as an interpretive guide, or as a relevant factor, or in interpreting substantive domestic rights, or in deciding their limitation). They testify to the numerous opportunities to consider the Convention and for it to manifest its legal-ness.

7.3 What Influences the Courts' Consideration of the CRC?

It emerges from the case law that the rules of reception, however generous or permissive, are not the only factor that influences the courts' engagement with the CRC or its effectiveness. A host of other factors facilitate or inhibit judicial engagement with the Convention. Some of these factors are CRC-related (and concern the special features of the CRC discussed in Chapter 1), while others relate to the intricacies of the domestic legal systems with which the CRC interacts, as detailed below.

Two general observations are necessary before proceeding. First, the factors discussed below are not exhaustive. The methodological focus on the rules of engagement does not capture important factors (e.g., litigation context or access to justice) because their consideration requires a different methodology. Second, many of the factors identified here may play an ambivalent role, both facilitating and inhibiting engagement. For example, the alleged vagueness of the CRC has sometimes been an obstacle to its application, but at other times it gave the Convention the flexibility needed for its application in unanticipated contexts – as amply demonstrated by the article 3(1) case law.[52] Further, a well-developed autochthonous children's rights case law may facilitate engagement with the CRC because it allows the courts to integrate the Convention into their reasoning. Conversely, if domestic law is well settled, it may be difficult for it to accommodate the CRC.

7.3.1 CRC Features

Several such features were identified in Chapters 1 and 2 as potentially relevant to the courts' engagement with the CRC. They included the juridical nature of the CRC, the nature and the novelty of its provisions, and the omission of the courts from among the means of CRC implementation in article 4.

The intrinsic juridical nature of the CRC has been largely uncontested by the courts, although some have rejected its *domestic* bindingness. Concerns that the CRC is vague, aspirational, or programmatic have preoccupied the courts unevenly. No such concerns have been raised in South Africa or the UK. French judges raised them extra-judicially, but the brevity of the judgments makes it difficult to ascertain if a general view exists among judges. In Australia, judges have occasionally considered the potentially aspirational nature of the Convention when questioning its ability to trigger the exercise of the external affairs power or to serve as an interpretive aid.[53] While theoretical certainty remains elusive in this area, the widespread application of the Convention speaks to an acceptance by the courts of its legal versatility or capacity to manifest itself as *legal*, as mentioned in Chapter 1. Thus, CRC provisions have operated as independent domestic rules; as aids in the interpretation or

[52] See Section 7.4.1.

[53] Callinan J in *MIMIA v. B* at para. 222; and, somewhat obliquely, Gleeson CJ and McHugh and Gummow JJ in *AMS v. AIF* at para. 50.

development of domestic law; as a context or framework for the application or development of domestic law; or as relevant considerations.

The nature of rights and their proximity to the judicial function correlates positively with the application of the CRC. For example, the engagement with article 3(1) by courts in France and South Africa has been linked with the article mentioning the courts.[54] The determination of the Family Court of Australia to extend its welfare jurisdiction beyond the traditional confines, with reference to the CRC, was borne out of the belief that it was within its function to do so.[55] Across the legal systems, CRC provisions concerning children's best interests (article 3(1)), their relationship with their parents (articles 7 and 9), and their right to be heard in proceedings (article 12), as well as juvenile justice provisions (articles 37 and 40), have been popular with the courts. By tradition or by nature, those rights involve some judicial processes over which the courts have a degree of control. This has made it easier for the courts to accommodate such rights than rights that may require enforcement against state organs or institutions – which may be reflected in the scarcity of case law on socio-economic rights that involve courts considering resource allocations or other policy-proximate considerations.

Two of the CRC's general principles, articles 3 and 12, have been popular with the courts, as discussed further in Section 7.4. In addition to their alignment with the judicial function, the general principles capture the essence of the CRC, as discussed in Chapter 1. They provide the courts with legal justification for a special legal treatment for children. Their flexibility or generality enables the courts to establish convergence with the domestic law, on which many instances of successful application rest. Their flexibility also facilitates their application to legal contexts where children's rights are not the dominant framework by enabling the identification and independent analysis of children's rights and interests, distinct from other interests.[56]

[54] *Director of Public Prosecutions, Transvaal v. Minister for Justice and Constitutional Development* 2009 (7) BCLR 637 (CC) (*DPP Transvaal*) at para. 77 (Ngcobo J); Pierre Bordry, 'Le Conseil d'État français et la Convention internationale relative aux droits de l'enfant' (2001) 205 *Journal du droit des jeunes* 16, 19; Jean-Luc Rongé, 'La Convention internationale relative aux droits de l'enfant: On avance ou on recule?' (2004) 10(240) *Journal du droit des jeunes* 9, 19.

[55] *B v. MIMIA* at para. 286 (Nicholson CJ and O'Ryan J) (see the emphasis on 'for judicial involvement').

[56] Helen Stalford, 'The Broader Relevance of Features of Children's Rights Law: The "Best Interests of the Child" Principle' in Eva Brems, Ellen Desmet, and Wouter Vandenhole

As discussed in Chapter 2, article 4 does not require states to ensure the judicial application of the CRC, leaving them with discretion in this regard. Among the courts surveyed here, only French and Australian judges have considered this article – and they have done so to justify their reluctance to give effect to the CRC. The French Court of Cassation used article 4 to justify denying direct application to the entire CRC, a position it later recanted. Australian High Court judges relied on it to argue that states enjoy discretion in terms of implementation measures, which need not include judicial application,[57] or that the state has chosen alternative institutions (i.e., human rights institutions) to give effect to the CRC.[58] The underlying consideration for these judges was that it is the legislatures or other state institutions, rather than the courts, that are to give domestic effect to the CRC. It appears, however, that with the growth in judicial application of the CRC, relying on article 4 to reject the consideration of the CRC has lost currency.

In brief, the special features of the CRC have a dynamic influence on how the courts engage with the Convention, which evolves with the uncovering of its legal dimensions and the development of its general principles.

7.3.2 Factors Not Related to the CRC: The Structure of Reception

The formal engagement rules are not the only domestic legal norms or institutions with which the CRC interacts. Instead, the domestic legal context or legal infrastructure (the 'structure of reception'[59]) in which the Convention operates plays an important role. This structure of reception

(eds.), *Children's Rights Law in the Global Human Rights Landscape: Isolation, Inspiration, Integration?* (Oxon: Taylor & Francis Group, 2017) 38, 40. This is abundantly demonstrated by the case law, especially in relation to the distinction between children's and parents' interests. See CE, No. 161364, 22 September 1997 (*Cinar*); CE, No. 285576, 7 June 2006 (*L'Association Aides*); *M v. S*; *Teoh*; *ZH*.

57 *MIMIA v. B* at para. 222 (Callinan J).

58 *Teoh* at paras. 40–41 (McHugh J), referring to the Parliament having chosen to give effect to the CRC through the remedial mechanisms of the Human Rights Commission.

59 Claudia Sciotti-Lam, *L'applicabilité des traités internationaux relatifs aux droits de l'homme en droit interne* (Brussels: Bruylant, 2004) 441. The relevance of the complexity of the domestic law to its interaction with the CRC is also acknowledged, albeit in slightly different terms, by Hoffman and O'Neil: Simon Hoffman and Sean O'Neil, *The Impact of Legal Integration of the UN Convention on the Rights of the Child in Wales* (Equality and Human Rights Commission, August 2018); Simon Hoffman and Rebecca Thorburn Stern, 'Incorporation of the UN Convention on the Rights of the Child in National Law' (2020) 28(1) *International Journal of Children's Rights* 133.

goes beyond the formal rules of reception. It is a complicated web of legal features that are selectively relevant, depending on the case.

Some components of the structure of reception are more obvious than others. Among the clearly evidenced components, this study has identified the substantive laws (including constitutional recognition of children's rights and human rights statutes), procedural laws, the institutional framework (the jurisdiction of the courts, federalism, the parliamentary system, and membership in effective regional human rights protection systems), and the legal tradition.[60] The more granular elements include the extent of the courts' discretion in particular systems;[61] sufficient flexibility in the law to tolerate *sui generis* methods;[62] and the judgment writing tradition.[63] Individual judges committed to applying the CRC are especially important in those systems where its consideration is not mandatory.[64] The structure of reception can be extended to non-legal features of domestic systems, with these 'softer' aspects (i.e., the social and political context) being relevant in the background. For example, the historical significance of human rights and their ability to support society's aspirations, their social legitimacy, and their political support are not mentioned in judgments, but they likely shape judicial attitudes and litigation. The South African case study illustrates this clearly.

It is seldom that the structure of reception is acknowledged as a factor (or a conglomerate thereof) that is significant for how the courts engage with the CRC. This should change. Children's rights writing is dominated by an internationalist perspective that approaches the CRC as the dominant instrument around which domestic law revolves. This perspective

[60] For example, the direct application of the CRC was a leap for the French courts. As courts with jurisdiction strictly determined by statute, they were called on to apply a complex treaty of a scope much wider than domestic statutes, without guidance from an international body.

[61] See Bell J in *Director of Public Prosecutions (Vic) v. TY (No. 3)* [2007] VSC 489 (*DPP v. TY*) (discussed in Section 4.6.2).

[62] See Section 4.7.2.

[63] Not all legal systems accommodate the writing of dissenting or concurring judgments. In France, for example, prior to the Court recanting its blanket denial of direct application of the CRC in 2005, Judge Ancel of the Court of Cassation was constrained to support the direct application of the CRC in academic publications because there was no practice of writing dissenting judgments. Nonetheless, separate and dissenting judgments can help the CRC jurisprudence to develop by espousing CRC-positive views, which could be embraced by other judges in the future.

[64] Kirby J in Australia; Ancel in France; Lady Hale and Lord Kerr in the UK.

has little domestic traction, as demonstrated by the Australian case law. When the Family Court attempted to address the fragmentation of child-related law by engaging in legal interpretation that was aligned with the CRC, it proved constitutionally unpalatable to the High Court and was rejected.[65]

The CRC and the domestic law have different logics. The CRC is reductionist because it conceptualises the legal issues as having the child in the centre and the state (mainly) as its debtor. Domestic law defies this reductionist perspective, with the child often being but one aspect of the decision-making. Even when children's rights are legally protected, litigation pulverises the matter brought to the court in inevitable legal questions that the CRC cannot answer, such as: Have the procedural rules been complied with? Which is the responsible state organ? Are the claims constitutionally sound? Are there other relevant interests, and how do they interact with children's rights? The potential exists, therefore, for the CRC to drown in technical domestic legal issues, especially when the law has not been transformed to accommodate it, and the Convention needs to be fitted into the domestic legal logic, language, and processes. It follows that the engagement of the courts with the CRC is seldom a matter of simply determining its legal status by applying the formal engagement rules and often involves attempts to articulate it into the domestic legal algorithm and its localisms. As Knop reminds us, 'the domestic interpretation of international law is not simply a conveyor belt that delivers international law to the people'.[66]

Domestically, therefore, the Convention is an element of the legal matrix and not the matrix itself.[67] At least two consequences arise from this. First, inevitably, the domestic law will dominate the courts' reasoning, both qualitatively and quantitatively. This is not, however, a licence to pay lip service to the CRC.[68] Cases in which the CRC is given

[65] See *Re Z* versus *GPAO*; *B v. MIMIA* versus *MIMIA v. B*. See Section 4.4.2.

[66] Knop, 'Here and There', 505.

[67] This aligns with McCrudden's observation that domestic judges are 'primarily domestic actors who use [the treaty] in order to advance domestic goals' and that '[t]he strategic goals they seek to further are mostly institutional rather than national': McCrudden, 'Why Do', 536.

[68] This occurs in cases where judges mention the CRC but do not even identify its relevant provisions. See, for example, *Re Woolley; Ex parte M276/2003* [2004] HCA 49 (*Re Woolley*) (the judgments of Gleeson CJ and McHugh J respectively) (Australia); Jafta J in *C v. Department of Health* (South Africa); CE, No. 400055, 27 July 2016; CE, No. 406256, 8 November 2017 (France).

little attention are not desirable,[69] although, admittedly, they reflect a judicial belief in the independent domestic *legal* value of the CRC and lay some groundwork for more meaningful engagement in the future. Quantitatively limited engagement is not necessarily meaningless, as long as it is effective (i.e., it extracts from the CRC what is relevant to a dispute). Second, the CRC influence depends not just on the nominal legal status conferred upon it by the rules of engagement, but also on its interaction with the other pieces of the matrix, from procedural rules to the division of power between different levels of government. These domestic contingencies must be well understood in order to develop locally effective CRC arguments and to prevent misleading generalisations. In brief, there is a need to diversify our understanding of the interaction between the CRC, domestic law and the courts, and to give more attention to the structure of reception.

As a part of the structure of reception, an autochthonous human rights framework has facilitated the interaction between the CRC and the domestic law, as illustrated by the improved application of the Convention by the VSC and the UK House of Lords/Supreme Court. Human rights statutes have facilitated the application of the Convention by, for example, recognising children's rights (such as in the Victorian Charter); containing mandatory or more permissive rules of engagement with international treaties (i.e., embracing the notion of ambiguity as choice or opportunity);[70] or aligning the domestic legal logic with the CRC (i.e., framing child-related issues as human rights). They also share some common features with the CRC (such as wider wording and application across legal fields, and the similar structure of the legal argument). Importantly, they have applied domestic human rights limitation clauses or reasoning to a CRC context. This not only complements the Convention, which lacks a limitation provision, but further confirms the confidence that the courts have in treating the CRC as a legal instrument. Ultimately, these statutes have all made it easier for the Convention to fit in domestically.

[69] They have been criticised for their superficiality (John Tobin, 'Judging the Judges: Are They Adopting the Rights Approach in Matters Involving Children?' (2009) 33(2) *Melbourne University Law Review* 579) or for being 'harmless window-dressing' (Melissa A. Waters, 'Creeping Monism: The Judicial Trend toward Interpretive Incorporation of Human Rights Treaties' (2007) 107(3) *Columbia Law Review* 628, 660).

[70] Sections 32(1) and (2) of the Victorian Charter (see Section 4.5); sections 2 and 3 of the Human Rights Act in the UK (see Section 6.5).

The structure of reception shapes what the courts extract from the CRC – that is, what they find useful in it. For example, in France, courts have used article 3(1) to mainstream the best interests of the child in decision-making because there is no domestic anchor for the concept. In South Africa, however, section 28(2) provides a strong anchor for the best interests of the child and has generated much case law, so domestic courts do not need to rely on article 3(1) as often. In Victoria, the novelty of the 2006 Charter means that the content of the rights is not fully developed, making the CRC a good source of inspiration in this regard.

The structure of reception influences the patterns of protection. The constitutional footing for children's rights in South Africa has generated a case law in which children most often appear as independent human rights holders. In the UK, on the other hand, the absence of child-specific statutory rights means that the CRC is predominantly raised in an HRA/ECHR context, with the consequence that the child often appears as part of the family under article 8 of the ECHR.

Convergent concepts, even if not created to give effect to the CRC, have been vehicles for CRC rights (such as welfare jurisdiction in Australia, ECHR rights in the UK, and statutory provisions accommodating of the subsidiarity principle in the context of intercountry adoptions in South Africa). However, caution is needed when relying on convergent concepts to give domestic effect to the CRC. First, it should not be assumed that alignment equates with identity of content, as that assumption may suppress the added value that the Convention can bring to the reasoning. For example, in the South African case of *AB v. Pridwin Preparatory School*,[71] the majority interpreted section 28(2) of the Constitution (the best interests provision) to include a child's right to be heard under article 12 of the CRC, which it defined similarly to procedural fairness under domestic law. Khampepe J, however, drew attention to the difference between article 12 and procedural fairness, from which she deduced an obligation to prioritise listening to children themselves whenever possible. Second, the structure of reception should not be overestimated as a vehicle for giving effect to the CRC, because, if the latter does not articulate with domestic norms, its application is in jeopardy. In the UK, for example, the ECHR has been the main vehicle for the CRC; when the former was not relevant, the application of the latter suffered.

[71] [2020] ZACC 12 (*Pridwin Preparatory School*).

The various components of the structure of reception have an ambivalent effect, even when the respective component was not designed with the CRC in mind. For example, the federal structure in Australia has resulted in a fragmentation of child-related laws, making the application of the CRC patchy, but it has also permitted States to be proactive in terms of passing human rights legislation that may facilitate its application. Similar considerations apply in the context of devolution statutes in the UK, where Wales and Scotland have passed more child rights-friendly legislation than has the Union.

The relationship between domestic laws and the CRC can be diverse, ranging from inconsistency to compliance or neutrality. When there was no overt conflict with the domestic law, the courts were amenable to considering the CRC, even without close attention to the formal reception rules. A weaker legal status of the Convention was at times compensated by identifying convergence with domestic norms able to act as carriers. This strategy is particularly visible in Australia, where the CRC is not given full domestic effect. Thus, in *Teoh*,[72] Gaudron J identified a potential common law right capable of carrying the substance of article 3(1) of the CRC and the Family Court used its welfare jurisdiction as a gateway for some CRC rights and the Convention spirit more generally.[73] The convergence between sentencing rules at common law and juvenile justice norms in the CRC has enabled the VSC to rely on the Convention in the exercise of sentencing discretion.[74] By contrast, when clear inconsistency existed between domestic law and the CRC, Australian courts rejected it.[75] This is not unique to Australia. The French Court of Cassation is argued to have applied article 12 of the CRC because statutes already gave it effect.[76] In South Africa, the alignment of section 28 of the Constitution with the CRC is the determining factor of the latter's application. And, in the UK, the judicial effect of the CRC is de facto quarantined by the scope of the ECHR, which acts as its vehicle.

The convergence between domestic law and the CRC is important for at least two reasons. First, it confirms to the courts that the values promoted by the CRC are supported by the executive and the legislature.

[72] *Minister for Immigration and Ethnic Affairs v. Teoh* [1995] HCA 20 (*Teoh*).
[73] *Re Z*; *B v. MIMIA*; *Re Jamie*.
[74] *DPP v. TY*.
[75] *MIMIA v. B*; *Re Woolley*.
[76] See Section 3.3.2.

This tripartite agreement on the 'domestic value'[77] of the CRC signals to the courts that its application is not contrary to the will of the political branches of the state, even in the absence of legislative incorporation or transformation. Second, this convergence has more than a symbolic nature. It enables the courts to ascertain that CRC provisions can be integrated into the existent domestic concepts, meaning that they are not of a nature so fundamentally different from domestic norms that they are not adaptable for domestic consideration.

Two relevant aspects of the reception framework arising from the case studies require further attention, as discussed in Sections 7.3.2.1 and 7.3.2.2 below.

7.3.2.1 The Jurisdiction of the Courts

Although the rules of engagement are binding on all courts in a particular state, the courts' jurisdiction may shape whether and how they engage with the CRC. The coexistence of multiple courts with jurisdiction to apply the Convention leads to jurisprudential fragmentation but also opportunities. In France, for example, administrative courts were quicker to apply the CRC because their jurisdiction included assessing the lawfulness of official action against international instruments. Judicial courts, however, do not exercise such control. Instead, they apply the CRC to resolve disputes between individuals and in relation to their rights. In Australia, the Family Court and the VSC surpass the High Court in the application of the CRC. The jurisdiction conferred by statutes on the first two courts creates opportunities for the CRC to be applied either by creating bridges between the domestic law and the CRC or by authorising its use through more permissive interpretive rules.

By engaging with the CRC from different jurisdictional perspectives and by using different tools, courts can capitalise on different normative facets of the CRC. For example, a norm that may not be of direct application because it is insufficiently specific could inform constitutional or judicial review of secondary legislation, which can be done against norms of a more abstract nature. A court with constitutional jurisdiction may be more accepting of the CRC because it is more accustomed to applying abstract norms. For example, courts in South Africa and the UK, which deal with both constitutional and human rights matters, have

[77] Waters, 'Creeping Monism', 701. Waters suggests that courts assess the 'domestic value' of a treaty from the perspective of the executive and the legislature; the higher the domestic value of a treaty, the more forward the courts can be in its application.

not expressed concern about the vagueness of the CRC. The French courts, however, which do not have constitutional jurisdiction, imply in their case law that some CRC provisions are insufficiently precise. Further, a CRC provision may not be directly applicable but could be used as an interpretive aid. Lastly, a provision that is not applicable in the immigration context may be applicable in a juvenile justice context.[78]

Although the engagement with the CRC by courts with different jurisdictions may be autonomous, the case law may be shaped by their interaction. In France, the case law of the Council of State has influenced the Court of Cassation and vice versa.[79] The ECtHR jurisprudence has encouraged the application of the Convention in France and the UK (as well as in other European jurisdictions[80]). However, the interaction between multiple courts has not always been favourable to the CRC. The attempts by the Family Court of Australia to expand the influence of the CRC have been rebuffed by the High Court.[81] In France, the Constitutional Council has confirmed the constitutionality of, for example, anonymous births and regressive juvenile justice legislation, dissuading the ordinary courts from considering the compatibility of the same with the CRC. In the UK, the Supreme Court largely follows the ECtHR, the case law of which caps the CRC and prevents the development of an authentically independent relationship with the domestic law.

At the same time, an imperfect alignment between the approaches of the courts allowed the CRC to develop in the interstices. In Australia, the limited application of the CRC by the High Court left space for the Family Court and the VSC to develop their Convention case law by taking advantage of their more favourable statutory position. In France, the Court of Cassation relied on the CRC to depart from the jurisprudence of the Constitutional Council and the ECtHR, and to take a position more favourable to children.[82] Similarly, the Council of State used its jurisdiction to take a different path from the Court of Cassation in the early stages of the CRC's application.

[78] See, for example, the position regarding article 37 by the High Court of Australia in *MIMIA v. B*, in contrast with that of the VSC in the *Certain Children* cases.

[79] See Section 3.6.2.2.

[80] Meda Couzens, 'Romanian Courts and the UN Convention on the Rights of the Child: A Case Study' (2016) 24(4) *International Journal of Children's Rights* 851.

[81] *GPAO*; *MIMIA v. B*.

[82] *Benjamin* and the application of article 7 of the CRC.

7.3.2.2 The Level of Jurisprudential Development of the CRC and the Rights of Children

This factor is also ambivalent. On the one hand, a developed children's rights jurisprudence may encourage the application of the CRC by providing a foundation on which to do so. In general, the more familiar courts are with applying children's rights, the more amenable they are to the application of the CRC. The ease with which the South African courts do so is a good illustration of how judicial familiarity with the CRC facilitates its application. In France, the gradual acceptance of the direct application of the CRC has increased the willingness of the courts to apply it and diversify its field of application (such as taxation, the working conditions of children, and healthcare access). The jurisprudence of the ECtHR deserves a mention as influential in facilitating judicial engagement with the CRC in Europe. The French and UK case law illustrate this, but the observation applies to other legal systems.[83] Thus, in France, the Court of Cassation accepted the direct application of the CRC in 2005 under the influence of, inter alia, the ECtHR case law. In the UK, the Convention is often applied as pre-interpreted in ECtHR judgments. The more widely applied the CRC provisions are, the better their diverse legal dimensions are understood, and the less likely it is for them to be perceived as imperfect, imprecise, or incomplete, and thus denied legal effect.

On the other hand, the absence of domestic case law may enable the application of the CRC. In Australia, for example, the limited application of the CRC by the High Court allowed other courts, which are better equipped to apply the Convention, to develop their jurisprudence. Courts have considered the CRC and the CRC Committee's output in the absence of domestic precedent or other sources of normative inspiration. The VSC, for example, relied on these to give content to the best interests and juvenile justice provisions in the Victorian Charter, in the absence of domestic authority in the context of relatively new human rights legislation.[84] In South Africa, the gaps in the case law enabled the Constitutional Court to use article 12 to complement the content of section 28(2) of the South African Constitution (the best interests section).[85] In the UK, the absence of a child-focused interpretation of

[83] For example, Romania: see Couzens, 'Romanian Courts'.

[84] *Certain Children (No. 2)*, for example. See Section 4.5.3.

[85] See especially *J v. National Director of Public Prosecutions* 2014 (7) BCLR 764 (CC) (*J v. NDPP*) and *Pridwin Preparatory School*, discussed in Section 5.4.2.

statutes or certain rights has oriented judges towards the CRC as a repository of legal tools that would enable them to develop the law.[86]

Entrenched domestic views and precedent may discourage the application of the CRC, as judges may be tempted to apply settled domestic principles. As acknowledged by Lord Mance, 'the domestic law position would be simpler'[87] if one would not consider international law. In Australia, the well-developed jurisprudence in relation to the welfare and *parens patriae* jurisdictions has made it difficult to rely successfully on the CRC to displace or develop the traditional views on the best interests of the child in line with article 3(1) of the CRC.[88] In South Africa, the thriving children's rights jurisprudence built on section 28 of the Constitution may lead to a marginalisation of the CRC, which can become problematic if courts assume, without close consideration, that the two sets of norms overlap. The ECtHR case law has had a largely positive impact on the acceptance of the CRC by domestic European courts by inserting the CRC into a legal pattern that is familiar to those courts. However, there is a risk that if the ECtHR case law becomes an absolute filter for the CRC, the courts will not consider it independently and on its own merits. In the UK, for example, the CRC is hardly applied independently of the ECHR. Thus, if domestic and supranational case law become the dominant reference framework for the application of the CRC, there is a risk that alternative legal views, such as those of the CRC Committee, will be overlooked and the influence of the CRC will be adjusted by the dominant perspective, which is not child-focused by design.

To conclude, an adequate understanding of the application of the CRC by domestic courts cannot be obtained merely by scrutinising their interaction with the CRC under the formal rules of engagement. Instead, proper recognition is needed for the domestic structure of reception, an intricate web of components that often play ambivalent roles in the application of the CRC. For effective CRC arguments before domestic courts, it is important to understand the complex relationship between the Convention and the domestic law and to make maximum

[86] Lord Cooke in *R v. G* [2003] UKHL 50 (see Section 6.4); Lord Kerr and Lord Wilson in *In the matter of an application by JR38 for Judicial Review (Northern Ireland)* [2015] UKSC 42 (see Section 6.5.1)

[87] Jonathan Mance, 'International Law in the UK Supreme Court' (speech, King's College, London, 13 February 2017) 1, www.supremecourt.uk/news/speeches.html.

[88] *MIMIA v. B* and *Re Woolley*.

use of the latter. The bewildering number of components of the structure of reception may make the relationship between the CRC and the domestic law volatile. Indeed, while the formal rules of engagement hardly change, the structure of reception is dynamic, being influenced by changes in legislation or the evolution of case law. The field is therefore constantly moving and in need of reassessment, but it is not anarchic. The formal rules of engagement remain the foundation of the relationship between the CRC and the domestic law, but it must be acknowledged that this relationship depends not only on the rules of engagement but also on the interaction of the Convention with other domestic laws and structures.

7.4 The Effect of the CRC on Judicial Reasoning

How the formal engagement rules have influenced the courts' application of the CRC was discussed in Section 7.2. This section turns to considering the *effect* of that engagement. This effect can be captured in the general idea that the CRC has prompted the courts to recognise children as a discrete category of rights holders who should benefit from a distinct legal treatment. Such recognition has often compensated for the lack of domestic rules in this regard.[89] There are numerous expressions of this, including the reshaping of the enquiries on the limitation of the rights of adults, often parents (in South Africa and the UK); introducing new special factors in decision-making (such as the best interests of the child); and making children's rights relevant to legal matters in which they have previously been neglected (such as parental extradition or expulsion, taxation, and labour relations). The CRC has been used, for example, by courts in Australia and France to mainstream children's rights in their reasoning. The Family Court in Australia relied on the CRC to extend its protective welfare jurisdiction beyond the confines of the parent–child relationship.[90] In France, the direct application of the CRC, especially article 3(1), has led to the rights of children being considered by administrative courts, despite them not being explicit statutory considerations.[91]

[89] Illustrative are, in France, *L'Association Aides* and *L'Observatoire* (CE, No. 293785, 31 October 2008) (see Section 3.5.3.2); in Australia, *DPP v. SE* [2017] VSC 13; *Director of Public Prosecutions v. SL* [2016] VSC 714 (see Section 4.5.2); and in South Africa, *M v. S*; *CCL*; *J v. NDPP* (see especially Section 5.4.2).

[90] *Re Z* [1996] FamCA 89; *B v. Minister for Immigration & Multicultural & Indigenous Affairs* [2003] FamCA 451 (*B v. MIMIA*).

[91] See Section 3.4.

The effect of the CRC on judicial reasoning is better understood as a continuum rather than an '"all-or-nothing question": does the international provision have *full* direct applicability or is it simply *irrelevant* for the judge?'[92] The continuum contains cases where the legal effects are difficult to discern, but also cases where the CRC contributes *something* to the legal reasoning, and, finally, cases where the Convention is determinant or very important for the legal reasoning (high-end impact). As discussed in Chapter 1, the effect that engaging with the Convention *can have* is conditioned by the constitutional framework of each jurisdiction and should be evaluated accordingly. For example, Australian, South African, and UK courts cannot set aside domestic legislation if it is contrary to the CRC, while French courts can do so. In France, however, the CRC does not inform the constitutionality control of laws, although this is possible in South Africa.[93]

Direct application, when recognised, is at the high end of the continuum because it equates the CRC provision with a domestic (usually) statutory norm that is binding on courts and may be applied as the 'rule of decision',[94] or as an autonomous source of domestic law or legal authority. When direct application is complemented (in specific systems) by the recognition of the domestic supremacy or primacy of international treaties, the CRC may prompt the courts not to apply the domestic norms that are in conflict with it. The French case law illustrates the high-end impact resulting from the combination of direct application and treaty supremacy. In *Benjamin*, the Court of Cassation applied article 7 of the CRC directly to fill a gap in the law and to protect a right not provided for in the domestic law; and, in several cases, the Council of

[92] Martin Scheinin, 'General Introduction' in Martin Scheinin (ed.), *International Human Rights Norms in the Nordic and Baltic Countries* (The Hague: Martinus Nijhoff, 1996) 11, 19 (emphasis in original). See similarly Julien Pieret, 'L'influence du juge belge sur l'effectivité de la Convention: retour doctrinal et jurisprudentiel sur le concept d'effet direct' in Vincent Chapaux, Julien Pieret, and Annemie Schaus (eds.), *Entre ombres et lumières: cinquante ans d'application de la Convention européenne des droits de l'homme en Belgique* (Brussels: Bruylant, 2008) 83, 110.

[93] It is worth remembering that, in Australia, the CRC can inform, to a limited extent, the constitutional review of statutes passed under the external affairs power (see Section 4.4.1) and, in the UK, statutes made by devolved parliaments can be judicially set aside if they are inconsistent with the ECHR, interpreted with reference to the CRC (see Section 6.3).

[94] The term used in David Sloss, 'Treaty Enforcement in Domestic Courts: A Comparative Analysis' in David Sloss (ed.), *The Role of Domestic Courts in Treaty Enforcement: A Comparative Study* (New York: Cambridge University Press, 2009) 1, 11.

State set aside domestic legislation or invalidated administrative decisions and secondary legislation that were inconsistent with the Convention.[95]

Indirect methods of application lack some of the strong features of direct application. Thus, the CRC does not operate independently because its use relies on the existence of domestic law that needs interpretation or development. At the same time, the case law illustrates that, *in concreto*, high-end effects are possible when the CRC is applied indirectly. In South Africa, it is the indirect methods of application that have secured the CRC's most powerful impact – namely, the shaping of the interpretation of children's constitutional rights and, consequently, its role in constitutional review. Constitutional interpretation has led to a constitutionalisation of selected aspects of the CRC, which ensures their domestic sustainability by entrenchment at the highest legal status. By comparison, self-execution would deliver much less to the CRC in South Africa, as it would place it in an under-constitutional and under-statutory position.

Australian cases also contain instances of high-end effect. In *Teoh*, the majority of the High Court developed a new method to give effect to unincorporated treaties, relying on, inter alia, the significance of the CRC. The comprehensive interpretation given by the majority in *Teoh* to article 3(1) of the CRC has been influential, both domestically and internationally, and is echoed in the CRC Committee's own interpretation of this article. The Full Family Court skilfully used the Convention to interpret relevant provisions in the FLA in ways that, if upheld by the High Court, would have mainstreamed children's rights protection beyond the boundaries of the Act.[96] In the UK, through the HRA and the ECHR, the scope of the best interests of the child has been judicially extended to numerous public law decisions.[97]

All in all, these effects, which have at times tested constitutional boundaries, are equally significant with the direct application of the CRC, albeit they are produced through different means. It should not be overlooked that consistent interpretation is not neutral; it has some constraining effect because it aims at aligning the meaning of domestic law with the CRC when that is possible. Lastly, the dualist systems

[95] *Cinar*; *Association Aides*; *L'Observatoire* (see Section 3.5.1.2).

[96] See Section 4.5.3.

[97] See, for example, *ZH*, discussed in Section 6.5.2.

discussed here are common law-based, and positive developments create binding legal precedents that ensure their sustainability.

Perhaps more useful than creating a hierarchy of effects is ascertaining whether the use of the CRC has added *something* (an added value[98]) to the reasoning that cannot be immediately derived from other legal instruments (national or international). Importantly, the added value of the CRC will look different in each legal system because it is contingent on the structure of reception and thus the level of children's rights development in each system.

In the jurisdictions analysed here, the Convention has contributed incrementally to enriching judicial reasoning rather than causing a major overhaul of the domestic law. This contribution need not be a specific outcome but can encompass the analytical add-on that the CRC may be bringing to the reasoning. Examples can be found in all the legal systems considered here. Prompted by the CRC, courts in France and Australia considered children's best interests as a primary consideration although the domestic law did not require it.[99] The VSC turned to the CRC to assist it in giving content to the newly enacted rights in Victoria's human rights legislation.[100] Careful consideration of the CRC in South Africa enabled the courts to absorb participation rights into the constitutional best interests provision or to refine the balancing of interests under the same provision.[101] In the UK, reliance on the CRC enabled the extension of the obligation to give a primary consideration to the best interests of children in public law;[102] offered protection to the right to be heard, which is not explicitly protected under the ECHR;[103] and supported child-focused interpretations of established legal concepts.[104]

While it is important to search for the value added by the CRC,[105] a cautionary note is needed. Identifying an added value assists with

[98] As defined in Section 1.5.

[99] Article 3(1) jurisprudence in France (see Section 3.5.3.2) and cases such as *Teoh* and *In re TLB* [2007] VSC 439 in Australia.

[100] See Section 4.5.3.

[101] Section 5.5.2.

[102] *ZH* in the UK (see Section 6.5.2).

[103] *In re D (a child)* [2006] UKHL 51.

[104] See Lord Cooke in *R v. G* and the interpretation of the term 'reckless' (see Section 6.4). See also Lord Kerr and Lord Wilson in *JR38* in relation to the interpretation of article 8 of the ECHR; Lord Carswell, who supported a child-focused interpretation of article 3 of the ECHR, *In re E (a child) (Northern Ireland)* [2008] UKHL 66 (see Section 6.5.1).

[105] As recognised also by other authors. See, for example, Eva Brems, Ellen Desmet, and Wouter Vandenhole, 'Children's Rights Law and Human Rights Law: Analysing Present

navigating normatively complex environments, but it may also create a hurdle in the application of a newer and less developed treaty such as the CRC. It may imply that it is a 'lesser' treaty that needs to prove itself. Thus, searching for the added value should be a tool for identifying the unique contribution of the CRC and uncovering its many normative layers, and not a prerequisite of its application.

One must also be wary of any assertion of perfect overlap with other legal instruments because the special features of the CRC, and especially its child-centred nature, are likely to deny this. In the absence of obvious distinctions with other relevant norms, a good starting point in searching for the added value of the CRC is to consider its general principles, which change the dynamic of its application and bring into the legal enquiry norms that are unlikely to be explicitly reflected in other international instruments. So far, articles 3 and 12 have done the heavy lifting of distinguishing the CRC from other instruments, and it is perhaps time to call on articles 2 and 6 to play their part.

When evaluating impact, the expectation is to do so based on concrete legal outcomes (such as individual remedies, the invalidation of administrative action, the setting aside of legislation, and the development or clarification of domestic law in a child-friendly direction). Its softer, more diffuse, and attitude-changing effects should, however, not be overlooked. The CRC has encouraged courts to think about the rights of children as relevant beyond the confines of areas of law where they have traditionally been encased (i.e., family law, child protection, and juvenile justice).[106] When ambiguity is defined as a choice of meaning, the CRC has enabled the courts to detect that ambiguity or, more accurately, to detect the potential for domestic law to be interpreted in a way that is

and Possible Future Interactions' in Eva Brems, Ellen Desmet, and Wouter Vandenhole, *Children's Rights Law in the Global Human Rights Landscape: Isolation, Inspiration, Integration?* (Oxon: Taylor & Francis Group, 2017) 1–2; Laura Lundy and Bronagh Byrne, 'The Four General Principles of the United Nations Convention on the Rights of the Child: The Potential Value of the Approach in Other Areas of Human Rights Law' in Eva Brems, Ellen Desmet, and Wouter Vandenhole, *Children's Rights Law in the Global Human Rights Landscape: Isolation, Inspiration, Integration?* (Oxon: Taylor & Francis Group, 2017) 52, 57, 67.

[106] *Teoh* (immigration); the best interests jurisprudence in France (e.g., taxation, immigration, deportation, and law enforcement against parents; see Section 3.5.3.2); the sentencing of parents or the horizontal application of children's rights in South Africa (*M v. S* and *Pridwin Preparatory School*).

aligned with the CRC.[107] Further, it has encouraged courts to create a distinct legal treatment for children in recognition of '*children* [being] a discrete community of rights holders'.[108] The CRC gives *legal* shape to child-related matters – that is, it speaks a legal language that many courts accept. It provides litigants and courts with a starting point and a child-specific rights framework, so that children's rights no longer need to be adjudicated within the more general rights framework.

Somewhat counter-intuitively, judgments in which the CRC is not applied, but reasons are provided, are not deprived of impact, as both successful and unsuccessful engagements contribute to negotiating its meaning domestically. These judgments have analytical value as they point to potential challenges raised by the application of the CRC, creating opportunities for those challenges to be discussed and, it is hoped, overcome. Thus, the reluctance of the French courts to apply the CRC has generated intense domestic debates about its direct applicability, which, in time, has become increasingly accepted. Judgments critical of the application of the CRC in South Africa have questioned the use of techniques of engagement that border on self-execution without due acknowledgement.[109] In Australia, McHugh J in *Teoh* questioned the wide scope of article 3(1), calling for closer attention to the implications of applying the best interests of the child to matters concerning children indirectly.[110] In *Re Woolley*, the judges pointed to the need to develop children's rights arguments that take into consideration the tensions between different rights of children[111] and frontally deal with situations where successful litigation may disadvantage children.[112] These sceptical judicial opinions are sounding boards for children's rights arguments. If carefully considered, they may assist in developing more sophisticated domestic arguments that deal more persuasively with the many complex issues inherent in the rights of children.

[107] See, for example, cases such as *R v. G* and *In re D* in the UK; and, in Australia, the Victorian Charter jurisprudence in general (Section 4.5).

[108] Stalford, 'The Broader Relevance', 47.

[109] See the discussion in Section 5.4.1.

[110] See Section 4.4.4.

[111] In *Re Woolley*, Gleeson CJ (para. 30) and McHugh J (para. 102) rejected a blanket approach to children's vulnerability and lack of capacity, which they saw as dependent on individual characteristics or circumstances.

[112] In *Re Woolley*, Callinan J (para. 254) raised the issue of children being potentially separated from their parents should the application succeed, which may increase the vulnerability of the children.

When considering judgments where the CRC is judicially rejected, one should, however, be particularly wary of courts doing so on the grounds that it is irrelevant. Terse statements of irrelevancy should be carefully scrutinised because they risk transforming relevance into another gatekeeper for the Convention. Such arguments are likely to be made in areas of law where children's rights are interlopers but where their application is most needed because of a lack of domestic transformation in accordance with the CRC (such as taxation, the allocation of resources, environmental decision-making, planning, and torts).[113]

An issue that stringently arises in a CRC context is the Convention's independent effect when applied jointly with other legal instruments, domestic or international. When the CRC is invoked as 'additional ballast'[114] to other arguments, its genuine effect is in question. This challenge is not unique to the CRC[115] and reasons advanced to 'normalise' this form of joint application include that the application of international law is 'contingent on domestic law'[116] and that legislative reform has reduced the need for direct reliance on international instruments.[117] To these, one can add the complexity of the domestic issues, which often cannot be addressed by giving the CRC the leading role.[118] Indeed, the Convention often blends with other norms, contributing *some* aspects to the reasoning rather than being its determining rule. The partial overlap between the CRC and domestic norms has enabled courts more readily to accept it. In France and the UK, the overlap with the ECHR has contributed to the acceptance of the Convention by the courts. In South Africa, the alignment of the CRC with the Constitution has achieved similar results. While this may dilute the impact of the CRC taken individually,

[113] In cases such as *Le Roux v. Dey* 2011 (6) BCLR 577 (CC) (see Section 5.4.2) in South Africa, or *R v. G* (see Section 6.4) in the UK, children's rights have been overlooked in legal matters not yet adapted to children's rights.

[114] Julia Sloth-Nielsen and Benyam D. Mezmur, '2 + 2 = 5? Exploring the Domestication of the CRC in South African Jurisprudence (2002–2006)' (2008) 16(1) *International Journal of Children's Rights* 1, 27.

[115] McCrudden, 'Why Do', 535.

[116] André Nollkaemper, 'The Duality of Direct Effect of International Law' (2014) 25(1) *European Journal of International Law* 105, 110.

[117] Magnus Killander and Horace Adjolohoun, 'International Law and Domestic Human Rights Litigation in Africa: An Introduction' in Magnus Killander (ed.), *International Law and Domestic Human Rights Litigation in Africa* (Pretoria: Pretoria University Law Press, 2010) 3, 14.

[118] For example, in the Australian cases of *Re Z*, *Re Woolley*, and *AMS v. AIF*, the core issues were of a constitutional nature and the CRC was not deemed relevant.

creating normative alliances with well-established domestic or international standards has facilitated its application and also buttressed its legal status.[119]

There is a risk that an apparent overlap between domestic law (or other international standards) and the CRC might lead to a summary dismissal of the latter.[120] This is to be avoided and the actual overlap of standards should not be assumed without careful consideration. One way to protect against such assumption (additional to considering its principles) is to consider the international jurisprudence, including by the CRC Committee, and comparative developments. Moving forward, closer consideration should be given to how and to what effect the CRC applies in cases of overlap with other legal instruments. The normative alliances with other instruments should be capitalised on as they can improve the acceptance of the CRC, but its individuality should be carefully guarded to avoid it dissolving into other instruments.

7.4.1 Article 3(1) of the CRC and the Courts

Despite being much criticised for its vagueness,[121] or for being 'indeterminate and opaque' and capable of being weaponised to justify divergent solutions,[122] article 3(1) has been popular with the courts.[123] Whatever legal weaknesses that article may have, it has become a source of legal tools to advance the rights of children.

[119] In South Africa, for example, the CRC aspects used to interpret constitutional provisions have arguably been indirectly constitutionalised. In the UK, the interpretive injunctions in the Human Rights Act, directed at the ECHR, have benefited the CRC.

[120] It should be remembered that article 41 of the CRC condones the priority application of domestic law or other treaties, provided that they contain superior protection.

[121] See, for example, Ursula Kilkelly, 'The Convention on the Rights of the Child after Twenty-five Years: Challenges of Content and Implementation' in Martin D. Ruck, Michele Peterson-Badali, and Michael Freeman (eds.), *Handbook of Children's Rights: Global and Multidisciplinary Perspectives* (New York: Routledge, 2016) 80, 85.

[122] Wouter Vandenhole, 'Distinctive Characteristics of Children's Human Rights Law' in Eva Brems, Ellen Desmet, and Wouter Vandenhole, *Children's Rights Law in the Global Human Rights Landscape: Isolation, Inspiration, Integration?* (Oxon: Taylor & Francis Group, 2017) 21, 26.

[123] This is true for other jurisdictions as well. Wouter Vandenhole, 'The Convention of the Rights of the Child in Belgian Case Law' in Ton Liefaard and Jaap E. Doek (eds.), *Litigating the Rights of the Child: The UN Convention on the Rights of the Child in Domestic and International Jurisprudence* (Dordrecht: Springer, 2015) 105; Laura Lundy et al., *The UN Convention on the Rights of the Child: A Study of Legal Implementation in 12 Countries* (UNICEF, 2012).

More concretely, trailblazing cases in which reliance was placed on article 3(1) have extended the caring considerations that inform that article well beyond the legal space in which they were previously relevant.[124] This has had significant impact on the public law in all four jurisdictions. Article 3(1) encouraged courts to extend the scope of domestic best interests norms beyond their traditional reach, to matters such as access to healthcare in France; immigration in Australia, France, and the UK; and the sentencing of parents in South Africa.[125] The Convention prompted the courts to acknowledge the complex dynamic between individual and collective best interests. The surrogacy cases in France and the benefits cap cases in the UK illustrate this most clearly. The dynamic has been central to the developing jurisprudence on crafting a special legal treatment for children that considers their age and vulnerability. In Australia and France, article 3(1) of the CRC compensated for the absence of an overarching rule that requires children to be treated differently. In France, the wide application of article 3(1) made it a powerful tool, especially in administrative cases. Importantly, article 3(1) has been used as a standard to assess the validity of laws and policies in France, South Africa, and the UK.[126] The Victorian Charter permits best interests assessments of legislation in Victoria, in which article 3(1) can play an interpretive role, and these assessments can result in statements of inconsistent interpretation with the Charter.[127] This accumulation of practice demonstrates that article 3(1), or the domestic correspondents more broadly, can serve as effective standards for assessing the quality and validity of domestic laws, contrary to concerns expressed in this regard.[128]

Article 3(1) provided the courts with a legal justification to consider independently the rights and interests of children in matters involving their parents but affecting the children, to avoid them suffering the negative consequences of parental behaviour (such as immigration breaches or criminal offending).[129] Article 3(1) has been an entry point

[124] *Cinar* (France); *Teoh* (Australia); *M v. S* (South Africa); *ZH* (UK).

[125] See especially *Re Z* and *B v. MIMIA* (Australia); *Cinar*, *L'Association Aides* and *L'Observatoire* (France); *M v. S* (South Africa); *ZH* (UK).

[126] See *L'Association Aides* (France); *J v. NDPP* (South Africa); *SG* and *DA* (UK).

[127] Section 36(2) read with section 17(2) of the Victorian Charter.

[128] Dominique Bureau, 'De l'application directe en France de la Convention de New York du 26 janvier 1990 sur les droits de l'enfant' (2005) 4 *Revue critique de droit international privé* III.A.20; *SG* at para. 149 (Lord Hughes).

[129] *Teoh* (Australia); *M v. S* (South Africa); France (see Section 3.5.3.2).

for rights of uncertain domestic status. For example, French courts have used it to protect socio-economic rights,[130] while the VSC drew into the content of the best interests provision of the Victorian Charter CRC rights that are not directly recognised in the Charter (i.e., articles 6 and 12).[131] Courts in South Africa, the UK, and Victoria have absorbed into the interpretation of article 3(1) (or related domestic provisions) some aspects of the right to be heard in article 12 of the CRC.[132] By doing so, the courts have covered a significant gap in the recognition of the right to be heard in those jurisdictions.[133]

There has been some judicial discomfort concerning the wide ambit recognised in best interests provisions,[134] variably expressed in relation to article 3 itself or the relevant domestic provisions. However, there is little articulation of principle in this regard, apart from the French Council of State, which decided that article 3(1) 'is not applicable only to decisions whose object is to address the personal situation of minor children but also to those decisions which can affect them in a manner sufficiently direct and certain'.[135]

Article 3(1) has revolutionised the legal nature of the best interests of the child, and there is now a growing understanding of the complexity of the concept.[136] As interpreted by the CRC Committee in General Comment No. 14,[137] the article has transformed the best interests of the child from a factual consideration into a legal norm that contains ascertainable entitlements and obligations. The Committee has interpreted article 3(1) to contain an interpretive principle, a right, and a rule

[130] See Section 3.5.2.

[131] See Section 4.6.1.

[132] *Certain Children* cases (Victoria); *J v. NDPP* and *Pridwin Preparatory School* (South Africa); *In re D* (the UK).

[133] See, for example, Sections 5.4.2.1 (South Africa), 6.4 (the UK), and 4.5.2 (Victoria). These systems give recognition to the wishes and views of children in some statutes, but the absorption in article 3(1) gives the views of children the wider scope that this article enjoys.

[134] McHugh J in *Teoh*; Callinan J in *Re Minister for Immigration and Multicultural and Indigenous Affairs; Ex parte Lam* [2003] HCA 6; Sachs J in *M v. S*; Lord Hughes in *SG* (para. 149).

[135] CE, No. 359359, 25 June 2014 at para. 1.

[136] Whether that complexity is inherent or (perhaps artificially) created by cramming too much into this concept to fulfil hopes and to fill potential gaps in the CRC is a matter for another day.

[137] CRC Committee, *General Comment No. 14 (2013) on the right of the child to have his or her best interests taken as a primary consideration (art. 3, para. 1)*, 29 May 2013, CRC/C/GC/14.

of procedure,[138] but it is not always clear which of the three roles is used and when. The roles are not identical and they carry different consequences. To borrow from Abramson, treating something as a general principle rather than a right may defeat its empowering message and encourage its limitation 'simply because the word principle contains the idea of exceptions'.[139] At the same time, the multifaceted nature of article 3 eased its application because the best interests of the child are 'recognisable' to judges as a legal principle that is historically protected by the law of many states.

With article 3(1), the best interests of the child become a human rights concept, which includes, but is not limited to, a child's welfare and well-being. Article 3(1) has offered the opportunity to develop a rights-based, non-paternalistic approach to children's best interests by integrating Convention rights in its interpretation. This opportunity has been taken in numerous cases across all four jurisdictions.[140] This *legalisation*, the effect of which is still to be fully understood, has several features. Notable is the predominantly procedural approach to article 3(1). In its most comprehensive document interpreting the article, the Committee refers to it in procedural terminology as containing, inter alia, 'a right of the child to have his or her best interests assessed and taken as a primary consideration when different interests are being considered'.[141] Various procedural guarantees accompany this, including the Committee's explicit statement that article 3(1) is also a rule of procedure accompanied by several guarantees.[142] Domestic courts have preceded the Committee in taking a similar route. *Teoh* in Australia put this approach on the map by connecting article 3 with procedural fairness in relation to children's interests. The South African Constitutional Court held that article 3(1) and implicitly its homologous provision in section 28(2) of the Constitution require the courts 'to apply the principle of best interests by considering how the child's rights and interests are, or will be, affected by their decisions'.[143] The French Court of Cassation requires lower

[138] CRC Committee, *General Comment No. 14*, para. 6.

[139] Bruce Abramson, *Article 2: The Right of Non-Discrimination*, volume in André Alen et al. (eds.), *A Commentary on the United Nations Convention on the Rights of the Child* (Leiden: Martinus Nijhoff, 2008) 54.

[140] *Association Aides* (France); *Certain Children (No. 2)* and *Re Jamie* (Australia); *J v. NDPP* and *Pridwin Preparatory School* (South Africa); and *ZH* (UK).

[141] CRC Committee, *General Comment No. 14*, paras. 6, 14.

[142] CRC Committee, *General Comment No. 14*, paras. 6, 14.

[143] *DPP Transvaal* at para. 79 (Ngcobo J).

courts to explain how they considered the best interests of the child in their decisions.[144] These procedural guarantees address some of the concerns about the 'disempowering . . . opacity'[145] and the 'unnervingly instinctive'[146] decision-making on children's best interests. The proceduralisation of the best interests of the child has also strengthened their mobility by enabling the independent application of wide-span best interests provisions by providing them with their own legal content.[147] However, this may foster a detachment of best interests provisions from other substantive rights, which threatens to void the former of content and should, therefore, be carefully managed by the courts.

Another feature of the legalisation of article 3(1) is that it does not require that an outcome favourable to the child is always achieved or that the child's interests always prevail. The absolutism of the traditional approaches to a child's best interests has been abandoned in favour of increased procedural guarantees against arbitrary decisions and a significantly wider scope.[148] Once co-opted as a human rights concept, the best interests of the child have become liable to limitations, with the silver lining that such limitations must be justified under the canon on human rights limitations in the relevant jurisdiction. However, there is no clear, discernible vision in relation to these limitations. In one sense, article 3(1) contains an inherent limitation by referring to *a* rather than *the* primary consideration. In this, some judges have seen an acknowledgement that other legitimate interests can be considered, and even prioritised over those of the children.[149] In South Africa, the Constitutional Court has used section 36 of the Constitution (the limitation clause) to ascertain the lawfulness of limitations to section 28(2) of the Constitution,[150] but the CRC Committee and the VSC (both applying rights-oriented best interests provisions) have not yet engaged closely with the issue. This remains an area in need of development – and one of growing

[144] See Section 3.5.3.1.

[145] Stalford, 'The Broader Relevance'.

[146] Stalford, 'The Broader Relevance', 43.

[147] Article 3(1) was considered, for example, largely independently of other CRC rights but coupled with ECHR rights in *SG* and *DA* in Britain.

[148] This is not to say that the best interests of the child can never be the determinative factor. See, for example, adoption and custody decisions.

[149] *AMS v. AIF* at para. 193 (Kirby J).

[150] *De Reuck v. Director of Public Prosecutions (Witwatersrand Local Division)* 2003 (12) BCLR 1333 (CC) at para. 55.

importance, considering the widespread use of article 3(1) or the domestic provisions it has inspired.

Perhaps the most far-reaching change in the legal nature of article 3(1) is bestowing upon it the status of an independent right that generates its own legal consequences and enforceable legal content.[151] There is an increasing number of cases supporting the independent legal content of best interests provisions (article 3(1) or convergent). The most illustrative are the extensive direct application of article 3(1) by the French courts; the equally extensive independent application of section 28(2) of the South African Constitution; and the emerging use of section 17(2) of the Victorian Charter to assess the lawfulness of official conduct.

Although united in their valuing of the independent clout of the best interests standard, the courts have differed in their approaches, prompted by the specificities of their domestic frameworks. In South Africa, for example, section 28(2) of the Constitution was declared an independent right.[152] In *Teoh*, Gaudron J argued the existence of a 'common law right . . . to have a child's best interests taken into account, at least as a primary consideration' in discretionary decisions that affect a child's welfare.[153] In France, powerful consequences are drawn from article 3(1) without it being declared an independent right. The VSC referred to section 17(2) of the Victorian Charter as containing a 'human right to protection';[154] notably, the concept of 'best interests' is not a part of the name of the right, although it is an element of its content.

This increasing recognition of independent power has emboldened the courts' reliance on the best interests provisions, resulting in their overuse. Byrne, Hanson, and Lundy have shown that the Committee often approaches the general principles as autonomous provisions rather than as cross-cutting principles that infuse other CRC provisions.[155] This has

[151] Earlier authors argued that article 3(1) does not create specific rights and duties: Philip Alston, 'The Best Interests Principle: Towards a Reconciliation of Culture and Human Rights' (1994) 8(1) *International Journal of Law and the Family* 1, 15; Geraldine Van Bueren, *The International Law on the Rights of the Child* (The Hague: Martinus Nijhoff, 1998) 46.

[152] *Fitzpatrick* at paras. 17–18.

[153] *Teoh* at para. 4 (Gaudron J).

[154] *ZZ v. Secretary, Department of Justice* [2013] VSC 267 at para. 71 (Bell J).

[155] Karl Hanson and Laura Lundy, 'Does Exactly What It Says on the Tin? A Critical Analysis and Alternative Conceptualisation of the So-called "General Principles" of the Convention on the Rights of the Child' (2017) 25(2) *International Journal of Children's Rights* 285, 293, 296; Lundy and Byrne, 'The Four General Principles'.

created the risk of marginalising other CRC provisions,[156] which has materialised in relation to article 3. In South Africa and France, more specific constitutional children's rights and other CRC rights, respectively, have been shunned in favour of best interests. A similar concern is emerging in other jurisdictions.[157] The risk is that should such trends develop in relation to all the general principles, it would be detrimental to other CRC rights. Those rights would regress to a pre-CRC position, where children's rights depended upon generous readings of general human rights norms. To avoid this, a more conscious effort is needed to use all relevant CRC provisions and give them an opportunity to develop, either independently or through a joint application with the general principles. A good practice in this regard comes from the VSC, which has used section 8(3) of the Victorian Charter (the right to equality before the law) to justify treating children differently from adults.[158] Article 2 of the CRC could be used in a similar fashion.

The reasons for the popularity of article 3(1) and the domestic provisions it inspired may be a matter of some speculation, but several explanations can be suggested. First, domestic judges were familiar with the concept of the best interests of the child or similar concepts extant in the domestic law prior to the CRC. This allayed judicial concerns about too radically departing from domestic rules to accommodate the CRC. Further, article 3(1) is user-friendly, ready to be applied by the courts, and, in truth, not very demanding because of the dominant procedural approach to its content. Its very wording mentions the courts, strengthening their view that they have a role to play in giving it effect.[159]

Stalford notes that this article is 'a neat, rhetorical device' usable by many kinds of decision-makers and a 'convenient shorthand' for factors that contribute to individual well-being.[160] Its flexibility generated mobility and opportunities to be applied to a wide range of legal contexts. The

[156] Lundy and Byrne, 'The Four General Principles', 61.

[157] Diana Bryant, 'It's My Body, Isn't It? Children, Medical Treatment and Human Rights' (2009) 35(2) *Monash University Law Review* 193, 207 (urging open consideration of children's rights rather than 'to quietly subsume human rights considerations under the rubric of "best interests"'); Nigel Cantwell, 'Are "Best Interests" a Pillar or a Problem for Implementing the Human Rights of Children?' in Ton Liefaard and Jaap E. Doek (eds.), *Litigating the Rights of the Child: The UN Convention on the Rights of the Child in Domestic and International Jurisprudence* (Dordrecht: Springer, 2015) 61.

[158] See Section 4.5.2.

[159] Courts in South Africa and France have drawn support in their application of article 3(1) from the article's explicit reference to courts.

[160] Stalford, 'The Broader Relevance', 38.

growing independent application of best interests provisions has also enabled the courts to pair them with provisions beyond the rights of children.[161] Further, article 3(1) has filled a gap left in the domestic law by the absence of a standard of wide application that would enable judges to justify a distinct legal treatment for children whenever relevant in response to the unique nature of children's interests and their need for special protection.

Lastly, article 3(1) has been of pragmatic importance to the courts because of its inbuilt evaluative feature ('a primary consideration') that assists the courts in balancing competing interests. Illustrative is its frequent use by the UK Supreme Court in the limitation enquiries under the ECHR. A cautionary note is needed in this regard. A preponderant use of article 3(1) or domestic best interests provisions in proportionality enquiries tends to portray children's interests in frequent conflict with other legitimate interests, suggesting that protecting children's interests often comes at the expense of either other individuals or general interests. Lady Hale's judgment in *HH*[162] is a timely encouragement to approach children's interests differently, namely as aligned with the public interest.

In a nutshell, article 3(1) has at its core the protection of children's dignity,[163] as reflected in association with the recognition of children's independent interests; transparency and accountability in decision-making; and a concern for the individual needs of each child. Its primary concern, at least as currently construed, is with children being recognised, seen, and heard and not with the absolute prioritisation of their interests.

This work has frequently drawn attention to the positive impact of the convergence between domestic norms and the CRC and the latter's application. Nonetheless, a cautionary note is needed and this can best be contextualised with reference to article 3(1). Nominally, the concept of the *best interests of the child* may populate the CRC, as well as the domestic law, but the type of protection it enjoys may differ. Article 3 (1) of the CRC is a norm of wide scope and requires application by all state bodies and in all decisions concerning the child. States in which the best interests of the child are protected only in sectoral statutes or selected areas of law do not fully respect this article.

[161] See its application with article 8 of the ECHR in the UK, for example.

[162] *HH v. Deputy Prosecutor of the Italian Republic, Genoa* [2012] UKSC 25.

[163] The best articulation of the relationship between the best interests of the child and dignity identified in this study is reflected in Ngcobo J's judgment in *DPP Transvaal*.

The Australian law illustrates the deleterious effect of fragmenting the protection of the best interests of the child. When the Family Court makes parenting orders, the best interests of the child are 'the paramount consideration'.[164] The 2006 Victorian Charter recognises the right of the child 'to such protection as is in his or her best interests and is needed by him or her by reason of being a child'.[165] *The best interests of the child* is a common 'keyword', but its meaning and reach differ considerably between instruments. When compared with article 3(1) of the CRC, both domestic sections are under-inclusive because they do not apply to all decisions concerning children (i.e., parenting orders versus all decisions, and Victorian official conduct versus Australian official conduct).[166] Section 17(2) of the Victorian Charter prima facie has a paternalistic, protection-only focus that is no longer associated with article 3(1).[167]

Subtle differences also exist between section 28(2) of the South African Constitution and article 3(1) of the CRC, or between the weight of the best interests of the child in *all* decisions concerning children (i.e., a primary consideration), as opposed to selected decisions concerning children (such as adoption or custody) where the best interests are determinant. Further, some best interests provisions have been declared independent rights (such as article 3(1) and section 28(2) of the South African Constitution) while others have not, retaining their traditional role of standards or principles. The type of applicable legal protection will vary, therefore, making it necessary to acknowledge that, despite monolithic references to 'the best interests of the child', not all protections of the concept are equal.

The best interests case law considered here converges with the general comment on article 3(1), where the Committee noted the tripartite nature of the article (a principle, a rule of procedure, and an independent right).[168] Echoes of this approach can be found across the four jurisdictions discussed here, albeit not in the same terms. The implications of this convergence, and whether it is the result of mutual influence, require further analysis. At a minimum, however, the convergence shows that it is possible for courts operating in vastly different systems to adopt similar

[164] Section 60CA of the FLA.

[165] Section 17(2) of the Victorian Charter.

[166] Similar comments have been made above in relation to the UK framework applied in *ZH*. See Section 6.7.2.

[167] Although, as previously mentioned, the VSC has given a non-paternalistic interpretation to this section in *Certain Children No. 2*.

[168] CRC Committee, *General Comment No. 14*, para. 6 (see Section 6.7.2).

views towards article 3(1) and that national courts and the Committee, despite their different institutional mandates, share some common views. These findings create opportunities for development, as discussed in Chapter 8.

7.5 Final Stocktaking

The CRC has had a significant impact on raising the legal profile of the rights of children. If any doubts linger about the legal strengths of these rights, or about the Convention itself, the widespread and varied case law discussed here demonstrates that such doubts are not shared by the courts. On the contrary, the CRC's extensive application is the ultimate confirmation of the strengths of its *legal* dimensions. Children's rights, as enshrined in the CRC, have not been placebo legal tools. They have demonstrated their versatility through their judicial application in many areas of law (such as immigration, access to services, contracts, sentencing, and gender identity), they have questioned many legal orthodoxies (such as the role of the best interests of the child in *all* decisions concerning children), and they have challenged contentious legal and political issues (such as the separation of powers, budgets, terrorism measures, and crime control). It can no longer be said that the Convention has a 'benign nature'.[169] The frequent interaction between the CRC and domestic law, including in fields where children's rights have not customarily been considered, has brought children's rights out of their (discipline) bubble. This is a sign of legal maturity, as children's rights can now hold their own among other legal rules. While the CRC is growing in black-letter legal maturity, its softer power should not be discounted. In some cases, the CRC has inspired more than directed, and, in an increasingly fractured international context, ideals and aspirations may become more effective than rules.

The formal rules of engagement have had an incontestable effect on how the courts have applied the CRC. They clarify the domestic status of the CRC and predict the techniques of engagement and their permissible consequences. They do not, however, capture or fully explain how domestic courts apply the CRC, and they do not determine the meaningfulness of the engagement – opportunities for which exist in all the legal systems discussed here. The rules of engagement are the first point of

[169] *Public Law Project v. Lord Chancellor* [2015] EWCA Civ 1193 at para. 27.

contact between the Convention and the domestic law, but they are not the sole point of contact. This makes them deficient in explaining the interaction between domestic courts and the CRC because they do not sufficiently account for its complexity. The CRC also interacts with sectoral laws that may have given some effect to the CRC, or with procedural rules, or with constitutional rules, or with rules governing the jurisdiction of the courts. The structure of reception, the relevant domestic legal infrastructure upon which the CRC operates, has a significant effect on the ability and the willingness of the courts to apply it. Finding convergence points between the CRC and the domestic law assists the courts from a pragmatic perspective, as Convention reasons can be latched onto similar domestic concepts or rules, but also from a more abstract perspective, by signalling to the courts that the CRC is not so fundamentally different from the domestic law that applying it risks trespassing into legislative domain.

The complex interaction between the CRC and judicial reasoning draws attention to the many junctures at which the Convention can contribute to that reasoning. The rules of engagement prompt us to think about this interaction in broad terms that do not capture some of its nuances. As illustrated most clearly in the case studies on Australia, South Africa, and the UK, the Convention contributes to different phases of the interpretation process, such as clarifying the substance of a domestic rule, assisting in the limitations enquiry, and informing the application of the law. Broadly, these may be classified as 'interpretation', but they should be acknowledged as distinct processes at least for analytical purposes. This is because these different interpretive purposes or different 'legal moments' draw out different aspects of the CRC's normative content – some require it to use its full normative force, while others would require less (i.e., what may not be useful for the interpretation of the substance of a domestic provision may be useful to inform the limitation enquiry).

There is a need to diversify our understanding of the domestic impact of the CRC, which is best understood as a matter of degree and not one of 'full effect' versus 'no effect'. The 'full effect'/'no effect' dichotomy does not recognise the significant number of cases in which the CRC adds *something* to the legal reasoning, or the diffuse effects that are not captured by conventional legal remedies or concepts. The dichotomy would also set the impact bar unreasonably high. Apart from in France, where CRC provisions can be the rules of decision, it is rare for them to be the sole or dominant reasons for a judgment. Most often, the CRC is applied together with domestic laws and other international instruments, contributing to some aspects of the reasoning. This is inevitable, given the coexistence of many legal instruments with potentially overlapping content.

Article 41 of the CRC provides that the Convention yields to instruments with higher protection standards, but this is not considered in the case law. More often, there is alignment between the applied instruments but no perfect overlap. For the Convention to be effectively applied and not to lose its judicial relevance, it is important that it offers *something* that other instruments do not – or, put differently, that it has an added value. This added value is highly contextual and will vary between legal systems, but the case studies demonstrate that however well endowed a legal system is, the CRC continues to contribute to developing the domestic law.[170] Thus, discovering the added value of the CRC is a gradual and non-linear process, which can stagnate at times only to be revived when a relevant case comes along. It is essential for this process that claims of similarity with other norms are not accepted without a close comparative consideration of the relevant CRC provisions.

It is possible that the yearning for added value has drawn the courts to articles 3(1) and 12, as flagbearers of the CRC's uniqueness. Article 3(1) and associated domestic concepts have become effective tools for asserting and justifying a distinct legal treatment for children. The recognition of the importance of this article is now reflected in the legal overhaul of the old conceptions of the best interests of the child, which has become an effective legal rule with ascertainable and independent legal content. Not only that, but it has now become a gateway for the protection of other rights in the Convention.

[170] For example, it was close to two decades after the ratification of the CRC that the South African Constitutional Court interpreted the best interests constitutional provision so as to include the voice of the child, with reference to article 12 of the CRC: *J v. NDPP*; *Pridwin Preparatory School.*

8

Looking to the Future of Judicial Application of the CRC

This brief chapter turns to the implications of this comparative study for the judicial application of the CRC in a decentralised legal order. The intricacies of the interaction of domestic courts with the Convention presented in this book have demonstrated the significant diversity of the ways in which courts can give it effect. These localisms make it difficult to capture the legal systems in categories other than the admittedly insufficiently informative categories of monist, dualist, and hybrid systems. Thus, no theory, model, or standard approach is advocated for here. Nonetheless, the study provides some insights that are general enough to be useful when considering the courts' engagement with the Convention, regardless of the formal category in which a legal system is placed. These insights can serve as an analytical tool for domestic self-reflection and, it is hoped, as aids in crafting more persuasive CRC arguments.

8.1 The Domestic Rules of Reception: An Inevitable Starting Point for the Courts

It remains an essential aspect of the courts' interaction with the CRC for them to do so through the filter of the reception rules, which permits them to establish its *legal* status. Generalisations about judicial engagements within specific categories of systems (monist, dualist, or hybrid) should be avoided beyond some very general basic features (direct or indirect application). This is because states belonging to the same category may conceptualise the relationship between international and domestic law differently, and the domestic structure of reception, which influences the judicial application of the CRC, is likely to differ widely between states.

This book argues strongly in favour of diversifying the understanding of the courts' interaction with the CRC. It calls for more attention to *sui generis* forms of engagement, but also for more nuance in terms of the orthodoxy of engagement or of engagement 'within' the rules of reception. We have grown accustomed to bundling many things into the concept of 'interpretation' as a domestic conduit for the CRC, some not fully fitting the label. This book, for example, draws attention to possible distinctions between the interpretation and the application of the law, or the interpretation of the substance of domestic rights and their limitation. These distinctions (and perhaps others) should be given more attention domestically because the location of the CRC in these discrete reasoning phases may have consequences for how it is used and what it can achieve.

8.2 Openness to Identifying and Analysing *Sui Generis* Methods

Reception rules play an important authorisation-to-engage function, but they also help to demarcate explicitly authorised forms of judicial engagement from those that are not explicitly authorised. Within the latter category one may find a grey space of 'permissible engagement' where courts engage with the Convention through *sui generis* methods. Local domestic actors should remain open to identifying such methods, which reflect a diversification of how the courts apply the CRC. The potential of these methods to expand the opportunities for the application of the Convention should be locally explored.

Sui generis methods seem to be a reality in at least some legal systems, but they remain insufficiently theorised. There are concerns that they may be used to avoid tackling difficult questions about the CRC's relationship with the domestic law. Questions also linger over these methods in terms of their legitimacy, cogency, and viability. There is, therefore, a need for closer analytical attention to, and more transparency in, using these methods.

8.3 The Importance of the Structure of Reception

One of the core insights of this study is that the domestic structure of reception is important for the courts' engagement with the CRC, and its influence thereon requires close consideration. The structure of reception is a mix of formal and informal concepts, institutions, and realities, with which the CRC interacts domestically. Ultimately, all relevant aspects of the domestic legal framework that have a bearing on the application of the CRC form its structure of reception, although the exact components are to be established within each jurisdiction.

The combination of formal rules of reception and diverse structures of reception makes the judicial interaction with the CRC unique in each jurisdiction. This structure of reception can enable the application of the CRC (e.g., through domestic 'carrier' norms that reflect CRC standards, a small gap between domestic law and the CRC, compatible laws, supporting precedent, or a domestic human rights protection system, to name but a few), but it may also inhibit it (e.g., if domestic laws conflict with the CRC, or courts that apply the CRC have limited jurisdiction, or there is no legislative protection for human rights). The structure of reception is dynamic, and any relevant change in legislation, policies, or case law can have consequences for the CRC.

The importance of the structure of reception for the application of the CRC puts the spotlight on the domestic legal knowledge essential for its optimal application. It is those who possess such knowledge who fully understand the strengths and weaknesses of the legal systems that host the Convention. They are able to identify convergent domestic norms that can carry the values of the CRC or, on the contrary, domestic norms that are contrary to the CRC and may need a consistent interpretation, invalidation, or setting aside. Local lawyers have the requisite knowledge to formulate CRC arguments packaged in domestic concepts that are cognisable by the domestic courts. International law and legal travellers such as this author can point to issues and prompt enquiry, but they can seldom suggest the most locally successful CRC arguments.

8.4 Differentiated Reception of CRC Provisions

One should be alert to the likelihood that courts may find it easier to engage with the CRC provisions that are closer to the functions traditionally performed by judges. When giving effect to these provisions, judges act as primary implementers rather than as enforcers of the CRC against other branches of the state. The domestic sensitivities in relation to the separation of powers may colour the judicial reception of CRC provisions and, arguably, a more conscious differentiation may be needed between courts as implementers and as enforcers of the CRC.

8.5 The Relationship between the CRC and Other Legal Instruments: Strengths and Concerns

Many jurisdictions are confronted by the overlap between the content of the CRC and that of other legal instruments. This generates complementarity and mutual normative support, but also normative competition. The courts have not yet formulated clear principles on how to address such overlap. A working relationship based on sound principles needs to be developed to ensure that the Convention remains relevant for the courts.

Courts are pragmatic and they are likely to consider that the sources of law most useful for the purpose of resolving a specific case – which are most often the sources with which they are familiar – are those that are more developed and more widely accepted. A newcomer source, such as the CRC, is often used to reinforce familiar sources or to address issues that are not sufficiently covered by them. Thus, some incentive may be needed for the courts to apply the CRC, beyond its mere existence and the formal rules of reception that permit its application. This incentive is what has been referred to in this book (and previously by other authors) as the *added value* of the CRC, which should, nonetheless, be navigated carefully so that it does not become a new obstacle to its application.

It is important that the CRC continues to be acknowledged, even when it overlaps with other instruments. The normative independence of the CRC must be safeguarded to avoid perceptions that its legal power depends on other instruments. Such dependency would lead to situations where if the companion norm does not apply, nor does the CRC. This does not mean that the CRC should be dissociated from other legal instruments. In some cases, this would be impossible (such as indirect application) and disadvantageous for the CRC (such as self-execution in South Africa or decoupling from the ECHR in the UK). What is needed is a balanced approach, whereby the CRC is applied whenever relevant and in a way that avoids its collapse into other legal instruments with the resultant loss of legal identity.

8.6 The Added Value by the CRC: Identification and Development

An identification of the CRC added value rests on a careful consideration of its provisions in the legal context in which it is applied. The added value is contingent on the structure of reception: the more a legal system has already given effect to the CRC, the less its added value will be for that system.

It is essential that however similar the CRC and other legal norms appear to be, their overlap or compatibility should not be assumed even when similar concepts (such as the best interests of the child) are used. When one considers the special features of the Convention and its child-focused nature, it is doubtful that complete overlap with other legal sources *can* exist. The special features of the CRC, especially its general principles, are repositories of added value. The openness of the courts to article 3(1) and the determination with which they turned a much-criticised provision into an effective legal tool that protects the uniqueness of children as legal subjects support this suggestion. Article 12 of the CRC comes close in popularity and was often used by courts to compensate for other legal instruments not accommodating children's views in matters concerning them.

A logical aid in identifying the added value of the CRC is the Committee's output (general comments, concluding observations, and views), which is distinctly child-focused and likely to contain views not expressed by other bodies or courts. However, the courts are only now starting to consider the Committee's output, and its current under-utilisation deprives the courts of opportunities to identify its added value and, more generally, an alternative reference discourse to that of powerful but not child-focused poles of legal authority (domestic or international).

The Committee should be proactive and promote the added value of the CRC in ways relevant to its judicial application. For example, it could give articles 2 and 6 a boost by developing them in general comments, or it could develop a child-focused approach to the limitation of children's rights. This is an increasingly relevant issue, considering the growing variety of areas of law in which the CRC is applied and, consequently, the increased likelihood that children's rights are in tension with other legitimate interests. The Committee has an opportunity to set the tone before other poles of legal authority generate a legal narrative from their own perspectives.

8.7 Assessing 'Impact': The Need for a Generous Approach

The domestic application of international law is premised on the latter having some impact. Judging impact is difficult because of the diversity of outcomes that may be included. A child-friendly outcome and an adequate remedy, the setting aside of domestic law, and a legal interpretation according to the CRC are indicators of impact.

However, impact can be more subtle. It can include, for example, how the reasoning is constructed, or the factors considered relevant for the resolution of the case. The acceptance of the CRC as an analytical tool for the domestic law or as a 'set of meta-norms'[1] against which to assess domestic developments is another subtle effect. Judgments critical of the CRC perform an important analytical function. Thus, they shed light on the reservations that some judges may have with the CRC and they permit a critical engagement with such reservations. They are useful self-learning tools for children's rights proponents that can be used to improve the cogency of Convention arguments.

Among the issues for reflection that arose from the CRC-sceptical judgments analysed in this study are the following: Is the Convention aspirational? Do all the substantive CRC articles create rights, and does this matter? Are the best interests of the child suitable for an *in abstracto* application? Is the Convention's scope too wide? Are child-focused judgments biased in favour of children, or inherently activist? In brief, critical judgments can be harnessed to improve the legal sophistication of children's rights arguments and to assist in articulating domestic legal reasoning more effectively.

8.8 Courts and the Committee: Understanding Their Different Approaches to Judicial Application

The maximalist, cosmopolitan-driven approach to judicial application promoted by the Committee and the parochial approach of the domestic courts coexist, but some tension exists between them. This study draws attention to two factors that explain the tension: the rules of reception and the different institutional positions occupied by the courts and the Committee.

Thus, the courts pass the Convention through the filter of the rules of reception, a step completely absent in the work of the Committee. The Committee is not called on to make judgments about the clarity or completeness of a CRC norm, nor is it called on to identify another legal norm, the content of which may need interpretation in line with the Convention. The Committee's engagement with the CRC is unconditional, but the same cannot be said of the courts.

Further, the different institutional positions account for some differences in the approaches of the courts and the Committee. Thus, courts

[1] The term used in Wouter Vandenhole, 'The Convention of the Rights of the Child in Belgian Case Law' in Ton Liefaard and Jaap E. Doek (eds.), *Litigating the Rights of the Child: The UN Convention on the Rights of the Child in Domestic and International Jurisprudence* (Dordrecht: Springer, 2015) 105, 118.

are domestic institutions, with roles and powers established by domestic law, while the Committee is an international oversight body in a decentralised legal order. For the Committee, the CRC is not only compulsory and binding but also existential. For the courts, however, the consideration of the CRC may not even be compulsory (as seen in Australia and the UK). Further, unlike that of the Committee, the role of the courts does not revolve primarily around the CRC, as the courts apply a wider range of domestic and international legal instruments. While the Committee barely considers legitimate interests other than those of children, domestic courts are forced to do so. They also resolve specific disputes rather than engage in abstract interpretations of the CRC, as the Committee has done until recently. Lastly, courts apply the CRC as one of the three branches of the state (judiciary, executive, and legislature) and have the responsibility not to trespass into the power of the other branches.[2] Constitutional limits on the powers of the courts affect how courts apply the Convention but are irrelevant for the Committee.

Thus, the generous vision of judicial application put forward by the Committee is likely beyond the reach of most courts but remains relevant to them as inspiration for potential developments. Ultimately, courts and the Committee bear primary allegiance to the dominant legal framework that gives them legitimacy, which means that the ways in which they engage with the CRC will continue to differ. This reinforces a point made throughout this study: namely, that there may be many ways of *being legal* and some ways may be activated by some actors but not others.

[2] A recent example illustrates this point. The request for an order obliging the state to take measures to repatriate the children of foreign fighters detained in camps in Northern Syria was rejected by the French administrative courts because it concerned foreign relations in regard to which the courts had no jurisdiction: Conseil d'État, Juge des référés, 23 April 2019, 429668, Inédit au recueil Lebon. Nonetheless, in the same matter, the ECtHR found a violation of article 3(2) of Protocol No. 4 to the ECHR (the right to enter the territory of the state of nationality): Protocol No. 4 to the Convention for the Protection of Human Rights and Fundamental Freedoms, securing certain rights and freedoms other than those already included in the Convention and in the first Protocol thereto as amended by Protocol No. 11, 16 September 1963, ETS 46. This was preceded by a finding by the CRC Committee that France violated several provisions of the CRC by failing to take measures to repatriate the children so detained: CRC Committee, *Constatations adoptées par le Comité au titre du Protocole facultatif à la Convention relative aux droits de l'enfant établissant une procédure de présentation de communications, concernant les communications nos 77/2019, 79/2019 et 109/2019*, 23 February 2022, CRC/C/89/D/77/2019; CRC/C/89/D/79/2019; CRC/C/89/D/109/2019.

8.9 Domestic Courts and the Development of the CRC

Courts are unique contributors to the CRC story and they are sites where the CRC can be observed in action. They affirm the CRC as a credible legal instrument and unveil its normative potential by testing it against domestic realities. Courts explore ways to integrate children's rights into mainstream legal reasoning. They are also sites of content-building, where the local meaning of the CRC is publicly negotiated in a rich context consisting of facts, legislation, policies, Committee outputs, and more. The outcomes – the domestic judgments – have an analytical authority that enjoys a higher degree of legal credibility than any other domestic interpretations. Taken collectively, courts are generators and repositories of substantial knowledge about the CRC, regardless of whether they consciously purport to contribute to its development or not. The question then becomes how to capitalise on that knowledge beyond jurisdictional boundaries.

With the caution needed when dealing with very diverse legal systems and leaving aside practical and other difficulties,[3] there is scope for courts to learn from each other. Convergent views in the article 3 jurisprudence discussed in this book suggest that cross-learning or 'horizontal' judicial communication is not unrealistic in a CRC context. Children's rights are fast moving, and one can expect that courts would at least be curious about how others have dealt with novel issues.

Court judgments can also inform the output of the CRC Committee through a process of 'vertical' communication, which is devoid of any hierarchical connotations. This process can take place in two directions: Committee-to-courts and courts-to-Committee. The Committee has an institutional position that enables it to identify, absorb, and disseminate good judicial practices from around the world. It is not an uncritical consumer of domestic input but distils domestic experiences in universally relevant material that it makes internationally available, including to domestic courts. The transnational potential of domestic CRC judgments requires close attention, but this book demonstrates that the Committee has much to learn from the courts about the CRC in action.

In the end, the CRC is what we make of it. The more we engage with it, the more meaning it develops and the more representative it becomes of the cosmopolitan community in which it operates. At its inception, the Convention rode on a wave of international goodwill and support for

[3] Such difficulties can include, for example, language, accessibility, and legal tradition.

human rights, which enabled it to inspire change. Human rights are now under multiple and conflicting pressures such as scepticism in relation to human rights, increased expectations to deliver protective outcomes, and a diminished state commitment to human rights protection. In this context, the judicial application of the CRC becomes even more important to maintain trust in the value of children's rights and to ensure that commitments in this regard are respected.

BIBLIOGRAPHY

Books

Abramson, Bruce, *Article 2: The Right of Non-Discrimination*, volume in André Alen, et al. (eds.), *A Commentary on the United Nations Convention on the Rights of the Child* (Leiden: Martinus Nijhoff, 2008).

Amos, Merris, *Human Rights Law* (Oxford: Hart Publishing, 2006).

Bailey, Peter, *The Human Rights Enterprise in Australia and Internationally* (Chatswood, NSW: LexisNexis Butterworths, 2009).

Bell, John, Sophie Boyron, and Simon Whittaker, *Principles of French Law*, 2nd ed. (Oxford: Oxford University Press, 2008).

Bonfils, Philippe, and Adeline Gouttenoire, *Droit des mineurs* (Paris: Dalloz, 2008).

Cassese, Antonio, *International Law*, 2nd ed. (New York: Oxford University Press, 2005).

Conforti, Benedetto, *International Law and the Role of Domestic Legal Systems* (Dordrecht: Springer, 1993).

Constantinesco, Vlad, and Stéphane Pierré-Caps, *Droit constitutionnel Français* (Paris: Presses Universitaires de France, 2010).

Craig, Paul, and Gráinne de Búrca, *EU Law: Texts, Cases and Materials*, 4th ed. (Oxford: Oxford University Press, 2008).

Crawford, James, *Brownlie's Principles of Public International Law*, 9th ed. (Oxford: Oxford University Press, 2019).

Cryer, Robert, et al., *Research Methodologies in EU and International Law* (Oxford: Hart Publishing, 2011).

Currie, Iain, and Johan de Waal, *The Bill of Rights Handbook*, 6th ed. (Cape Town: Juta, 2013).

Dickey, Anthony, *Family Law* (Sydney: Thomson Reuters 2014).

Dugard, John, *International Law: A South African Perspective* (Lansdowne: Juta, 2005).

Fatima, Shaheed, *Using International Law in Domestic Courts* (Oxford: Hart Publishing, 2005).

Fortin, Jane, *Children's Rights and the Developing Law*, 3rd ed. (Cambridge: Cambridge University Press, 2009).

Herzfeld, Perry, and Thomas Prince, *Statutory Interpretation Principles* (Sydney: Thomson Reuters, 2014).

Heyns, Christof, and Frans Viljoen, *The Impact of the United Nations Human Rights Treaties on the Domestic Level* (The Hague: Kluwer Law International, 2002).

Hickman, Tom, *Public Law After the Human Rights Act* (Oxford: Hart Publishing, 2010).

Hoffman, David, and John Rowe, *Human Rights in the UK: An Introduction to the Human Rights Act 1998*, 4th ed. (Harlow: Pearson, 2013).

Hoffman, Simon, and Sean O'Neil, *The Impact of Legal Integration of the UN Convention on the Rights of the Child in Wales* (Manchester: Equality and Human Rights Commission, August 2018).

Kang-Riou, Nicolas, Jo Milner, and Suryia Nayak (eds.), *Confronting the Human Rights Act: Contemporary Themes and Perspectives* (London: Routledge, 2012).

Killander, Magnus (ed.), *International Law and Domestic Human Rights Litigation in Africa* (Pretoria: Pretoria University Law Press, 2010).

Lundy, Laura, et al., *The UN Convention on the Rights of the Child: A Study of Legal Implementation in 12 Countries* (United Kingdom: UNICEF, 2012).

Liefaard, Ton, and Jaap E. Doek (eds.), *Litigating the Rights of the Child: The UN Convention on the Rights of the Child in Domestic and International Jurisprudence* (Dordrecht: Springer, 2015).

Nolan, Aoife, *Children's Socio-Economic Rights, Democracy and the Courts* (Oxford: Hart Publishing, 2011).

Nollkaemper, André, *National Courts and the International Rule of Law* (Oxford: Oxford University Press, 2011).

Office of the United Nations High Commissioner for Human Rights, *Legislative History of the Convention on the Rights of the Child: Volume I* (New York: United Nations, 2007).

Rivero, Jean, and Jean Waline, *Droit Administratif* (Paris: Dalloz, 2002).

Sanson, Michelle, *Statutory Interpretation* (Melbourne: Oxford University Press, 2012).

Sciotti-Lam, Claudia, *L'applicabilité des traités internationaux relatifs aux droits de l'homme en droit interne* (Brussels: Bruylant, 2004).

Shaw, Malcolm N., *International Law*, 8th ed. (Cambridge: Cambridge University Press, 2017).

Shelton, Dinah (ed.), *International Law and Domestic Legal Systems: Incorporation, Transformation, and Persuasion* (Oxford: Oxford University Press, 2011).

Sloss, David (ed.), *The Role of Domestic Courts in Treaty Enforcement: A Comparative Study* (New York: Cambridge University Press, 2009).

Van Bueren, Geraldine, *The International Law on the Rights of the Child* (The Hague: Martinus Nijhoff, 1998).

Vandenhole, Wouter, Gamze Erdem Türkelli, and Sara Lembrechts, *Children's Rights: A Commentary on the Convention on the Rights of the Child and Its Protocols* (Cheltenham: Edward Elgar Publishing, 2019).

Verhellen, Eugeen, *Convention on the Rights of the Child: Background, Motivation, Strategies, Main Themes* (Leuven: Garant, 1994).

Book Chapters

Abdelgawad, Elisabeth Lambert, and Anne Weber, 'The Reception Process in France and Germany' in Helen Keller and Alec Stone Sweet (eds.), *A Europe of Rights: The Impact of the ECHR on National Legal Systems* (New York: Oxford University Press, 2008) 108.

Alen, André, and Wouter Pas, 'The UN Convention on the Rights of the Child's Self-Executing Character' in Eugeen Verhellen (ed.), *Monitoring Children's Rights* (The Hague: Martinus Nijhoff, 1996) 165.

Aust, Anthony, 'United Kingdom' in David Sloss (ed.), *The Role of Domestic Courts in Treaty Enforcement: A Comparative Study* (New York: Cambridge University Press, 2009) 476.

Brems, Eva, Ellen Desmet, and Wouter Vandehnole, 'Children's Rights Law and Human Rights Law: Analysing Present and Possible Future Interactions' in Eva Brems, Ellen Desmet and Wouter Vandenhole (eds.), *Children's Rights Law in the Global Human Rights Landscape: Isolation, Inspiration, Integration?* (Oxon: Taylor & Francis Group, 2017) 1.

Buergenthal, Thomas, 'Self-Executing and Non-Self-Executing Treaties in National and International Law' in Hague Academy of International Law, *Collected Courses of the Hague Academy of International Law/Recueil des cours*, vol. 235 (Leiden: Brill, 1992) 303.

Cantwell, Nigel, 'Are "Best Interests" a Pillar or a Problem for Implementing the Human Rights of Children?' in Ton Liefaard and Jaap E. Doek (eds.), *Litigating the Rights of the Child: The UN Convention on the Rights of the Child in Domestic and International Jurisprudence* (Dordrecht: Springer, 2015) 61.

'Are Children's Rights Still Human?' in Antonella Invernizzi and Jane Williams (eds.), *The Human Rights of Children: From Visions to Implementation* (Burlington, VT: Ashgate, 2011) 37.

Carter, Anne, 'Understanding Facts' in Anne Carter (ed.), *Proportionality and Facts in Constitutional Adjudication* (Oxford: Hart Publishing, 2021) 40.

Charlesworth, Hilary, 'The High Court and Human Rights' in Peter Cane (ed.), *Centenary Essays for the High Court of Australia* (Chatswood, NSW: LexisNexis Butterworths, 2004).

Charlesworth, Hilary, and Gillian Triggs, 'Australia and the International Protection of Human Rights' in Donald Rothwell and Emily Crawford (eds.), *International Law in Australia* (Sydney: Thomson Reuters, 2017) 117.

Couzens, Meda, 'CRC Dialogues: Does the Committee on the Rights of the Child "Speak" to the National Courts?' in Ton Liefaard and Julia Sloth-Nielsen (eds.), *The United Nations Convention on the Rights of the Child: Taking Stock after 25 Years and Looking Ahead* (Leiden: Brill/Nijhoff, 2016) 103.

de Graaf, Coby, 'The Application of the United Nations Convention on the Rights of the Child in Dutch Legal Practice' in Alison Diduck, Noam Peleg and Helen Reece (eds.), *Law in Society: Reflections on Children, Family, Culture and Philosophy* (Leiden: Brill Nijhoff, 2015) 589.

Devereux, Anne, and Sarah McCosker, 'International Law and Australian Law' in Donald Rothwell and Emily Crawford (eds.), *International Law in Australia* (Sydney: Thomson Reuters, 2017) 23.

Donson, Fiona, 'Commentary on *R (on the Application of Castle) v Commissioner of Police for the Metropolis*' in Helen Stalford, Kathryn Hollingsworth and Stephen Gilmore (eds.), *Rewriting Children's Rights Judgments: From Academic Vision to New Practice* (Oxford: Hart Publishing, 2017) 275.

Ganguly Thukral, Enakshi, and Anant Kumar Asthana, 'Children's Rights in Litigation: Use of the CRC in Indian Courts' in Ton Liefaard and Jaap E. Doek (eds.), *Litigating the Rights of the Child: The UN Convention on the Rights of the Child in Domestic and International Jurisprudence* (Dordrecht: Springer, 2015) 31.

Gunew, Sneja, 'Estrangement as Pedagogy: The Cosmopolitan Vernacular' in Rosi Braidotti Patrick Hanafin and Bolette Blaagaard (eds.), *After Cosmopolitanism* (London: Routledge, 2012) 132.

Gouttenoire, Adeline, 'Les droits de l'enfant en droit français' in Olga Cvejić Jančić (ed.), *The Rights of the Child in a Changing World* (Cham: Springer, 2016) 109.

Hale, Brenda, 'High Points and Low Points in the First Ten Years: A View from the Bench' in Nicolas Kang-Riou, Jo Milner and Suryia Nayak (eds.), *Confronting the Human Rights Act: Contemporary Themes and Perspectives* (London: Routledge, 2012) 49.

Himes, James, 'Monitoring Children's Rights: Cutting Through the Confusion and Planning for the Effective Action' in Eugeen Verhellen (ed.), *Monitoring Children's Rights* (The Hague: Martinus Nijhoff, 1996) 113.

Hollingsworth, Kathryn, 'Commentary on *R v JTB*' in Helen Stalford, Kathryn Hollingsworth and Stephen Gilmore (eds.), *Rewriting Children's Rights Judgments: From Academic Vision to New Practice* (Oxford: Hart Publishing, 2017) 421.

Keller, Helen, and Alec Stone Sweet, 'Assessing the Impact of the ECHR on National Legal Systems' in Helen Keller and Alec Stone Sweet (eds.), *A Europe of Rights: The Impact of the ECHR on National Legal Systems* (New York: Oxford University Press, 2008) 678.

Kilkelly, Ursula, 'The Convention on the Rights of the Child After Twenty-Five Years: Challenges of Content and Implementation' in Martin D. Ruck, Michele Peterson-Badali and Michael Freeman (eds.), *Handbook of Children's Rights: Global and Multidisciplinary Perspectives* (New York: Routledge, 2016) 80.

Kilkelly, Ursula, and Laura Lundy, 'Children's Rights in Action: Using the Convention on the Rights of the Child as an Auditing Tool' in André Alen, et al. (eds.), *The UN Children's Rights Convention: Theory Meets Practice*, 2nd ed. (Antwerp: Intersentia, 2007) 57.

Killander, Magnus, and Horace Adjolohoun, 'International Law and Domestic Human Rights Litigation in Africa: An Introduction' in Magnus Killander (ed.), *International Law and Domestic Human Rights Litigation in Africa* (Pretoria: Pretoria University Law Press, 2010) 3.

Lanotte, Johan Vande, and Geert Goedertier, 'Monitoring Human Rights: Formal and Procedural Aspects' in Eugeen Verhellen (ed.), *Monitoring Children's Rights* (The Hague: Martinus Nijhoff, 1996) 73.

Latty, Franck, 'Observations, *GISTI et FAPIL*' in Alain Pellet and Alina Miron (eds.), *Les grandes décisions de la jurisprudence française de droit international public* (Paris: Dalloz, 2015) 674.

Limbeek, Manuela, and Marielle Bruning, 'The Netherlands: Two Decades of the CRC in Dutch Case Law' in Ton Liefaard and Jaap E. Doek (eds.), *Litigating the Rights of the Child: The UN Convention on the Rights of the Child in Domestic and International Jurisprudence* (Dordrecht: Springer, 2015) 89.

Lundy, Laura, and Bronagh Byrne, 'The Four General Principles of the United Nations Convention on the Rights of the Child: The Potential Value of the Approach in Other Areas of Human Rights Law' in Eva Brems, Ellen Desmet and Wouter Vandenhole (eds.), *Children's Rights Law in the Global Human Rights Landscape: Isolation, Inspiration, Integration?* (Oxon: Taylor & Francis Group, 2017) 52.

Marotta, Vince P., 'The Cosmopolitan Stranger' in Stan van Hooft and Wim Vandekerckhove (eds.), *Questioning Cosmopolitanism: Studies in Global Justice Volume 6* (Dordrecht: Springer, 2010) 105.

Murphy, Sean D., 'Does International Law Obligate States to Open Their National Courts to Persons for the Invocation of Treaty Norms That Protect or Benefit Persons?' in David Sloss (ed.), *The Role of Domestic Courts in Treaty Enforcement: A Comparative Study* (New York: Cambridge University Press, 2009) 61.

Ngidi, Karabo, 'The Role of International Law in the Development of Children's Rights in South Africa: A Children's Rights Litigator's Perspective' in Magnus Killander (ed.), *International Law and Domestic Human Rights Litigation in Africa* (Pretoria: Pretoria University Law Press, 2010) 173.

Nollkaemper, André, 'The Netherlands' in David Sloss (ed.), *The Role of Domestic Courts in Treaty Enforcement: A Comparative Study* (New York: Cambridge University Press, 2009) 326.

Nussbaum, Martha C., 'Patriotism and Cosmopolitanism' in Garrett Wallace Brown and David Held (eds.), *The Cosmopolitan Reader* (Cambridge: Polity Press, 2010) 155.

O'Shea, Andreas, 'International Law and the Bill of Rights' in Lexis Nexis Butterworths, *Bill of Rights Compendium* (looseleaf publication; South Africa: LexisNexis Butterworths, 2004).

Pieret, Julien, 'L'influence du juge belge sur l'effectivité de la Convention: retour doctrinal et jurisprudentiel sur le concept d'effet direct' in Vincent Chapaux, Julien Pieret and Annemie Schaus (eds.), *Entre ombres et lumières: cinquante ans d'application de la Convention européenne des droits de l'homme en Belgique* (Brussels: Bruylant, 2008) 83.

Pierik, Roland, and Wouter Werner, 'Cosmopolitanism in Context: An Introduction' in Roland Pierik and Wouter Werner (eds.), *Cosmopolitanism in Context: Perspectives from International Law and Political Theory* (Cambridge: Cambridge University Press, 2010) 1.

Porras, Ileana M., 'Liberal Cosmopolitanism or Cosmopolitan Liberalism?' in M. N. S. Sellers (ed.), *Parochialism, Cosmopolitanism, and the Foundations of International Law* (Cambridge: Cambridge University Press, 2011) 118.

Quennerstedt, Ann, 'Transforming Children's Human Rights: From Universal Claims to National Particularity' in Michael Freeman (ed.), *Law and Childhood Studies: Current Legal Issues Volume 14* (Oxford: Oxford University Press, 2012) 104.

Rayner, Moira. 'The State of Children's Rights in Australia' in Bob Franklin (ed.), *The New Handbook of Children's Rights: Comparative Policy and Practice* (London: Routledge, 2002) 345.

Reynaert, Didier, et al., 'Introduction: A Critical Approach to Children's Rights' in Wouter Vandenhole, et al. (eds.), *Routledge International Handbook of Children's Rights Studies* (London: Routledge, 2015) 1.

Roberts, Anthea, et al., 'Conceptualizing Comparative International Law' in Anthea Roberts, et al. (eds.), *Comparative International Law* (New York: Oxford University Press, 2018) 3.

Rosenczveig, Jean-Pierre, 'The Self-Executing Character of the Children's Rights Convention in France' in Eugeen Verhellen (ed.), *Monitoring Children's Rights* (The Hague: Martinus Nijhoff, 1996) 187.

Scheinin, Martin, 'General Introduction' in Martin Scheinin (ed.), *International Human Rights Norms in the Nordic and Baltic Countries* (The Hague: Martinus Nijhoff, 1996) 11.

Shackel, Rita, 'The UN Convention on the Rights of the Child: Tracing Australia's Implementation of the Provisions Relating to Family Relations' in Olga Cvejić Jančić (ed.), *The Rights of the Child in a Changing World* (Cham: Springer, 2016) 37.

Shelton, Dinah, 'Introduction' in Dinah Shelton (ed.), *International Law and Domestic Legal Systems: Incorporation, Transformation, and Persuasion* (Oxford: Oxford University Press, 2011) 1.

Skelton, Ann, 'South Africa' in Ton Liefaard and Jaap E. Doek (eds.), *Litigating the Rights of the Child: The UN Convention on the Rights of the Child in Domestic and International Jurisprudence* (Dordrecht: Springer, 2015) 13.

Skrbiš, Zlatko, and Ian Woodward, 'Cosmopolitan Openness' in Maria Rovisco and Magdalena Nowicka (eds.), *The Ashgate Research Companion to Cosmopolitanism* (Farnham: Ashgate, 2011) 53.

Sloss, David, 'Treaty Enforcement in Domestic Courts: A Comparative Analysis' in David Sloss (ed.), *The Role of Domestic Courts in Treaty Enforcement: A Comparative Study* (New York: Cambridge University Press, 2009) 1.

Stalford, Helen, 'The Broader Relevance of Features of Children's Rights Law: The "Best Interests of the Child" Principle' in Eva Brems, Ellen Desmet and Wouter Vandenhole (eds.), *Children's Rights Law in the Global Human Rights Landscape: Isolation, Inspiration, Integration?* (Oxon: Taylor & Francis Group, 2017) 38.

Tobin, John, 'Article 4: A State's General Obligation of Implementation' in John Tobin (ed.), *The UN Convention on the Rights of the Child: A Commentary* (Oxford: Oxford University Press, 2019) 108.

'The Development of Children's Rights' in Lisa Young, Mary Anne Kenny and Geoffrey Monahan (eds.), *Children and the Law in Australia*, 2nd ed. (Chatswood, NSW: LexisNexis Butterworths, 2016) 25.

'Introduction: The Foundation for Children's Rights' in John Tobin (ed.), *The UN Convention on the Rights of the Child: A Commentary* (Oxford: Oxford University Press, 2019) 1.

'Understanding a Human Rights Based Approach to Matters Involving Children: Conceptual Foundations and Strategic Considerations' in Antonella Invernizzi and Jane Williams (eds.), *The Human Rights of Children: From Vision to Implementation* (Burlington: Ashgate, 2011) 61.

Van Alstine, Michael P., 'The Role of Domestic Courts in Treaty Enforcement: Summary and Conclusions' in David Sloss (ed.), *The Role of Domestic Courts in Treaty Enforcement: A Comparative Study* (New York: Cambridge University Press, 2009) 555.

van Ert, Gib, 'Canada' in David Sloss (ed.), *The Role of Domestic Courts in Treaty Enforcement: A Comparative Study* (New York: Cambridge University Press, 2009) 166.

Vandaele, Arne, and Wouter Pas, 'International Human Rights Treaties and Their Relation with National Law: Monism, Dualism and the Self-Executing Character of Human Rights' in Arabella Weyts (ed.), *Understanding Children's Rights: Collected Papers Presented at the Seventh International Interdisciplinary Course on Children's Rights* (Ghent: Children's Rights Centre, University of Ghent, 2004) 269.

Vandenhole, Wouter, 'The Convention of the Rights of the Child in Belgian Case Law' in Ton Liefaard and Jaap E. Doek (eds.), *Litigating the Rights of the Child: The UN Convention on the Rights of the Child in Domestic and International Jurisprudence* (Dordrecht: Springer, 2015) 105.

'Distinctive Characteristics of Children's Human Rights Law' in Eva Brems, Ellen Desmet and Wouter Vandenhole (eds.), *Children's Rights Law in the Global Human Rights Landscape: Isolation, Inspiration, Integration?* (Oxon: Taylor & Francis Group, 2017) 21.

Wallace Brown, Garrett, and David Held, 'Editor's Introduction' in Garrett Wallace Brown and David Held (eds.), *The Cosmopolitan Reader* (Cambridge: Polity Press, 2010) 1.

Williams, Jane, 'England and Wales' in Ton Liefaard and Jaap E. Doek (eds.), *Litigating the Rights of the Child: The UN Convention on the Rights of the Child in Domestic and International Jurisprudence* (Dordrecht: Springer, 2015) 53.

'Multi-Level Governance and CRC Implementation' in Antonella Invernizzi and Jane Williams (eds.), *The Human Rights of Children: From Visions to Implementation* (Burlington, VT: Ashgate, 2011) 239.

Journal Articles

Abraham, Ronny, 'Les effets juridiques, en droit interne, de la Convention de New York relative aux droits de l'enfant' (1997) 3 *Revue française de droit administratif* 585.

Akandji-Kombé, Jean-François, 'De l'invocabilité des sources européennes et internationales du droit social devant le juge interne' (2012) 11 *Droit social* 1014.

Allars, Margaret, 'One Small Step for Legal Doctrine, One Giant Leap Towards Integrity in Government: *Teoh's* Case and the Internationalisation of Administrative Law' (1995) 17(2) *Sydney Law Review* 204.

Alston, Philip, 'The Best Interests Principle: Towards a Reconciliation of Culture and Human Rights' (1994) 8(1) *International Journal of Law and the Family* 1.

'Out of the Abyss: The Challenges Confronting the New U.N. Committee on Economic, Social and Cultural Rights' (1987) 9(3) *Human Rights Quarterly* 332.

Ancel, Jean-Pierre, 'La Convention de New York relative aux droits de l'enfant devant la Cour de cassation' (2011) *Justice & Cassation* 13.

'La Cour de cassation et la Convention internationale relative aux droits de l'enfant' (2001) 5(205) *Journal du droit des jeunes* 20.

Bastarache, Michel, 'La révision judiciaire des décisions ministérielles à la lumière de l'arrêt *Baker c. Canada*' (2004) 5(2) *Revue de la common law en français* 399.

Bates, Frank, '"Out of Everywhere into Here": The Disparate Bases of Childrens' [sic] Rights in Australia' (2007) 15(2) *Asia Pacific Law Review* 235.

Bishop, Michael, and Jason Brickhill, 'Constitutional Law' (2011) 1 *Annual Survey of South African Law* 188.

Bonnet, Baptiste, 'Le Conseil d'État et la Convention internationale des droits de l'enfant à l'heure du bilan: de l'art du pragmatisme' (2010) 17 *Recueil Dalloz* 1031.

Bordry, Pierre, 'Le Conseil d'État français et la Convention internationale relative aux droits de l'enfant' (2001) 205 *Journal du droit des jeunes* 16.

Bossuyt, Marc, 'The Direct Applicability of International Instruments on Human Rights' (1980) 15(2) *Revue belge de droit international* 317.

Botha, Neville, 'Justice Sachs and the Use of International Law by the Constitutional Court: Equity or Expediency?' (2010) 25(1) *South African Public Law* 235.

'Public International Law' (2010) 2010(1) *Annual Survey of South African Law* 1269.

'Rewriting the Constitution: The "Strange Alchemy" of Justice Sachs, Indeed!' (2009) 34(1) *South African Yearbook of International Law* 253.

Botha, Neville, and Michèle Olivier, 'Ten Years of International Law in the South African Courts: Reviewing the Past and Assessing the Future' (2004) 29(1) *South African Yearbook of International Law* 65.

Boulanger, François, 'Applicabilité directe de la Convention de New York et intérêt supérieur de l'enfant' (2006) 8 *Recueil Dalloz* 554.

Bradley, Curtis A., 'Self-Execution and Treaty Duality' (2008) 1 *Supreme Court Review* 131.

Bryant, Diana, 'It's My Body, Isn't It? Children, Medical Treatment and Human Rights' (2009) 35(2) *Monash University Law Review* 193.

Buergenthal, Thomas, 'Modern Constitutions and Human Rights Treaties' (1998) 36 *Columbia Journal of Transnational Law* 211.

Bureau, Dominique, 'De l'application directe en France de la Convention de New York du 26 janvier 1990 sur les droits de l'enfant' (2005) 4 *Revue critique de droit international privé* 679.

Cameron, David Edwin, 'Constitutionalism, Rights, and International Law: The *Glenister* Decision' (2013) 23 *Duke Journal of Comparative & International Law* 389.

Charlesworth, Hilary, 'The UN and Mandatory Sentencing' (2000) 25 *Australian Children's Rights News* 1.

Chauvaux, Didier, and Thierry-Xavier Girardot, 'Les clauses d'un traité international dépourvues d'effet direct ne peuvent être invoquées à l'encontre d'un acte réglementaire' (1997) *L'Actualité juridique: Droit administratif* 435.

Chénedé, François, and Pascale Deumier, 'L'oeuvre du Parlement, la part du Conseil constitutionnel en droit des personnes et de la famille' (2013) 39 *Les nouveaux Cahiers du Conseil constitutionnel* (online).

Chénedé, François, 'Les arrêts Mennesson et Labassée ou l'instrumentalisation des droits de l'homme' (2014) 14 *Recueil Dalloz* 1797.

Ciobanu, Viorel, 'Independenţa judecătorului şi principiul legalităţii în procesul civil' (2010) 2 *Revista Română de Drept Privat* 43.

Claes, Eric, and Arne Vandaele, 'L'effet direct des traités internationaux: Une analyse en droit positif et en théorie du droit axée sur les droits de l'homme' (2001) 34(2) *Revue belge de droit international* 411.

Collins, Tara M., 'The General Measures of Implementation: Opportunities for Progress with Children's Rights' (2019) 23(3) *International Journal of Human Rights* 338.

Collinson, Jonathan, 'Making the Best Interests of the Child a Substantive Human Right at the Centre of National Level Expulsion Decisions' (2020) 38(3) *Netherlands Quarterly of Human Rights* 169.

Courbé, Patrick, 'L'application directe de la Convention des Nations unies sur les droits de l'enfants' (2006) (22) *Recueil Dalloz* 1487.

Coutou, Claire, and Bénédicte Vassallo, 'Rapport de Mmes Coutou et Vassallo, Conseillers référendaires' (2008) 674 *Bulletin d'information* 12.

Couzens, Meda, 'Romanian Courts and the UN Convention on the Rights of the Child: A Case Study' (2016) 24(4) *International Journal of Children's Rights* 851.

de Búrca, Gráinne, 'Human Rights Experimentalism' (2017) 111(2) *American Journal of International Law* 277.

Decaux, Emmanuel, 'Le régime du droit international en droit interne' (2010) 62 (2) *Revue internationale de droit comparé* 467.

Dekeuwer-Défossez, Françoise, 'La convention relative aux droits de l'enfant, qui ne crée des obligations qu'à la charge des Etats parties, n'est pas directement applicable en droit interne' (1994) *Recueil Dalloz* 34.

'La Convention internationale des droits de l'enfant: quelles répercussions en droit français?' (2006) 5 *Cahiers de la recherche sur les droits fondamentaux* 39.

'L'effectivité de la CIDE: rapport de synthèse' (2010) 200 *Les petites affiches* 35.

Dubouis, Louis, 'Droit international et juridiction administrative' (2006) *Répertoire de droit international Dalloz* January, 1

Dugard, John, 'International Law and the "Final" Constitution' (1995) 11(2) *South African Journal on Human Rights* 241.

'International Law and the South African Constitution' (1997) 8(1) *European Journal of International Law* 77.

'The Role of International Law in Interpreting the Bill of Rights' (1994) 10(2) *South African Journal on Human Rights* 208.

Dumortier, Gaëlle, 'L'effet direct des conventions internationales' (2012) 3 *Revue française de droit administratif* 547.

Dyzenhaus, David, Murray Hunt, and Michael Taggart, 'The Principle of Legality in Administrative Law: Internationalisation as Constitutionalisation' (2001) 1(1) *Oxford University Commonwealth Journal* 5.

Edgar, Andrew, and Rayner Thwaites, 'Implementing Treaties in Domestic Law: Translation, Enforcement and Administrative Law' (2018) 19(1) *Melbourne Journal of International Law* 24.

El Boudouhi, Saida, 'The National Judge as an Ordinary Judge of International Law: Invocability of Treaty Law in National Courts' (2015) 28(2) *Leiden Journal of International Law* 283.

Engle, Eric, 'The Convention on the Rights of the Child' (2011) 29 *Quinnipiac Law Review* 793.

Fenton-Glynn, Claire, 'Austerity and the Benefit Cap: In Whose Best Interests?' (2015) 37(4) *Journal of Social Welfare and Family Law* 467.

Fernando, Michelle, 'Express Recognition of the UN Convention on the Rights of the Child in the Family Law Act: What Impact for Children's Participation?' (2013) 36(1) *UNSW Law Journal* 88.

Ferreira, Gerrit, and Werner Scholtz, 'Has the Constitutional Court Found the Lost Ball in the High Weeds? The Interpretation of Section 231 of the South African Constitution' (2009) 42(2) *Comparative and International Law of Southern Africa* 264.

Fortin, Jane, 'Are Children's Best Interests Really Best? *ZH (Tanzania) v Secretary of State for the Home Department*' (2011) 74(6) *Modern Law Review* 947.

'Children's Rights: Flattering to Deceive?' (2014) 26(1) *Child and Family Law Quarterly* 51.

Fulchiron, Hugues, 'La constitutionnalisation de l'intérêt supérieur de l'enfant' (2019) 13 *Recueil Dalloz* 709.

Gallinetti, Jacqui, '2kul2Btru: What Children Would Say About the Jurisprudence of Albie Sachs' (2010) 25(1) *South African Public Law* 108.

Garlicki, Lech, 'Constitutional Courts Versus Supreme Courts' (2007) 5(1) *International Journal of Constitutional Law* 44.

Gay, Laurence, 'L'affirmation d'un droit aux soins du mineur étranger ou l'inconventionnalité partielle d'une loi jugée conforme à la Constitution' (2006) 11 *Revue de droit sanitaire et social* 1047.

Gelblat, Antonin, and Robert Medard Inghilterra, 'L'intérêt supérieur de l'enfant: radiographie d'une exigence constitutionnelle' (2019) 16 *Revue des droits de l'homme* 1.

Gilmore, Stephen, 'Use of the UNCRC in Family Law Cases in England and Wales' (2017) 25(2) *International Journal of Children's Rights* 500.

Gouttenoire, Adeline, 'Cohérence des contrôles de conventionnalité et de constitutionnalité en matière de droit des personnes et de la famille' (2013) 2 *Les nouveaux Cahiers du Conseil constitutionnel* 63.

'L'application de la Convention internationale des droits de l'enfant' (2012) 50 *Les petites affiches* 17.

'Le domaine de l'article 3-1 de la CIDE: la mise en oeuvre du principe de primauté de l'intérêt supérieur de l'enfant' (2010) 200 *Les petites affiches* 24.

'Surrogacy Agreements: At Last, the Primacy of the Child's Interests' (2015) 1 *Montesquieu Law Review* 103.

Gowar, Christin, 'The Status of International Treaties in the South African Domestic Legal System: Small Steps Towards Harmony in Light of *Glenister*?' (2011) 36(1) *South African Yearbook of International Law* 307.

Groves, Matthew, 'Treaties and Legitimate Expectations: The Rise and Fall of Teoh in Australia' (2010) 15(4) *Judicial Review* 323.

Guyon-Renard, Isabelle, 'Rapport de Mme Guyon-Renard, Conseiller rapporteur' (2012) 777 *Bulletin d'information* 7.

Hanson, Karl, and Laura Lundy, 'Does Exactly What It Says on the Tin? A Critical Analysis and Alternative Conceptualisation of the So-called "General Principles" of the Convention on the Rights of the Child' (2017) 25(2) *International Journal of Children's Rights* 285.

Harland, Christopher, 'The Status of the International Covenant on Civil and Political Rights (ICCPR) in the Domestic Law of State Parties: An Initial Global Survey Through UN Human Rights Committee Documents' (2000) 22(1) *Human Rights Quarterly* 187.

Hauser, Jean, 'Droits de l'enfant: il y a CIDE et CIDE!' (1994) *Revue trimestrielle de droit civil* 581.

'La référence à la Convention internationale des droits de l'enfant (CIDE) fait recette à la Cour de cassation mais est-elle nécessaire?' (2006) *La revue trimestrielle de droit civil* 101.

Hill, Daniel, 'Estimating the Effects of Human Rights Treaties on State Behavior' (2010) 72(4) *Journal of Politics* 1161.

Hoffman, Simon, and Rebecca Thorburn Stern, 'Incorporation of the UN Convention on the Rights of the Child in National Law' (2020) 28(1) *International Journal of Children's Rights* 133.

Hovell, Devika, and George Williams, 'A Tale of Two Systems: The Use of International Law in Constitutional Interpretation in Australia and South Africa' (2005) 29(1) *Melbourne University Law Review* 95.

Hudson, Graham, 'Neither Here nor There: The (Non-) Impact of International Law on Judicial Reasoning in Canada and South Africa' (2008) 21(2) *Canadian Journal of Law & Jurisprudence* 321.

I'Anson, John, Ann Quennerstedt, and Carol Robinson, 'The International Economy of Children's Rights: Issues in Translation' (2017) 25(1) *International Journal of Children's Rights* 50.

Jean, Jean-Paul, 'Observations de M. Jean, Avocat général' (2013) 777 *Bulletin d'information* 31.

Kalantry, Sital, 'The Intent-to-Benefit: Individually Enforceable Rights Under International Treaties' (2008) 44 *Stanford Journal of International Law* 63.

Khaïat, Lucette, 'La défense des droits de l'enfant, un combat inachevé' (2010) 296 *Journal du droit des jeunes* 20.

Killander, Magnus, 'Judicial Immunity, Compensation for Unlawful Detention and the Elusive Self-Executing Treaty Provision: *Claassen v Minister of Justice and Constitutional Development* 2010 (6) SA 399 (WCC)' (2010) 26(2) *South African Journal on Human Rights* 386.

King, Michael, 'Against Children's Rights' (1996) 50 *Acta Juridica* 28.

'Children's Rights as Communication: Reflections on Autopoietic Theory and the United Nations Convention' (1994) 57(3) *Modern Law Review* 385.

Kirby, Michael, 'Chief Justice Nicholson, Australian Family Law and International Human Rights' (2004) 5(1) *Melbourne Journal of International Law* 221.

Knop, Karen, 'Here and There: International Law in Domestic Courts' (2000) 32 (2) *New York University Journal of International Law and Politics* 501.

Lacey, Wendy, 'In the Wake of *Teoh*: Finding an Appropriate Government Response' (2001) 29(2) *Federal Law Review* 219.

'Judicial Discretion and Human Rights: Expanding the Role of International Law in the Domestic Sphere' (2004) 5(1) *Melbourne Journal of International Law* 108.

'A Prelude to the Demise of *Teoh*: The High Court Decision in *Re Minister for Immigration and Multicultural Affairs, Ex parte Lam*' (2004) 26(1) *Sydney Law Review* 130.

Lachaume, Jean-François, 'Droit international et juridiction judiciaire' (2009) *Répertoire de droit international Dalloz* October, 1

'Jurisprudence française relative au droit international (année 1997)' (1998) 44 *Annuaire français de droit international* 663.

Lagarde, Pierre, 'La convention de New York du 26 janvier 1990 sur les droits de l'enfant n'est pas directement applicable en droit interne' (1993) 3 *Revue critique de droit international privé* 449.

Lasser, Michel de S.-O.-l'E., 'Judicial (Self-)Portraits: Judicial Discourse in the French Legal System' (1995) 104(6) *Yale Law Journal* 1325.

Lazerges, Christine, 'Les limites de la constitutionnalisation du droit pénal des mineurs' (2008) 1 *Archives de politique criminelle* 5.

Lebreton, Gilles, 'Le droit de l'enfant au respect de son "intérêt supérieur". Critique républicaine de la dérive individualiste de droit civil français' (2003) 2 *Cahiers de la recherche sur les droits fondamentaux* 77.

Lundy, Laura, Ursula Kilkelly, and Bronagh Byrne, 'Incorporation of the United Nations Convention on the Rights of the Child in Law: A Comparative Review' (2013) 21(3) *International Journal of Children's Rights* 442.

Marguénaud, Jean-Pierre, 'De l'indifférence des juridictions judiciaires à l'égard de la Convention internationale relative aux droits de l'enfant' (1999) 2 *Revue trimestrielle de droit civil* 509.

Massip, Jean, 'L'application par la Cour de cassation de conventions internationales récentes relatives à l'enfance' (1995) 53 *Les petites affiches* 41.

'La Convention relative aux droits de l'enfant, qui ne crée des obligations qu'à la charge des Etats parties, n'est pas directement applicable en droit interne' (1993) *Recueil Dalloz* 361.

'La cour de cassation et le caractère directement exécutoire en France de la Convention sur les droits de l'enfant' (1998) 39 *Les petites affiches* 25.

Maynial, Patrice, 'Observations de M. Maynial, Premier avocat général' (2008) 674 *Bulletin d'information* 33.

McCrudden, Christopher, 'Why Do National Court Judges Refer to Human Rights Treaties? A Comparative International Law Analysis of CEDAW' (2015) 109(3) *American Journal of International Law* 534.

Meagher, Dan, 'The Common Law Presumption of Consistency with International Law: Some Observations from Australia (and Comparisons with New Zealand)' (2012) 3 *New Zealand Law Review* 465.

Monéger, Françoise, 'Enfant (droits de l')' (2006) *Répertoire de droit international Dalloz* January, 1.

'La Convention des droits de l'enfant devant les juridictions administratives' (1996) *Revue de droit sanitaire et social* 137.

'Le Conseil d'État met en avant l'intérêt supérieur de l'enfant contenu dans la Convention des Nations Unies sur les droits de l'enfant' (1998) 3(1) *Revue de droit sanitaire et social* 174.

'Rapport de Mme Monéger, Conseiller rapporteur (Pourvoi no 09-69.052)' (2011) 747 *Bulletin d'information* 20.

Mosikatsana, Tshepo L., 'Children's Rights and Family Autonomy in the South African Context: A Comment on Children's Rights Under the Final Constitution' (1998) 3(2) *Michigan Journal or Race and Law* 341.

Neirinck, Claire, 'L'application de la Convention internationale de l'enfant à la découpe: à propos d'un revirement de jurisprudence' (2005) 5 *Revue de droit sanitaire et social* 814.

Neudorfer, Sonja, and Claudia Wernig, 'Implementation of International Treaties into National Legal Orders: The Protection of the Rights of the Child within the Austrian Legal System' (2010) 14 *Max Planck Yearbook of United Nations Law* 409.

Nicholson, Alastair, 'The United Nations Convention on the Rights of the Child and the Need for Its Incorporation into a Bill of Rights' (2006) 44(1) *Family Court Review* 5.

Nivard, Carole, 'L'effet direct de la Charte sociale européenne devant les juridictions suprêmes françaises' (2012) 28 *Revue des droits et libertés fondamentaux* (online).

'Précision et organes institués par des conventions internationales et européennes' (2015) 7 *Revue des droits de l'homme.*

Nollkaemper, André, 'The Duality of Direct Effect of International Law' (2014) 25(1) *European Journal of International Law* 105.

Olivier, Michèle, 'International Human Rights Agreements in South African law: Procedure, Policy and Practice (Part 2)' (2003) 3 *Tydskrif vir die Suid Afrikaanse Reg* 490.

Otto, Diane, 'From "Reluctance" to "Exceptionalism": The Australian Approach to Domestic Implementation of Human Rights' (2001) 26(5) *Alternative Law Journal* 219.

Peleg, Noam, 'Developing the Right to Development' (2017) 25(2) *International Journal of Children's Rights* 380.

Poole, Melissa, 'International Instruments in Administrative Decisions: Mainstreaming International Law' (1999) 30(1) *Victoria University of Wellington Law Review* 91.

Powell, Emilia Justyna, and Jeffrey K. Staton, 'Domestic Judicial Institutions and Human Rights Treaty Violation' (2009) 53(1) *International Studies Quarterly* 149, 154.

Provost, René, 'Judging in Splendid Isolation' (2008) 56(1) *American Journal of Comparative Law* 125.

Quennerstedt, Ann, 'Children, But Not Really Humans? Critical Reflections on the Hampering Effect of the "3 P's"' (2010) 18(4) *International Journal of Children's Rights* 619.

Reydellet, Michel, 'La convention des droits de l'enfant n'est pas un traité "hors-jeu"' (1998) 11 *Les petites affiches* 17.

Rongé, Jean-Luc, 'La Convention internationale relative aux droits de l'enfant: On avance ou on recule?' (2004) 10(240) *Journal du droit des jeunes* 9.

Rosa, Solange, and Mira Dutschke, 'Child Rights at the Core: The Use of International Law in South African Cases on Children's Socio-Economic Rights' (2006) 22(2) *South African Journal on Human Rights* 224.

Roux, Theunis, 'Judging the Quality of Legal Research: A Qualified Response to the Demand for Greater Methodological Rigour' (2014) 24(1) *Legal Education Review* 178.

Ruddle, Lara, and Sally Nicholes, '*B & B and Minister for Immigration and Multicultural and Indigenous Affairs*: Can International Treaties Release Children from Immigration Detention Centres?' (2004) 5(1) *Melbourne Journal of International Law* 256.

Sandberg, Kirsten, 'The Role of National Courts in Promoting Children's Rights: The Case of Norway' (2014) 22(1) *International Journal of Children's Rights* 1.

Scheffler, Samuel, 'Conceptions of Cosmopolitanism' (1999) 11(3) *Utilitas* 255.

Schwartz, Rémy, 'La jurisprudence du Conseil d'État et les droits de l'enfant' (2010) 296 *Journal du droit des jeunes* 37.

Scott, Craig, and Patrick Macklem, 'Constitutional Ropes of Sand or Justiciable Guarantees? Social Rights in a New South African Constitution' (1992) 141 *University of Pennsylvania Law Review* 1.

Seibert-Fohr, Anja, 'Domestic Implementation of the International Covenant on Civil and Political Rights Pursuing to Its Article 2 Para. 2' (2001) 5 *Max Planck Yearbook of United Nations Law* 399.

Sharp, Naomi, 'Procedural Fairness: The Age of Legitimate Expectation Is Over' (2016) 90(11) *Australian Law Journal* 797.

Sifris, Adiva, 'Children in Immigration Detention: The Bakhtiyari Family in the Family Court' (2004) 29(5) *Alternative Law Journal* 212.

Single, Jennifer, 'The Status of the UN Convention on the Rights of the Child in Australian Law' (1999) 9(1) *Polemic* 36.

Skelton, Ann, 'Child Justice in South Africa: Application of International Instruments in the Constitutional Court' (2018) 26(3) *International Journal of Children's Rights* 391.

Sloss, David, 'Executing *Foster v. Neilson*: The Two-Step Approach to Analyzing Self-Executing Treaties' (2012) 53(1) *Harvard International Law Journal* 301.

'Non-Self-Executing Treaties: Exposing a Constitutional Fallacy' (2002) 36(1) *University of California Davis Law Review* 1.

'Self-Executing Treaties and Domestic Judicial Remedies' (2004) 98 *Proceedings of the American Society of International Law* 346.

'When Do Treaties Create Individually Enforceable Rights?: The Supreme Court Ducks the Issue in *Hamdan* and *Sanchez-Llamas*' (2006) 45(1) *Columbia Journal of Transnational Law* 20.

Sloth-Nielsen, Julia, 'Chicken Soup or Chainsaws: Some Implications of the Constitutionalisation of Children's Rights in South Africa' (1996) 27 *Acta Juridica* 6.

'Children's Rights in the South African Courts: An Overview Since Ratification of the UN Convention on the Rights of the Child' (2002) 10(2) *International Journal of Children's Rights* 137.

'Ratification of the United Nations Convention on the Rights of the Child: Some Implications for South African Law' (1995) 11(3) *South African Journal of Human Rights* 401.

'The Role of International Human Rights Law in the Development of South Africa's Legislation on Juvenile Justice' (2001) 5(1) *Law, Democracy & Development* 59.

Sloth-Nielsen, Julia, and Benyam D. Mezmur, '2 + 2 = 5? Exploring the Domestication of the CRC in South African Jurisprudence (2002–2006)' (2008) 16(1) *International Journal of Children's Rights* 1.

Sloth-Nielsen, Julia, and Helen Kruuse, 'A Maturing Manifesto: The Constitutionalisation of Children's Rights in South African

Jurisprudence 2007–2012' (2013) 21(4) *International Journal of Children's Rights* 646.

Smolin, David, 'Overcoming Religious Objections to the Convention on the Rights of the Child' (2006) 20(1) *Emory International Law Review* 81.

Stewart, Linda, 'The Grootboom Judgment, Interpretative Manoeuvring and Depoliticising Children's Rights' (2011) 26(1) *South African Public Law* 97, 101.

Taggart, Michael, '"Australian Exceptionalism" in Judicial Review' (2008) 36(1) *Federal Law Review* 1.

Taxil, Bérangère, 'Les critères de l'applicabilité directe des traités internationaux aux États-Unis et en France' (2007) 59(1) *Revue internationale de droit comparé* 157.

Taylor, Rachel, 'Putting Children First?: Children's Interests as a Primary Consideration in Public Law' (2016) 28(1) *Child and Family Law Quarterly* 45.

Tobin, John, 'Finding Rights in the "Wrongs" of Our Law: Bringing International Law Home' (2005) 30(4) *Alternative Law Journal* 164.

'Increasingly Seen and Heard: The Constitutional Recognition of Children's Rights' (2005) 21(1) *South African Journal on Human Rights* 86.

'Judging the Judges: Are They Adopting the Rights Approach in Matters Involving Children?' (2009) 33(2) *Melbourne University Law Review* 579.

Todres, Jonathan, 'Emerging Limitations on the Rights of the Child: The U.N. Convention on the Rights of the Child and Its Early Case Law' (1998) 30(1) *Columbia Human Rights Law Review* 159, 193.

Tully, Stephen, 'Momcilovic v The Queen (2011) 245 CLR 1' (2012) 19(1) *Australian International Law Journal* 279.

Tuovinen, Juha, 'The Role of International Law in Constitutional Adjudication: *Glenister v President of the Republic of South Africa*' (2013) 130(4) *South African Law Journal* 661.

Tushnet, Mark, 'The Possibilities of Comparative Constitutional Law' (1999) 108 (6) *Yale Law Journal* 1225.

Twomey, Anne, 'Minister for Immigration and Ethnic Affairs v Teoh' (1995) 23(2) *Federal Law Review* 348.

van Ert, Gib, 'Canadian Cases in Public International Law in 2003–4' (2004) 42 *Canadian Yearbook of International Law* 583.

Vassallo, Bénédicte, 'La Convention des droits de l'enfant à la cour de cassation' (2010) 296 *Journal du droit des jeunes* 25.

Vasseur-Lambry, Fanny, 'Les message troublants du juge de la filiation: l'accouchement sous X en question' (2012) 137 *Les petites affiches* 13.

Vázquez, Carlos Manuel, 'Treaties as Law of the Land: The Supremacy Clause and the Judicial Enforcement of Treaties' (1995) 122 *Harvard Law Review* 599.

Velu, Jacques, 'Les effets directs des instruments internationaux en matière de droits de l'homme' (1980) 15(2) *Revue belge de droit international* 293.

Verdier, Pierre, 'Pour en finir avec l'intérêt de l'enfant' (2008) 280 *Journal du droit des jeunes* 34.

Verhoeven, Joe, 'La notion d'"applicabilité directe" du droit international' (1980) 15(2) *Revue belge de droit international* 243.

Walker, Kirsten, and Penelope Mathew, 'Minister for Immigration v Ah Hin Teoh' (1995) 20(1) *Melbourne University Law Review* 236.

Waters, Melissa A., 'Creeping Monism: The Judicial Trend toward Interpretive Incorporation of Human Rights Treaties' (2007) 107(3) *Columbia Law Review* 628.

Weiss-Gout, Béatrice, 'Trois décisions, une même deception' (2011) 146 *Gazette du Palais* 7.

Williams, Jane, 'Incorporating Children's Rights: The Divergence in Law and Policy' (2007) 27(2) *Legal Studies* 261.

Woolhandler, Anne, 'Judicial Enforcement of Treaties: Self-Execution and Related Doctrines: Remarks' (2006) 100 *Proceedings of the American Society of International Law* 439.

Wu, Tim, 'Treaties' Domain' (2007) 93(3) *Virginia Law Review* 571.

Young, Lisa, '*B and B: Family Law Reform Act* 1995 (Cth): Relocating the Rights Debate' (1997) 21(2) *Melbourne University Law Review* 722.

Reports, Working Papers, Lectures, Speeches, and Theses

Ancel, Jean-Pierre, 'Les opinions dissidents' (5ème conférence du Cycle de conférences annuelles sur les méthodes de jugement, 18 October 2005).

Attorney-General's Department, *Australia's Report under the Convention on the Rights of the Child* (1995).

Australian Law Reform Commission, *Traditional Rights and Freedoms: Encroachments by Commonwealth Laws* (ALRC Report 129, 2016).

Canivet, M. Guy, 'Vision prospective de la Cour de cassation' (l'Académie des sciences morales et politiques, 13 November 2006).

Conseil d'État, *Groupe de travail sur la rédaction des décisions de la juridiction administrative: rapport final* (May 2012).

Cour de cassation, *Rapport annuel 2005* (2006).

Cour de cassation, *Rapport annuel 2009* (2010).

Cour de cassation, *Rapport annuel 2013* (2014).

Défenseur des droits, *Rapport du Défenseur des droits au Comité des droits de l'enfant des Nations-Unies* (2020).

de Gouttes, Régis, 'Le dialogue des juges' (paper presented at the Colloque du Cinquantenaire du Conseil Constitutionnel, 3 November 2008).

Duncan, Beatrice, *Global Perspectives on Consolidated Children's Rights Statutes* (UNICEF, Legislative Reform Initiative, 2008).

Errera, Roger, 'L'application de la Convention Internationale relative aux droits de l'enfant et l'incidence de la Convention européenne des droits de l'homme sur les droits de l'enfant' (Comité franco–britannique de coopération judiciaire, Colloque de Rennes sur l'enfant en justice, 19–21 May 2005) 7.

French, Robert, 'Oil and Water?: International Law and Domestic Law in Australia' (The Brennan Lecture, Bond University, 26 June 2009).

Gobert, Michelle, 'Le droit de la famille dans la jurisprudence de la Cour de cassation' (Neuvième conférence le droit de la famille dans la jurisprudence de la Cour de cassation, 11 December 2006).

Home Office, UK Border Agency, *Every Child Matters: Change for Children, Statutory Guidance to the UK Border Agency on Making Arrangements to Safeguard and Promote the Welfare of Children* (November 2009).

Joint Standing Committee on Treaties, Parliament of the Commonwealth of Australia, *United Nations Convention on the Rights of the Child* (1998).

Laurent-Boutot, Carine, 'La Cour de cassation face aux traités internationaux protecteurs des droits de l'homme' (unpublished PhD thesis, University of Limoges, 2006).

Louvel, Bertrand, 'Discours prononcé en ouverture des travaux de la commission de réflexion dédiés à la motivation' (14 September 2015).

Mance, Jonathan, 'International Law in the UK Supreme Court' (speech, King's College, London, 13 February 2017) 1, www.supremecourt.uk/news/speeches.html.

Nicholson, Alastair, 'Australian Judicial Approaches to International Human Rights Conventions and "Family Law"' (Miller Du Toit Conference, Cape Town, 26 March 2002).

Scrutiny of Acts and Regulations Committee, Parliament of Victoria, *Review of the Charter of Human Rights and Responsibilities Act 2006* (2011).

Slama, Serge, 'Adoption de nouveaux critères de détermination de l'effet direct des normes internationales sans consacrer leur invocabilité systématique' (CREDOF, 2012).

South African Law Commission, *The Review of the Child Care Act: First Issue Paper* (Project 110, 18 April 1998).

Triggs, Gillian, 'Human Rights across the Tasman: a Widening Gulf' (Hotung Fellowship Public Lecture, 6 April 2016).

Vandaele, Arne, and Eric Claes, 'L'effet direct des traités internationaux. Une analyse en droit positif et en théorie du droit axée sur les droits de l'homme' (Institut de droit international, Working Paper No. 15, 2001).

Venice Commission, *Report on the Implementation of International Human Rights Treaties in Domestic Law and the Role of the Courts* (CDL-AD(2014)005, 2014).

Venice Commission, *Report on the Protection of Children's Rights: International Standards and Domestic Constitutions* (CDL-AD(2014)005, 2014).

Internet Materials

Ancel, Jean-Pierre, 'La protection des droits de la personne dans la jurisprudence récente de la Cour de cassation' in Cour de cassation, *Rapport de la Cour de cassation 2000* (2001), www.conseil-constitutionnel.fr/conseil-constitutionnel/francais/la-constitution/la-constitution-de-1958-en-20-questions/quelle-place-la-constitution-de-1958-fait-elle-au-droit-international.17499.html.

Australasian Legal Information Institute (Austlii), www.austlii.edu.au/.

Australian Human Rights Commission, 'Common Law Rights, Human Rights Scrutiny and the Rule of Law', https://humanrights.gov.au/our-work/rights-and-freedoms/common-law-rights-human-rights-scrutiny-and-rule-law.

Conseil d'État, https://conseil-etat.fr/.

Constitutional Assembly, Constitutional Committee, *Supplementary Memorandum on Bill of Rights and Party Submissions* (not dated), www.justice.gov.za/legislation/constitution/history/REPORTS/tc4-SUPPL.PDF.

Cour de cassation, www.courdecassation.fr/.

Cour de cassation, 'Conseil d'État: rencontre à la Cour de cassation' (26 January 2015), www.courdecassation.fr.

Cour de cassation, 'Lancement des travaux de groupes de reflexion visant à développer les relations institutionnelles de la Cour' (10 October 2014), www.courdecassation.fr.

de Vos, Pierre, '*Glenister*: A Monumental Judgment in Defence of the Poor', *Constitutionally Speaking* (blog, 18 March 2011), https://constitutionallyspeaking.co.za/glenister-a-monumental-judgment-in-defence-of-the-poor/.

Legifrance, www.legifrance.gouv.fr/.

Mathieu, Bertrand, 'Qu'est-ce que la Constitution?', *Conseil constitutionnel* (2008), www.conseil-constitutionnel.fr/.

Panel of Constitutional Experts, 'Memorandum, Re: Children' (5 February 1996), www.justice.gov.za/legislation/constitution/history/LEGAL/CP005026.PDF.

Pellet, Alain, 'Quelle place la Constitution de 1958 fait-elle au droit international?', *Conseil constitutionnel* (2008), www.conseil-constitutionnel.fr/la-constitution.

'Ratification Status for CRC: Convention on the Rights of the Child', *UN Treaty Body Database*, https://tbinternet.ohchr.org/_layouts/15/TreatyBodyExternal/Treaty.aspx?Treaty=CRC&Lang=en.

Sloss, David, 'Domestic Application of Treaties' (Santa Clara Law Digital Commons, 2011), https://digitalcommons.law.scu.edu/facpubs/635.

South African History Online, 'The June 16 Soweto Youth Uprising' (2013), www.sahistory.org.za/article/june-16-soweto-youth-uprising.

'Status of Treaties: Convention on the Rights of the Child', *United Nations Treaty Collection*, https://treaties.un.org/Pages/ViewDetails.aspx?src=IND&mtdsg_no=IV-11&chapter=4.

United Nations Materials

Committee on Economic, Social and Cultural Rights, *General Comment No. 9: The Domestic Application of the Covenant*, 3 December 1998, E/C.12/1998/24.

Committee on the Elimination of Discrimination against Women and Committee on the Rights of the Child, *Joint General Recommendation No. 31 of the Committee on the Elimination of Discrimination Against Women/General Comment No. 18 of the Committee on the Rights of the Child on Harmful Practices*, 14 November 2014, CEDAW/C/GC/31–CRC/C/CG/18.

Committee on the Protection of the Rights of All Migrant Workers and Members of Their Families and Committee on the Rights of the Child, *Joint General Comment No. 3 (2017) of the Committee on the Protection of the Rights of All Migrant Workers and Members of Their Families and No. 22 (2017) of the Committee on the Rights of the Child on the General Principles Regarding the Human Rights of Children in the Context of International Migration*, 16 November 2017, CMW/C/GC/3–CRC/C/GC/22.

Committee on the Rights of the Child, *Concluding Observations: Australia*, 20 October 2005, CRC/C/15/Add.268.

Concluding Observations: France, 25 April 1994, CRC/C/15/Add.20.

Concluding Observations: France, 30 June 2004, CRC/C/15/Add.240.

Concluding Observations: France, 22 June 2009, CRC/C/FRA/CO/4.

Concluding Observations: South Africa, 27 October 2016, CRC/C/ZAF/CO/2.

Concluding Observations: United Kingdom of Great Britain and Northern Ireland, 20 October 2008, CRC/C/GBR/CO/4.

Concluding Observations of the Committee on the Rights of the Child: France, 22 June 2009, CRC/C/FRA/CO/4.

Concluding Observations on the Combined Fifth and Sixth Periodic Reports of Australia, 1 November 2019, CRC/C/AUS/CO/5-6.

Concluding Observations on the Fifth Periodic Report of France, 23 February 2016, CRC/C/FRA/CO/5.

Concluding Observations on the Fifth Periodic Report of the United Kingdom of Great Britain and Northern Ireland, 12 July 2016, CRC/C/GBR/CO/5.

Concluding Observations on the Second Periodic Report of South Africa, 27 October 2016, CRC/C/ZAF/CO/2.

Constatations adoptées par le Comité au titre du Protocole facultatif à la Convention relative aux droits de l'enfant établissant une procédure de présentation de communications, concernant les communications nos 77/2019, 79/2019 et 109/2019, 23 February 2022, CRC/C/89/D/77/2019; CRC/C/89/D/79/2019; CRC/C/89/D/109/2019.

General Comment No. 4 (2003): Adolescent Health and Development in the Context of the Convention on the Rights of the Child, 1 July 2003, CRC/GC/2003/4.

General Comment No. 5 (2003): General Measures of Implementation of the Convention on the Rights of the Child (arts. 4, 42 and 44, para. 6), 27 November 2003, CRC/GC/2003/5.

General Comment No. 6 (2005): Treatment of Unaccompanied and Separated Children Outside Their Country of Origin, 1 September 2005, CRC/GC/2005/6.

General Comment No. 7 (2005): Implementing Child Rights in Early Childhood, 1 November 2005, CRC/C/GC/7.

General Comment No. 8 (2006): The Right of the Child to Protection from Corporal Punishment and Other Cruel or Degrading Forms of Punishment (arts. 19; 28, para. 2; and 37, inter alia), 2 March 2007, CRC/C/GC/8.

General Comment No. 9 (2006): The Rights of Children with Disabilities, 27 February 2007, CRC/C/GC/9.

General Comment No. 10 (2007): Children's Rights in Juvenile Justice, 9 February 2007, CRC/C/GC/10.

General Comment No. 11 (2009): Indigenous Children and Their Rights Under the Convention, 12 February 2009, CRC/C/GC/11.

General Comment No. 12 (2009): The Right of the Child to Be Heard, 20 July 2009, CRC/C/GC/12.

General Comment No. 13 (2011): The Right of the Child to Freedom from All Forms of Violence, 18 April 2011, CRC/C/GC/13.

General Comment No. 14 (2013) on the Right of the Child to Have His or Her Best Interests Taken as a Primary Consideration (art. 3, para. 1), 29 May 2013, CRC/C/GC/14.

General Comment No. 15 (2013) on the Right of the Child to the Enjoyment of the Highest Attainable Standard of Health (art. 24), 17 April 2013, CRC/C/GC/15.

General Comment No. 16 (2013) on State Obligations Regarding the Impact of the Business Sector on Children's Rights, 17 April 2013, CRC/C/GC/16.

General Comment No. 21 (2017) on Children in Street Situations, 21 June 2017, CRC/C/GC/21.

General Guidelines Regarding the Form and Content of Initial Reports to Be Submitted by States Parties Under article 44, paragraph 1 (a), of the Convention, 30 October 1991, CRC/C/5.

General Guidelines Regarding the Form and Content of Periodic Reports to Be Submitted by States Parties Under article 44, paragraph 1 (b), of the Convention, 29 November 2005, CRC/C/58/Rev.1.

List of Issues to Be Taken Up in Connection with the Consideration of the Third and Fourth Periodic Reports of Romania, 9 March 2009, CRC/C/ROM/Q/4.

List of Issues to Be Taken Up in Connection with the Consideration of the Third Periodic Report of the Netherlands, 22 October 2008, CRC/C/NLD/Q/3.

Summary Record of the 1054th Meeting, 22 September 2005, CRC/C/SR.1054.

Treaty-Specific Guidelines Regarding the Form and Content of Periodic Reports to Be Submitted by States Parties under article 44, paragraph 1 (b), of the Convention on the Rights of the Child, 25 November 2010, CRC/C/58/Rev.2.

Economic and Social Council (ECOSOC), *UN Economic and Social Council 2005/20: Guidelines on Justice in Matters Involving Child Victims and Witnesses of Crime*, 22 July 2005, E/RES/2005/20.

Human Rights Committee, *Bakhtiyari v. Australia*, Communication No. 1069/2002, 6 November 2003, CCPR/C/79/D/1069/2002.

United Nations Standard Minimum Rules for the Administration of Juvenile Justice ('The Beijing Rules'), General Assembly Resolution 40/33, 29 November 1985, A/RES/40/33.

INDEX

www.ingramcontent.com/pod-product-compliance
Lightning Source LLC
LaVergne TN
LVHW011703200926
848484LV00004B/1055
* 9 7 8 1 1 0 8 8 3 3 7 1 4 *